More Praise for *Hitler in Los Angeles*

"A remarkable tale, one that pits a secretive, chess-playing Jewish spymaster—attorney Leon Lewis—and a group of courageous German-American war veterans that he recruited as his spies against a cast of villains straight out of a classic Warner Bros. film . . . Mr. Ross has a novelist's eye for characters and detail." —*The Wall Street Journal*

"Reveal[s] the hitherto untold story of Jewish resistance to Nazi infiltration, not in Berlin or Warsaw but in Los Angeles during the 1930s, a time when Nazism, a distant rumble on the horizon for most Americans, was for tens of thousands of others a siren call to action . . . Ross has a blockbuster revelation." —*The Chronicle of Higher Education*

"Nazis, spies, assassination plots, a planned putsch to topple Franklin Roosevelt—these are the ingredients for a World War II movie. But in Steve Ross's compelling history, they make for a true-life thriller about an episode that has been almost completely ignored: the attempt by the Nazis to take over America." —Neal Gabler, author of *Walt Disney*

"The director of the Casden Institute for the Study of the Jewish Role in American Life and an award-winning film historian, Ross tells a shocking story of Nazi efforts to infiltrate America . . . Ross puts his experience in film history to good use, and he creates lively portraits of the men and women whom Lewis recruited as spies and who succeeded in putting some dangerous Nazis behind bars. A vivid history of home-grown resistance." —*Kirkus Reviews*

"[This] nonfiction revelation . . . reads like an exciting spy novel. Ross reveals this true story of resistance by American Jews and Gentiles with an exciting, evocative writing style." —*New York Journal of Books*

"Steven J. Ross has the verve of a spellbinding novelist and the skill of a master historian. This story has every bit the drama of Roth's *The Plot Against America* or Dick's *The Man in the High Castle*, except it actually happened! The all-important takeaway of *Hitler in Los Angeles*? Good people can and must prevail against bad." —David N. Myers, president/CEO, Center for Jewish History

"Thrilling . . . Dramatic." —*Daily Express*

"This is a truly brilliant history by a superbly talented historian. More importantly, it's a damn fine read, a true-life thriller that's a powerful reminder of how hate, if left to fester, can destroy us all." —Alex Kershaw, author of *Avenue of Spies*

"A riveting and terrifying chapter of Nazi American history . . . Ross has a flair for thriller-writing and this history is a captivating read . . . Enthralling . . . Important and compelling . . . *Hitler in Los Angeles* is crammed with twists and turns involving double-agents, movie stars, and big-time studio moguls. Netflix needs to turn *Hitler in Los Angeles* into a television series." —*PopMatters*

"Readers interested in a detailed look at this spy operation can have confidence in this well-sourced account." —*Library Journal*

"Steven J. Ross, one of our foremost authorities on the entwined histories of American Jewry, domestic politics, and Hollywood, presents a chilling tale of the Nazi plot to destroy America; the small spy network who helped defeat it; and the official indifference to the threat posed by German agents and homegrown extremists bent on sabotage and political murder." —Glenn Frankel, Pulitzer Prize–winning journalist and author of *High Noon*

"Outstanding and compelling . . . Parts of *Hitler in Los Angeles* read almost like a spy novel, except that these events really—and frighteningly—happened." —*Truthdig*

"This little-known chapter of 1930s history—captured by Steven J. Ross with impeccable research and an intriguing narrative—needs to be told; it will challenge assumptions about the power of citizens to shape world events from their own backyard." —Ted Johnson, senior editor, *Variety*

"Remarkable and meticulously researched." —*Times Higher Education*

HITLER IN LOS ANGELES

HITLER IN LOS ANGELES

How Jews Foiled Nazi Plots Against
Hollywood and America

STEVEN J. ROSS

BLOOMSBURY PUBLISHING
NEW YORK · LONDON · OXFORD · NEW DELHI · SYDNEY

BLOOMSBURY PUBLISHING
Bloomsbury Publishing Inc.
1385 Broadway, New York, NY 10018, USA

BLOOMSBURY, BLOOMSBURY PUBLISHING, and the Diana logo are trademarks of
Bloomsbury Publishing Plc

First published in the United States 2017
This paperback edition published 2019

ISBN: HB: 978-1-62040-562-8; eBook: 978-1-62040-564-2; PB: 978-1-62040-563-5

LIBRARY OF CONGRESS CATALOGING-IN-PUBLICATION DATA

Names: Ross, Steven Joseph, author.
Title: Hitler in Los Angeles : how Jews foiled Nazi plots against
Hollywood and America / Steven J. Ross.
Description: New York : Bloomsbury USA, [2017] | Includes bibliographical references.
Identifiers: LCCN 2017012324 | ISBN 9781620405628 (hardcover)
Subjects: LCSH: Jews—California—Los Angeles—History—20th century. | Lewis,
Leon L.—Friends and associates. | Lewis, Leon L.—Adversaries. | Roos, Joseph,
1908–1999—Friends and associates. | Roos, Joseph, 1908–1999—Adversaries. | Jewish
Federation Council of Greater Los Angeles—Political activity. | Motion pictures—Political
aspects—United States—History—20th century. | National socialism and motion pictures. |
Los Angeles (Calif.)—Ethnic relations.
Classification: LCC F869.L89 J564 2017 | DDC 979.4/94004924—dc23
LC record available at https://lccn.loc.gov/2017012324

6 8 10 9 7 5

Typeset by Westchester Publishing Services
Printed and bound in the U.S.A. by Berryville Graphics Inc., Berryville, Virginia

To my mother, Esther Ross, and the memory of my father,
Benjamin Ross

And to the memory of my in-laws, Kurt and Olga Kent

CONTENTS

Map of Nazi and Fascist Los Angeles x
Prologue 1

I CREATING A SPY NETWORK, 1933–1934
1. "The Most Dangerous Jew in Los Angeles" 7
2. The Spying Begins 21
3. Plots Revealed, Spies Uncovered 35
4. Going for Help 44
5. A Bitter Lesson: The German-American Alliance Trial 53

II THE NAZI AND FASCIST ATTACK ON HOLLYWOOD, 1933–1935
6. The Moguls and the Nazis 67
7. Inside the Fascist Front 79
8. HUAC Comes to Town 94
9. The Most Charming Nazi in Los Angeles 108

III NEW THREATS, NEW SPIES, 1935–1939
10. Spy and Divide 133
11. The Plots to Kill the Jews 152
12. Nazi versus Nazi 166
13. Silver Shirts, Nazis, and Movie Stars 186
14. Slaughter the Hollywood Jews 198
15. The Most Hated Nazi in Hollywood 214
16. The Three Most Dangerous Enemies List 228
17. The Race Is On 247

IV ESPIONAGE, SABOTAGE, AND THE COMING OF WAR, 1938–1941
18. Closing In 263
19. Sabotage, Secret Agents, and Fifth Columnists 279
20. Darkening Skies, New Dangers 298
21. Pearl Harbor Roundup 316

Epilogue: Vigilant till War's End and Beyond 331

Guide to Spies, Nazis, and Fascists 341
Acknowledgments 345
Notes 347
Index 399

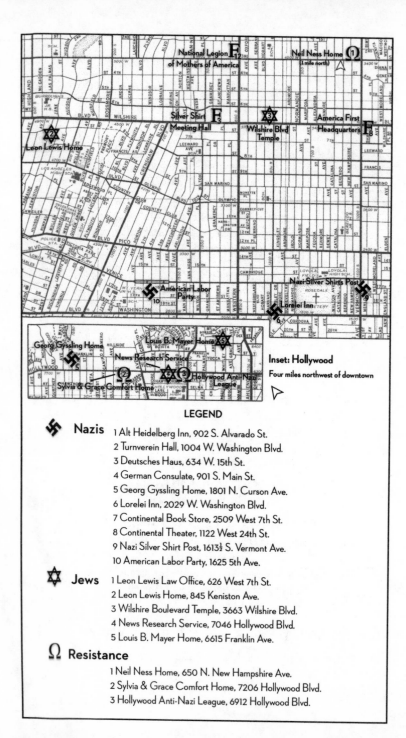

National Legion of Mothers of America **F** 12380

Neil Ness Home Ω (1 mile north)

Silver Shirt Meeting Hall **F**

Wilshire Blvd Temple ✡3

America First Headquarters **F** 8

✡2 Leon Lewis Home

🌀10 American Labor Party

Nazi Silver Shirts Post 🌀9

Lorelei Inn 🌀6

Inset: Hollywood

Four miles northwest of downtown

Georg Gyssling Home 🌀5

Louis B. Mayer Home ✡5

News Research Service ✡4

Hollywood Anti-Nazi League Ω3

Ω2 Sylvia & Grace Comfort Home

LEGEND

🌀 **Nazis**
1 Alt Heidelberg Inn, 902 S. Alvarado St.
2 Turnverein Hall, 1004 W. Washington Blvd.
3 Deutsches Haus, 634 W. 15th St.
4 German Consulate, 901 S. Main St.
5 Georg Gyssling Home, 1801 N. Curson Ave.
6 Lorelei Inn, 2029 W. Washington Blvd.
7 Continental Book Store, 2509 West 7th St.
8 Continental Theater, 1122 West 24th St.
9 Nazi Silver Shirt Post, 1613½ S. Vermont Ave.
10 American Labor Party, 1625 5th Ave.

✡ **Jews**
1 Leon Lewis Law Office, 626 West 7th St.
2 Leon Lewis Home, 845 Keniston Ave.
3 Wilshire Boulevard Temple, 3663 Wilshire Blvd.
4 News Research Service, 7046 Hollywood Blvd.
5 Louis B. Mayer Home, 6615 Franklin Ave.

Ω **Resistance**
1 Neil Ness Home, 650 N. New Hampshire Ave.
2 Sylvia & Grace Comfort Home, 7206 Hollywood Blvd.
3 Hollywood Anti-Nazi League, 6912 Hollywood Blvd.

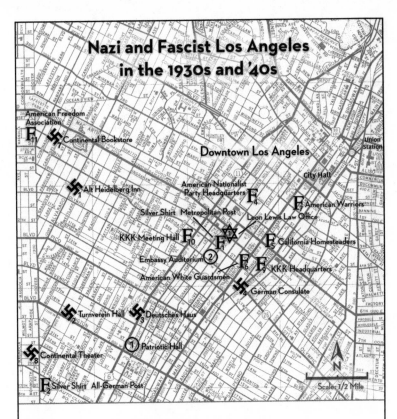

Nazi and Fascist Los Angeles in the 1930s and '40s

Downtown Los Angeles

F₁₁ American Freedom Association
卐 Continental Bookstore
Union Station
City Hall
卐 Alt Heidelberg Inn
American Nationalist Party Headquarters **F₄**
F₇ American Warriors
Silver Shirt Metropolitan Post
Leon Lewis Law Office
KKK Meeting Hall **F₁₀**
F₁ ✡
F₅ California Homesteaders
Embassy Auditorium ②
F₆ **F₉** KKK Headquarters
American White Guardsmen
卐 German Consulate
卐 Turnverein Hall
卐 Deutsches Haus **F₃**
① Patriotic Hall
卐 Continental Theater **₈**
F₂ Silver Shirt All-German Post
Scale: 1/2 Mile
N

F Fascists
1 Silver Shirt Metropolitan Post, 730 S. Grand Ave.
2 Silver Shirt All-German Post, 2600 S. Hoover Blvd.
3 Silver Shirt Meeting Hall, 659 S. Andrews Pl.
4 American Nationalist Party Headquarters, 630 W. Fourth St.
5 California Homesteaders, 541 S. Spring St.
6 American White Guardsmen Headquarters, 761 S. Broadway
7 American Warriors, 257 S. Spring St.
8 America First Headquarters, 3142 Wilshire Blvd.
9 Ku Klux Klan Headquarters, 704 S. Spring St.
10 Ku Klux Klan Meeting Hall, 845 S. Figueroa St.
11 American Freedom Association Headquarters, 2802 West 7th St.
12 National Legion of Mothers of America, 241 S. Western Ave.

○ Meeting Halls
1 Patriotic Hall, 1816 S. Figueroa St.
2 Embassy Auditorium, 851 S. Grand Ave.

©2017 Cartography by Philip J. Ethington and Steven J. Ross
Base Map, 1946 by the Automobile Club of Southern California. Reproduced by permission.

Prologue

We will undermine the morale of the people of America . . .
Once there is confusion and after we have succeeded in undermining the faith of the American people in their own government,
a new group will take over; this will be the German-American
group, and we will help them assume power.
— ADOLF HITLER, 1933

Every evening throughout my childhood, the Gestapo broke into our
home and terrorized my mother. Some nights they would only drag
her away; other nights they took her, my sister, and me to Gestapo headquarters. Each morning my mother, who had survived the Auschwitz,
Bergen-Belsen, and Salzwedel concentration camps, woke up exhausted
and drenched in sweat. And every morning she told me about her
nightmares.

My father had no nightmares—at least, not ones he shared with his
family. He simply never talked about his years in the Warsaw Ghetto or
his time in Dachau. Ironically, Dachau is where he learned how to be a
baker—a skill he used when he came to the United States. Although he
was not well-known beyond his circle of friends, for over three decades
New Yorkers who patronized Zabar's or Balducci's enjoyed his Russian
coffee cake and strudels.

As a teenager, I wanted to know how these horrors could have
happened to my parents and to millions of Jews. I swore that I would
have fought to save them, and I did not understand how Jews
could have been so passive in the face of such evil. Why was there not
more resistance at home and abroad? I promised myself that one day I
would try to answer these disturbing questions.

Yet for forty years I have been an American historian who ignored his own past. I have written about poverty in eighteenth-century New York City; experiments in free black labor conducted during the Civil War; nineteenth-century working-class history; and twentieth- and twenty-first-century Hollywood politics. It is now time to honor my youthful promise and write about the world of my parents and the millions of Jews who found themselves terrorized by Nazis and fascists, not just in Europe but also in the United States.

In the course of my research, I discovered that my youthful self—along with many historians—had been asking the wrong question. Many American Jews *did* rise to oppose Hitler, but they could not agree on the best path of resistance. A divided strategy and inability to implement a single vision is not the same as passivity or a failure of will. Indeed, one might rightly ask why the U.S. government did not do more to stop the spread of Nazism and fascism at home. Why did local authorities in so many cities turn a blind eye to Nazi activities in their own backyards?

My earlier assumptions about American Jewish resistance changed after I came across a special exhibition at California State University Northridge's Oviatt Library, *In Our Own Backyard*.[1] This remarkable exhibit documented the activities of Nazis and fascists in Los Angeles and, most surprisingly, the existence of a Jewish spy ring that operated from August 1933 to the end of World War II. Delving into the library's collection of over two hundred boxes of spy reports, I discovered the amazing story of Leon Lewis and the courageous group of men and women—Christians and Jews—who risked their lives to undermine Nazi and fascist activity in Los Angeles.

Drawing extensively on the spy reports sent to Lewis on a near-daily basis, *Hitler in Los Angeles* tells the story of thirteen years of Jewish resistance to American Nazis and fascists. It is a story almost too amazing to be true. But it is. As I soon discovered, American Jews were far more active in fighting Hitler and fascism in the United States during the 1930s and early 1940s than were our Communist-obsessed government authorities.

Hitler in Los Angeles is a history written from the point of view of Leon Lewis and his spies as they saw events evolving in real time. Many of their reports contain dialogue of actual conversations between the spies and those upon whom they were spying. I use their own words— spies, Nazis, fascists, and government authorities—as much as possible to describe the unpredictable world they encountered. The men and women Lewis and his able assistant Joseph Roos recruited as undercover operatives never knew if American Nazis and fascists would carry out their numerous threats to murder Jews. They did not know whether Hitler would ease his policies toward Jews. And they certainly did not know a Holocaust would occur throughout Europe. But they knew they had to take the Nazi threat seriously, for they repeatedly heard fellow Americans openly talk about overthrowing the American government and killing every Jewish man, woman, and child they could find.[2]

FOR NAZI PROPAGANDA MINISTER Joseph Goebbels, no American city was more important to the cause than Los Angeles, home to what he deemed the world's greatest propaganda machine, Hollywood. Although many people in the United States and around the world viewed New York as the capital of Jewish America, Goebbels saw Hollywood as a far more dangerous place where Jews ruled over the motion picture industry and transmitted their ideas throughout the world. Goebbels and Adolf Hitler had one thing in common with Soviet dictator Joseph Stalin: they saw Hollywood as central to their efforts to win over the American public and the world to their cause. The power of the cinematic image, Hitler wrote in *Mein Kampf*, had far "greater possibilities" for propaganda than the written word, for people "will more readily accept a pictorial representation than read an article of any length."[3] Hitler and Goebbels knew that American films were eagerly watched throughout Europe, Latin America, and Asia; if properly controlled, they could help advance Germany's quest for world domination. While Reds tried to control Hollywood through infiltration, Nazis planned to do it through intimidation and murder.

Los Angeles seemed the perfect place to establish a beachhead for the Nazi assault on the United States. Not only did Southern California have a long history of anti-Semitism and right-wing extremism, but the Los Angeles port was less closely monitored than New York (or "Jew York," as Nazis often referred to it), which made it easier to use as the central depot for sending spies, propaganda, money, and secret orders from Germany—all of which were then distributed throughout the United States.

Nazi plans to conquer an industry, a city, and a nation were not idle fantasies. But what Hitler, Goebbels, and their American disciples did not know was that Los Angeles also served as the epicenter of Jewish efforts to spy on Nazis and thwart their plans. Smug in their sense of racial superiority, Nazis believed they had little to fear from these cowardly less-than-human people.

Beginning in August 1933 and lasting until the end of World War II, Jewish attorney Leon L. Lewis used his connections with the American Legion and Disabled American Veterans of World War I (DAV) to recruit military veterans—and their wives and daughters—to go undercover and join every Nazi and fascist group in Los Angeles. Often rising to leadership positions, this daring group of men and women uncovered a series of Nazi plots to kill the city's Jews and to sabotage the nation's military installations. Plans existed for hanging twenty Hollywood actors and power figures, including Al Jolson, Eddie Cantor, Charlie Chaplin, Louis B. Mayer, and Samuel Goldwyn; for driving through Boyle Heights and machine-gunning as many Jewish residents as possible; for fumigating Jewish homes with cyanide; and for blowing up defense installations and seizing munitions from National Guard armories on the day Nazis planned to launch their American putsch.

From 1933 until 1945, while many Americans closed their eyes, Lewis's operatives risked their lives to stop Hitler's minions and alert citizens to the dangers they posed to American democracy.

This is the story of those plots, the spies who uncovered them, the men who hired them, and how a small cadre of Los Angeles Jews— including Hollywood actors and studio heads—thwarted Nazi plans to lay the groundwork for Germany's New Order in America.

I

CREATING A SPY NETWORK, 1933–1934

1.

"The Most Dangerous Jew in Los Angeles"

L eon Lewis never imagined he would ask the German-born son of a Bavarian general to spy on his fellow countrymen. Lewis knew Captain John H. Schmidt from years of attending meetings of the local Disabled American Veterans (DAV). He considered the German émigré a "highly intelligent" man who "has given every proof of his loyalty to his country." The fellow veterans, however, were by no means close friends.[1] Moreover, Lewis was asking a Christian to help a Jew spy upon fellow Germans.

As he paced his downtown office on Seventh Street waiting to meet his first potential recruit in late July 1933, Lewis reflected upon the recent events that had led him to embark on a new career as spymaster. In March 1933, two months after Adolf Hitler became the Reich's chancellor of Germany, Berlin officials sent Captain Robert Pape to Los Angeles and charged him with building a Nazi organization in Southern California. Four months later, Nazis began their invasion of Los Angeles.

On the evening of July 26, a hundred Hitlerites, many dressed in brown shirts and sporting red, white, and black swastika armbands, held their first public meeting at their spacious downtown headquarters in the Alt Heidelberg building. Standing in front of American and swastika flags and flanked by storm troopers "whose arms bulged with excess power," Hans Winterhalder, handsome propaganda chief of the Friends of the New Germany (FNG), told the gathered crowd of their plans to unify the fifty scattered German American organizations of Southern California and their 150,000 members into a single body. Hitlerism would succeed in the United States, he promised in heavily accented English, if loyal Germans flocked to the cause. "My position here is like a priest. It is my job to teach the Nazi system."[2]

The front page of the next day's *Los Angeles Record* and *Los Angeles Examiner* featured a picture of four Brownshirts dressed in full regalia giving the Nazi salute. What most frightened Leon Lewis was a small paragraph in the *Record* describing how Los Angeles–based Nazis had turned the basement of their headquarters into a barracks for unemployed Germans, who would be fed, bathed, and housed at no cost other than being instructed in National Socialism by Winterhalder. Lewis understood that this was not done out of kindness. Nazis were raising an army from among the unemployed and discontented, just as Hitler had done in the 1920s.

What the Nazis had not counted on was that Lewis was just as familiar with Hitler's strategy as they were. If the FNG wanted to build an American army of discontented veterans, then he would present them with a perfect recruit: a decorated veteran who had served in both the German and American armies, but had fallen on hard times because of draconian government cuts to his military pension. If Lewis could convince John Schmidt to become his first undercover agent, it would help him recruit other ex-servicemen to spy on the Nazi movement before it was too late. As far as he was concerned, the meeting with Schmidt would be the most important of both their lives.

There was little in Leon Lewis's early background to suggest that the modest midwesterner would become a spymaster. As his close associate Joseph Roos recounted, "Lewis was a very private person, a reclusive person."[3] He was someone who enjoyed serving others but drew little attention to himself. He left no diaries or accounts of his life, only his correspondence with his spies and colleagues at the Anti-Defamation League. Few people talk about him in their memoirs, and there is little trace of his personal life in newspapers. The spymaster was a ghostly presence: always there but rarely seen.

Leon L. Lewis was born in Hurley, Wisconsin, on September 5, 1888, to German Jewish immigrants Edward and Rachel Lewis. He attended public school in Milwaukee, went to college at the University of Wisconsin and George Washington University, and earned a law degree from the University of Chicago Law School in 1913.[4]

Upon graduating, the six-foot-one Jew with light brown eyes and black hair had little desire to assimilate into the mainstream of American life. Instead, Lewis devoted himself to the Jewish concept of *tikkun olam*, "world repair." After an Atlanta jury wrongfully convicted local

B'nai B'rith president Leo Frank of murdering a thirteen-year-old girl in 1913, the B'nai B'rith's national organization—the oldest and largest Jewish fraternal association in the United States—responded by creating the Anti-Defamation League (ADL). When the ADL opened its headquarters in Chicago that year, Lewis accepted president Sigmund Livingston's offer to serve as its first national executive secretary. The ADL began operating with a modest $200 budget, two desks, and lofty ambitions to fight anti-Semitism wherever it occurred.

A lawyer with a social worker's heart, Lewis spent the next several years deeply entrenched in Jewish life, speaking to B'nai B'rith groups throughout the Midwest, documenting instances of discrimination, and aiding vulnerable Jews in need. An indefatigable worker, he also served as executive director of Chicago's Sinai Social Center from 1915 to 1917 and began monitoring movies on behalf of the ADL, looking for anti-Semitic images.[5]

Lewis's work for the ADL was put on hold after the United States entered World War I in April 1917. Two months later, he enlisted in the U.S. Army infantry and was sent to France that November. During his eighteen months of military service, which included combat in the Somme, Lewis rose through the ranks from private to captain. When the war ended in November 1918, the recently promoted Major Lewis remained in Europe, where he continued his humanitarian work by serving as deputy chief of the army's War Relief Section, organizing Red Cross aid for wounded American soldiers in Great Britain.[6]

Lewis's time in the trenches and subsequent postings in Coblenz (Germany), Paris, and London gave him an intimate look at the devastation, poverty, and hopelessness brought by war: over 16 million military and civilian deaths and 20 million people wounded. While stationed in Europe, Lewis witnessed the cruelties inflicted not only by the enemy but also by American and Allied soldiers. He saw how normally decent men would kill without a second thought when ordered to do so. The nightmarish idea that Americans could just as easily turn against each other, especially Christian against Jew, haunted him for the rest of his life.

Returning to Chicago in 1919 with heightened organizational skills and numerous military commendations, Lewis resumed his position as the ADL's national executive secretary. That August, the thirty-one-year-old bachelor married twenty-seven-year-old Ruth Lowenberg. The following year he presented his first of many reports on the dramatic rise of anti-Semitism in Europe and the United States to the Central Conference of American Rabbis.

Leon Lewis ca. 1918

Over the next several years, few Americans watched Hitler's ascent from Brownshirt leader to Reich chancellor more carefully than Leon Lewis. Keeping track of Hitler and the threat he posed to Jews was both his job and his obsession. In 1923, after reading Lewis's reports of growing anti-Semitism in Germany, ADL president Livingston asked him to take on the additional role of executive secretary of their new international division. A tireless worker, Lewis also served as founding editor of the *B'nai B'rith Magazine* and helped organize the Hillel foundation to further Jewish life on college campuses. He continued his multiple jobs until 1925, when newly elected B'nai B'rith president Boris Bogen, the ADL's governing body, moved the organization's headquarters to Cincinnati. Rather than relocate his family, Lewis resigned his position and went to work for the recently created law firm of Rosenthal, Mayer, and Lewis.[7]

No longer officially in charge of the ADL's international division, Lewis continued monitoring Hitler's improbable rise to power. Many Americans viewed Hitler and his followers either as thugs or fools. They assumed that the Nazi leader's virulent anti-Semitism was a passing phase, and once in office he would moderate his policies toward the nation's Jews. But Lewis realized Hitler was using violence to get into power, and once in office, Nazi leaders would likely eliminate all political opposition.

In March 1931, suffering from lingering health issues, Lewis moved his family from Chicago to the more amenable climate of Los Angeles. Setting up a law practice specializing in business affairs, he also served as the Anti-Defamation League's representative to Hollywood, monitoring films for anti-Semitic images. As in Chicago, he plunged into the city's Jewish life, speaking at synagogues and to local Jewish groups about events at home and abroad. By the summer of 1933, the army veteran had emerged as an important leader in local American Legion and DAV posts, heading up the Americanism Committee for both organizations.

Lewis and his family, which now included daughters Rosemary and Claire, found the nation's fifth largest city of 1.4 million a vibrant place for Jews to live and work. Lured by sunshine and economic opportunity, Los Angeles's Jewish population had risen from 2,500 in 1900 to 30,000 in 1930 to 70,000 on the eve of World War II. The most rapid growth came during the 1920s and 1930s, when recent Jewish arrivals, many of them from Eastern Europe, increased by 225 percent.[8]

Nowhere was the expansion of Jewish life more visible than in the lively eastside neighborhood of Boyle Heights. In 1908 only two Jewish families inhabited the area. By 1929, it was home to 10,000 Jewish households, two synagogues, nine hotels, two theaters, a variety of cultural institutions, and many inexpensive homes and apartments. A decade later, 35,000 Jews called Boyle Heights their home.[9]

Much to his chagrin, Lewis discovered that Los Angeles was experiencing the same rising tide of anti-Semitism he had witnessed in Chicago during the 1920s. Few Southern California hate groups proved more powerfully entrenched than the Ku Klux Klan, an organization that believed the United States would be far better off without Jews, Catholics, and blacks. When district attorney Thomas Lee Woolvine raided the Klan's Los Angeles headquarters in April 1922, his men found a local membership list of 1,500 people that included the Los Angeles County sheriff and chief of police. Anti-Semitism also took more subtle forms. Covenants and gentlemen's agreements among real estate agents excluded Jews and other minorities from home ownership in many areas. Elite social and business organizations that once welcomed Jews to their ranks—such as the California Club and Chamber of Commerce—now began excluding them.[10]

Much of the anti-Semitism and right-wing activism Lewis witnessed was driven more by fear than hatred. Writing in the *New Republic* in January 1931, Edmund Wilson captured the sense of desperation that gripped so many Americans during the Great Depression. With 9 million men out of work, he wrote, "our cities are scenes of privation and misery on a scale which sickens the imagination; our agricultural life is bankrupt; our industry, in shifting to the South, has reverted almost to the horrible conditions of the Factory Acts of England of a hundred years ago." Banks were failing, and newspapers were afraid to tell the truth. Wilson wondered whether what had broken in America was "not simply the machinery of representative government but the capitalist system itself."[11]

Lewis shared Wilson's concerns about the fragility of capitalism and democracy. He had seen communism take over Russia, fascism take over Italy, and Nazism take over Germany in 1933. What would happen in the United States if the effects of the Great Depression worsened was anyone's guess.

Poverty in Los Angeles was as bad as in most cities. The local Community Chest received a daily average of 590 requests for relief and public assistance in 1930. As the Depression worsened, city agencies across Southern California proved incapable of aiding an unemployed population that soared to over 350,000.[12]

Lewis saw how many Angelenos were attracted to colorful yet dangerous demagogues such as Gerald B. Winrod, the far-right Kansas evangelist known as the Jayhawk Nazi, who was later shown to be in the service of the Reich Ministry of Public Enlightenment and Propaganda; Father Charles Coughlin, whose weekly anti-Semitic rants reached 14 million people; and William Dudley Pelley, head of the Silver Legion of America (commonly known as the Silver Shirts), a fascist and anti-Semitic organization whose members donned uniforms much like the ones Brownshirts wore that they sewed themselves so as not to wear anything touched by Jews.[13]

Like their counterparts in Germany and Italy, American fascists and Nazis blamed Jews for causing the worldwide economic crisis and exerting undue influence on the national government. Shortly after Franklin D. Roosevelt assumed office in March 1933, the nation's 103 Nazi and fascist organizations denounced what they derisively referred to as his "Jew Deal" and demanded that the president remove all Jews from public office.[14]

On January 30, 1933, the day Lewis and Jews around the world had long dreaded finally happened: Adolf Hitler became the Reich's chancellor of Germany. In the weeks following his appointment, the news coming out of Germany was filled with horror after horror. The führer was turning anti-Semitism into a national policy. Over the next several months, Jews were gradually barred from civil employment, from owning businesses, from teaching in or attending universities, and from participating in any organized German sport. That May, a jubilant crowd of 40,000 cheered as 5,000 students marched to the square in front of the opera house and burned 20,000 "subversive" books that reflected an "un-Teutonic spirit." Worse yet, Americans fleeing Germany told reporters of mass violence against the nation's Jews. As early as March 1933, the *London Daily Herald* predicted that Nazis would soon launch a pogrom "on a scale as terrible as any instance of Jewish persecution in 2,000 years."[15]

Jewish leaders across the nation could not agree on the best ways to deal with the rise of Nazism abroad and at home. They were not alone. It took president Franklin D. Roosevelt until May 1934 to convene his top advisers to discuss whether Nazis posed a threat to national security and whether they should be put under surveillance.

Responding to the Nazi threat, representatives from the American Jewish Committee, B'nai B'rith, and the American Jewish Congress—the three leading national groups—met in New York in March 1933 and agreed to form a joint committee to monitor the evolving situation. What they could not agree upon was how openly militant Jews should be in responding to growing German violence.

Lewis read newspaper accounts of how the 1,500 Jewish representatives who met in New York were divided between those who favored quiet diplomacy and those who demanded forceful public action. New York Supreme Court justice Joseph Proskauer and Judge Irving Lehman of the American Jewish Committee counseled restraint. Public protests in America would only further endanger German Jews, they warned. However, it was the charismatic rabbi Stephen Wise who swayed the delegates. How could Jews "ask our Christian friends to lift their voices in protest against the wrongs suffered by Jews if we keep silent?" What was happening in Germany, he warned, could "happen tomorrow in any other land on earth unless it is challenged and rebuked."[16] Wise called on all parties to join his upcoming protest rally at Madison Square Garden.

On March 27, 1933, 65,000 people poured into the New York arena to hear Senator Robert F. Wagner, former New York governor Al Smith, Rabbi Wise, and several Christian clergy endorse a worldwide boycott of German goods and call on the Hitler regime to halt its brutal treatment of German Jewry. Those who could not attend listened to the speeches being broadcast worldwide on radio; others went to similar rallies held in over seventy cities, including a mass demonstration of 50,000 in Chicago.

The response from German authorities was swift and brutal. Denouncing accusations concerning the persecution of Jews as slanderous lies, Nazi Party officials called on all Aryan Germans to hold a one-day boycott of Jewish-owned businesses on April 1. If the American press ceased their pernicious charges against the Nazi regime, minister of propaganda Joseph Goebbels promised to halt any further boycott. However, if press attacks continued, Goebbels warned, the "the boycott will be resumed . . . until German Jewry has been annihilated."[17]

On April 1, German storm troopers watched as incensed protestors throughout Germany smashed windows, harassed customers, and threw stink bombs inside Jewish-owned businesses. Although U.S. secretary of state Cordell Hull issued a mild statement condemning these "unfortunate incidents," he, like many government officials, privately believed that the reports of violence against German Jews were greatly exaggerated.[18]

Alarmed by the news coming out of Germany and by the formation of "Hitler cells" in numerous American cities, Jewish leaders in Los Angeles held several meetings that winter and spring aimed at forging a united body that could act on behalf of the city's Jews. Attending the gatherings in his official capacity as the ADL's representative to Southern California, Lewis discovered that Los Angeles Jews were no more united than their counterparts across the nation: some called for aggressive boycotts, while others favored enlisting the support of sympathetic Christian leaders who could quietly pressure Hitler into easing his anti-Semitic policies.

Leon Lewis hoped for something more than boycotts, rallies, and denunciations. These were all reactive measures; he wanted Jews to pursue a far more proactive approach to dealing with the Nazi threat—a threat most Americans did not yet fully understand. Lewis knew from years of monitoring the foreign press that the Nazi government encouraged Germans living in the United States to form "active 'cells' wherever sufficient numbers of National Socialists can be gathered into proselytizing units."[19] He had witnessed the Nazi movement come to Chicago in October 1924, when Hitler's German-born followers organized the Free Society of Teutonia, and saw it quickly spread to cities throughout the East and Midwest.

In March 1933 former German captain Robert Pape and his Nazi cohort established a beachhead in Los Angeles, setting up quarters at the Alt Heidelberg on Alvarado Street and opening the Aryan Bookstore, a propaganda center that "teem[ed] with Nazi and Adolf Hitler books and literature." Reports in the local *B'nai B'rith Messenger* warned that representatives "direct from Germany" were bringing National Socialism to Los Angeles "in a quiet and secret fashion."[20]

Several weeks later, the Nazis emerged from the shadows and held a meeting at Turnverein Hall, where a packed hall of Germans came to hear Pape and his brethren sing the praises of the New Germany. Pape predicted that Communists and their Jewish allies would eventually try to seize control of the American government. On that day, Nazis would rise and save America by destroying the Communists and eliminating the Jewish menace. Pape and his fellow speakers left the stage to enthusiastic applause and numerous requests for applications to join the Friends of New Germany.[21]

Lewis discovered that Nazis were holding closed weekly meetings at their headquarters and attracting dozens of sympathizers. One tipster told him how Hans Winterhalder was fostering "bitterness and animosity towards the Jews." The local propaganda chief warned German-speaking residents that one day they would "awake and be forced to take similar action [against Jews] as the Germans for their own preservation."[22]

Following their first public gathering on July 26, Nazi speakers stepped up their weekly attacks. "Jews hate Gentiles and cheat us whenever they can," exclaimed one Friends of New Germany orator. Jews, insisted another speaker, "are fresh, indecent, conceited and know no scruples . . . They are not of the White Race, they are Semites (Half Niggers). Gentiles beware of Jewish Domination."[23]

By late summer, Pape and Winterhalder had attracted 400 new disciples to their cause. Lewis was far more concerned with the Friends of New Germany's ability to recruit among the city's 150,000 Germans, 17,000 Poles, and 13,000 Austrians, as well as the area's tens of thousands of unemployed.[24]

Nazis had every reason to believe their strategy of appealing to disgruntled veterans would succeed. In May 1932, 10,000 World War I veterans, many of them unemployed since the onset of the Great Depression, marched to Washington, D.C., to demand that Congress give them an early payment of their military service bonus. When legislators refused to do so, the Bonus Army, as the press dubbed them, camped out near the Capitol in peaceful protest. Three months later, after receiving a request from President Herbert Hoover to disband the orderly protestors, General Douglas MacArthur led an armed force of 400 infantry, 200 cavalry, and 6 tanks, attacking and gassing the veterans and burning their makeshift tent camps to the ground. Two marchers were killed, 55 injured, and 135 arrested. That July, angry Bonus March veterans in Pennsylvania set out to recruit 1 million men into their "Khaki Shirt" movement.[25]

The election of Franklin D. Roosevelt did little to quell growing discontent among veterans. Shortly after taking office, Roosevelt tried to balance his budget by ordering severe cuts in veterans' benefits. Pensions for 20,000 former servicemen were slashed by over 40 percent, while monthly stipends for those on disability were reduced by 25 percent. Faced with outrage from veterans' groups and the threat of a second Bonus March, Congress restored many of the cuts that June. But under another series of reductions, many disabled veterans who had been supporting their families on $60 to $80 a month were permanently cut off from all benefits.[26]

Since approximately one-third of all disabled veterans lived in Southern California, Los Angeles was fertile ground for Nazi recruiters. Lewis observed, "Many of the men are disgruntled over recent legislation cutting down their compensation, they are out of work and discouraged and a great many of them are ripe for conversion to Fascism." Nazis remained confident that these angry men would make "easy prey for the spreading of un-American and anti-American doctrines and the concoction of anti-American plots."[27]

The U.S. government was not closely monitoring Nazi activities in America. Curt Riess, a Berlin-born Jew who covered Hollywood for the French magazine *Paris Soir*, noted in 1934 that the United States was the only great power that "possessed neither an espionage system nor a counterespionage system." The FBI did not engage in espionage unless asked to do so by naval or army intelligence, which had an annual budget of $30,000 between them. Even if asked, the FBI had only 300 agents in November 1933, none of whom were trained in counterespionage. "Every day and every hour since Hitler had taken power, Nazi agents in the United States were plotting against America," Riess warned. "No wonder that Hitler and Goebbels often declared to their intimates, that nothing would be easier than 'to produce unrest and revolution in the United States.'"[28]

In July 1933, Leon Lewis, dubbed "the most dangerous Jew in Los Angeles" by local Nazis, launched an undercover operation under the auspices of the newly created Community Committee. As he told one friend, he had done secret intelligence work for the military during World War I.[29]

Far from being a lone wolf, Lewis began the Community Committee as a local "civic protective group" with close ties to the local ADL and B'nai B'rith. Drawing on his military planning background, Lewis spent the next two months designing a command structure that included subcommittees in charge of information gathering, dissemination, and support. His core "Advisory Committee" consisted of nine major Jewish leaders and was chaired by Mendel Silberberg, an Army Air Force veteran and Los Angeles's most powerful entertainment attorney.[30]

RECRUITING UNDERCOVER AGENTS

An inner circle of prominent Jews was great, but to succeed, the Community Committee had to be more than just a Jewish organization. Lewis attracted several prominent leaders from Disabled American Veterans and American Legion posts to his advisory board by framing his operation not as a defense of Jews but as a patriotic effort to root out "un-American" groups that sought to subvert democratic values. The men who joined Lewis's board were veterans he knew and trusted—and who trusted him—from years of attending meetings at Patriotic Hall and from his work heading the Americanism Committee of both organizations.

To give his undercover operation greater legitimacy, Lewis persuaded the Disabled American Veterans county board to pass a resolution that August condemning Nazism and demanding that "Germans do not organize any Nazist groups in these democratic United States" built "upon racial hatreds or prejudice." Several days later, delegates to California's American Legion convention, at Lewis's urging, passed a similar resolution condemning "groups holding their primary allegiance to foreign governments." They called on American authorities "to take prompt and efficient steps to prevent such attempts to undermine the principles of our free and democratic form of government."[31]

Sending a copy of the latter resolution to ADL national director Richard Gutstadt, a pleased Lewis noted that "there is no direct reference to persecution of Jews in the resolution. The action is based upon a direct appeal to patriotism and the prevention of foreign propaganda in America."[32]

With his advisory board set and his operation endorsed by veterans' groups, Lewis focused on launching an undercover operation. To succeed, he needed the right kind of men and women working alongside him. The Nazis desperately wanted to recruit American war veterans into the FNG. Hitler's American followers hoped to build their movement by persuading disgruntled veterans to join their cause, just as the führer had done in the 1920s. "The major objective of this [FNG] organization," Lewis observed, "was to build centers of Anti-Jewish hatred in American groups and organizations and for several months no effort was spared by the Nazis to convert groups within the various veteran organizations to their cause."[33]

Nazis were likely to recognize any Semitic-looking men or women who tried to infiltrate their organization. Consequently, Lewis needed Christians to work as his undercover operatives. Knowing that his best chance of success lay with selecting people attractive to the Nazi group, Lewis first turned to his fellow DAV post member John Schmidt for help. It proved a brilliant but problematic choice: brilliant because of the German's background but problematic because he had been hospitalized for a nervous breakdown after World War I and placed on permanent disability.[34]

Lewis was willing to take a chance on a man he knew the Nazis would welcome as a dream recruit: a decorated but disgruntled veteran who had served in both the German and American armies with distinction. The son of a general in the Bavarian field artillery, Schmidt was born in February 1886 and trained as a cadet in the German army before coming to the United States around 1903. Enlisting in the U.S. Army in February 1915, he fought with General John J. Pershing in Mexico and

Capt. John Schmidt
USC Libraries Special Collections

then in France with the U.S. Infantry during World War I. He retired with the rank of captain in December 1918.[35]

Schmidt, the DAV deputy chief of staff for California, was drawn into espionage after Lewis explained how Friends of New Germany leaders were using discontent surrounding the Economy Act of 1933 to "foment discord among disabled veterans." Like many of his countrymen, Schmidt hated what Hitler was doing to his beloved Germany. He believed all Nazis "ought to be lined up against the wall and filled full of lead." After Lewis appealed to his patriotism and promised the cash-strapped veteran a modest monthly stipend, Schmidt—who operated under the code names Agent 11, 74, and Elf—agreed to pose as a Nazi sympathizer and work his way into the leadership ranks of the FNG.[36]

THE SPY OPERATION

In mid-August 1933, Lewis began conducting his spy operation out of his small law office on the fourth floor of the downtown Roosevelt Building, located at the northeast corner of Seventh and Flower Streets. Risking his family's safety, Schmidt enlisted the help of his wife, Alice Schmidt (Agent 17), who, like her husband, was fluent in German and a staunch foe of the Nazis. Lewis also recruited his only Jewish operative, William C. Conley, the national commander of the DAV, who agreed to join the FNG and pose as a Nazi sympathizer.

With three spies on board, Lewis used his respected positions in the veteran community to persuade several more DAV leaders and their wives to join every local Nazi and fascist group and report back on their activities. Lewis wanted experienced soldiers who would not be prone to fear or exaggeration. If these seasoned veterans came to see Nazis as posing a threat to Americans, the government agencies he eventually hoped to contact could not accuse Lewis of engaging in Jewish paranoia. Lewis did not plan to remain a spymaster for long. As soon as his agents gathered sufficient evidence of wrongdoing, he intended to turn their reports over to the government and let them run the spy operation. Once they did, he would return to practicing law.

Lewis understood that spying was a dangerous business that could "jeopardize the personal safety" of his spies, their families, and his own. To protect their identities, he assigned each spy a code name and insisted that they communicate all information under their secret identity.

"These men and woman had never done intelligence work before," he recounted. "They required careful guidance and direction." Lewis instructed them to discover what Nazis, fascists, and other hate groups were doing. Their ultimate goal was to "blow the Nazi movement in America to smithereens and to discredit completely all anti-Semitic organizations and American bigots who have any truck with them."[37]

Before turning them loose, Lewis gave his spies a final set of instructions aimed at protecting them from foul play. First, he told them never to use their home address but instead to open a post office box where they could receive correspondence from Nazi and fascist groups. Second, he warned them "never to write anything while they were in the presence of Nazis or anti-Semites." Lewis either met his operatives in person or talked to them on the phone, taking down their reports in shorthand.[38] Finally, he wanted his agents to keep close tabs on the Nazis' most prominent allies: the Silver Shirts, the Ku Klux Klan, and the American Labor Party and its military wing, the Lode Star Legion.

Lewis asked Schmidt to begin the spy operation by attending Nazi and Silver Shirt meetings and befriending their members. Executing that mission, as Schmidt soon discovered, proved far more dangerous than anyone anticipated.

2.

The Spying Begins

John Schmidt planned his strategy for penetrating the Friends of New Germany in the same way he would plan an undercover military operation: lull the enemy into a false sense of security and then have them welcome him into their ranks. That meant visiting FNG headquarters, mingling with the Nazi faithful, and convincing them he would be a valuable addition to their cause.

Schmidt certainly did not look like a spy. At five foot eleven, the forty-eight-year-old veteran weighed a portly 200 pounds and looked more like a kindly grandfather. But with blond hair and piercing blue eyes, he certainly looked like an Aryan grandpa.

The former army captain who spoke with a heavy German accent began his campaign on Thursday, August 17, 1933, by visiting the Aryan Bookstore. Housed on the ground floor of the Alt Heidelberg building, the bookstore served as the chief distribution center for Nazi propaganda on the West Coast. A lively haunt of the city's German community, the multipurpose building also contained a beer garden, a large German restaurant, several private dining rooms, and, on the second floor, the FNG headquarters. Its regular patrons referred to the Alt Heidelberg as the Brown House, the name given to Nazi headquarters in Munich.

At Leon Lewis's urging, Schmidt returned to the bookstore several times over the next week, browsing through its shelves and talking to patrons. He found the place crammed with anti-Communist literature and the latest German books, pamphlets, and anti-Semitic newspapers like Julius Streicher's *Der Stürmer*, Joseph Goebbels's *Der Angriff*, and the local *California Staats Zeitung*—all intended to update German émigrés and their American offspring on the great strides Hitler was

Aryan Bookstore Vandalized, January 1934; Hermann Schwinn on left
Jewish Federation Council of Greater Los Angeles, Community Relations Committee Collection, Part 2,
Special Collections and Archives, Oviatt Library, California State University, Northridge

making in rebuilding the fatherland. Those who preferred English reading matter could purchase copies of the infamous *Protocols of the Elders of Zion*. The fabricated anti-Semitic text published in Russia in 1903 purported to reveal Jewish plans for world domination and subversion of Christian morals. Auto manufacturer and anti-Semite Henry Ford popularized the book in the United States by distributing 500,000 copies during the 1920s.[1]

After multiple visits, Schmidt began discussing the bookstore's literature with two fellow Germans. As their conversation veered toward politics, the men lectured him on how Jews and Communists posed the greatest threat to America. "The favorite subject of conversation among these men and any visitor who came into the store," Schmidt reported to Lewis, was that "President Roosevelt was a tool in the hands of the International Jew" and that he "must be replaced by someone whom the veterans and the Nazis would select."[2] Schmidt listened sympathetically and feigned agreement with their anti-Semitic views. Believing they had met a kindred spirit, his new acquaintances invited him to lunch.

As they walked into one of the Alt Heidelberg's private dining rooms, Schmidt learned that his hosts were Captain Robert Pape, *Obergauführer* (local leader) of the FNG, and Hans Winterhalder, their propaganda chief. Pape was a World War I veteran and active Nazi party member who came to the United States in late 1931. Two years later, Heinz Spanknöbel, the FNG's national leader, sent him to Los Angeles to organize Nazi branches along the Pacific Coast. Pape was currently living at the Alt Heidelberg on a modest military pension he received from Germany. (Only later would Leon Lewis learn that Pape was reporting directly to Hitler and propaganda minister Joseph Goebbels.)[3]

Winterhalder was another die-hard Hitlerite who had traveled throughout the United States since 1925, building support for the budding National Socialist movement. Soon after settling in Los Angeles in 1929, he claimed his service station went bankrupt "on account of animosity of Jewish customers." In addition to running the FNG's propaganda operations, Winterhalder also served as its *Werbeleiter*, the officer in charge of recruiting new members.[4]

Suspecting Schmidt might be an infiltrator, Pape and Winterhalder grilled him about his background. The Nazi leaders were impressed when Agent 11 told them his father had been a general in the Bavarian field artillery and his brother a lieutenant colonel in the Bavarian army who fought in World War I. Schmidt described his own military service in the German army, fighting with General John J. Pershing in Mexico and with the American Expeditionary Forces in France during the Great War. Acting the part of a disgruntled veteran, Schmidt explained how he sustained serious injuries during the war but had been denied disability payments because he failed to file his claim on time. Without his military pension, the ex-soldier could not afford needed medical care. Everything Schmidt said was the truth; he had been seriously injured and subsequently denied his pension. He was angry with the government for its shabby treatment of veterans. What he did not mention was that he was even angrier at what Hitler was doing to his former homeland.[5]

Pape and Winterhalder continued to quiz Schmidt "about my early experiences in Germany and asked me to bring and show to them my German army papers . . . also my American army papers, American Legion and D. A. V. papers." Insisting that a military man like Schmidt "could be very useful to them," the Nazi leaders asked him to join their organization. Although it usually took four weeks to investigate an applicant's background, given his family's distinguished military service, Pape and Winterhalder assured him they could accelerate the process.[6]

Convinced they were in the presence of a sympathetic German, Pape and Winterhalder revealed why they wanted more American veterans. The FNG hoped to train a group of former military leaders "who in turn can train others so that in a few months time the organization will

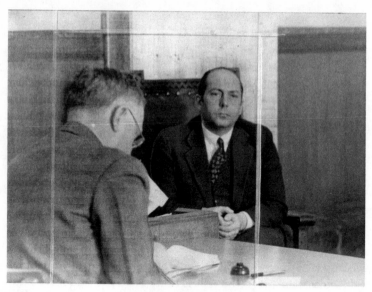

Capt. Robert Pape, January 1934
USC Libraries Special Collections

be functioning on a broad scale." The FNG operated along paramilitary lines similar to those Hitler had used with his Brownshirts in the 1920s. Like the führer, they maintained an elite storm trooper (*Sturmabteilung*) unit limited to a few well-trained men who wore brown-shirt uniforms with black swastika armbands surrounded by a red circle. As their meal drew to an end, Pape and Winterhalder asked Schmidt to introduce them to like-minded DAV and American Legion officers who could help recruit others to their cause.[7]

Schmidt made quite an impression on the two Nazis. Returning to the Aryan Bookstore a few days later, he discovered that the word had gone out "that special respect is to be shown to me." Bookstore owner Paul Themlitz made a point to greet his latest customer. Themlitz gave Schmidt some anti-Semitic literature and recommended he read the fascist Silver Shirt newspaper *Liberation* to learn the "truth about the Jews in America." When Themlitz brought him upstairs to meet the men who staffed the FNG's main offices, Schmidt saw that this was no ordinary bookstore owner. As he would later learn, the tall, blond, thirty-one-year-old German served as the FNG's number-two man and its liaison to their Silver Shirt allies.[8]

Hans Winterhalder and Paul Themlitz, January 1934
USC Libraries Special Collections

Schmidt returned to Nazi headquarters several times over the next week, often accompanied by his wife, Alice. The couple visited the bookstore, mingled with patrons, and at one point dined with fifteen "inside initiates," including Los Angeles Police captain William "Red" Hynes, head of the city's notorious Red Squad. During one of their meals, Winterhalder boasted how Nazis were secretly infiltrating the Jewish-dominated studios. Six of his men were working in Hollywood as film extras and "gathering information in the studios on how the Jews were ruining 'white girls.'"[9]

On the evening of August 22, John Schmidt attended his first FNG meeting, along with eighty-two other men and women. He listened as a series of Nazi speakers described themselves as loyal Americans who were leading the fight against communism. When the German orators were done, Pape asked Schmidt to address the gathering. Telling them what they wanted to hear, Schmidt insisted that "America needs shaking up and waking up from what is known in America as communism." He described the work of PAL (Patriotism, Americanism, and Loyalty), a recently organized veterans' group. Schmidt hoped the veterans and the FNG would unite "to rid America of communism, and Bolshevism which is a thorn in the side of this country."[10]

RECRUITING NEW SPIES

Lewis's spy could not have made a better first impression. To gain the Nazis' full confidence, Schmidt had to deliver on his promise to recruit other veterans. Several days later, he brought Captain Carl Sunderland and Hugh Harold, a former Disabled American Veteran commander, to lunch at the Alt Heidelberg. To make their reactions more convincing, Schmidt never told his companions the true reason for their visit. As they walked through the restaurant, many of the diners greeted Schmidt as a welcome friend. Sitting down to dinner, the three men were joined by Pape, FNG secretary Hermann Schwinn, and Karl Specht, head of the local storm trooper unit. The Nazi contingent told their guests about the great work being done to promote the German cause in America, especially among ex-soldiers. Seeing an opportunity to do his own recruiting, Specht invited Sunderland to attend the storm troopers' next English-only meeting.

As they left the restaurant, Schmidt's companions were confused by their friend's relationship to the Nazis. "This is a dangerous mob," Harold warned. "They are smart, systematic, highly educated men." Waiting until no one could hear them, Schmidt finally told Harold and Sunderland he was there to spy on the Nazis. "I have no sympathy with foreign spies, even if they are German." Now that they saw what the Nazis were like, Schmidt wanted them to join Lewis's undercover operation. Agreeing that "such a mob has no place in the United States," Sunderland volunteered to help in whatever way he could and told Schmidt he could call on him "day or night if necessary."[11]

Schmidt was delighted. Carl Sunderland seemed a perfect recruit to the Nazi cause. Born in Fort Wayne, Indiana, in 1884, the onetime salesman had a long military career. He'd served three stints with the Thirteenth Cavalry beginning in 1906, and fought in World War I until discharged with the rank of captain in February 1919. Wounded in combat, the forty-nine-year-old veteran was incensed when his disability payment was reduced to $45 a month in August 1933. As post commander of L.A. Chapter No. 5 DAV, Sunderland could bring a sizable number of men into the Nazi fold.[12]

Friends of New Germany leaders were equally impressed with Sunderland's family background. His grandparents were German, as was his wife's grandmother. What his hosts did not know was that the five-foot-nine midwesterner had taken three years of German in high school, and although he could not speak the language very well, he could comprehend what Nazis said when they thought they could speak without being understood.[13]

After Schmidt delivered his first recruits, Schwinn informed him that his application for membership had been approved. Schmidt agreed to take the secret oath required of all initiates: "I am prepared to enter the League of Friends of New Germany. The aims and purpose of the League are known to me, and I pledge myself to support them without any reservation whatsoever. I acknowledge unconditionally the leadership principle upon which the League is formed. I belong to no Semitic organization (Freemasonry, etc.). I am of Aryan stock and have neither Jewish nor colored blood in me."[14]

Now that Schmidt was one of them, Schwinn asked Schmidt to drive him to San Pedro Harbor to meet the recently arrived German ship *Este*. This was the first time a Lewis spy got a clear sense of the group's intimate ties to the Nazi regime and their plans for potential sabotage. As they walked around the docks, Schmidt observed how Schwinn "seemed particularly well versed on Japanese boats and Japanese interests in certain canneries. He also told me the names of some of the battleships in the Harbor and sneeringly remarked that . . . [Germans] could blow them all out of the water with great ease." The Nazi leader boasted that "this coast line here is open very easily to air attack at any time." Schmidt let him go on talking about our coast defenses, "about which he seemed to know quite a good deal."[15]

As the two men boarded the *Este*, sailors greeted them with a round of "Heil Hitler" and Nazi salutes. Schwinn introduced his companion as "a great fuehrer in the American Legion and D. A. V." who was "lining up the Veteran organizations with the Nazis." Delighted to meet a new ally, fourth officer Kurt Waldman, one of the likely Gestapo agents who traveled on each German vessel, described their great progress in recruiting new FNG members in Vancouver (450), Seattle (600), Portland (400), and San Francisco (300). As they prepared to leave the boat, Schmidt observed a ship officer pass Schwinn a large package of money. This was the first of many instances in which Lewis's spies saw money and propaganda being illegally smuggled into the Los Angeles port, something the Nazi government vehemently denied doing.[16]

Impressed by the efficiency of the local Nazi operation, a troubled John Schmidt contacted Lewis later that evening to report on his initial findings. He confessed that at first he thought the men he met at the dock and at FNG headquarters were "cranks and fanatics." But he had come to realize they were dangerous foes and that it was "up to me as an American citizen and lover of this country to use every possible effort to bring these men to the end they deserve."[17]

Having glimpsed the Nazis' potential for destruction, Schmidt told Lewis, "I want you to help me by putting under my direction a few

absolutely loyal men so they can become members of the Nazi organization. And so I can help to put them in key positions." Lewis agreed to
do so.[18]

With Lewis's approval, Schmidt and Sunderland recruited another
veteran into their spy operation, Major C. Bert Allen (Agent 7), and
brought him to meet the FNG leadership. The Nazis were impressed.
The thirty-six-year-old Missouri Baptist had won a Distinguished Service
Cross, was head of the PAL organization, and served as state adjutant
for Disabled American Veterans. After introducing their guest to Hans
Winterhalder and discussing the current plight of American veterans,
the Nazi hosts asked Allen to help them "throw the united force of the
DAV with their [Nazi] movement and the movement of the Silver
Shirts."[19] Feigning interest, the major suggested PAL and the Nazis
could work together to eliminate communism.

Shortly afterward, Allen convened a meeting of the PAL executive
board and told them what he had learned. Appalled by what they heard,
the board granted Allen authority to string the Nazis along, provided
PAL did not "become involved in anything that would place them in
the wrong position with the government."[20]

By early September Schmidt had become an important member of
the FNG and a valuable conduit to local veterans' groups. During the
next few weeks he bore deeper into the Nazi ranks, bringing more
potential recruits and attending every weekly FNG meeting. Turnout at
Nazi gatherings had grown so great, upward of 400, that the group
moved their headquarters to Turnverein Hall on 1004 West Washington
Boulevard, where they also opened a second Aryan Bookstore.

Schmidt's wife, Alice (Agent 17), who spoke and wrote German, was
one of those recruits. She attended so many meetings that she was asked
to become president of the FNG's Ladies Auxiliary and help with
needed translation and paperwork in the group's offices. This gave the
bilingual spy an opportunity to read their mail and send her own reports
to Leon Lewis, who operated under the code name L1. John and Alice
gained the confidence of the Nazi inner circle and loosened their
tongues by inviting them to their home on multiple occasions to dine
with Sunderland, Allen, and their wives. Carl and Blanche Sunderland also welcomed FNG leaders into their home for meals and
conversation.

After spending considerable time working in the FNG offices, Alice
warned Lewis that Winterhalder was "a very dangerous man. He has
the eyes of a fanatic. He is very nervous." He and Pape were "working

very systematically to bring Nazism to America."[21] Most of what she and John had heard up to this point was just talk: talk about the need to create a united front of disgruntled veterans, dedicated fascists, and American Nazis who would rid the nation of the Communist and Jewish menace—which Nazis saw as one and the same. Once they became more deeply entrenched in the FNG, the couple learned that several Nazis planned to do more than just spread propaganda.

Winterhalder felt so confident about Schmidt's loyalty that he told him about the FNG's secret long-term plan to seize control of the American government. The "time would not be so long before" the Nazis would launch "armed revolts and uprisings against the Jews" and "overthrow this, our present form of government." To accomplish that, the Nazi propaganda chief needed Schmidt to "take those American veterans who would not line up with the Germans into the Silver Shirt organization" and create an army of anti-Communist, anti-Semitic ex-soldiers willing to join the upcoming revolution.[22]

Robert Pape's wife confided to Alice that she and her husband knew John could be a great help by becoming "the backbone of the local organization." When Winterhalder and Themlitz dined at the Schmidt home one evening along with Allen, the Nazis casually queried them about the arms and military equipment the American Legion possessed and whether the National Guard would be loyal "in case of a revolt."[23]

Nazi leaders believed they could count on the local law enforcement officials for help. Police captain William "Red" Hynes was a regular presence at FNG headquarters and could often be found dining with its leaders. Schwinn boasted to Sunderland that Hynes "was a true friend of ours. Any time we want any help or information from him, I either go to his office or we have lunch together."[24] He had suggested FNG members stop wearing brown shirts to meetings so as not to antagonize citizens who associated the garb with Hitler's forces.

Schwinn misread Hynes's loyalties. The police captain cared about only one thing, catching Communists, and would use anyone—Nazi or Jew—to do so. The captain of the Los Angeles Police Department's intelligence bureau—or Red Squad, as it was popularly known—had worked for the city's police the previous eleven years and headed the Red Squad for seven years. Like FBI director J. Edgar Hoover, Hynes took Soviet leaders at their word when in March 1919 they declared their intention to launch a worldwide revolution aimed at destroying capitalism. Hoping to prevent that from happening on American soil, the young police officer went undercover in 1922 and joined the Communist Party while also serving as state secretary of the radical Industrial Workers of the World. Hynes made himself a welcome presence at the FNG by providing them with useful information and police protection from time to time. But he was no true friend; he was using them to gather information about their mutual enemy, the Communists. The Nazis earned his favor by providing him with lists of people belonging to Red groups, but Hynes was no fool. Although far more concerned with Reds, he kept an eye on the Nazis and purchased a copy of its secret membership list for $250 from the cash-strapped Winterhalder.[25]

Uncertain of Hynes's loyalties but needing his help, Lewis asked fellow B'nai B'rith member and DAV national commander Colonel William C. Conley to alert the Red Squad leader to the Nazi threat. In early September, Conley (Agent WC) met with Hynes and described the FNG as preaching messages "just as bad, if not worse, than the communistic propaganda in the United States." Hynes responded that he "had been watching them [Nazis] for some time and that he had a man out there who was sending him reports." However, he lacked the money needed to keep monitoring the group (though there always seemed to be sufficient funds to keep the city's Reds under constant surveillance).[26]

The Jewish colonel believed he was swaying the police captain to his cause until Hynes revealed his anti-Semitic leanings. The FNG's ideology, Hynes told him, "is based upon the foundation that all American troubles are due to communists and that all Jews are communists," an ideology that seemed to jibe with his own. He closed by warning Conley that the *B'nai B'rith Messenger* "was doing a lot of harm to the Jews."[27]

Refusing to be discouraged, Conley met Hynes outside the downtown Los Angeles police building a few days later, where they could talk without being overheard. He told Hynes he had raised the money needed to maintain police presence inside the FNG. The Red Squad captain seemed uninterested until Conley added that "there would be a piece of change in it for him, to which he said, 'all right' and warmed up considerably more in the balance of the conversation." Happy to accept the payment, Hynes made no promises about how the money would be used.[28]

Even without Hynes's assistance, Schmidt accomplished everything Lewis had hoped he would. As he brought more veterans to meetings, Nazi leaders grew increasingly comfortable revealing confidential information about their inner workings. Swearing the former captain to secrecy, Hermann Schwinn explained that the local FNG, which now had 425 members, took orders from New York, which in turn received instructions from Berlin. Schwinn confided that his group was plotting to take over the wealthy German-American Alliance (Deutsch Amerikanischer Stadtverband, a consortium of all German American associations in Los Angeles) in order to seize control of its considerable bank account of $30,000 ($549,000 in 2015 dollars) and its large plot of land in nearby La Crescenta. The Nazis would use the money for more aggressive recruiting and propaganda campaigns, and the land as a picnic area for Nazi functions. Hoping to garner support among veterans, Schwinn asked Schmidt to serve as a delegate to the forthcoming German-American Alliance elections.[29]

IS ANYONE PAYING ATTENTION?

Sitting in his downtown office on Seventh Street, Leon Lewis read the reports from Schmidt, Sunderland, and Allen with growing concern. Ignoring his law practice, he spent his days talking to them on the telephone or meeting at places where they would not be seen. His spies had found enough evidence of hatred and plotting to be concerned about the fate of Los Angeles's Jews and American democracy. These plans might never be realized, but could he take a chance? No one had believed Hitler's Brownshirts could seize control of Germany, but they had.

Knowing the potential threat was greater than he and his spies could handle, Lewis turned to government officials for help. On the morning of September 15, he and Community Committee treasurer Armin Wittenberg met with Los Angeles police chief James "Two Gun" Davis. The colorful chief had earned his sobriquet because of his ability to shoot with both hands and his policy of instructing men to fire first and ask questions later. He enjoyed posing with two guns aimed at the camera and demonstrating his skill by shooting cigarettes out of the mouths of frightened volunteers.[30]

Meeting in Davis's office, Lewis introduced himself as an attorney and former national secretary of the B'nai B'rith who had been conducting an investigation of Nazi activities in Southern California. He had discovered that "their ultimate objective was to foster a fascist form of government in the United States." He knew that Captain Hynes was also investigating subversive groups and was prepared to turn over important information his undercover agents had obtained so that the police could take action.[31]

Lewis was shocked when, three minutes into his talk, Davis interrupted him to defend Hitler. The police chief calmly explained that when Hitler realized that "Germans could not compete economically with the Jews in Germany," his government had "been forced to take the action which it did take." Davis spent the next fifteen minutes lecturing Lewis and Wittenberg on the causes of Hitlerism and ended by saying he would accept their reports but would not provide them with any police data.[32]

The normally calm Lewis was barely able to contain his anger at Davis's "implication that our sole interest in this matter was as Jews." He informed the chief that he had been a captain in the U.S. Army and had served eighteen months overseas. Moreover, he was acting not as a Jew but as chair of the American Legion's Americanism Committee. The reports he received from his operatives, all war veterans, "clearly demonstrated the anti-American purposes of the leaders of the Nazi group both here and generally throughout the country." Nazi efforts "to create a fascist action in the United States," he warned Davis, "were an attack on life and property."[33]

Unmoved by the attorney's appeal, Davis curtly responded that Communists posed a far greater menace to the city than Nazis, and that the greatest threat to democracy emanated from the Jewish-dominated Boyle Heights area. "In fact," Lewis later noted, "one could conclude from his talk that all Jews are communists." The police chief ended the conversation by promising to discuss the matter with Captain Hynes.[34]

Police captain William "Red" Hynes and police chief James Davis
Los Angeles Daily News Negatives, Collection 1387, UCLA Library Special Collections, Charles E. Young Research Library, UCLA

Returning to his office, a deeply upset Lewis wrote a memo recounting the visit. He now believed rumors that the police chief had joined the Silver Shirts, "or at least that he promised them the support of the Police Department."[35]

Lewis thought about sending State Department officials evidence of foreign propaganda being shipped into Los Angeles, but—knowing the department to be rife with anti-Semites who might leak his reports—he decided to wait because "a premature disclosure of this information would jeopardize the personal safety of five families, including my own."[36]

Undeterred, Lewis asked his spy Bert Allen to arrange a meeting with Joe Dunn, the Justice Department's Secret Service chief for Southern California. Gathering at the home of a mutual friend in late September, Allen told Dunn about Lewis's undercover investigation of local Nazis and suggested that the Secret Service could pursue matters far more effectively than Lewis's small band of spies. Although moved by Allen's appeal, Dunn explained, his office "could not do anything about the matter on its own initiative without the commission of some overt act." The Secret Service head suggested Allen contact Justice Department officials in Washington, D.C., and ask them to launch a local investigation. In the meantime, Dunn recommended that Lewis's group make use of their findings "by giving widespread publicity to the results of the[ir] investigation."[37]

FOMENTING DISCORD FROM WITHIN

Convinced there would be no help from government authorities at any level, Lewis and his agents set out to undermine the local Nazi movement by fueling dissension among its leaders. Although sharing a common cause and quarters at the Alt Heidelberg, Schwinn, Pape, and Winterhalder shared no love for one another. "Captain Pape is all right in Germany," Winterhalder confided to Schmidt, "but here in American life he is only too slow, but too dumb, and can not grasp opportunities. Neither does he understand the American public or the American veteran." Winterhalder's assessment of Pape was accurate. The captain had lost his taste for militant action and wanted nothing more than to return to Germany. As Pape confided to Schmidt, he would never take out citizenship papers "in a rotten country . . . run by Jews and Catholics."[38]

Not only was Pape homesick, but he talked too much, especially after consuming alcohol. That became clear when he asked Schmidt and Conley to travel down to the docks to meet the German vessel *Seattle*. As they spent the afternoon socializing with the ship's officers, Lewis's agents pretended to get drunk, hoping an inebriated Pape might slip and reveal confidential information. He soon did. Slurring his words, Pape promised that once "the nations of the earth were awakened to the menace of Jewry," they "would purify themselves by following the example of Germany." What "Hitler has done for the German nation, he could do for America."[39]

Pape was burned out, and the FNG's ambitious secretary, Hermann Schwinn, knew it. The only naturalized citizen among the FNG's four leaders, the Hamburg-born Schwinn had moved to Canton, Ohio, with his parents in 1924, and worked as a bank clerk until settling in Los Angeles in 1928 to take a similar position with a German-American bank. After losing his job in the Depression, the slender twenty-eight-year-old German with a Hitler mustache accepted a position as Pape's assistant and secretary of the newly formed FNG. But the ambitious Schwinn was never happy being anyone's assistant. Desperately wanting to take over the leadership reins, he pulled Schmidt aside one afternoon and insisted it was time to unseat Pape and Winterhalder. Schwinn wanted to "send the whole damn bunch back to Germany as they need a better type of material who can keep their mouths shut and act like gentlemen."[40]

Schmidt, Sunderland, and Allen listened to the Friends of New Germany leaders complain about each other and urged them to unseat their rivals. "We have made the whole gang suspicious of each other," Schmidt told Lewis. Pape now felt certain that Winterhalder was double-crossing him; and Schwinn was double-crossing both of them. At the very least, they would slow down the Nazis' progress.[41] But Lewis's spies soon discovered that Nazi plans for sabotage were far more advanced than they had realized.

3.

Plots Revealed, Spies Uncovered

In late September, Carl Sunderland heard rumors that Nazi diehard Dietrich Gefken was planning to overthrow the American government. Leon Lewis quickly devised a strategy aimed at gaining Gefken's trust and discovering more about his plot. Lewis's sole Jewish spy, William C. Conley, was scheduled to give a talk at Patriotic Hall. Alerting Conley to Gefken's rumored plot, Lewis asked him to attack President Roosevelt and his chief economic adviser, Bernard Baruch, in a manner the anti-Semitic German would find appealing.

On the evening of September 25, with 350 people packed into Patriotic Hall, Conley blasted Roosevelt and Baruch for their callous treatment of veterans. As per Lewis's instructions, Conley and his wife, Emma, along with John and Alice Schmidt, Carl and Blanche Sunderland, and Bert Allen, invited Gefken to join them afterward at the Lorelei Inn, a popular Nazi haunt on West Washington Boulevard. The group spent the rest of the evening dancing and consuming considerable amounts of alcohol.[1]

After many rounds of beer, the Nazi praised Conley for denouncing the Jew-loving president. "The 'Goddamn' kikes" are running the country," Gefken spat out. "Barney Baruch" is "the real president," and that is why the veterans are getting "such a rotten deal." Nazis were prepared to rise up and "take over the Government just as the veterans did in Germany." There "are enough Dutchmen in this country to put the Goddamn Jews where they belong—six feet under the ground," Gefken told his dining companions. Germans are ready "at a minute notice to strike for their freedom" and fight shoulder to shoulder with American veterans.[2]

Col. William Conley
USC Libraries Special Collections

The spies had heard similar threats before, but Gefken confided that within six months Nazis and their American allies would be strong enough to launch a "bloody revolution" in several heavily Jewish cities.[3]

Uncertain if it was the booze talking, Schmidt, Sunderland, and Allen invited Gefken to lunch to learn more about his past history and current plans. Gefken told them he had been in United States for ten years. Prior to that he worked as an organizer for the Brownshirts and had participated in the Munich putsch in November 1923 that led to Hitler's arrest. He boasted how he traveled around Germany with two pistols in his pocket "and let the Jews have the lead before they had any chance to get him." After suffering "the most severe beating he ever got" from Nazi opponents, Gefken fled to the United States. Over the next few years, he worked as a cook while conducting Nazi propaganda work in New York, Omaha, Denver, San Francisco, and Los Angeles, where he now served as first sergeant in the FNG's secret storm trooper unit.[4]

Hoping to enlist their aid, Gefken explained how he had already laid the groundwork for a Nazi takeover of the West Coast. After joining Company K, 159th Infantry of the California National Guard in San Francisco, he mapped out "the Armory plans, floor plans, location of ammunition and lockers and rifles, the list of addresses of the officers and all that was needed to take over the Armory on a given notice." The building housed nine machine guns, coastal artillery weapons, and enough rifles and ammunition to supply a full regiment. Having scoped out the San Francisco armory, he needed the three veterans to help him obtain blueprints for the National Guard armory in San Diego. He planned on traveling there to meet with navy men who were illegally selling rifles and ammunition to local Silver Shirts who were part of his plot. He would then return to San Francisco and reenlist in the National Guard.[5]

Once everything was in place, Gefken would launch simultaneous uprisings in San Francisco and San Diego intended to spark similar violence along the entire West Coast. FNG storm troopers who were secretly training in street fighting and the use of bombs every Friday night at the Alt Heidelberg would lead the revolt. Most of these men had fought in the German army or trained with National Guard units. They would be joined in battle by Silver Shirts in San Diego, disgruntled American veterans, 400 storm troopers operating in Southern California, and storm troopers who traveled on every German ship landing in California.[6]

Once the battle began, Gefken and his allies would use machine guns to corral army officers and lock them up. Nazis would then confer with captured American troops. Those willing to pledge their loyalty to Hitler would be taken into the storm troopers. Those who refused would be killed on the spot.[7]

Lewis's agents took Gefken seriously. "This man was not boisterous," Schmidt reported, but spoke like someone "who had gone through the same kind of experience before and knew how to handle any emergency." Schmidt found Gefken "a fearless fellow, neither radical nor fanatical, but absolutely believes in the supremacy of the Aryan race, by which he means the Germans." Gefken was a trained street fighter who had not hesitated to throw acid in the faces of his enemies while living in Germany.[8]

When a worried Schmidt told Lewis that Gefken was ready to rejoin the San Francisco National Guard machine gun unit, the Jewish spymaster devised an elaborate plan to thwart him. Lewis asked William Conley to write Police Chief Davis detailing Gefken's plans for sabotage along the Pacific Coast. Conley assured Davis that he was no "amateur Sherlock Holmes" but had worked "along this line as an Intelligence Sergeant during the late war." Gefken's plot was "a very dangerous one," and Conley promised to send the police chief further information. Suspecting this was something more than the usual Jewish complaining, Davis ordered Red Squad captain William Hynes to cooperate with Lewis's investigation, which he now believed was being conducted under the auspices of various veterans' groups.[9]

Lewis telephoned Captain Hynes and filled him in on Gefken's plans to join the National Guard. The two men agreed on a plan. Two weeks later, Hynes called Lewis to say he had alerted Captain Hoffman of the San Francisco National Guard to Gefken's imminent attempt to join his machine gun unit. Hoffman promised to have an officer of the U.S. Army's Military Intelligence Division present and ensure Gefken would get no further information. In the meantime, Hynes told Lewis they should inform Gefken that everything had been arranged for him to reenlist in the National Guard.[10]

Hoping to obtain hard evidence that could be forwarded to the Justice Department, Leon Lewis engaged in his first serious piece of spycraft: he obtained a Dictaphone and planted a microphone in Gefken's hotel room. Lewis would record the Nazi's meeting with his operatives and secure proof of his plans; he arranged for Hynes and four witnesses to listen in on the meeting from a nearby room.[11]

When Allen and Sunderland met in Gefken's bugged hotel room, the unsuspecting Nazi asked the ex-soldiers to obtain machine guns, rifles, and ammunition needed for the revolt. The PAL leaders protested, "We have no means of getting them." Gefken brusquely responded, "Yes you have, they are right here in your town, in your armory." Sitting in another room with headphones fixed to their ears, Hynes and Lewis heard the entire conversation.[12]

Following Lewis's orders, Schmidt told Gefken everything had been arranged; he had spoken with Captain Hoffman on the phone and called in a favor. Gefken would receive a warm welcome when he tried to rejoin his former San Francisco National Guard unit. Delighted with the news, Gefken left Los Angeles to set his plot into motion. But when he arrived at National Guard headquarters and asked Captain Hoffman how he knew John Schmidt, Hoffman responded he had never met the man and had no idea who he was. Leon Lewis had made his first mistake. He assumed Captain Hynes would tell the National Guard leader to let Gefken know that Schmidt had made the call that paved the way. But whether intentionally or not, Hynes never did. The operation was blown. Gefken knew he had been betrayed; there would be no rejoining the Guard. He returned to Los Angeles to seek revenge.[13]

Fortunately, Lewis had a backup plan in place. Not trusting Police Chief Davis or Captain Hynes, Lewis alerted naval intelligence authorities in San Diego and warned them about Gefken's plot to secure guns. Launching their own undercover investigation, navy agents arrested two marine corporals who were selling government rifles and 12,000 rounds of ammunition to local Silver Shirts. Naval intelligence also dismantled storm trooper units that "were all armed and were trained in the use of their weapons."[14] Preferring to remain under the radar, Lewis never took credit for the subsequent arrests.

UNDER SUSPICION

Whatever joy Lewis and his spies may have taken in foiling Gefken's scheme was short-lived. The Nazi suspected Schmidt was a spy. Gefken shared his concerns with Friends of New Germany number-two man Paul Themlitz and propaganda chief Hans Winterhalder. Much to Gefken's surprise, they told him they also suspected Schmidt. They had wondered how a sickly veteran on a limited pension could afford to buy so many books and dine out so often. (A well-trained spy would have known to cover his tracks better. But with the exception of William Conley, none of Lewis's group had any training in espionage work.)

Disappointed that his plans for sabotage had been thwarted, Gefken set his own trap. The following week, he asked Winterhalder, Bert Allen, and Carl Sunderland to join him at FNG headquarters to discuss a highly confidential matter. As they gathered in a private room, the former Brownshirt informed them that John Schmidt was a spy. Gefken told them about his encounter with National Guard captain Hoffman and Schmidt's non–phone call. Schmidt was either working for the Jews or a government agency. "We always suspected" Schmidt, Winterhalder added. If the former German soldier was working for the American government, "that is not so bad as he is then only doing his duty to his country, but . . . if he is working for the [Jewish] adversary, he is a traitor."[15]

Schmidt was not the only one under suspicion. Allen and Sunderland were startled when Winterhalder turned to them and remarked, "Of course, we don't know about you fellows and whether you have anything to die for or not." The two undercover agents insisted they did not believe Schmidt was a spy. As for their own loyalties, they explained that they joined the FNG to "interest the German Americans in the PAL." Several minutes later, when Hermann Schwinn and FNG head Robert Pape walked into the room, Winterhalder repeated what had been said. Schmidt "imagined himself to be a smart fellow," Schwinn told the group, but we have been "wise to him and had known this for several months."[16]

Discussing the best way to proceed, Gefken suggested they tail Schmidt, find out where he got his mail, steam it open, and see what he was up to. "Doing away with Schmidt would be a patriotic duty if it was true that he was spying on us."[17]

Pape intervened and offered a different strategy. "We could use Schmidt just as he hoped to use us." They would provide false information to lead him and his bosses off the track. Hoping to deflect suspicion from themselves, Allen and Sunderland volunteered to head up the tailing operation. If they discovered Gefken's accusations were true, they promised that Schmidt would be a dead man. Showing he meant business, Gefken pulled out a twelve-inch knife and told the group he would continue carrying it "for protection."[18]

The day after Gefken's secret meeting, the forewarned Schmidt walked into the Aryan Bookstore and asked a clearly rattled Paul Themlitz, "Will you shake hands with a spy?" He told the startled bookstore owner he knew his FNG friends suspected him of espionage, but they were wrong. He planned to continue attending meetings and working on their behalf. Schmidt had chutzpah, but he was not stupid. Knowing this day might come, he had taken out a gun permit in September and carried a loaded revolver with him at all times. As Schmidt left the bookstore, Themlitz wondered who had tipped him off.[19]

Several days later, Allen and Sunderland met Gefken at his room in the Barbara Hotel to report the results of their investigation. When they entered the room, they found Schwinn, Themlitz, and storm trooper head Karl Specht waiting. Themlitz opened the meeting by describing his recent encounter with Schmidt and wanted to know how the German captain had learned he was under suspicion. Someone in Nazi headquarters must have warned him, but who? Jumping in before the men turned on him, Sunderland explained that he and Allen had followed through on their promised investigation and discovered Schmidt was spying, but not in the way they thought. He told them the army's Military Intelligence Division had asked Schmidt to investigate whether there was a connection between fascist Silver Shirts and prominent leaders belonging to the veteran group PAL. After discovering Schmidt's mission and fearing a government investigation, PAL leaders had decided to shut down their operations. The Nazis, Sunderland assured them, were in no danger from Schmidt.[20]

Sunderland was so convincing that his Nazi companions agreed that PAL had done the right thing; no one wanted a government investigation, especially since the Germans knew they were violating the law by smuggling in money and propaganda through the Los Angeles port.[21]

Breaking the tension that filled the room, Sunderland suggested they adjourn to the hotel's restaurant for a round of beer—which they happily did. Over the course of the evening, the Nazis kept coming back to the question of how Schmidt knew he was under suspicion and whether he was really working for army intelligence. "During all of the conversation," Sunderland and Allen later told Lewis, "the persons present were apprehensive and acted as though they wanted to open up but would first like to be sure that eleven [Schmidt] was not working with someone in the group."[22] Sunderland and Allen, like Schmidt, remained under suspicion.

DANGER

On November 6, a week after the hotel meeting, Schmidt went to his mailbox and opened an official letter from FNG head Robert Pape. "Considering your peculiar conduct as a member of the league of the Friends of the New Germany, I feel constrained to suspend your membership in the league until further notice." Pape also withdrew Schmidt's appointment as a delegate to the German-American Alliance.[23]

After receiving Pape's letter, Schmidt paid a visit to the recently arrived German vice consul Georg Gyssling and told him about the suspension. Gyssling became furious and promised that "he would bawl out Pape very thoroughly and that Pape would have to apologize to me." They agreed to meet with Pape at the consul's office the following morning. Gyssling, Schmidt wrote Lewis, "impressed me that he was the superior of 22 [Pape's code name] and that he could dictate to 22 in any matter."[24] Gyssling was in fact a rising star in the diplomatic service and a friend of German ambassador Hans Luther.

When the captain showed up the next morning, the vice consul offered his apologies; Pape was busy writing a speech and was unable to attend. "Gyssling told me that Pape had said to him that Schmidt had represented himself to Pape as a federal agent of some kind." Schmidt denied the charges, calling them "a damn lie." He had no connection to the government. Gyssling told him that he had bawled Pape out and ordered him to restore Schmidt into the good graces of the Nazi organization. He also ordered the FNG head to put Schmidt on its executive committee to give "some of the idiots Pape has around him sound advice."[25]

Gyssling did not fool Schmidt. "The consul played the innocent immigrant boy . . . He wants to whitewash everyone and everybody. He is worried about what we may have found out about the local organization and he wants me to bring my file to his office for study." When Schmidt asked which files he meant, Gyssling dropped all pretenses and replied that he knew the veteran had official records and affidavits from Secret Service men who had been watching FNG headquarters. "I laughed at him and I told him that he had the usual misinformation." As he got up to leave, the vice consul again apologized and begged him to meet with Pape to straighten matters out.[26]

Schmidt left Gyssling's office having obtained two vital pieces of information. First, it was clear that the vice consul, not Pape, was the real Nazi power in Los Angeles. Second, Gyssling had his own spies who were conducting undercover work. How else could he have known about the Secret Service men?

Despite Gyssling's seeming sympathies, Schmidt was in danger. Fearing for his operative's safety, Lewis arranged for protection. That night, when the Schmidts showed up for a memorial service in Turnverein Hall, they were greeted by plainclothes police officer Frank Irvine, who told him, "Captain Schmidt, I am to be guarding you tonight." Entering the hall, John and Alice were given the cold shoulder by their former FNG compatriots. As the service concluded, the couple ran into German-American Alliance president Max Socha, who was part of the Nazi scheme to seize control of the wealthy Alliance. Recognizing Schmidt's police companion, Socha warned, "Bodyguard, well you may need one, or you may need each other for mutual protection."[27]

Lewis's spy operation had begun to unravel. Sunderland and Allen had remained calm when Winterhalder questioned their loyalties. But they, too, were feeling the pressure. Alice Schmidt paid close attention to the pair while working in the FNG offices. She warned her husband that Sunderland "is too pessimistic, a fellow that could throw anyone in to a frightened state of mind." As for Allen, he "either must change his habits of booze and social nights, or get the 'Goodbye-forever-tag.'"[28]

The three spies would never again be trusted by the Nazis, but they had nevertheless succeeded in disrupting FNG operations. When Schmidt and Sunderland returned to Nazi headquarters in mid-November, Fritz Schaeffer, a former lieutenant in the German Imperial

Guard, informed the pair that Pape was no longer head of the FNG and that the group had temporarily closed down its storm trooper unit to avoid trouble with authorities. The FNG's leadership now feared that a government investigation of their operation was inevitable.[29]

Gefken had been stopped, the threat to the San Francisco armory ended, and the San Diego Silver Shirts rounded up. Yet Lewis, his agents, and their wives knew the Nazis were gaining strength, not just in Los Angeles but also across the nation. Local storm troopers were getting increasingly proficient in their military training. Schmidt had seen Specht and his men conducting military drills dressed in uniforms with tall black boots, black trousers, white shirts, black neckties, and the familiar swastika armbands. Lewis's operatives also discovered that Nazis were training in street fighting and rifle practice in isolated parts of the Hollywood Hills.[30]

Captain Hynes and Police Chief Davis had cooperated with Lewis and his agents, but grudgingly so. Neither man had any sympathy for Jews; nor did they see Nazis as posing the same threat as Communists. FNG leaders had ingratiated themselves with the police by feeding them useful information about Red activity in Los Angeles, which was more than could be said for Lewis's group.

Lewis needed help if the Nazi menace was to be stopped. Schmidt's exposure reminded the Jewish attorney that he was not an experienced spymaster; nor were his undercover agents sufficiently trained in avoiding detection. Determined to get help, Lewis traveled to Washington, D.C., in mid-November 1933 to meet with Jewish congressman Samuel Dickstein, the man who earlier that year had called for a congressional investigation of Nazism. With the police, sheriff's office, and Secret Service either unable or unwilling to help, Dickstein seemed their only hope. Someone in the government had to listen, even if Lewis had to force them to do so. The stakes were simply too high.

4.

Going for Help

In October 1933, a month before leaving for Washington, D.C., Leon Lewis received encouraging news from John Schmidt about the growing cleavage between the city's old-guard Germans, whom he described as men "40 and more years," and younger, recently arrived pro-Nazi immigrants. Schmidt predicted the animosity between the two groups would erupt into open warfare at the upcoming elections of the German-American Alliance, the wealthy umbrella organization for the city's German voluntary associations.[1]

Several weeks before their falling-out, Hans Winterhalder and Paul Themlitz told Schmidt about their plan to stack the October 13 election with delegates, vote their men into office, seize control of the Alliance's substantial bank account, and use the funds to expand their operations throughout Southern California. The time has arrived, they confided, "to kick out of office the old type German and supplant him with those of the Hitler's followers."[2] There was only one problem. Alliance bylaws required that all voting organizations be incorporated and provide its president with their membership lists; but the FNG had never incorporated, and its leaders refused to hand over their roster for fear it might fall into Jewish hands.

Two days before the slated elections, FNG leaders secretly met with Alliance president Max Socha, a man anti-Nazi Germans accused of being a dictator who used the office "for personal and political gain."[3] Knowing the Alliance's longtime leader seemed unlikely to be reelected, Schwinn promised Socha that if he allowed their group to vote in the election, they would reelect him president. The ambitious Prussian-born businessman eagerly agreed to the deal.

When delegates gathered at Turnverein Hall on Friday, October 13, the Schwinn-Socha group defeated anti-Nazi presidential candidate John Vieth by a single vote. The results sparked outrage among the old-guard Germans. Following the election, Philip Lenhardt, the Alliance's well-respected former secretary, did something unimaginable: he sent a letter to the Jewish *B'nai B'rith Messenger* accusing Socha of corruption. Socha had ignored democratic principles and gotten reelected by "steam rolling" the final count with unqualified votes from Friends of New Germany delegates. Lenhardt vowed that loyal German Americans would not "tolerate the creation of any hate against any race or creed as sponsored by Max Socha, who forgets that we, the German-Americans, are here also a class of racial minorities."[4]

The swelling anger over the election surfaced again when older members of the Turnverein blasted the "entire young tribe" of Nazis, whose efforts "to spread Hitler propaganda" would turn "the American people against the Germans living within her border."[5] Over the next few weeks, several other German associations issued similar statements condemning the rigged elections.

Hoping to take advantage of the growing rift, Lewis urged Schmidt to contact the dissident leaders and chart a course of action. Wasting no time, Schmidt met with Philip Lenhardt and John Vieth, the defeated presidential candidate. As a fellow German, he understood why they were so pained by the growing Nazi presence in their community. They saw themselves as loyal Americans who had built a happy life in the United States. While proud of their German heritage, they were equally proud of the contributions Germans had made to America. The old guard bristled at Robert Pape's efforts to impose the orders and ideas of a foreign leader on the city's German Americans. Worse yet, Nazis threatened to destroy the good reputation that German Americans had struggled so hard to restore after World War I.

Revealing that he had been investigating the FNG on behalf of veterans' groups, Schmidt asked these respected German elders to lead the anti-Nazi fight. Lenhardt and Vieth promised to appeal the election results at the Alliance's next meeting. Yet both men understood that challenging the Nazis put them at risk. After receiving several anonymous threats, Vieth went to see police commissioner Barry Munson. After listening to Vieth's account of corruption and intimidation, Munson promised to send a plainclothesman to the next Alliance gathering to keep peace between the warring factions.[6]

On Friday night, November 11, Schmidt, Vieth, and Lenhardt walked into the Alliance meeting, accompanied by police officer Frank Irvine. The gathering opened with its pro-Nazi secretary reading aloud letters from members objecting to the illegal elections. As each letter was read, "the male and female Nazi delegates screamed and regular bedlam started." When the shouting died down, Lenhardt stood up to address the body. "As an old member of the *Stadtverband*," he could not recognize Socha as its legitimately elected president. His remarks were greeted by "pfuis and catcalls" and cries of "traitor" from the Nazi crowd.[7] Buoyed by the police presence, dissenting delegates moved to reject the results of the election. But Socha tabled the motion without permitting further discussion.

Unwilling to admit defeat, Vieth met with Schmidt to plan a more aggressive course of action. Vieth now believed "that proper court action should be taken without delay to unseat Max Socha and his cohorts." To show Schmidt how serious he was, Vieth signed an affidavit testifying to the events of the past several weeks.[8]

Up to this point, Schmidt and Lewis had planned their moves together. But once the spymaster left for Washington, Schmidt operated on his own. Over the next two weeks he met with Philip Lenhardt, John Vieth, and seventy-year-old Otto Deissler, one of the city's most venerated German leaders, to discuss the best way of overturning the election results. Schmidt urged the three men to file a lawsuit in their names so that "the fight really is a fight of Germans to clean out their own house." Rather than possibly prejudice the case by hiring a Jewish attorney, Schmidt advised them to hire a Christian American like Hugo Harris. Taking Schmidt's urging to heart, the four men met with Harris, who suggested they could strengthen their case by marshaling support from the city's German associations—which they did. Over the next few weeks they collected money for the court battle from wealthy Germans opposed to the Nazi cohort.[9]

The decision to bring their battle into open court was not taken lightly. Lenhardt, Deissler, and Vieth knew that going public would garner sensational publicity that would not reflect well on the German American community. On the other hand, allowing Americans to see Nazis as the face of the German American community would prove even more disastrous. After much soul-searching, Vieth, Lenhardt, and Deissler hired Hugo Harris and his partner David Field, both Christians, to represent them in a lawsuit against Max Socha and the Alliance's illegally elected officers.

GOING TO WASHINGTON, D.C.

On November 15, 1933, as John Schmidt plotted strategy with Vieth, Lenhardt, and Deissler, Leon Lewis boarded the train to Chicago and then on to Washington, D.C., to meet with New York congressman Samuel Dickstein. The Lithuanian-born Jew who represented New York's Lower East Side had traveled to Berlin a year earlier and witnessed Hitler's Brownshirts roaming the city streets, attacking Jews at random. Upon returning home, he discovered that the anti-Semitic Nazi propaganda he had read in Germany was now coming into his country.[10]

Launching his own one-man investigation, Dickstein discovered that "there were so-called Nazi 'cells' in this country which had been collecting money to propagandize our people with Nazi philosophy." By the time Franklin D. Roosevelt was elected in November 1932, the House Immigration and Naturalization Committee chair had gathered enough information to call upon Congress to launch a formal investigation of Nazism in the United States. "I appealed to everyone," Dickstein wrote, "but nobody would pay much attention to me."[11]

Lacking any appropriations, the feisty silver-haired representative dug into his own pocket and brought a number of witnesses to Washington, D.C. "I had to pay their fares to Washington. I built up a record sufficient for an investigation."[12] However, as long as Republicans controlled the Senate and Herbert Hoover was still in the White House, the Jewish representative found little support, even among Democrats, for his proposed investigation on un-American activities by Nazis and fascists.

Dickstein was troubled by Hitler's increasing grip on power. During recent German elections, National Socialists swept all offices and the persecution of Jews continued unabated. American newspapers, however, were more focused on the pending repeal of Prohibition and the hunt to find the kidnappers who had murdered aviation hero Charles Lindbergh's one-year-old son.

Before leaving Los Angeles, Lewis had met with recently elected congressman Charles Kramer to discuss what could be done in Washington. Kramer was not a Jew, but his campaign manager was an Anti-Defamation League member and a close friend of Leon Lewis; moreover, his district included 50,000 Jewish constituents. As a member of the House Immigration and Naturalization Committee, Kramer had been asked by Dickstein to investigate Nazism on the West Coast and report his findings to the full committee. With hard evidence in hand,

Kramer was confident Congress would pass an appropriation bill sufficient to hire twenty-five full-time investigators and launch a series of hearings aimed at uncovering Nazi and fascist activities throughout the country.[13]

Lewis remained skeptical. As he told Kramer, any investigation would prove fruitless unless the House committee had the power of subpoena and the right to administer an oath. Without such powers, witnesses could lie with impunity. Lewis saw Kramer and Dickstein as well-intentioned but naive allies. He would not turn over his spy reports to either man "unless it were found that the Committee investigation was being conducted in such a manner as to insure the results desired."[14] Lewis needed to go to Washington and judge for himself.

Boarding the elegant Super Chief, Lewis stopped in Chicago three days later to discuss strategy with longtime ADL colleagues Richard Gutstadt and Sigmund Livingston. The reports Livingston had received from Lewis and from similar Jewish undercover operations in midwestern and eastern cities proved far more revealing than anything Dickstein had discovered. However, upon learning of Dickstein's proposed hearings, most local leaders halted their investigations. Only Lewis's group continued penetrating Nazi groups and providing firsthand accounts of their activities.[15]

Before Lewis left Chicago, Gutstadt gave him the names of trusted contacts in Washington and New York who were well acquainted with Dickstein. If these men agreed that the congressman was progressing in meaningful fashion, Lewis would turn over his spy reports; if not, he and his ADL colleagues would proceed on their own.

Lewis arrived in Washington the next day and met with Livingston's friends. Dickstein had very little evidence to back up his charges, they told him, and they feared his actions were "based on political opportunism."[16] Nevertheless, they had arranged for Lewis to meet the congressman.

When Lewis showed up at Dickstein's office the next morning, the congressman apologized that he had to return to New York, but invited his guest to stay and read his files. As Lewis looked over the documents, his heart sank. Most of the so-called evidence Dickstein had compiled was based "entirely on hearsay." He "had very little, if anything to support his conclusions" and was "desperately groping for a means of saving face with the other members of the Committee and with the press."[17] The lawyer in Lewis knew such uncorroborated testimony was unlikely to hold up in court.

When the two men met the next day, Lewis got right to the point. "I earnestly warned the congressman against continuing the hearings with the type of evidence he had in his possession." Dickstein's dossier on the Silver Shirts contained practically nothing of any value. "I had considerable evidence," Lewis wrote, but would not "present it before the Committee."[18] Lewis would not risk exposing the identities of his spies, thereby placing their lives and those of their families—and his own—at risk.

The flummoxed Dickstein promised to write Congressman Kramer asking him to arrange for a private meeting where statements by Lewis's operatives "could be taken down and placed in the record." The ensuing affidavits could provide the kind of concrete evidence that would spur Congress into action and bring national attention to the growing Nazi danger.[19]

Lewis misjudged Dickstein's apparent incompetence. Lacking congressional funds and undercover agents to investigate right-wing hate groups, Dickstein hoped that his hearings, however flawed, would make Americans realize the Nazi threat was far more than just a "Jewish" issue; democracy itself was under attack. The congressman had already shelled out $6,000 ($110,000 in 2015 dollars) of his own money on behalf of his cause. Moreover, right-wing groups had threatened Dickstein's life. "I had to have a bodyguard to protect myself for a period of a year or two. My home wasn't safe at all, I had to change addresses several times." Nazis denounced him as a "loud-mouthed Jew with a talent for making the *Goyim* [Christians] Jew-conscious."[20]

Dickstein also faced considerable opposition from anti-Semites in Congress, most notably Pennsylvania's outspoken Republican representative Louis T. McFadden, who insisted that there was "no persecution of Jews in Germany." McFadden repeatedly accused Jews of controlling the nation's financial institutions, its media outlets, and even the presidency. "Do you not see the *Protocols of Zion* manifested in the appointment of Henry Morgenthau as Secretary of the Treasury?" he asked on the floor of Congress. "It is not by accident, is it, that a representative and a relative of the money Jews of Wall Street and foreign parts have been so elevated?" With only ten Jewish representatives in the Seventy-Third Congress, less than 3 percent of its 435 members, Dickstein could scarcely count on many colleagues to come to his defense or the defense of his people.[21]

Lewis left the Capitol disappointed that there would be no serious help from Washington. He spent the next three days in New York meeting with prominent Jewish leaders. "I found that there was absolutely no coordination of counter-propaganda activities by the Jewish organizations in that city, that there had been no investigation carried on there in any way parallel to that which we had done here." Worse yet, many New York groups had hesitated to take action because they assumed Dickstein would soon do so. Lewis's efforts at securing unified action provided fruitless. Jewish groups remained as divided as they had been eight months earlier.[22]

Unwilling to return home empty-handed, Lewis met with a handful of like-minded New Yorkers and proposed creating a national "non-Jewish organization based not on anti-Semitism or anti-Hitlerism, but upon pro-Americanism." The Nazi threat had to be met by coordinated national action and not simply on a city-by-city basis. Voicing their support, the ad hoc group asked Lewis to present his plan to ADL leaders in Chicago and report back to them. Feeling hopeful for the first time, Lewis telephoned Livingston and asked him to set up a meeting.[23]

The following Sunday morning, hastily assembled representatives from Indianapolis, St. Louis, and Chicago gathered at Chicago's Standard Club. They agreed to follow a strategy similar to the one Lewis had adopted in Los Angeles. They would create local undercover groups comprising Jews, Christians, veterans, and German Americans that would investigate and share information about Nazi and fascist activity. Jews might do the planning, but they needed to remain in the background. "Evidence of German political interference in the United States," Lewis explained, would be most effective if pressure on German anti-Semitic groups was "asserted from within by German Americans" who opposed Nazism. Lewis insisted "that no publicity of any kind be given" to their plans. If this were seen as a Jewish operation, it would likely lose outside support. Gutstadt and Livingston agreed to travel to New York to meet with their counterparts and urge them to create a series of decentralized independent civic investigative bodies in each major city.[24]

After ten days, Lewis boarded the Super Chief back to Los Angeles and began devising a plan of action he hoped would rouse a complacent nation.

PLOTTING A NEW STRATEGY

The thirty-six-hour train ride across the Great Plains and over the Rocky Mountains gave Leon Lewis plenty of time to think about his next move. Dickstein had the right idea but the wrong method. The Nazi danger to America had to be exposed, but it needed to be done in a manner far more convincing than the congressman's flawed one-man show. Too many people saw New York's Lower East Side representative as a Jew pursuing the interests of his people and not those of the American nation. That perception had to be changed.

The Chicago meeting provided Lewis with the seeds of a two-part strategy he had been contemplating even before his departure: first, encourage the city's German American community to lead the attack against local Nazis; second, having secured the cooperation of the local Disabled American Veterans and American Legion posts, seek the endorsement and participation of their state and national bodies. If he could convince these patriotic groups that Nazis posed a threat to democracy, their leaders might demand a full-fledged congressional investigation of un-American activities.

GERMAN VERSUS GERMAN

Spending hours deep in thought as he traveled the Super Chief to Los Angeles, Leon Lewis devised a plan of action. He would use the German-American Alliance lawsuit as a vehicle for exposing Nazi plans for sabotage and subversion. As his train pulled into Union Station, Lewis decided that he would ask Schmidt to take the lead while he worked behind the scenes.

The next day, Schmidt met Lewis and brought him up to speed on recent events. The Nazis were feeling pressured. Growing opposition within the German American community and rumors of an impending court battle had turned FNG leaders against one another. Hans Winterhalder and the ambitious Herman Schwinn had grown impatient with Captain Robert Pape's seeming incompetence. The FNG leader had been unable to quell the swelling opposition to the Alliance elections.

When Schmidt entered FNG headquarters on December 8, Paul Themlitz pulled him aside and asked to have a private conversation over lunch. For whatever reason, Themlitz still liked Schmidt. As they dined in the Turnverein restaurant, the Aryan Bookstore owner told him about a recent confrontation between Pape and Winterhalder. The FNG propaganda chief wanted to deliver a militant speech at an FNG meeting, but Pape turned him down, arguing it was too anti-Semitic. When Winterhalder went ahead and gave it anyway, Pape expelled him.

During the course of an ensuing argument, the local führer threatened to "box the ears off" Winterhalder. But Winterhalder landed the first blow, hitting Pape "in the face and knocking him on the floor," whereupon Schwinn rushed in and "applied the finishing touches by kicking 22 [Pape] in the pants."[25] As a result of the scuffle, Pape had been removed as western *Gauleiter* (head of all FNG branches in the west), and Schwinn was temporarily in charge. Berlin hoped to deflect criticism by appointing an American citizen to head the group.

This was welcome news to Lewis. The upcoming trial offered the perfect occasion for Germans, not Jews, to alert Americans to the dangers posed by the growing Nazi movement. Lewis was ready to seize an opportunity beyond his "wildest dreams"; a "real opening has been created for a complete cessation of German anti-Semitic efforts in America at last."[26]

Flush with the prospects of success, Lewis was delighted to learn Dickstein had followed through on his promise to have Charles Kramer launch an investigation of Nazi and fascist activities on the West Coast. Hoping to make use of Lewis's extensive undercover reports, Kramer sent the attorney a letter granting him official congressional status: "I hereby delegate you, as counsel, to assist me in this work and to carry on the investigation either in my presence or in my absence." Lewis could now emerge from the shadows if needed.[27]

During the first week of January 1934, confident that they had a majority of the German community behind them, Otto Deissler and Philip Lenhardt filed a lawsuit against the German-American Alliance. Judge Guy F. Bush informed the plaintiffs that opening arguments would be delivered in Los Angeles Superior Court on January 9, 1934.

5.

A Bitter Lesson: The German-American Alliance Trial

In the world of spying, nothing is ever quite what it seems. At first glance, the German-American Alliance court case seemed a simple battle between rival German groups. Otto Deissler and Philip Lenhardt asked judge Guy Bush to overturn the results of the recent election, arguing that Max Socha had violated bylaws by allowing Nazis to cast illegal ballots, thereby enabling them to seize control of the organization. Although Leon Lewis would have preferred a jury trial to secure maximum publicity, both plaintiffs and defendants wanted the decision rendered by a judge, believing he would be less swayed by emotions than a jury.

For Lewis, the trial over a disputed election—and hoped-for ensuing publicity—was a way to expose Nazi activities to unsuspecting Americans in Los Angeles and across the nation. With a court date set, Lewis faced a dilemma: should he expose his three main spies—John Schmidt, Carl Sunderland, and Bert Allen—by putting them on the stand and blowing their cover, or save their testimony for Kramer's projected congressional investigation? The spymaster decided to bet everything on the court case. The trial was a certainty, while the proposed congressional investigation might never happen.

Learning from Samuel Dickstein's mistake in relying on uncorroborated evidence, Lewis had Deissler, Lenhardt, and his three operatives swear out detailed affidavits before the trial. He then gave the documents, along with several hundred dollars in legal fees, to plaintiff attorneys Hugo Harris and David Field. If the court case did not go as expected, Lewis planned to turn over the affidavits to Dickstein's Immigration and Naturalization Committee or any "other branches of the Federal Government as may be interested in the subject matter."[1]

On Tuesday morning, January 9, 1934, as Hitler was busily rearming Germany's military, Superior Court judge Guy Bush convened the case of *Otto Deissler et al. v. Max E. Socha et al*. Attorney Hugo Harris opened by having Deissler testify to the events surrounding the October 13 election. After recounting the technical reasons why votes by the Friends of New Germany should not have been counted, the German charged Socha and the twenty other defendants (all FNG members) with plotting to place Hitler's sympathizers in charge of the Alliance in order to spread Nazi beliefs throughout Southern California.[2]

On Monday, January 15, after several days of testimony by Deissler and Lenhardt, Carl Sunderland took the stand before a packed courthouse. Sunderland, the *Los Angeles Times* reported, "recited an amazing story of intrigue, bordering at times on sedition." Upon hearing about Nazi activities from fellow veteran John Schmidt, he decided to conduct his own investigation of the FNG. He told the court how Dietrich Gefken approached him about forming "some connection between the Friends of New Germany and the disabled veterans." The soldiers "had received a raw deal under the economy bill," and he felt "they would welcome a change." To that end, Gefken asked him to obtain weapons and blueprints for armories in Los Angeles and San Diego. "He said that when the time came these armories could be seized, and the arms and ammunition used" for the "purpose of taking over the United States Government."[3]

Sunderland concluded his testimony by revealing that two groups of well-trained storm troopers were operating in the area: those who secretly drilled at FNG headquarters and those aboard every German vessel that docked in Los Angeles Harbor. Sunderland had been told that, in case of a crisis, the latter group of storm troopers "would come ashore and defend the flags with their lives."[4]

After being cross-examined by defense attorney H. H. L. Carnahan, Sunderland stepped out of the witness box, and John Schmidt took his place. Schmidt explained how he began a painstaking investigation of the FNG in August, was made a member in September, and was expelled in November for being "a spy against Hitlerism in the United States." Frequently glancing at his memorandum book to refresh his memory, Schmidt told of visiting German ships in the harbor and hearing officers discuss the progress being made in America. He had seen bundles of propaganda in English and German being brought ashore and a large packet of money being handed over to Hermann Schwinn with the warning "You had better be careful, don't lose it."[5]

Schmidt left reporters and spectators aghast as he described FNG plans to recruit veterans for a potential insurrection. Nazi chieftains "wanted me to take them around and introduce them to different leaders of the veteran organization" with the aim of starting "a general uprising by reason of the veterans getting a raw deal from our present administration." The American government, they insisted, "was Communistic" and Roosevelt a mere puppet of the Jews. Gefken and Winterhalder had asked him to secure plans for the Los Angeles armory and find out where "guns and equipment and especially machine guns" were kept.[6]

When court adjourned for the day, reporters flocked to Max Socha, who called the provocative testimony "bunk" and promised it would all be refuted when his side of the case was presented. Also speaking to the press was New York attorney Samuel H. Untermyer, the man responsible for organizing the international boycott of German goods. After spending the afternoon sitting alongside the plaintiffs' attorneys, Untermyer told reporters, "I have come here because of the international importance this case may assume." The American people would now have proof "that there exists and is being conducted an insidious, traitorous, countrywide propaganda and conspiracy aimed at the peace and security of our country." He expected that the trial's sworn testimony would be submitted to a congressional committee that would continue investigating Nazi subversion in America.[7]

Following Untermyer's attack on the FNG, German vice general consul Georg Gyssling felt compelled to respond. In an official statement released the next day, the consul insisted that "neither the German government nor the German National Socialistic party has any connections whatsoever, official or unofficial, with said organization [the Alliance] or the Friends of New Germany." Not only did Hitler disapprove of German citizens spreading "propaganda for National Socialism in foreign countries," but he promised to expel any party member "involved in such activities." Gyssling's government expected that any German who became an American citizen would be "exclusively loyal to his adopted country, just as we expect our citizens to be exclusively loyal toward Germany."[8]

The one person who remained anonymous throughout the hearings was Leon Lewis. At no point in the trial did any of his operatives mention they were working with the Jewish Community Committee leader. His undercover operatives presented themselves as patriotic soldiers investigating allegations of un-American activities. When the defense counsel asked Sunderland if he had joined the FNG as a spy or "investigator for anyone," the captain lied: "I went on my own accord."[9] The only one Lewis kept from testifying was his sole Jewish agent, William Conley.

The following day's headlines were everything Lewis had hoped for, a stark warning that Nazis had invaded Los Angeles and were up to no good: "Alleged L.A. Nazi Conspiracy Told," "Nazis Scheme to Stir Up Trouble Here Related," "Bold Nazi Plot Here Disclosed," "Nazi Troops Here, Asserts Trial Witness."

Tuesday's court session resumed with Schmidt explaining that he had joined the FNG to find out what Hitler's followers were planning. "All these men [indicating the defendants] are very likeable men, just in a bad spot. I went slow. I didn't want to hurt them." Despite his personal affection for many of its members, his investigation led him to conclude that the FNG "was anti-United States, anti-Jew and anti-Catholic." The group took its orders from national leader Heinz Spanknöbel in New York, who in turn received instructions from Nazi propaganda minister Joseph Goebbels in Berlin. Captain Pape, the FNG's local führer, told Schmidt "that he was an officer in the German army and was receiving 300 marks a month for his services in organizing the Nazi group" for the "purpose of driving the Catholics and Jews out of the Government . . . [and] to Germanize the United States of America."[10]

After Schmidt was cross-examined by defense attorney Carnahan, the plaintiffs rested their case. Carnahan began the defense by calling Alliance secretary Ludwig Leithold to the stand to describe the events surrounding the elections. Fellow defendants Karl Specht, Robert Pape, Paul Themlitz, Konrad Burchardi, Hans Winterhalder, and Max Socha followed and denied all accusations of un-American activities. Responding to charges that the FNG maintained a secret storm trooper unit, its alleged leader Karl Specht explained that its *Sportabteilung* (sports section) was organized to further sports such as swimming and hiking. He denied the group had any militaristic intentions or that it engaged in secret armed drilling.[11]

The star witness of the day was Hermann Schwinn, who insisted, "We are loyal American citizens standing fairly and squarely behind the man who has given this country a new deal just as Adolf Hitler has given Germany a new deal." Schwinn and his associates had organized the Friends of New Germany not to bring Hitlerism to America but "to tell the truth about the happenings in Germany." A "minority group [Jews]," he told the court, "was spreading malicious propaganda and atrocity stories against Germany." FNG members considered it "our duty to take steps against this."[12] Sounding a theme the Nazis would repeat for the rest of the decade, Schwinn portrayed the FNG as a patriotic organization fighting to protect the nation against the evils of communism.

The trial proceeded relatively smoothly until Thursday, January 18, when the packed courtroom heard Judge Bush suddenly announce, "Threats of violence have been made against the court." The judge ordered the bailiff to "lock the doors and allow no one to leave the courtroom." Speculating that those who threatened him might be present at that very moment, he instructed *Los Angeles Times* photographer Fred Coffey to take pictures of everyone in the room. Bush created a further sensation by ordering Schwinn and three of his companions to re-create the Nazi salute they had given while taking their oath. As the men thrust their right arms upward, Coffey took their picture, which appeared on the front page of the next day's newspaper.[13]

The case took an even more sensational turn on Friday when plaintiff attorney David Field rushed into the courtroom during a break and breathlessly informed Judge Bush that Captain Schmidt's life had just been threatened in the corridor. Leaping off the bench with little concern for his safety, Bush ran into the hallway and "encountered an excited throng, arguing and gesticulating widely." Pushing his way through the crowd, the judge confronted a shabbily dressed man arguing with Schmidt and Lewis. When Bush demanded to know what had happened, Schmidt replied, "I have been threatened."[14] As a crowd gathered around the antagonists, Judge Bush ordered them to disperse.

Returning to the courtroom after calm had been restored, Bush adjourned the case until Monday. When a worried Hugo Harris asked the judge to provide Schmidt with police protection, Bush ordered special detectives to guard the witness. As the bailiff cleared the courtroom, Schmidt informed the judge that his life had been threatened several times before. "I expected trouble. I had received a telephone call [this morning] informing me that if I dared to testify again I would meet with the same fate as the Jews who were killed in Germany." Overhearing Schmidt's complaint, the Nazi defendants let loose "with loud guffaws of laughter which was instantly stopped by the Judge." Sitting in the back of the courtroom, Leon Lewis overheard the judge warn how "threats against witnesses in court or under subpoena were worse than the anonymous threats received by him and that it was a serious matter."[15]

The next day's newspapers were filled with detailed descriptions of the startling events. What the public did not know is that Leon Lewis, fearing the worst, rushed Schmidt and his wife, Alice, to a notary, where all three gave sworn statements about the threats to his life. Schmidt recounted how he was sitting in the rear of the courtroom, a row behind Lewis, listening to Max Socha give his testimony, when a man in a yellow leather jacket whom he knew to be an FNG storm trooper sat down beside him and whispered in his ear, "We'll kill you, you son of a bitch," and then walked out of the courtroom. Jumping to his feet, Schmidt shouted to Lewis, "My life has been threatened." The spymaster rushed to the rear door and intercepted the Nazi. Schmidt returned to the courtroom surrounded by "a crowd of legionnaires," at which point Alliance secretary Ludwig Leithold's wife sneered, "You dirty son of a bitch, you dirty liar." Schmidt told Lewis how Themlitz and Winterhalder made similar remarks "every time they caught my eye" in the courtroom.[16]

The trial resumed Monday, with uniformed and plainclothes detectives patrolling the courtroom. The plaintiffs' attorneys asked to call a final witness, C. Bert Allen, to the stand. The major testified he had learned from Dietrich Gefken that "the FNG is a cover organization for the Storm Troops," who "planned to operate in North America as they had in Germany." Gefken "told me that they had arms and supplies and that 30 men were holding secret drills each week, particularly in street fighting and in the use of bombs." America, the Nazi insisted, "is on the brink of a revolution," and FNG members planned "to step in and take command just as Hitler did in Germany."[17]

Defense attorney Carnahan responded to Allen's testimony by calling Max Socha and several FNG officers to the stand. The defendants told the same story: as soon as they discovered Gefken's true aims, they had expelled him from the FNG. Socha denied knowing of any Nazi influence in the Alliance and once again insisted that the election was conducted in an orderly and legal manner. Following Socha's testimony, the defense rested its case.

Judge Bush announced that closing arguments would be delayed a week because several attorneys were obliged to be in the U.S. district court for another trial. Before he adjourned, Bush startled the courtroom yet again by revealing that his wife had received a threatening phone call and that he had received similar messages in the mail. "Any more threats," he told the crowd, "and somebody will go to jail."[18]

Despite the warning, there was one more threat. On Thursday, January 31, at 5:57 p.m., John Schmidt answered his home telephone only to hear a voice at the other end of the wire warn, "If you intend to testify in court again you had better stay away or you will be bumped off." The caller "laughed in a menacing manner and I heard the click of a receiver being slammed down."[19]

The following Friday morning, February 9, Judge Bush startled the courtroom attendees by ruling in favor of the defense. Basing his decision entirely on technical grounds, he explained that the Sons of Herman and Liederkranz Society, on behalf of whom Deissler and Lenhardt brought suit, were not incorporated associations and there-fore, according to Alliance bylaws, not legal members of the organiza-tion. As such, they had no standing in court and therefore no right to contest the October election. The Alliance results would remain unaltered. The Nazis had won. The dramatic trial had come to an anti-climactic end. "No demonstration greeted Judge Bush's decision," one newspaper reported. "The crowd quietly left the assembly room of the State Building."[20]

As he left the courtroom, Lewis understood the frustration Samuel Dickstein must have felt. Despite the sensational testimony, he had lost the trial on a technicality. Yet, ever the optimist, Lewis focused on the trial's positive aspects. As he wrote Richard Gutstadt, "the influence of the Nazi group in the German-American Alliance from now on will be practically nil and the methods and purposes of the Friends of New Germany have been dragged into the open and have had their effect on public opinion."[21]

But the national reaction he hoped for did not materialize. Although it had received extensive and often sensational coverage in the local press, the trial's dramatic exposés drew scant national attention. Only a single article appeared in the *Washington Post* and nothing in the *New York Times*, *Wall Street Journal*, or Lewis's hometown *Chicago Tribune*. The Jewish Telegraphic Agency gave widespread coverage to the trial, but it was highly unlikely that anyone in power was reading its columns.

The Nazi leadership proved far more wily than expected. Following the trial's conclusion, the FNG experienced a rapid recovery and began turning many within the German community against Deissler and Lenhardt. Attorneys Harris and Field urged their clients to appeal the verdict. The Germans, however, were now broken men. When Lenhardt and his close ally John Vieth went to a German-American Alliance meeting in mid-February, Hans Winterhalder, Paul Themlitz, and Hermann Schwinn greeted them with screams of "traitor" and "Jew friend." Alliance members were so loud and hostile that the despondent pair was forced to leave.[22]

Similar insults were shouted again several days later when Lenhardt, Vieth, and Schmidt attended a meeting of the Sons of Herman Lodge #12. The lodge secretary denounced Schmidt "as a traitor against the fatherland" and warned the three men that they and their families would soon "receive their proper lessons by Nazis." A week later, a suspicious-looking German followed Alice Schmidt down Wilshire Boulevard. She ducked into Bullocks Wilshire, hoping to lose him, but when she emerged a half hour later, "she saw the same German again, following her to Vermont [Avenue] where 17 [Alice] took a car to town." Even the usually unflappable John Schmidt was worried. "Much upset about threats that have been made against my children," he wrote Lewis. "Sheriff Cooper is cooperating with me in this matter." Several days later, Schmidt's children were placed under police guard.[23]

When Schmidt dared to attend an FNG meeting two days later, perhaps to discover who had tailed his wife, he heard Lewis's name mentioned for the first time by Schwinn and Paul Themlitz. As the rattled undercover agent told his boss, they knew "who you were" and that he "went to Washington" to meet with Samuel Dickstein. The Nazis had an inside man passing them confidential information, probably police captain William Hynes. As a local Silver Shirt leader told Schmidt, Hynes "is our big support against the Communists and lets us know in advance anything that may happen so that we can prepare to fight off any attack."[24]

When attorney David Field wrote his clients on March 19, explaining the technical aspects of the court decision and suggesting that they appeal the verdict, Deissler and Lenhardt never bothered to answer. Lewis wanted to pursue the matter, but as far as the pair of Germans was concerned, the case was closed. They could not bear to suffer further abuse and threats from former friends and Nazi enemies.[25]

A DANGEROUS NEW ENEMY

The Friends of New Germany had won a major victory in court and secured control of the Alliance and its substantial treasury. With sufficient funds in hand, Nazis were in a position to build a more powerful organization. The initial publicity surrounding the trial had caused FNG membership to fall from a previous high of 350–500 to approximately 130 men and women.[26] Lewis even considered dropping his spy operation if the Nazi decline continued. But once Schwinn, Socha, and their allies knew a trial was imminent, they launched a counteroffensive by forging a fascist front with the city's numerous right-wing groups, especially the rapidly expanding Silver Shirt movement (also known as the Silver Legion), which by February 1934 had four posts in Los Angeles.

William Dudley Pelley, the group's eccentric national leader, was so impressed with FNG chief propagandist Hans Winterhalder that he placed him in charge of the Silver Shirt post on Vermont Avenue and encouraged him to open a bookstore that sold Nazi and fascist literature. The Nazi did so well that Pelley appointed him to the editorial staff of the *Silver Ranger*. Winterhalder, in turn, asked Paul Themlitz to assist him. By late March, Winterhalder's post was composed almost entirely of German Nazis.[27]

Leon Lewis knew all about the Silver Shirts. Alice and John Schmidt and Carl Sunderland had been sending him reports about their meetings since September 1933. They told Lewis how Silver Shirt fascism and FNG Nazism were similar, but with several key distinctions. Adolf Hitler was opposed to Christianity and religion in general. Yet, although Nazis in Germany were anti-Communist, anti-Semitic, and anti-Catholic, their FNG brethren abandoned anti-Christian rhetoric because they feared it would turn off potential American supporters. The Silver Shirts considered themselves a Christian organization that shared a hatred of Communists and antipathy for Jews with their Nazi brethren. Nevertheless, while all FNG members Schmidt met were rabid anti-Semites, not all Silver Shirts hated Jews. In that sense, Silver Shirt fascism was closer to that advocated by Italian dictator Benito Mussolini, who did not make anti-Semitism state policy until pressured by Hitler. Many American fascists would have been happy to see the Jews simply leave the country voluntarily. But others, as Schmidt soon learned, preferred a more permanent solution to the Jewish problem.[28]

Lewis's spies discovered that Silver Shirts had maps of Los Angeles showing all the houses in which Jews lived. Schmidt understood the ominous potential for such maps. He had heard Silver Shirt leader Walter Sigafoose declare at a recent meeting, "The Jewish race is not the Chosen People—not the salt of the earth, it is a race guided by the forces of darkness and evil. The Jewish race is under the influence of the Dragon, or Satan or the Devil." Schmidt warned Lewis that the 150 to 300 who regularly attended most Silver Shirt gatherings were not crazy anti-Semites. They were well-dressed men and women "of a better class," the educated kind who had excluded Jews from their clubs and neighborhoods without ever thinking of themselves as anti-Semitic.[29]

After testifying at the German-American Alliance trial, the Schmidts and Sunderlands were no longer welcome at Silver Shirt meetings. When Carl Sunderland drove up to a Silver Shirt gathering in late January, two men approached his car and warned him in no uncertain terms not to attend the gathering. Rather than protest, the exposed spy drove off.[30]

Worse yet, police captain William Hynes was not the Silver Shirts' only government ally. As one Silver Shirt told Schmidt, the "entire Los Angeles Police Department, Sheriff's Office, Federal Office, including the Department of Justice," had "all taken the oath of the Silver Legion." Lewis received a similar report from Long Beach attorney N. Nagel. After hearing Police Chief Davis give a speech at a Masonic luncheon in which he implied that "all Jews are communists," a rattled Nagel wrote Lewis that he was convinced "the rumors of his [Davis] joining the Silver Shirts, or at least that he promised them the support of the Police department, is true." Over the next several years, Lewis would discover that the police and sheriff's departments were indeed filled with men sympathetic to the Silver Shirts, the Nazis, and the Ku Klux Klan.[31]

THE AMERICAN CRUSADE

Realizing that revelations of Nazi conspiracies would soon be forgotten, Lewis now had to pin his hopes on Kramer's upcoming hearings and trust they would lead to a full House investigation of Nazis and fascists. He knew Kramer and Dickstein needed help if they were to overcome the opposition of congressional skeptics and anti-Semites such as Louis McFadden. Having lost in the courtroom, Lewis worked to solicit support from veterans' groups—groups that could pressure Congress far more effectively than any Jewish association. Lewis enlisted the support of national Disabled American Veterans leader Volney P. Mooney—who was also a member of the Community Committee—and succeeded in persuading the DAV's county and national bodies to pass resolutions calling on Congress to "co-operate with other patriotic groups to combat all subversive movements," especially "the Nazi and Silver Shirt crowd."[32]

Lewis also convinced the far more conservative American Legion to join the anti-Nazi campaign. Since its formation in 1919, the American Legion proved to be one of the nation's leading anti-Communist organizations. Like police captain Hynes, few Legionnaires seemed overly troubled by the growing presence of Nazis and fascists. But Los Angeles was a different case. Downtown American Legion Post 8, the most important unit in Southern California, was founded and led by Community Committee chair Mendel Silberberg. When Lewis addressed the group, he spoke to them not as a Jewish spymaster but as chair of the Post's Americanism Committee. He convinced the Legionnaires to propose a resolution at its national convention requesting "all proper governmental authorities to take prompt and efficient steps to condemn such attempts to undermine principles of our free and democratic government."[33] The national body adopted their resolution.

Lewis's strategy worked. Due to his efforts, Dickstein received the outside support he needed. On March 20, 1934, the first day of the newly elected Seventy-Third Congress, legislators voted to establish a special House Un-American Activities Committee (HUAC) to investigate all subversive activities within the United States. Most people expected Samuel Dickstein to chair the committee. However, the New York congressman approached Speaker of the House Henry Rainey and shrewdly argued, "There are plenty of newspaper stories about the Jews being persecuted in Germany. If I head this Committee, since I am of Jewish blood, those babies will say that I will not give them a fair deal. I wouldn't want that on my conscience. I'll take the second place— vice-chairman of the Committee." Following his suggestion, Rainey appointed John McCormack of Boston as chair, Dickstein as vice chair, and Charles Kramer as its West Coast representative.[34]

Despite his momentary pleasure at Dickstein's long-awaited victory, Lewis realized he faced a new set of problems. By allowing Schmidt, Sunderland, and Allen to testify, he had exposed his three most important assets. Schmidt and Sunderland could no longer penetrate the inner circles of Los Angeles Nazidom. Only Walter Clairville, the former acting chief investigator for the city of Los Angeles, who had joined Lewis's operation in February, remained unknown to the Nazis and Silver Shirts.

With the FNG reviving and the Silver Shirts expanding, Lewis needed to rebuild his cadre of spies and obtain more money to fund his operation. He had a plan: he would approach the men who ran Hollywood and ask them to finance his investigations. Having worked with many of them since before the war, monitoring anti-Semitic cinematic images on behalf of the Anti-Defamation League, Lewis knew they were hardscrabble men who had risen up from poverty to wealth and power. Louis B. Mayer and his fellow moguls were not likely to fund him simply out of Jewish kinship; he needed to appeal to their business interests as well as their patriotism. Not only would he provide the overwhelmingly Jewish group with proof of Nazi and fascist subversion in America but he would also alert them to the fact that Nazis and fascists had succeeded in penetrating their studios. Without the moguls' financial assistance, Lewis was afraid he would be unable to continue his operations on any significant scale.

With the aid of MGM's Irving Thalberg and Rabbi Edgar Magnin, the city's most powerful Jewish leader, Lewis succeeded in setting up a secret meeting with the moguls. He would present his findings and appeal for aid. The future of his operation—and, as far as he was concerned, the future of the nation—depended on convincing these men to support his cause.

II

THE NAZI AND FASCIST ATTACK ON HOLLYWOOD, 1933–1935

6.

The Moguls and the Nazis

On the evening of March 13, 1934, a procession of limousines pulled into the luxurious Hillcrest Country Club on Pico Boulevard. Forty of Hollywood's most powerful studio heads, producers, and directors—men such as Louis B. Mayer, Irving Thalberg, Jack Warner, Harry Cohn, and Ernst Lubitsch—came to hear what Leon Lewis considered so important that their meeting had to be held in the utmost secrecy. As they entered the club's large private dining room and took their seats, each man found several copies of the Silver Shirt periodicals *Liberation* and *Silver Ranger* placed in front of him. Leafing through the publications, the Hollywood contingent was undoubtedly taken aback by a stream of vicious articles denouncing the Jewish-dominated movie industry and its immoral leaders. They likely flinched as they read a story blasting Hollywood Jews who would "rip our Divine Constitution to shreds and hand it over, HEADS BENT LOW, SPIRITS CRUSHED, MORALE DESTROYED, TO THE BULBOUS NOSED LORDS OF INTER-NATIONAL JEWRY." They saw similar articles in other issues denouncing them for producing "Filth," "Debauchment," and "Anti-Christ Desecration."[1]

Lewis had gained their attention.

Following the dinner, the men adjourned to the club room. Mendel Silberberg, chair of the Community Committee, the group overseeing Leon Lewis's operation, explained how he had brought them together for the purpose of creating a war chest to fund Lewis's investigations. Silberberg then ceded the floor to Lewis. He described how over the past seven months his spies had infiltrated the Friends of New Germany and uncovered evidence of espionage, sabotage, and rebellion, findings

Nazi Poster Calling for Boycott of Hollywood Movies
Jewish Federation Council of Greater Los Angeles, Community Relations Committee Collection, Part 2,
Special Collections and Archives, Oviatt Library, California State University, Northridge

that had been well documented by the local press during the recent
German-American Alliance trial.

Lewis ended his speech by asking whether the studio leaders were
willing to support his investigation or allow it to die. The moguls had
donated thousands of dollars to help Jews in Germany. Lewis now
asked them for thousands of dollars to help Jews combat Nazis in Los
Angeles. With the cash-starved Community Committee virtually out of
money, the moguls' answer would shape the fate of Lewis's operation.[2]

FROM THE START, Lewis knew money would be an issue. When he held
the Community Committee's first meeting at Judge Isaac Pacht's home
in August 1933, he invited "fifty or more of the monied element" of
Jewish Los Angeles to attend: bankers, lawyers, doctors, judges, and
merchants. The group of "big shots" pledged $5,000 ($91,400 in 2015
dollars) to fund the spy operation; however, eight weeks later, they had
only given Lewis $1,000.[3]

When the big shots failed to deliver, Lewis turned to the wealthy
Jews who ran the movie industry. To help, he enlisted the support of
three Los Angeles power figures: Mendel Silberberg, Irving Thalberg,
and Rabbi Edgar Magnin. Lewis began by asking Silberberg to help
"secure a special committee of movie magnates" who could "be very
useful to us" in raising needed funds. The spymaster could not have
chosen a better person to chair the Community Committee. Silberberg gave him immediate legitimacy with studio chieftains and local

Leon Lewis Receives American Legion Americanism Award, June 1939
USC Libraries Special Collections

patriotic groups. A prominent figure in veteran circles, Silberberg was also the nation's most powerful entertainment attorney. In addition to serving as counsel to the Motion Picture Producers and Distributors Association, the founding partner of Mitchell, Silberberg and Knupp represented MGM, Columbia Pictures, and RKO. His personal clients included Hollywood's who's who—among them Louis B. Mayer, Harry Cohn, Sol Lesser, and Jean Harlow. Silberberg was also a major power broker in the Republican Party. Considered one of the GOP's five "kingmakers"—one of the five men who chose the party's presidential nominee—he chaired Herbert Hoover's Southern California presidential campaign in 1928 and served as a delegate to the Republican convention that year and again from 1948 to 1960.[4]

The man many considered the most powerful secular Jew in Los Angeles came to Judaism late in life. Born in Los Angeles in 1886 to assimilated Austrian and Russian Jewish parents, Silberberg was raised a Christian Scientist. After law school and a stint as an air force officer in World War I, he founded the city's first and most important American Legion post, Post 8. By the early 1930s, Silberberg's close contacts with movie industry personnel and friendship with Leon Lewis (whom he knew from veteran circles), Louis B. Mayer, and Rabbi Edgar Magnin sparked a renewed interest in Judaism. "Evidently the moguls were beginning to groom him as their 'front man' in the Jewish community," Lewis's assistant Joseph Roos recounted.[5]

When Lewis approached Silberberg in the summer of 1933 and explained his plans to mount a spy operation aimed at penetrating the city's Nazi organization, the entertainment attorney agreed to chair the new group. Silberberg was a man who knew how to get things done quickly. "When he was in a meeting," recalled one colleague, "his charisma was so strong that everybody focused on Silberberg. He was an incredible force. Everybody liked him."[6] Silberberg shared one key trait with Leon Lewis: he was never concerned with taking credit. Others could have the glory so long as the job was done right.

Silberberg was not entirely selfless; there was one aspect of the chair's job the recently rediscovered Jewish attorney especially enjoyed. Throughout Lewis's spy operation, the Community Committee's executive committee met every other Friday at noon for a private working lunch held at the Federation of Jewish Welfare Organizations headquarters on Temple Street. Much to the chairman's delight, the group hired a cook to prepare the meal. "Silberberg had never been exposed to Jewish cuisine and was delighted to discover the wonders of lox and cream cheese," a bemused Roos observed.[7]

With Silberberg serving as Community Committee head, Lewis gained immediate entry into the studio offices and private homes of the Hollywood elite. In early September 1933 he visited film and radio star Eddie Cantor's beach house and met with "a group of Jewish actors, writers, and directors who are very much het-up" to fight the city's Nazi cohort. Cantor agreed to help. Several weeks later, Lewis secured $2,600 ($47,500 in 2015 dollars) in pledges from thirty employees at Warner Brothers and expected similar amounts from people at MGM and Universal.[8]

Lewis's longtime work with the movie industry also brought him into contact with Irving Thalberg, the man known throughout Hollywood as the "Boy Wonder." Considered the creative genius of MGM, an accolade that annoyed Louis B. Mayer to no end, the Brooklyn-born son of German immigrants was only too happy to run the studio while his boss was off for weeks at a time pursuing his political interests in California and Washington, D.C. In December 1931, when most studios were facing bankruptcy, twelve New York bankers praised Thalberg and

Mayer as the only two executives who had "made the grade during the past year."[9]

Whereas Mayer's intimates considered him the greatest studio chief and actor in Hollywood—"He could put on an act and cry and make the actors break down and do what he wanted," remarked Rabbi Magnin—others saw Thalberg as the far more imposing figure. "Thalberg, not Mayer, was the toughest and most ruthless man in the industry," observed actor Robert Montgomery. "He was a shrewd, tough, hard, cold operator, with a complete ruthlessness toward people." What interested Lewis, however, was Thalberg's considerable skill as a fundraiser for Jewish causes. During 1933–34, the MGM production chief whom *Fortune* magazine condescendingly referred to as "a small fine-made Jew" proved amazingly successful heading the motion picture division of the local United Jewish Appeal, securing pledges of $40,000 at its first meeting.[10]

Fighting Hitler was not an abstract cause for Thalberg. The studio executive had witnessed Nazi repression while recuperating from a heart attack in Bad Nauheim, Germany, in 1933. He returned to Los Angeles determined to help his European kinsmen and, at Silberberg's urging, Leon Lewis. Thalberg would be the spymaster's point man in dealing with studio heads.

Edgar Fogel Magnin was the bridge between Silberberg, Thalberg, and the rest of the Jewish moguls. Born in San Francisco in 1890 to a wealthy department store family and ordained at Hebrew Union College in 1914, Magnin assumed his first rabbinical appointment at Wilshire Boulevard Temple in 1915—and remained there for the next sixty-nine years. Like many men to the manor born, he expected to be heeded by those beneath him. Magnin, noted one acquaintance, "was the kind who preferred for Jews not to be seen too much in the limelight, especially Jews who did not look or act 100% American." Over the next several decades, the strong-minded "Rabbi to the Stars" built his reform temple into the most powerful synagogue in Los Angeles and home to Hollywood's Jewish elite. Its members included Silberberg and most of the men who sat on Lewis's advisory committee. Magnin considered temple member Louis B. Mayer, the industry's most powerful figure, as one of his closest friends. "Louie would do anything for me," the rabbi boasted. "He loved me."[11] As for Lewis, he first met Magnin in 1927, when they worked together pressuring Cecil B. DeMille to remove offensive scenes from *King of Kings*.

By late September 1933, as money ran low, Lewis remained confident that with Silberberg, Magnin, and Thalberg behind him, studio heads and their Jewish stars would rally to his cause. He needed money to pay modest stipends to several spies, reimburse their expenses, cover general operating costs, and pay himself a monthly retainer. All told, he needed at least $17,000 a year to sustain his operation. "Have already succeeded in selling one or two of them on the idea," he wrote Richard Gutstadt. "These moguls are hard to pin down for more than a few minutes talk—however I have joined Hillcrest [Country Club] and am making progress between the drive and the approach shot."[12] Excluded from most of the city's Christian-only clubs, Jews had opened Hillcrest in 1920 to have a place where they could golf, play tennis, socialize, and, in Lewis's case, raise money.

When Lewis returned home in November from his meeting with Samuel Dickstein, he faced yet another disappointment: the Community Committee was broke. The moguls had given him a modest sum, but not enough to sustain his operation. Earlier in the month, a deeply frustrated Lewis complained of being "chronically out of pocket for $200 to $600 . . . At the present writing there is about $1,000 on hand in the Treasury, and I have about $300 due for monies I have advanced."[13]

By the end of the month, matters had grown even worse. "There are barely enough funds on hand to take care of amounts I have already laid

Rabbi Edgar Magnin (l) and Mendel Silberberg (r)
USC Libraries Special Collection

out for expenses." He had received over $10,000 in pledges, yet the promised support had not come in. Lewis was desperate for money; for the Community Committee, for himself, and for his family, which now included two young daughters aged ten and five. Lewis had never expected to devote so much time to running his undercover operation; as a result, his more profitable legal work suffered. "I cannot afford as I have done for the past four and a half months to devote all my time to this work. My practice has been completely shot to hell and I have just lost my best client I had—the West Coast Textile Association—because of the way I have neglected their work during the past few months." Strapped for funds and seeing his business slip away, the distraught attorney was ready to quit his undercover work. Nothing would please him more, he confessed to Richard Gutstadt, "than to pass the entire burden on to someone else."[14]

Needing money to survive, Lewis turned to Silberberg, who immediately swung into action. The Community Committee head arranged for Thalberg and Magnin to meet with him and Lewis at the Federation of Jewish Welfare Organizations offices. Over the next several months, the four men laid the groundwork for a secret meeting of movie industry leaders.[15]

Before appealing to the moguls, Lewis and Silberberg made a last attempt to forge a broad coalition of Jewish groups that would join the Community Committee. The demands of preparing for the German-American Alliance trial forced Lewis to delay any potential meeting. But on March 9, one month after Judge Bush delivered his verdict, Mendel Silberberg assembled two dozen representatives of the city's leading Jewish groups—the B'nai B'rith, the American Jewish Congress, the American Jewish Committee, the Council of Jewish Women, and others—in hopes of raising a war chest and forging a united front behind a newly reorganized Community Committee.[16]

Unfortunately, when it came to deciding on a common course of action for the Community Committee, some, like Rabbi Magnin, wanted to fold Lewis's group into a larger national organization that could work with the Catholic Church to pass legislation prohibiting the persecution of any group in America. Others favored a more aggressive approach and wanted to work with national groups to confront Hitler's minions in Germany and in Los Angeles. Few, however, seemed concerned with focusing on the best way to continue Lewis's local spy operation.

With twenty-odd men and women expressing twenty different opinions, the fractured group was eventually swayed by the arguments of

Louis Greenbaum. The past commander of the Disabled American Veterans spoke against diluting the success of their current work by placing it under the wing of a large national body. Lewis's spy operation had proven itself more efficient and effective than any other local or national Jewish group. The Community Committee, Greenbaum insisted, had "done with less than $10,000 what no other group has been able to do with all the money they have been able to gather." Seconding Greenbaum's argument, judge Lester Roth moved that the Community Committee should remain an independent local body with loose ties to the ADL and "do the best we can under the circumstances."[17]

Taking the floor after considerable debate, Lewis offered a compromise. In the "interest of harmony and effective cooperation for the entire community," he invited the gathered organizations to be part of a larger Community Committee that would operate under the chairmanship of Mendel Silberberg. However, a much smaller advisory board, also chaired by Silberberg, would oversee Lewis's spy operation; only they would know the full dimensions of the Community Committee's undercover work. Following a positive vote to adopt Lewis's proposal, the gathered leaders agreed that his law office would serve as a central clearinghouse for all questions and information; advisory board members would meet for lunch every other Friday to discuss ongoing operations.[18] The group did not, however, offer to give Lewis any money. The time had come to call upon the Hollywood moguls for financial assistance.

THE HILLCREST MEETING CONCLUDES

As the assembled group adjourned to Hillcrest's club room after dinner on March 13, Leon Lewis knew that to persuade these tough-minded men to donate serious money, he needed to appeal to their self-interest and not just their Jewish loyalties. He planned to frighten them into generosity. Thus far, Lewis explained, he had gathered over 200 reports from his spies. Many of those findings had been disclosed during the course of the German-American Alliance trial. The moguls knew this. What they did not know was that Nazis and fascists had invaded their studios and were firing Jewish employees. Many studio heads had heard rumors about Lewis's operation, but only a handful knew the full extent of its workings, and fewer still knew how strong the Nazi movement had grown since the summer of 1933.

Although studio heads paid close attention to their above-the-line personnel—an industry term for the stars, writers, directors, and producers whose names were featured at the start of a film—they knew far less about their below-the-line employees, the craftspeople who comprised 80 to 90 percent of studio employees. After interviewing every Jew who had worked as an extra over the past several years, Lewis discovered widespread discrimination by studio foremen, many of whom were openly sympathetic to the Silver Shirts. "There has never been a time when Jewish employment in the studios has been at such a low ebb." Paramount's two studio managers had fired so many Jewish employees in the past several months that "the number of Jews can be counted on the fingers of one hand." One manager was eventually fired "because he attempted to adopt Hitlerism as a policy in running the studio." Paramount was not unique. Other studios, Lewis warned, had also "reached a condition of almost 100% [Aryan] purity."[19]

In return for funding his undercover operation, Lewis promised that his spies would continue gathering information on Nazi and fascist activities in their studios and, more importantly, find out more about the hated German vice consul Georg Gyssling. Since arriving in Los Angeles in June 1933, Gyssling had been pressuring Hollywood not to make any film that disparaged Hitler or the Nazi regime. He threatened that any studio ignoring his warning would have all its films banned in Germany. His constant demands for script changes were slowing down production and costing the studios money. Worse yet, the Jewish men resented having the representative of a foreign government—a Nazi, no less—tell them what they could or could not make. Angry as they were, the moguls had to cooperate with Gyssling; they were beholden to stockholders and could not risk being excluded from the German market.

Lewis knew the diplomat exercised considerable influence over the city's German community, especially its nascent Nazi groups. Even the leaders of the FNG bowed to his demands. The German consul was a man far more powerful than he claimed to be, but how much more, and what his exact duties were, remained a mystery. With adequate funding from the moguls, Lewis promised to find out what Gyssling was up to and perhaps discover his Achilles' heel.

Following Lewis's revelations and promises, Rabbi Magnin, Irving Thalberg, and Louis B. Mayer each rose to voice his opinion as to what needed to be done. Mayer, who liked to dominate any meeting he attended, insisted that "there could be no doubt as to the necessity of carrying on and he for one was not going to take it lying down and that there were two things required, namely money and intelligent direction: that he believed it was the duty of the men present to help in both directions."[20] MGM producer Harry Rapf seconded his boss's recommendation and moved that Silberberg appoint a special studio committee, to be composed of one representative from each studio. The motion was carried, and members of the newly appointed committee remained behind after the meeting adjourned at 10:30 p.m.

Silberberg and the group agreed upon a quota from each studio sufficient to cover Lewis's operating costs for the year. Thalberg pledged to raise $3,500 from MGM; Emanuel Cohen promised Paramount would raise the same, and he would ask Warner Brothers for $3,500 as well. Universal's representative agreed to contribute $2,500, while Pandro Berman noted that RKO had only eight Jewish executives, so they would give a more modest $1,500. The studio representatives agreed to ask Twentieth Century, United Artists, and Columbia to raise $1,500 each. Producer Phil Goldstone volunteered to raise funds from the remaining independents, while RKO head of production David Selznick offered to solicit contributions from Hollywood agents. By the end of the evening, the studio leaders had received pledges totaling $24,000 (approximately $425,000 in 2015 dollars).[21]

Amazingly, the normally loquacious moguls managed to keep the proceedings relatively quiet. As Joseph Roos, Lewis's able assistant, later recounted, the Community Committee "was known to the inner circles of the Jewish community and film industry but escaped public notice entirely. Not even the well informed journalist and attorney Carey McWilliams seems to have noted it."[22]

Lewis left the Hillcrest meeting greatly relieved. Hollywood money would allow him to recruit more spies and continue his undercover operations. "For the first time," he wrote an ADL colleague, "we have established a real basis for co-operation with the Motion Picture Industry and I look for splendid results hereafter." Equally heartening, the anticipated funds meant Lewis could now be paid a regular monthly retainer of $500 ($8,850 in 2015 dollars). Although industry pledges proved harder to collect than anticipated, within four months Lewis had deposited $11,806 into the Community Committee's bank account. The vast bulk of his financial support came from the newly organized studio committee chaired by Irving Thalberg.[23]

The Hollywood contributions slowed down that fall as industry leaders from both parties turned their attention and money to defeating Upton Sinclair's California gubernatorial campaign. The longtime socialist had stunned the political establishment by capturing the Democratic nomination for governor of California in August 1934. Sinclair ran on a platform that scared the hell out of the wealthy Hollywood crowd. In addition to calling for a graduated income tax, starting at $5,000 and increasing to a point where all incomes over $50,000 would be taxed 50 percent, he also promised to initiate a special tax on the state's highly profitable movie industry.[24]

Sinclair's tax plans threatened both the personal and business fortunes of the studio heads. During the mid-1930s, movie industry leaders earned nineteen of the twenty-five highest salaries in America. Mayer reigned as the nation's highest salaried executive in 1937, earning $1.3 million, more than the heads of General Motors and U.S. Steel. When polls that fall announced that Sinclair was running neck and neck with Republican candidate Frank Merriam, Mayer and Thalberg produced a series of three staged newsreels, *California Election News*, that succeeded in frightening voters and turning the tide against the Democratic hopeful. On November 6, Californians elected Merriam to office by a considerable margin. When actor and Democratic activist Fredric March blasted MGM's scurrilous newsreels as "a dirty trick" and "the damndest unfairest thing I've ever heard of," Irving Thalberg quickly shot back, "Nothing is unfair in politics. We could sit down here and figure dirty things out all night and every one of them would be all right in a political campaign."[25] Robert Montgomery was right: Thalberg, despite his genial appearance, was not a man to be trifled with.

With the Sinclair problem resolved, the moguls once again turned their attention to helping Lewis. A month after the election, Mayer arranged for executives from nearly every studio to meet with Lewis over lunch on the MGM lot. Lewis told them about the investigations his agents had embarked upon over the past year. But he needed more money to sustain the work and asked if they would support his efforts to expose Nazis and fascists operating in their city and inside studio lots.

When Louis B. Mayer called for a vote, the sentiment was unanimous: Lewis's work needed to continue, and the men present would arrange for its adequate financing. Mayer appointed a committee consisting of himself, Emanuel Cohen of Paramount, Jack Warner, and Harry Rapf to arrange another meeting at Hillcrest in which those present would be asked to renew or make new contributions to fund the CC's operations.[26] Mayer's advisory group asked Eddie Cantor, Paul Muni, Al Jolson, and Edward G. Robinson to solicit funds from fellow actors and actresses.

The moguls had saved Lewis's financially strapped operation from going bankrupt, but none of this money came without strings attached. Within a few weeks of the Hillcrest meeting, he had sufficient funds to recruit new undercover agents to replace exposed spies John Schmidt, Carl Sunderland, and C. Bert Allen. He now had to fulfill his promise to provide the moguls with information about Nazi consul Georg Gyssling and about Nazi and fascist activities within their studios. But first he had to prepare for the House Un-American Activities Committee hearings scheduled to run in Los Angeles between August 1 and 8, 1934. Given the national attention HUAC was likely to garner, Lewis was determined to provide the committee with sufficient information to alert citizens that the enemy was operating within its borders and had to be stopped.

7.

Inside the Fascist Front

L eon Lewis was a busy man. Not only was he raising money, recruiting new operatives, and spying on Nazis, but he found himself dealing with yet another hate group: William Dudley Pelley's Silver Shirts. On March 20, 1934, a week after the Hillcrest Country Club meeting, Congress authorized the creation of the House Un-American Activities Committee and asked it to recommend "any necessary remedial legislation."[1] When recently elected congressman Charles Kramer was appointed as head of the HUAC subcommittee investigating un-American activities on the West Coast, he asked Leon Lewis to serve as counsel to the local investigation. Kramer told Lewis he would begin by focusing on the Silver Shirt leader's headquarters in Asheville, North Carolina.

Over the next five months, three groups set out to investigate Nazi and fascist activities in Los Angeles: HUAC investigators, the FBI, and Leon Lewis's spies. Only one would prove truly successful.

When the fledgling Silver Shirts began meeting at Friends of New Germany headquarters in September 1933, Lewis had asked John and Alice Schmidt, Carl and Blanche Sunderland, and Bert Allen to attend their gatherings. To become a member, Schmidt told Lewis, an applicant needed to be a citizen of the United States, a member of the Aryan race, "and must recognize Christ as a *factor* in the S.S. movement." Jews, Catholics, and "Colored Race members" were barred from the organization.[2]

Far more troubling than the group's anti-Semitism was Silver Shirt leader William Dudley Pelley's prophesies of a hoped-for national revolution. The slender, charismatic New Englander with piercing blue eyes, a silver mustache, Vandyke goatee, and slicked-back salt-and-pepper hair led the nation's largest and most dangerous anti-Semitic fascist movement. Born in Lynn, Massachusetts, to devoutly Methodist parents in 1890, Pelley spent his early years working as a highly successful journalist, fiction writer (he won an O. Henry Award in 1930), and Hollywood screenwriter. Between 1917 and 1929, studios produced sixteen of his films, many featuring prominent stars such as Lon Chaney, Tom Mix, and Colleen Moore.[3]

On May 28, 1928, while living in Altadena, a suburb several miles north of downtown Los Angeles, Pelley underwent an experience that changed the course of his life. In "Seven Minutes in Eternity—The Amazing Experience That Made Me Over," published in the March 1929 *American Magazine*, he recounted how between 3:00 and 4:00 a.m., he was awakened by an inner voice shrieking, "I'm dying! I'm dying!" After experiencing a physical sensation akin to a "combination of heart attack and apoplexy," he plunged "down a mystic depth of cool blue space" and found himself naked on a marble slab, surrounded by two male "Spiritual Mentors." They told Pelley he belonged to a group of spiritual counselors whose "mission it is to guide humanity in times of stress." Moreover, he was destined to become the "head of a great spiritual movement" that would transform American politics. Seven minutes after entering the "Higher Realm" of the afterlife, he woke up certain this had not been a dream. For the rest of his life, Pelley insisted that his heavenly mentors helped guide his earthly actions.[4]

The response to Pelley's article was extraordinary. The *American Magazine* received thousands of letters from readers wanting to know more about his experiences. Happy to abandon a film career that brought him into contact with the Jewish studio heads he loathed, Pelley moved to New York in the summer of 1929 and then to Asheville, North Carolina, in 1932, determined to usher in a "New Order Among men."[5]

On January 30, 1933, Pelley's political crusade assumed a frighteningly new dimension. He had been following Hitler's rise to power with great admiration, and the moment Hitler assumed the chancellorship of Germany, "something clicked in my brain." Calling together his office staff, Pelley announced, "Tomorrow we launch the Silver Shirts!" If a "young house-painter" could take control of the German government, he told them, then it was time to bring "the work of the Christian Militia into the open."[6]

Over the next two years, Pelley built the Silver Legion, popularly known as the Silver Shirts because of the color of their uniform tops, into a formidable quasi-religious, quasi-paramilitary organization. He divided the United States into nine divisions, each presided over by a commanding officer, who in turn answered to Pelley and his general staff in Asheville. Pelley ordered each post to organize a paramilitary band of a hundred "actionists," known as Silver Rangers, who would serve as the military vanguard in his quest to establish an American theocratic state. Members were expected to pay a $10 initiation fee, $12 in annual dues, and $16 for Nazi-style uniforms that consisted of leggings, blue corduroy pants, a tie with the individual's membership number stamped on it, and a silver shirt with a scarlet *L* (which stood for Love, Loyalty, and Liberation) stitched over the heart. Germany had its Brownshirts, Italy its Blackshirts, and now America had its Silver Shirts.[7]

Claiming that Christ had asked him to transform America's spiritual character, Pelley set out to rid the nation of its two greatest dangers, Jews and Communists. Jesus, he told his followers, hated Jews for violating God's precepts, and Jews responded by killing him. Pelley's weekly newspaper, the *Silver Ranger*, which moved production to Los Angeles in early 1934, featured anti-Semitic articles and news of German actions against Jews that warmed the heart of the Nazi faithful. Repeatedly referring to America as the "Jewnited States" and the Roosevelt government as the "Jewish administration in Washington," secretly run

William Dudley Pelley
Jewish Federation Council of Greater Los Angeles, Community Relations Committee Collection, Part 2, Special Collections and Archives, Oviatt Library, California State University, Northridge

by Bernard Baruch and Felix Frankfurter, the periodical called upon loyal Christians to free the nation from the chains of "Alien Jewry."[8]

Jewish leaders took the Silver Shirt leader's anti-Semitic preaching seriously. Long before Hitler's "Final Solution," Pelley's 1933 book *No More Hunger: The Compact Plan of the Christian Commonwealth* promised a "permanent Solution to the Jewish Problem." Under Pelley's plan, all Jews would be required to cluster in one city per state, in areas known as "Beth Havens." A secretary of Jewry would administer each ghetto and guarantee their safety. However, any Jew who tried to leave the area would be subject to execution. Pelley's book called on Silver Shirts to defeat the rapacious Jews who controlled the world's banking and financial institutions, and restore prosperity and true Christian values to America. Pelley "is the most rabid anti-Semite I have yet met," one HUAC investigator later observed; "he is bound to wipe out Jews from the map of the United States and expects to accomplish this in the next five years."[9]

Many of his contemporaries dismissed Pelley as a madman, but Lewis understood that no truly crazy person could create a national organization, run a press and newspaper, conduct national speaking tours, and attract the support of anti-Semitic congressmen. In ordinary times, a narcissistic and delusional man such as Pelley would be little more than a sideshow in national politics. But his message might resonate among the nearly 13 million Americans who were unemployed in 1933, roughly one-fourth of the civilian labor force.

Pelley attracted a wide array of respectable and not-so-respectable Americans to his cause. The men and women who attended Silver Shirt meetings came for multiple reasons: some enjoyed Pelley's forceful Christian messages; some came to hear weekly denunciations of Jews and Franklin D. Roosevelt; and some came out of loneliness, despair, or hope. The diverse crowd of 365 people attending a December 10, 1933, Los Angeles Silver Shirt meeting at Odd Fellows Temple "had the appearance of the middle class with a sprinkling of intelligentsia and also men out of work."[10] These were not crazy people, Lewis's agent warned. They were ordinary men and women looking for answers. Their ordinariness made the anti-Semitic organization all the more frightening.

While much of Pelley's political ideology was filled with spiritual mumbo jumbo, Leon Lewis watched the Silver Shirts attract a large and devoted following. Los Angeles proved especially fertile soil for the fascist movement, establishing six posts—the largest of any city in the nation—and additional posts in nearby Pasadena and Whittier. "The Silver Shirts now are fighting for that what the weak Legionnaires cannot do," an admiring Hans Winterhalder told John Schmidt. "They are fighting for an America for the Whitemen, while the American Legion stands satisfied for an America under Russian Recognition." Pelley's group, Winterhalder bragged, had 10,000 members in Southern California "armed and ready for action against the Communists." Although Lewis placed local Silver Shirt membership at a more modest 500 and active national membership at 5,000, he knew it only took a few determined men to launch a massacre.[11]

Like Hitler and Mussolini, the self-inflated William Dudley Pelley enjoyed parading around in military garb. Prepared for violence at any moment, he always carried a gun strapped to his left hip. As Silver Shirt membership continued to rise, Lewis and the Community Committee worried about the prospect of an alliance between the Silver Shirts and the city's far better organized and more disciplined Nazis. Throughout the fall of 1933, Sunderland and Schmidt provided the attorney with reports of the growing links between the two groups. Lewis doubted that Pelley's followers could create a national army on their own. But what if the Nazis saw a way of recruiting like-minded men who could serve as a potential military force? Veterans who would never ally with Nazis might well flock to the American-dominated Silver Shirts. Many of their local leaders had served in the military as officers and now spoke of the need for armed action to save the nation from the Jewish-Communist threat.

Was the possibility of a Silver Shirt coup a delusional dream? Perhaps, but Lewis reminded himself that highly educated Germans had never thought a man like Adolf Hitler could come to power. As militant fascist Henry Allen wrote Congressman Kramer, "Christians of the United States . . . are faced with the same problems concerning the preservation of our Government from Jew domination as the people in Germany before Hitler rescued them from Jewish strangulation. I am but one of those millions who would gladly give my life to cast off the yoke of the lecherous Jewry rapidly fastening itself upon us . . ."[12]

As in Germany and Italy, a number of conservative business leaders found themselves attracted to fascism. In one of the least-known instances of traitorous American actions, a group of wealthy industrialists plotted to overthrow President Roosevelt in 1933 and replace him with the extraordinarily popular Major General Smedley Butler. Testifying before Congress in a closed executive session in November 1934, the Marine Corps' highest-ranking officer told how he had been offered a small fortune to lead 500,000 World War I veterans in a military coup against the Roosevelt administration and impose a fascist dictatorship similar to Mussolini's Italian government. Although the businessmen involved all denied the existence of such a plot, a final report by a special House committee confirmed much of Butler's testimony.[13]

Nazi leaders reacted to the imminent start of Kramer's investigation by curtailing their public activities and building a united front with other right-wing American organizations: local Silver Shirts, the American Labor Party and its military wing, the Lode Star Legion, the Ku Klux Klan, and the American White Guard, a militant "secret organization" comprising breakaway Metropolitan Post men and Ku Klux Klan members.

AGENT 33 AND THE FASCIST FRONT

With his initial agents exposed following the German-American Alliance trial, Lewis turned to his last remaining undercover operative, Walter Clairville. He charged Agent 33 with infiltrating as many of the city's fascist groups as possible, discovering the extent of their alliances with local Nazis, and uncovering any potentially violent plans. He also instructed Clairville to act as an agent provocateur, sowing discord and suspicion among the city's fascists and Nazis.

Clairville was a far more experienced and cunning operative than Lewis's previous spies. Born in Oakland, California, in 1879, he learned his investigative skills while working in military intelligence during World War I. Wounded during the war and discharged in July 1919, the former sergeant moved to Los Angeles in 1922 and began working as assistant—and later chief—investigator for the city attorney's office. His membership in the Disabled American Veterans brought him into contact with Schmidt and Lewis. Eager for new agents, the spymaster hired the veteran in February 1934 and instructed him to begin attending as many weekly fascist meetings as possible.

Clairville worked for Lewis in two capacities: as a member of the Disabled American Veterans' secret investigative committee (which Lewis chaired) and as an investigator aiding Lewis in his official position as counsel for the upcoming local HUAC hearings.[14]

Over the next several months, the amiable Clairville rose to leadership positions in a number of the city's fascist groups. Silver Shirts and

Nazis saw Clairville as an ideal recruit: a seemingly disgruntled military veteran who was given an inadequately small disability pension for his wartime service. When he applied for membership in Silver Shirt Metropolitan Post 47-10—the nation's largest and most active post—that February, he attracted the attention of its leaders by "condemning the Jews and praising the Silver Legion."[15] Introducing himself as an unemployed investigator, Clairville offered to do similar work for the Silver Shirts.

Post leader Eugene R. Case was especially delighted with his latest recruit and invited him to work at their downtown headquarters at 730 South Grand Avenue. As luck would have it, while working for the city attorney's office, Clairville had been asked to determine whether there was sufficient information to arrest Case on charges of criminal libel. The investigator suspected Case of wrongdoing, but concluded there was insufficient evidence to issue an arrest warrant. Consequently, when Clairville began working at Silver Shirt headquarters, a grateful Case introduced him as "the man who kept me out of jail."[16]

Case's blessing eased Clairville's entry into the Metropolitan Post's inner circle. Spending his days working at headquarters and nights attending meetings, Clairville soon became close friends with the Post's secretary, Mark L. White. The two veterans hit it off and spent time socializing and discussing their war experiences. Clairville saw White as the kind of man Nazis and fascists loved to embrace: an unhappy, impoverished World War I veteran whose military pension had been cut to a miserly $7.50 a month ($133 in 2015 dollars). By the time he met Clairville, the thirty-year-old sole supporter of a pregnant wife, child, and mother was unemployed and desperate for a job.[17]

Within a matter of weeks, White and Case invited their new recruit to join a secret inner circle that included Silver Shirt leaders Colonel Walter A. McCord and Major W. C. Fowler, and Mr. Byrnes, the local post's chief investigator. When queried if he was a member of the Ku Klux Klan, Clairville responded, "No I am not a Klansman, but I am in sympathy with their aims regarding Jews and Negroes and while I was in the office of City Prosecutor, I cooperated with Klan members." Clairville proved himself so invaluable that he was asked to serve as one of the Post's two undercover investigators, checking the backgrounds of all applicants and making sure no Jews or spies joined their organization. The married White grew so comfortable with Clairville that he asked if he could use his car on "a date with a 'flusey.'"[18]

Like John Schmidt, Clairville knew he was far more likely to obtain confidential information about the Silver Shirts over beer and food than in a meeting hall. He frequently took White to restaurants and bought him several rounds of drinks "in order to loosen him up." During the course of their meals, Clairville learned that the Silver Shirts were divided into two distinct factions: those, like White, who saw themselves as loyal Christian Americans who opposed communism and wanted nothing to do with Nazis, and those who embraced Nazis, Klansmen, and other fascist groups as like-minded allies in the struggle to rid the nation of Reds, Jews, Catholics, and blacks.[19]

As he drank more and more, the loose-lipped White spoke frankly about the growing tensions within the local movement. Over the past several months, White and many other Silver Shirt members had become disenchanted with Pelley. Calling the Silver Shirt leader "a big slob," White explained how the downtown Metropolitan Post (which Pelley dubbed the "Rebel Post") had broken away from the national group and vowed to clean up a corrupt Silver Shirt "racket" in which many leaders lined their pockets with members' dues and the profits from charging $16 for uniforms that cost them $2.50. Yet despite their breakaway, post leader Eugene Case proved no better than other corrupt officers. Case was a drunk who frequently missed important meetings because he was hungover. Worse yet, White and others suspected him of embezzling local funds. As one disgruntled Silver Shirt carped, "If Case had a chance to get $1,000, he would take it and leave right away."[20]

After learning about the divisions within the Silver Shirt movement, Lewis urged Clairville to see if he could turn White against Metropolitan Post leaders. Following the conclusion of a meeting in mid-March, White complained about the keynote speaker's rabid denunciations of President Roosevelt. "Even though I am a Republican," White said, he did not like listening to attacks on the president "when he is doing the best he can." The rampant corruption within his organization had led him to dislike Nazis and Silver Shirts alike. He was so disgusted, he told Clairville, that he was ready to go to the Justice Department and "spill the beans" about their un-American activities.[21] Upon hearing that, Clairville revealed his true identity and told him about Leon Lewis, whom he described as a counsel working for the House Un-American Activities Committee. He then asked White to accompany him to Lewis's office so they could put his testimony on record.

The next day, as the three men met inside the downtown Roosevelt Building, the canny Lewis assessed his potential new recruit: "White is a young man of very little education, a bad look in his eye—evidently has a guilty conscience." At first, the exceedingly nervous White denied any knowledge of Germans in the Silver Shirts, insisting it was "a strictly American organization, supporting the Constitution and standing squarely upon it." However, as the three veterans continued talking, White grew more comfortable and finally admitted that Eugene Case had strayed far beyond the Constitution and was perverting American values. The majority of Silver Shirt members were "clean cut American people." They were not anti-Jewish, anti-Catholic, or pro-Nazi; they were just anti-Communist.[22]

When Lewis offered to pay him a "small weekly stipend" to help Clairville investigate "Un-American activities" on behalf of the Disabled American Veterans, the impoverished veteran opened up about Nazi involvement with the Silver Shirts. White confessed that he knew Hermann Schwinn, Paul Themlitz, and Hans Winterhalder, now in charge of the Silver Shirts' Vermont office. Winterhalder's post, he told Lewis, was a Nazi front composed entirely of Germans who openly wore "a swastika in the coat lapel." No American was permitted to join. White promised to assist Lewis and Clairville "in 'busting up' the organization" and investigating every possible Silver Shirt–Nazi connection. He began by turning over the names and addresses of local Silver Shirt organizers and all new applicants.[23]

Meeting again the next day, White confirmed what Lewis's spies had learned from Dietrich Gefken: Nazis and Silver Shirts from San Diego were plotting an armed rebellion against American forces. Leaders from both groups frequently met with their counterparts in Los Angeles to plot a common course of action. One San Diego post, he added, regularly used "graphic pictures of a dead Christ being feasted on by Jewish communists to get a rise from the audience."[24] Before leaving Lewis's office, White promised to go to San Diego and bring back more specific information about the Nazi–Silver Shirt alliance.

Over the next several weeks, White and Clairville reported that a small cadre of militant leaders in Los Angeles was building an armed fascist front that would be ready to kill Jews and Communists at a moment's notice. White described how he and twenty local Silver Shirts were preparing for such an eventuality by holding secret military maneuvers at a factory owned by one of the post leaders. Captain Case told him how groups in Los Angeles and San Diego were stockpiling heavy weapons for any future eventuality, explaining, "We need machine guns if the Communists start trouble." Knowing White's military background, Case ordered him to train a squadron of four men, who would "carry guns and travel in one car." They, in turn, would train a platoon and then a company of well-drilled Silver Shirt soldiers who would lead the anticipated battle against Reds and their Jewish allies.[25]

As Lewis spent time that spring with Congressman Kramer preparing for the local hearings scheduled for August, Clairville uncovered yet another plan for armed confrontation. He told Lewis about attending his first meetings of the newly formed American White Guard.[26] Disgusted with the disorganization and corruption of the Silver Shirts, AWG organizers Major W. C. Fowler and Colonel Walter McCord—who had come to know and trust Clairville and White while working at the Metropolitan Post—invited the ex-soldiers to become leaders in their new organization.

In late March, the two undercover agents met at Fowler's downtown office on Seventh and Broadway, just a few blocks from Lewis's law firm. Fowler, a former Ku Klux Klan organizer and current provost marshal of the AWG's Mobilization Department, planned to raise a military regiment of 1,954 veterans, which he hoped to expand to 30,000. These men were not playing at being soldiers, Clairville warned; they were experienced combat officers. Fowler "has a military appearance, square broad shoulders, supposed to have been in the Department of Justice" and "weighs about 240 pounds." Likewise, Walter A. McCord, commanding officer of the Ninth Division of the Silver Shirts (which included all of California) and an AWG cofounder, was a former machine gun battalion commander who now served as a colonel in California's 353rd Reserve Infantry. When McCord asked Clairville to help organize the group's intelligence unit, Lewis's spy agreed. "I did that kind of work in the army, 5th Field Artillery 1st Division," he told the impressed AWG leader.[27]

Despite their violent aims, American White Guard leaders expected little trouble from local police. So long as they continued denouncing Communists, Los Angeles police captain "Red" Hynes would not trouble them. Far from it, the police captain welcomed their help in battling what he saw as America's number-one enemy. When the superintendent of Patriotic Hall wrote Hynes asking if it was OK to let the American White Guard hold meetings in his facility—the same facility that housed the DAV and American Legion—the police captain answered that, given the "aims, purpose, and objectives of this organization," he saw no reason to deny them "the privilege of meeting in any of our patriotic halls."[28]

Lewis asked Clairville to burrow deeper and discover any immediate plans for violence. Within a matter of days, the highly effective agent reported that he, Case, and White had met with California Ku Klux Klan leader Gus W. Price to discuss a possible fascist alliance. "We are the front line of defense," Case told the KKK chief. "We are militant. Ex-service men. 500 strong. 80 percent overseas men." Although Price could not guarantee official cooperation with the state's 26,000 Klan members, he promised his unofficial support. "I have men in your organization," he remarked, as well as men in the police department. "At one time we had 400 policemen in our Klan." To prove his point, he called the Hollywood police station and asked to speak to the acting captain. The police officer confirmed he was a Klan member. Before his visitors left, Price offered two pieces of advice: be careful of the Jews who were secretly investigating their operations, and "don't underestimate Mendel Silberberg."[29]

Leon Lewis understood that sometimes the best results came not from foiling a plot but from making sure it never developed. The Community Committee leader hoped Clairville and White could accelerate the split between Pelley and Case, as well as between the Silver Shirts and White Guardsmen. "There is a lot of double crossing going on," Clairville reported. "Each one [Pelley and Case] is suspicious of one another, claiming that money is collected, and is not properly split." Clairville and White did their best to fuel that discord by sowing "more seeds of discontent, knocking Case, etc." They also convinced many Metropolitan members to oppose Winterhalder's creation of a Silver Shirt post dominated by local Nazis. When Hitler sympathizer Harold Generes spoke at a Silver Shirt executive meeting in early April, Mark White's brother Joseph denounced him: "You are a lousy Nazi. We are Americans. I served in the Army eight years. I don't intend to be connected with any God damned Nazis."[30]

As internal dissension grew more overt, William Dudley Pelley traveled to Los Angeles in late March 1934 hoping to mend the rift with the breakaway Metropolitan Post. But that would not happen. Clairville had so impressed his rebel post brethren that they asked him to write an article criticizing Pelley. The article, secretly written by Leon Lewis, exposed the direct connection between Pelley and the Friends of New

Germany. The one-inch banner headline of the newspaper's special April 6 edition boldly asked, "Pelley Allied with the Nazis?" Answering in the affirmative, the article detailed the leader's close relationship with Los Angeles Nazis. Pelley had asked Hermann Schwinn to organize a Nazi post for the Silver Shirts and then placed the FNG's propaganda chief, Hans Winterhalder, in charge of its office on Vermont Avenue and entrusted recent Silver Shirt enlistee Paul Themlitz with selling its publications.[31]

The Lewis-Clairville article closed by calling upon "every sincere American who is a member of the Silver Legion" to bring the Metropolitan Post any "evidence that they have of Nazi interference in American affairs and Silver Legion of America affairs; our corps of investigators will trail down these facts and will submit them without delay to the United States Department of Justice." As loyal Americans, they wanted "no Nazi interferences," or "foreign entanglements of any kind" in their movement.[32]

Schwinn denounced the article as a pack of lies. There was no Nazi–Silver Shirt connection. Winterhalder was not a member of the FNG. Themltiz was not in charge of distributing Silver Shirt literature. No meetings were ever held at Schwinn's office, and the alleged storm trooper unit had no connection to the FNG. Despite Schwinn's denials, the damage had been done. The Nazi–Silver Shirt alliance had been exposed in their own newspaper, and Pelley's personal appeal for reconciliation with the Metropolitan Post had failed. Clairville also succeeded in undermining the White Guardsmen's organizing efforts by pitting its leaders, McCord and Fowler, against one another.[33]

There was one discordant note in the affair. After a similar series of articles exposing the Nazi–Silver Shirt connection appeared in the left-wing periodical Today, several Silver Shirt officials suspected Clairville of writing the articles, or at least leaking the information to the magazine. Silver Shirts knew that Jews were "operating an espionage system," and chief investigator Byrnes thought Clairville might be one of them. Once again, another of Lewis's spies faced the threat of death. It would be easy, Byrnes told Clairville, to throw a man out of the sixth-floor office bathroom, where the casement was very low, and make it look like an accident. "Operator has been extremely cautious of this situation," he wrote Lewis; he did not intend to become the victim of such an "accident."[34]

Despite the risk to his safety, Clairville scored a major coup by persuading Eugene Case to testify against his Silver Shirt comrades.

Lewis's spy had taken the discredited leader out for drinks, hoping the alcohol might lead "a moron of his type" to reveal secrets about the group's military operations. In late April, several weeks after the publication of the *Silver Ranger* and *Today* articles, Clairville achieved his goal. Fearing his arrest for un-American activities, Case told him that he withdrew from the Silver Shirt movement "when he found out about Foreign [i.e. Nazi] involvement." Having saved Case from jail once before, Clairville suggested he could do so again by arranging for him to meet with local Secret Service agent Ash, whom he knew from his city investigator days.[35]

Wasting no time, Lewis arranged for Clairville and Case to meet with the Justice Department official the following day. Despite an earlier conversation with Lewis, Ash was unprepared for the meeting. Clairville had called Lewis's office and asked him "to give this man some idea of what line of questions to ask Case." The Silver Shirt leader told Ash how San Diego Nazis and Silver Shirts were working together "collecting arms and ammunition" and had obtained "an armored car." Despite these revelations, the unprepared Secret Service man did not press Case further. Ash "could have moved in and asked incriminating questions no matter whether he was familiar with the picture or not." As they left the government building, Case turned to Clairville and snorted, "Ash was dumb." Despite Clairville's disappointment, Lewis cautioned his agent not to make a fuss. "If Mr. Ash is antagonized it will create a non-co-operating attitude for any future that this subversive matter may hold."[36]

THE FBI ENTERS THE SCENE

Leon Lewis was not the only one concerned with uncovering Nazi activity. On May 9, 1934, President Roosevelt summoned the attorney general, the secretary of treasury, the secretary of labor, the Secret Service chief, and FBI director J. Edgar Hoover to the White House to discuss whether "Nazi groups in the United States should be investigated." Answering in the affirmative, the gathered officials agreed that immigration laws offered solid grounds for investigating the foreign connections of all domestic groups. Assigning the FBI the lead role, Roosevelt asked Hoover to cooperate with the Secret Service and the Department of Immigration. The FBI head instructed each field office to open an investigation in its area to determine whether any foreign agents were working with domestic Nazis or fascists and whether any of these groups posed a threat to national security.[37]

The FBI, however, proved too small and ill-equipped to handle such a sweeping investigation. When Henry Dolan joined the G-men, as they were popularly known at the time, in November 1933, there "were only 300 agents in the entire country" and "eighty of them were stationed in New York alone." Little wonder, then, that Nazis soon decided to ship the bulk of their propaganda materials through the less guarded port of Los Angeles. As Dolan trained at FBI headquarters for six weeks, neither he nor any other agent was given instruction in domestic espionage. His daily regimen included a "review of Federal laws, the laboratory work of fingerprinting, typewriter identification, and the various guns and the various things that go into making laboratory crime detection."[38] Given the modest number of agents and their lack of training in counterespionage, Hoover's men proved incapable of efficiently carrying out the president's orders.

To the extent that FBI agents conducted surveillance work, the Communist-obsessed Hoover ordered them to tail suspected Reds rather than Nazis or Silver Shirts. Ever since the Russian Revolution of 1917, and especially after the Communist Third International—a worldwide body of Communists from forty-one nations—met in Moscow in 1919 and proclaimed destruction of capitalism as its goal, the FBI leader had been obsessed with uncovering Red activity in the United States. The bombing of Attorney General A. Mitchell Palmer's home in 1919 and numerous reports of mail bombs being sent to government officials that year led Hoover to believe that the Red revolution had come to America.

Hoover was especially concerned about the power of movies and movie stars to affect the political consciousness of a nation. Following World War I, he ordered FBI agents to maintain close surveillance over suspected Hollywood radicals such as Charlie Chaplin, Upton Sinclair, and radical working-class filmmakers. During the early 1920s, his agents filed over 1,900 pages of reports just on Chaplin.[39]

Lewis was not surprised that the FBI and local police had little interest in combating the Silver Shirts. Although Los Angeles police chief James Davis insisted that his department was opposed to the organization, Lewis received reports about police officers who were sympathetic to the Silver Shirts and even passed out their literature while on duty.[40]

With the police turning a blind eye to the Silver Shirts and with no meaningful help from the FBI, it was up to Lewis, Congressman Charles Kramer, and HUAC to stop the growth of Nazism and fascism in Los Angeles. Having forwarded his spy reports to Kramer, the Secret Service, and naval intelligence, Lewis hoped that the upcoming Los Angeles HUAC hearings would expose the subversive activities of Nazis and fascists and spark the national outrage the German-American Alliance trial had failed to generate.

8.

HUAC Comes to Town

On April 26, 1934, in a room packed with reporters, Samuel Dickstein announced that the House Un-American Activities Committee, created by Congress a month earlier to investigate Nazi propaganda in the United States, would begin preliminary hearings in nine cities, including Los Angeles. Dickstein told how an early investigation of Silver Shirts by his fellow congressman Charles Kramer had uncovered information about subversive activities that would startle the nation. After traveling to North Carolina to investigate William Dudley Pelley, Kramer returned to Los Angeles and began hiring investigators to gather information for the local hearings set to begin in August 1934.

Samuel Dickstein's long-sought-after victory was only a partial one. The congressman's love of publicity and his playing loose with evidence turned many colleagues against him. Congress appointed the Jewish politician as committee vice chair, but, "in order to show him up," instead of appropriating the $50,000 Dickstein requested to hire twenty-five investigators, they allocated $25,000, enough for only ten agents. "How much can you do with ten investigators?" the Jewish politician complained.[1]

Leon Lewis had agreed the previous month to serve as Kramer's special counsel to the House investigations, but recommended that Volney P. Mooney, national judge advocate of the Disabled American Veterans and a member of Lewis's Community Committee, be appointed chief counsel. Lewis believed Americans were more likely to listen to the findings of a respected Christian inquisitor than a Jewish one. With Mooney preparing to take over as the DAV's national commander, Lewis took charge of HUAC's day-to-day operations in Los Angeles. "I am practically doing all the work and have the complete confidence and cooperation of Congressman Kramer who is leaving the matter of arrangements for the forthcoming hearings here *almost entirely in my hands.*"[2]

Lewis hoped to uncover enough evidence to convince the FBI to take over his operation and launch their own investigation of Nazi and fascist activities. He would have liked nothing better than to return to his work as a lawyer and the Anti-Defamation League's representative to Southern California. Lewis still believed that trained government agents could do a better job than his ad hoc assortment of spies. For that to happen, he had to make sure that Kramer and his investigators would succeed.

On May 5, 1934, Kramer appointed R. Robert Carroll as his chief field representative and instructed him to begin investigating Silver Shirts and other fascist groups linked to local Nazis. He told Carroll to get help from Leon Lewis and police commissioner Ray Kleinberger, a Jew whose brother served as Kramer's campaign manager. Born in Missouri to parents of German descent, Carroll had previously worked as a caterer, clerk, and correctional facility guard. Despite his lack of undercover experience, he proved a highly capable spy.[3]

Attending numerous meetings over the next several weeks, the thirty-six-year-old investigator documented the connection among Silver Shirts, Nazis, and American White Guard. Working sixteen to twenty hours a day, Carroll discovered that violence was the end goal of these groups. Aryan Bookstore owner Paul Themlitz told him how Nazis and Silver Shirts would "restore the country to the real Americans and take it back from the Jews who were putting us all into slavery." Based on his preliminary findings, Carroll predicted this could "turn into one of the biggest if not the biggest investigation which the United States has ever sponsored."[4]

Not everyone in Los Angeles shared Carroll's assessment of the dangers posed by Nazis and fascists. In a May 12 editorial, the *Los Angeles Times* insisted that there was "no probability the local Nazis will ever succeed in making more of a nuisance of themselves than did the late unlamented Ku Klux Klan, which barely rippled the surface of our serenity." Instead, the editors argued that HUAC should focus on investigating Communists. "While the underlying principle of Fascism and Communism is identical," the editors noted, "and both foment hatred and intolerance, Communists constitute a real threat to the public peace and safety and the Fascists do not—at least not yet."[5]

Whatever the *Times* may have thought, Carroll was convinced that Nazis and fascists threatened democratic institutions. "I can get all the evidence you need to prove your contentions that the Silver Shirts and the Nazis are one and the same," he wrote HUAC members. To do so, he needed "ten or fifteen good men and two or three clever women."[6] Unfortunately, with funds limited, HUAC decided to focus its investigations on the East Coast. Kramer's colleagues appointed six investigators for New York, two for Washington, D.C., and one each for Boston and Detroit. HUAC did not see the West Coast as an especially important center of right-wing activism.

Carroll refused to back down. After pressuring Kramer, he received permission to hire two men and one woman—with a caveat: the congressman ordered his chief investigator to cut Leon Lewis out of the loop. "Of course he is giving us splendid cooperation, but naturally he wants some of his friends on the job, please don't mention this to Lewis or anyone just yet."[7] Kramer instructed Carroll to keep meeting with the Jewish lawyer but not to reveal the names of the people he hired, nor share their findings. If there was glory to be had from the investigation, the congressman wanted it for himself.

Unlike Lewis, who chose his spies based on ability, Kramer selected his based on political considerations. As Carroll interviewed people on Kramer's list, he realized they were mediocre, incompetent, or obsessed with uncovering Reds. Emile Normile, his boss's favored candidate, was "a typical policeman utterly unfit for this type of work . . . a man about 65 years of age, slightly deaf, not so quick at catching an idea" and the type "who would attract suspicion by his very manner in this kind of an investigation." The unemployed former cop spent most of his time at local Democratic headquarters. "Normile may be a good precinct worker," Carroll told Kramer, but "he hasn't the qualities for this job." He needed agents he could trust, "for one false step may mean my life. You have no idea of the intense hatred among these people for the committee, their investigators, and all who are not sympathetic with them [the Silver Shirts]."[8]

Kramer had the last word. "Have known Normile for a long time and believe him to be loyal and trustworthy." Despite his repeated objections, Carroll hired Normile. As for the others on Kramer's list, only William F. Lucitt seemed vaguely competent. The former prison guard had spent the past eight years working as an electrician at Sears, Roebuck. Lucitt had one positive virtue: a considerable knowledge of German.[9]

Having agreed to hire two of Kramer's people, Carroll insisted on selecting a woman not on his boss's list, Florence Shreve. She had worked with him on previous investigations and had been attending Silver Shirt and Friends of New Germany meetings for the past several weeks. Shreve, he wrote, "is the most valuable assistant that I could have at this time, since she understands the language, can catch all their German telephone conversations and talks freely with those in charge." But Kramer refused his request; he wanted Shreve to work on his reelection campaign. Instead, he instructed Carroll to hire Mary Spalione, even though she did not speak German.[10]

Knowing his life was on the line, Carroll refused to bend and persuaded Kramer to hire Shreve. She would begin her official position as "Investigator and Stenographer" for the special HUAC hearings on June 1; Lucitt and Normile would commence their duties the same day, but at a salary higher than their female colleague.

With his agents in place, Carroll instructed them to attend Nazi and fascist meetings, join their organizations, and make themselves useful to their leaders. Their effectiveness, however, would be limited by more political gamesmanship. Soon after Carroll's appointment in May, Leon Lewis took him to meet B. E. Sackett, the Justice Department agent in charge of the Los Angeles office. Sackett explained that the U.S. attorney general wanted both men to turn over a report on their investigations by early June. Lewis agreed to do so, but not Kramer. "Under no circumstances," he instructed Carroll, "make any report to anyone except our committee."[11]

Kramer was not the only one playing games. On June 13, HUAC's national chair John McCormack ordered the four Los Angeles investigators to bypass Kramer and send all reports about Reds directly to him. Samuel Dickstein had created the committee to focus on Nazis and fascists, but McCormack was far more interested in uncovering "subversive communistic activities."[12]

GOING UNDERCOVER

Carroll's team was officially in place on June 1, only two months before the beginning of the Los Angeles hearings. Since Emile Normile could neither speak nor read German, Carroll assigned him to monitor Silver Shirt headquarters on South Vermont Avenue. His charge: identify the people coming in and out of the office and write down their license plates whenever possible.

As Carroll feared, Normile proved useless. In one report, Normile observed that Hans Winterhalder always sat directly in front of his office window in order to see everyone who came in and out of the building. Normile, in turn, spent his days sitting on a bench directly outside the Silver Shirt office. It apparently never occurred to him that if he could see Winterhalder, Winterhalder could see him. Later that month, Normile saw two men he had met at a meeting of the newly organized American Labor Party enter the office. "Winterhalder called their attention to me. I was sitting across the street on a bench. They focused a small camera on me, but I had my face partially covered so I do not think they succeeded in getting much of a picture." The Nazis proved smarter than the HUAC agent. After grabbing a streetcar on Vermont Avenue, they "doubled back on another car passing my spot, got off a block beyond and walked back to Ranger office," where they spotted Normile sitting in the same place, writing down notes.[13] His spying was over.

William Lucitt proved a far more capable investigator. Assigned the task of attending Silver Shirt meetings in Los Angeles and nearby Pasadena, he sent back detailed accounts of their antigovernment and anti-Semitic messages. Even after he was ordered to focus on the city's Reds, the German-speaking Lucitt spent many evenings socializing with Nazis at the Old Vienna Café on Santa Monica Boulevard, a festive haunt where patrons and musicians dressed in Tyrolean-style outfits joined in singing German songs. On one of his frequent visits to the popular "storm trooper hangout," he learned from one of its inebriated leaders that Nazis planned a "Putsch" over the summer "during which all Jews and Catholics 'will be taken care of.'"[14]

Los Angeles Nazis were growing in strength. Fortunately, Florence Shreve accomplished what no agent since John and Alice Schmidt had achieved: she was invited into the inner circle of the Friends of New Germany. Her ability to speak fluent German made it easy for the convivial agent to engage Nazis at FNG meetings and in the Aryan Bookstore, where she soon became a familiar figure. When Paul Themlitz complained about the burdensome task of writing letters and keeping track of mail for both the Silver Shirts and the FNG, the bilingual stenographer volunteered to help. She also agreed to work with Hans Winterhalder editing the *Silver Ranger* newspaper. By the middle of June, her German friends had invited Shreve to take notes at secret meetings of the FNG's core leaders. On one evening she heard Themlitz speak about "the necessity of taking decided action against the Jewish menace in America."[15]

Shreve's success placed her in danger. The higher she rose, the greater the possibilities of being exposed as a spy. The inner circle meetings she attended, Carroll explained to Kramer, "are held behind locked doors." This put her in jeopardy "because none of us can go with Mrs. Shreve, and if there is ever a leak, she would be in a jam."[16]

That July, Shreve began working closely with Franz Ferenz, who replaced Winterhalder as the FNG's head of recruitment and publicity. Ferenz needed an assistant to help edit his manuscript, *Hitler: What Every American Should Know about the Man Whose Influence Is Felt the World Over*, and Shreve offered her services. It did not take her long to assess the Austrian-born Ferenz. He had been in Germany during the 1920s and established close contacts with many of Hitler's friends, contacts he maintained after coming to America. "If he can be believed, he is receiving direct information from Germany and Austria from people close to '*Der Fuehrer*' as he calls Hitler, on what is really going on there." By the middle of the month, Shreve was serving as personal secretary to Themlitz and Ferenz, and both expressed "every confidence in her."[17]

After several weeks on the job, Robert Carroll was smart enough to see that working with Lewis was far more likely to thwart the Nazi threat than relying on the self-serving Kramer. Ignoring the congressman's order, Carroll and Shreve spent several hours in mid-July conferring with Lewis "in preparation for the taking of testimony for the sub-committee." They reviewed all the information that had been gathered and "prepared to get this evidence into proper shape" for the hearings.[18]

Lewis suspected Kramer of double-dealing. He knew the congressman had been withholding information and feared that the opportunity to expose Nazi activity in Los Angeles was slipping away. Taking no chances, Lewis ordered Walter Clairville and Mark White to continue investigating right-wing groups. They had penetrated deeper into the fascist front than any of the HUAC investigators.

Lewis was not above playing his own games. He did not tell Carroll and Shreve that Clairville and White were working for him, nor did he reveal the identities of the HUAC agents to his own spies. When the two sets of agents attended a meeting of a recently formed German Silver Shirt post on South Hoover Boulevard, neither knew the others worked for Lewis.

INSIDE THE AMERICAN LABOR PARTY

While attending a Silver Shirt meeting in late May, Clairville and White met the blue-eyed and blond-haired John Riemer. After sharing the usual pleasantries, White explained that he and Clairville were ex-servicemen and former Metropolitan Post leaders interested in joining a more militant organization. The Silver Shirts, he scoffed, "are all Pacifists."[19] After hearing this, a delighted Riemer revealed that he was starting the American Labor Party (ALP), an action-oriented group that would supersede the Silver Shirts. He invited the two agents to his home to discuss the best ways of organizing the new militant body.

After leafing through a copy of the former German Army reservist's book *Bread and a Home, Protection Against Want in Old Age: Program of the American Labor Party*, the two agents concluded that Riemer's proposed party was "just the same Party set-up as over there [Nazi Germany]." Joining them for dinner was FNG storm trooper leader and ALP cofounder Rafael Demmler. "There are about fourteen million niggers in this country," he told the possible recruits. "I figure they could have a State of their own. Our Program will go over Big in the South."[20] Impressed with their conversation, Riemer invited the two men to an informal council to plan a strategy for selling the ALP to the American people.

Leon Lewis recognized the ALP as a Nazi front: "It is the NSDAP all over again and . . . adopts the same restrictions as the Nazi Party in Germany."[21] Not trusting Kramer with the information, Lewis sent his agents' reports directly to his Justice Department contact, B. E. Sackett. Robert Carroll was also monitoring the ALP. He met Riemer while attending the same Silver Shirt meeting as Clairville and White, and accepted his invitation to attend the party's first public meeting in mid-June.

When Clairville visited the Aryan Bookstore several days later, Themlitz confided that the Nazis planned to use Riemer as their puppet in forging a well-armed militant fascist front. Riemer would be easy to control, the Nazi boasted, for he "has not the appearance or the ability to take the lead, he is a machine type of man. You wind him up in the morning and he runs down at 5 o'clock."[22]

Over the next several weeks, Clairville, White, and Carroll (still unaware that the other two were working for Lewis) attended private meetings at Riemer's home, where he announced his intentions to form the Lode Star Legion, the ALP's military wing. "This organization directed by known Nazi agents," Clairville warned, "has for its purpose the inciting and the forming of a drilled and armed force to harass the constituted authorities of the United States." Sending a similar warning, Carroll told HUAC members that Riemer "is very militant and all he is interested in is having an army so that they can take over the government."[23]

Carroll was convinced that Riemer was just a front. "Demmler is the brains behind Riemer, the brains behind everything that was said or done." A cabinetmaker by trade, Rafael Demmler was an experienced soldier who had fought with Brownshirts in Germany and organized the paramilitary Steel Helmets on the East Coast before coming to Los Angeles. After joining the FNG, he supervised the local storm trooper unit that drilled behind the Aryan Bookstore in the evening. Unlike Riemer, he knew how to train men in both formal combat and street fighting. Demmler in turn took orders from Paul Themlitz, the man Carroll deemed the most dangerous Nazi of all. Carroll overheard Themlitz order Demmler to gather "hand grenades and machine guns."[24]

Carroll, White, and Clairville soon gained leadership positions within the ALP and Lode Star Legion. But just as the investigators were getting closer to exposing a direct link between the subversive militant organization and the local Nazis, the operation was compromised. On July 5, less than a month before the Los Angeles hearings were to begin, Lucitt and Normile received letters from HUAC headquarters in Washington, D.C., notifying them that due to drastic budget cuts, they were being let go as of July 15; Shreve received a similar letter, but her employment was extended until August 15.[25]

The news did not go over well with Robert Carroll. Unlike HUAC chair John McCormack, he saw the Nazis as far more cunning than Communists. "The Communists, while very dangerous and radical," he wrote the full committee, "work more in the open and their material is easier to get. Riemer, the Silver Shirts and Friends of New Germany are very subtly organized and one has to dig further to get the facts."[26] To get those facts, he needed his full complement of agents. Carroll's argument fell on deaf ears. It was now up to him and Shreve to uncover as much as they could before August 1.

Carroll's rapid rise within the ALP and Lode Star Legion ended in late July, when Riemer suspected him of being a spy. The Nazis had their own informants within the police and sheriff's departments. Themlitz knew HUAC agents and Jewish spies were trying to infiltrate their organization; he just did not know who they were. He and Winter-halder had figured out that Normile was working either for HUAC or the Jews. Riemer had become suspicious of the overly enthusiastic Carroll and shared his concerns with Walter Clairville. "You see those men with Carroll [Lucitt and Normile], they don't look so good to me." Wondering if Carroll was on the level and knowing Clairville's back-ground as a former city investigator, he asked him "to get a line" on Carroll.[27]

Fortunately, several weeks earlier Lewis had told Clairville that Carroll was working undercover for HUAC. Hoping to protect Carroll's identity, Clairville agreed to interview him. Afterward, he sent Riemer a report stating that the suspected spy "seems to be in perfect accord" with the ALP program.[28] Riemer still had his suspicions, and Carroll rose no further in the organization.

HUAC's investigation of Nazi and fascist activity suffered a fatal blow in late July 1934 when its national chair, John McCormack, ordered Kramer's Los Angeles agents to focus mainly on Reds. "Without disre-garding Nazi evidence, I feel that we should go extensively into Commu-nism."[29] With only Carroll and Shreve still in place, it was impossible to continue investigating the Friends of New Germany or the American Labor Party. HUAC had emerged out of Samuel Dickstein's burning desire to halt the growth of Nazism in the United States. But his strategy of legitimizing the investigation by turning the chairmanship over to a non-Jew had backfired. McCormack saw Russia, not Germany, as posing the greatest threat to American security.

THE HUAC HEARINGS

On August 1, congressman Charles Kramer and his chief counsel, Volney P. Mooney, armed with months of reports from Leon Lewis and weeks of information from HUAC investigators, began the formal hearing into subversive activities on the West Coast. During the next eight days, operating mostly in closed executive hearings, they heard testimonies from Nazi, Silver Shirt, and Communist leaders.

The German witnesses denied any connection between the FNG and Hitler's National Socialist German Workers' Party or the American Silver Shirts. They denied receiving funds from Germany or from local

German general vice consul Georg Gyssling. They denied that the FNG operated an active storm trooper regiment, insisting that their SA unit was a *Sportsabteilung* that engaged in hiking, singing, gymnastics, and occasional drilling in preparation for parades. They denied knowing anything about Dietrich Gefken's plan to infiltrate National Guard units and foment a revolt along the Pacific Coast. They denied that Rafael Demmler and the ALP secretly followed Hermann Schwinn's orders. The only thing they did admit was that the FNG had 500 paid members along the Pacific Coast and 140 in Los Angeles, half of whom were not citizens.

Over the course of the hearings, Schwinn and his fellow Nazis repeatedly portrayed themselves as patriotic Americans ready to lead the fight against any Communist effort to overthrow the government. "Quite a few of our members have had experience with Communism in Germany," Schwinn told the committee, "and we therefore believe we are qualified to judge as to the danger of Communism." As Hans Winterhalder added, "I concede that we are un-Jewish, but not un-American."[30]

The Nazis were well prepared for the investigation. They had been tipped off by their own inside sources. The ambitious but naive Kramer never bothered to consult the more experienced Lewis as to which local law enforcement officials could be trusted. Consequently, Kramer shared confidential information with men who maintained close ties to Nazi and fascist groups. Sheriff Eugene Biscailuz enjoyed socializing with German consul Gyssling, and his deputy James Foze was an outspoken anti-Semite with friends in the FNG and Silver Shirts. Likewise, when Police Chief Davis and Captain Hynes discovered what HUAC was planning, at least one of them informed their Nazi and fascist friends about the committee's intentions. So long as Nazis and Silver Shirts kept feeding them information about Communists, police officials were happy to turn a blind eye to their activities. The Los Angeles Police Department submitted sixty-five pieces of evidence to HUAC, but not a single document pertained to Nazis or fascists. They only reported on alleged Red subversion.[31]

Knowing that Nazis were unlikely to reveal any startling information, Lewis arranged for counsel Mooney to call San Diego–based marine corporal E. T. Gray and Virgil Hays, a police officer and former marine, to the stand. The two men told the same story. After being tipped off in late 1933 (by Leon Lewis, who remained anonymous in the press and throughout the hearings), the U.S. Marine Corps intelligence service asked Gray and Hays to join the San Diego Silver Shirts and see what they were planning. Hays discovered that Silver Shirts and local storm troopers intended "to remove all Jews from public office and deport them from the United States . . . by the use of force if necessary." He told the committee about the presence of 200 armed men being taught how to storm and take command of a city. Local law enforcement officials, Hays warned, were supporting the San Diego Silver Shirts. W. W. Kemp, their West Coast commander, had assured him that no one would be bothered when the time came to act. "Firearms of both the Sheriff's office and the Police Department will be turned over to us. The under-sheriff [a Jew] will be liquidated."[32]

The Silver Shirts meant business. When they suspected Corporal Gray of being a spy, five men beat him so badly they fractured his skull and sent him to the hospital for two weeks. After receiving death threats if they testified, the pair traveled to Los Angeles accompanied by armed marines.[33]

Despite the riveting testimony of the two marines, following the conclusion of the hearings, Kramer told the press the committee was unable to prove a direct connection between the Silver Shirts and the Friends of New Germany. Lewis was incredulous. Corporal Gray had testified under oath that Silver Shirts "were in sympathy with the Nazi rule in Germany," that they flew the swastika flag at meetings, and that many members decorated their homes with swastikas. Walter Clairville testified that the Silver Shirts "are endeavoring to take this country over." Yet the committee failed to ask him or Mark White about the links between the FNG and the emerging fascist front.[34]

After months of supplying Kramer, the Justice Department, and naval intelligence with information, Leon Lewis and his agents walked away from the HUAC hearings disappointed. Because most of the witnesses were questioned in closed executive sessions, the public learned little about the proceedings until printed copies of selected testimony were released in December 1934. The committee's discovery of Nazi activities and their control of several fascist groups were never leaked to the press. The committee heard "testimony which probably never will be disclosed," Kramer told reporters on August 7, "because it is of such a poisonous nature it might cause serious international complications."[35] Only two stories made national headlines that August: Silver Shirt activity in San Diego, and Communist activity among movie stars.

Reporting only the bare bones of their closed-session testimony, the *Los Angeles Times, New York Times, Atlanta Constitution, Wall Street*

Journal, and *Washington Post* told how Gray and Hays had discovered that "armed men known as the Silver Shirts with a secret auxiliary called Storm Troopers" were drilling in San Diego with machine guns, rifles, and over 2,000 rounds of .30-caliber ammunition illegally purchased from members of the U.S. Armed Forces. These men were trained "members of the United States Navy, United States Marine Corps, and the California National Guard."[36]

The press paid far greater attention to William Hynes's revelation that "certain world-famous" movie stars were making large contributions to the Communist Party. Refusing to name specific individuals until "the proper time," Hynes told reporters that most of "those who have contributed thousands of dollars to advance the Red cause in America believe they are guided by philanthropy." The captain knew better. He estimated that there were 2,000 dues-paying members of the Communist Party in Los Angeles and an additional 20,000 to 25,000 sympathizers, whom he characterized as well-intentioned dupes. Not once in the course of his lengthy testimony did Hynes mention investigating Nazis or fascists.[37]

Disappointed that months of investigating Nazis had yielded few public results, Lewis was pleased that one piece of vital information emerged during the hearings. Unable to prove a direct connection between Nazis and Silver Shirts, the committee exposed a link between the Nazi government and the American Labor Party. William Lucitt discovered a check for $215 signed by German consul Georg Gyssling and cashed by ALP head John Riemer. When subpoenaed by the committee, Gyssling claimed diplomatic immunity and refused to testify. Unfortunately, Lucitt was furloughed before he could confirm whether foreign drafts rumored to be as much as $1 million were being sent from Germany and laundered through Walter Brunsweiger, vice president of the Bank of America branch on Seventh and Olive.[38]

Although falling short of what Lewis had hoped for, the Los Angeles hearings had damaged the Nazi cause. There was now an official record of a German diplomat funding an American organization. But many questions remained. Had the German government wired $1 million into the Bank of America branch, as Samuel Dickstein reported to John McCormack?[39] Was Gyssling running a spy network? Were the rumors of a bitter rivalry between Gyssling and Schwinn true? Could the two Nazi leaders be played against one another? Lewis could no longer rely on Clairville and White. After testifying at the HUAC hearings, they could no longer continue burrowing from within.

Convinced that the police were "part of the problem, not the solution, of the growing menace of fascism," Lewis asked Robert Carroll to meet with Captain Jesse Hopkins of the Los Angeles Police Department and James Foze of the Los Angeles County Sheriff's Office and discover their views on subversive activities. After Carroll introduced himself as a congressional investigator on furlough, "both Foze and Hopkins made the categorical statement that 'all Jews in Los Angeles are Communists and that most of the outstanding Jewish leaders are Communists.'" Foze got very excited and told him "that all the Jews here ought to have 'their nuts cut out' and kicked out of the city." Captain Hopkins proved an equally virulent anti-Semite. When asked who the city's leading Communists were, he answered "Rabbi Magnin, Louis B. Mayer, Carl Laemmle, James Cagney and plenty of others." As for the Silver Shirts, he thought they "are absolutely right."[40]

Deeply disappointed with the committee's preference for focusing on Reds rather than Nazis, Leon Lewis played one last card. In early September, HUAC chair John McCormack, hoping to placate the city's Jewish community, sent Lewis a letter asking for his thoughts about possible legislative recommendations. A week later the spymaster spent twenty-four hours with the Boston congressman, carefully laying out what he knew about the Nazis and what might be done.[41]

On February 15, 1935, the House Un-American Activities Committee presented Congress with a series of legislative recommendations, many of them drawn from Lewis's meeting with McCormack. Warning that Nazi propaganda had been smuggled into the country in an effort to bring the "twenty-odd-million Americans of German birth or descent . . . into the Nazi program," HUAC recommended enacting a law requiring all propaganda agents working on behalf of foreign governments to register with the State Department. Responding to testimony of alleged Communist and fascist plots to overthrow the American government, especially Nazi efforts to recruit disgruntled war veterans, HUAC urged Congress to adopt two more laws: one making it illegal to "counsel or urge any member of the military or naval forces of the United States, including reservists, to disobey laws or regulations"; and a second that would make it illegal to incite "the overthrow or destruction by force and violence the government of the United States, or of the republican form of government guaranteed by the Constitution." It took Congress three years to pass the Foreign Agents Registration Act.[42]

With the hearings over, Lewis shifted his attention to discovering the precise role being played by the enigmatic Georg Gyssling. Adored by the city's social elite, the German consul proved a nightmare for Hollywood studio heads. Realizing they needed to know more about their archenemy, the moguls turned to Leon Lewis and his spies for help. It was time for Lewis's undercover operation to provide a return on their investment.

9.

The Most Charming Nazi
in Los Angeles

Georg Gyssling was a man of many faces. He revealed one face to Los Angeles's social elite, another to its studio heads, and yet another to the city's German and Nazi communities. A continual thorn in the side of the city's Jewish movie moguls, Gyssling proved extraordinarily popular with Los Angeles elites, fulfilling the social obligations that accompanied his position with the greatest aplomb. Respectable Angelenos who would never invite outspoken Nazis such as Hermann Schwinn or Paul Themlitz into their homes vied to see who could host Gyssling's soirees or grab his arm for a spin around the dance floor. He was indeed the most charming Nazi in Los Angeles.

Leon Lewis's spies and the moguls who dealt with Gyssling sent him wildly conflicting reports as to the vice consul's true leanings. Some described him as a militant Nazi who strictly toed the party line; others said Friends of New Germany leaders considered Gyssling insufficiently militant and too soft on Jews; others still suspected the diplomat was running an espionage network along the Pacific Coast. What the vice consul really believed and what his actual duties were remained shrouded in mystery.

Born on June 16, 1893, Gyssling was raised in the village of Walce, Opolskie, Poland, then part of Germany. Passionate about archaeology and ancient languages, he attended a special high school (*Gymnasium*) in Davos, Switzerland, that taught Hebrew, Aramaic, and Sanskrit. Following the outbreak of World War I, he interrupted his legal studies to enlist in the German army. Like Leon Lewis, Gyssling experienced the devastation of war firsthand, fighting in the trenches as a frontline soldier (*Frontkämpfer*) and low-ranking officer (*Unteroffizier*) until wounded and discharged from active service in December 1916. After returning to civilian life, Gyssling earned a doctorate of law, joined the Foreign Service in December 1919, and underwent training in Poznań, the Hague, Kraków, and Amsterdam. Entering the diplomatic corps before Hitler's rise to power, the bright young lawyer so impressed his superiors that they assigned him to the German consulate in New York.[1]

On August 5, 1927, the thirty-four-year-old diplomat arrived in New York City accompanied by his twenty-six-year-old wife, Ingrid, their brain-damaged infant son, Georg, and their twenty-one-year-old maid, Margarete Rihn. Settling his family in suburban Hackensack, New Jersey, just across the Hudson River from Manhattan, the vice consul performed a number of ceremonial duties: speaking at the funeral of an Iron Cross veteran, welcoming a German zeppelin crew, and appearing as the friendly face of the German government at local German celebrations. In March 1928 the Gysslings welcomed the arrival of their American-born daughter, Angelica.

Much to his government's delight, the handsome six-foot-three consul with a thinning hairline, dark mustache, and winning smile proved a remarkable athlete. After a series of bone-crushing accidents sent members of Germany's Olympic bobsled team to the hospital, authorities in Berlin ordered the agile diplomat to Lake Placid, New York, in February 1932 to compete in the Winter Olympics. Although he had never set foot in a bobsled, Gyssling served as a brakeman on Germany's four-man bobsled B-team. His team finished seventh— and last—in the event. Still, it was quite an achievement for an amateur to participate in a sport he knew little about and to do it in the Olympics.[2]

Gyssling may have walked away disappointed that he did not earn a medal, but his status as an Olympian gave him an air of glamour among fellow diplomats. In April 1933, Hans Luther, ambassador to the United States and former chancellor of Germany, assigned the rising star to Los Angeles, then considered the second most important consular post in the United States. Far from being demoted, Gyssling, who had joined the Nazi Party in 1931, now served as Hitler's official representative to the Jewish-dominated motion picture industry. The no-nonsense ambassador knew that Gyssling was a tough negotiator who could handle the equally tough moguls. He charged the consul with taking quick action in overseeing "film business-matters" in Hollywood.[3]

Gyssling's entry into Los Angeles's elite circles was eased by the popularity of his predecessor, Gustav Struve. Sent to Los Angeles in 1931 to promote the 1936 Berlin Olympics, the city's elites warmly embraced Struve, viewing him as a socially graceful diplomat who did not appear to be a rabid Nazi. Far from it, he befriended Albert Einstein and his wife on their three visits to Los Angeles in 1932 and 1933, meeting them upon arrival and seeing them off when they departed for Europe. When Struve was ordered to Washington, D.C., in March 1933 to work for the German ambassador, gossip columnists noted how his friends engaged in "fits of weeping over Gustav's departure" and added, "It was probably better luck than we deserved having him here this long."[4]

Arriving in Los Angeles in the spring of 1933, Georg Gyssling settled into Struve's spacious office in the Garland Building on 901 South Main Street, the city's official Nazi headquarters. A huge photo of Hitler greeted those entering the German consulate's reception room; inside Gyssling's private office was an even bigger painting of the führer. The new vice consul began his tenure by denying that German authorities were mistreating Jews. "Tales of persecution of Jews in Germany are absolutely false," he told reporters. The "few Jews who have met with violence have not been singled out because of their race, but because they were Communist leaders and agitators." The consul assured the press that "Einstein would be perfectly welcome in Germany. My chief mission here will be to correct misinterpretations."[5]

Gyssling also rebuffed claims that Nazi groups were being formed in Los Angeles or that National Socialism was being spread in America by propaganda sent from Germany. "National Socialism is purely German

German Consul Georg Gyssling
Courtesy Angelica Gyssling McNally

and no article of export," he explained in a letter to the *Los Angeles Record*. He had been sent to Los Angeles to combat "the many slanderous attacks directed against the Hitler regime by world Jewry."[6]

Gyssling proved far less strident when it came to conducting the ceremonial duties that were part of a consul's responsibilities. Local newspapers featured pictures of the smiling consul greeting German war ace Major Ernst Udet, who had come to participate in the National Air Races held in Los Angeles that June. Gyssling's other duties included driving to the docks to greet incoming German vessels, hosting lavish receptions to honor visiting German dignitaries, giving speeches at local German celebrations, and going on the radio to reassure the public of Hitler's peaceful aims.

Gyssling succeeded in charming the city's press with his "jovial" demeanor and willingness to answer their questions in a gracious and articulate manner.[7]

THE CONSUL AND THE SOCIAL SET

The tall, chubby-faced vice consul with the proverbial million-dollar smile was the perfect choice to represent the German regime in a city whose most famous industry was dominated by Jews. Always immaculately dressed and exuding a cultured European sophistication, the charming multilingual consul embraced his social duties with skill and enthusiasm. Yet Gyssling understood that his social activities were deeply entwined with his political mission. By establishing himself as the amiable face of the new Germany, he could more easily sway public opinion and sell Hitler and his policies to the city's power elite.

Within months of his arrival, Dr. Gyssling, as he was usually referred to, won over the city's two social leaders: Jo Alderman, the widely recognized head of the city's elite social circles, and Alma Whitaker, the leading society gossip columnist. Whitaker's columns gushed about Gyssling's social skills. She marveled at the lavish receptions held at his stately home, admired his grace at diplomatic gatherings, noted his keen abilities as a gardener, and heralded him as one of the "four most ardent bridge players in town."[8]

The consul's wife, Ingrid, was equally welcomed into Los Angeles society. Attending an April 1934 party at their "gorgeous hilltop castle, regal with German flags flying" in honor of the Nazi vessel *Karlsruhe* and its crew, Whitaker told her readers how Mrs. Gyssling "won all hearts . . . She is patrician, charming, gentle." Hitler's persecution of Jews did not prevent "200 socially prominent Angelenos" from attending Gyssling's receptions. "Everyone seemed to be there," Whitaker observed. "Bankers, university professors, doctors, judges, civic nabobs galore, together with their ladies, decided the fatherland had sent an excellent contingent of handsome and well-bred ambassadors—most of them speaking delightful English." Gyssling and his wife, the sympathetic columnist noted, were "doing their best for troubled Germany."[9]

Yet all was not well within the Gyssling household. While Angelenos welcomed the couple to Los Angeles, Ingrid never felt comfortable either in her new city or the United States. Moving to Los Angeles with her children six months after her husband's posting, she rented a second home for herself three hours from the city center. When a *Los Angeles Times* reporter arrived at her distant abode to interview her, she was told that "Mrs. Gyssling was indisposed" and could not get out of bed. Initially annoyed, the reporter changed her tune when a contrite Ingrid showed up at the *Times*'s offices to apologize. "My dear," she told the reporter, "it is quite simple. I am simply a German housewife. You see, I'm a mother." The "poor little girl," as the reporter described Ingrid, managed to charm the press. She could swim, ride, and "knows a thing or two about music and literature."[10]

But Ingrid was no hausfrau. According to the *Los Angeles Times*, she was an orthopedist with a medical degree from Heidelberg University— an orthopedist who could not practice her calling. Unhappy with her life in the United States, Ingrid frequently traveled back to Germany, sometimes with her children, more often by herself. In September 1935 she took her final trip home, never to return to the United States. Upon her arrival, she entered a sanatorium in Holstein, where she spent the next six months being treated for a "neurasthenic-depressive disorder." One year later the German courts granted Georg's request for a divorce and custody of his children.[11]

The Gysslings' estrangement and subsequent divorce may have proven difficult for their children, but it opened the doors for society women to vie for his attention. It was not much of a battle, for social leader Jo Alderman soon assumed the position of his regular hostess, helping his housekeeper, Christine Boone. Known for running the city's preeminent salon, Alderman regularly entertained diplomats from Russia, Britain, France, Brazil, and Germany at her home. "Jo's a lovely

Georg Gyssling Attending Jo Alderman's Salon (back row, right side)
Courtesy Angelica Gyssling McNally

girl," one reporter noted, "enveloped in an aura of tact!" The thirty women attending her Tuesday-afternoon salons, which included the likes of screenwriter Anita Loos, were widely considered to be the "best-informed group in town on international affairs."[12]

Over the next several years Alderman, girlfriend of Gyssling's close friend Hans Wolfram, helped steer salon conversations "on current events and politics along lines most favorable to Germany." She also helped the consul mount some of the most sought-after parties in Los Angeles. After Ingrid Gyssling left the city, Alderman began holding salons at Georg Gyssling's spacious home on North Curson Avenue.[13]

Gyssling also succeeded in charming a number of Los Angeles Jews. Publicly, the skilled diplomat parroted the official party line coming out of Berlin. Yet privately, not all Jews were convinced he was an anti-Semite or a dedicated Nazi. "One of the finest Jews in the West told me on Monday of this week," *B'nai B'rith Messenger* columnist Nayer Tomid (a pen name that, translated from Hebrew, means "candle of truth") wrote in October 1933, "Dr. Gyssling is outraged by the Jewish excesses in Germany. He is too fine a gentleman to subscribe to the anti-Semitic program of the Hitler government." Angered by what he regarded as sheer stupidity, the columnist warned, "Let none of us be fooled. The Gysslings are no better than the Hitlers or the Spanknoebels . . . They subscribe to the whole Nazi program, the main plank of which entrails the declassing of the Jews. It makes me laugh, then, when I hear or read in the newspapers that one of our rich Jewish fools gave a party for Dr. Georg Gyssling." Those who thought Gyssling was "any better than the rest of the 'friends of New Germany,'" Tomid warned his readers, were "merely deluding themselves."[14]

When it came to the Jews who ran the city's movie studios, there was no division of opinion about Georg Gyssling. He was universally hated and considered far more dangerous to their business fortunes than the Nazis belonging to the Friends of New Germany or their Silver Shirt allies. For the Jewish moguls, Gyssling was the most dangerous Nazi in Los Angeles.

THE CONSUL AND THE MOGULS

Adolf Hitler understood that military action was not the only way to influence a population. The führer begrudgingly admired the ways the American and British governments used film as vehicles of propaganda during World War I. He saw how movies such as *The Beast of Berlin* (1918) and *To Hell with the Kaiser!* (1918) generated profound hatred of the German enemy. "The present government of Germany," observed United Press Paris correspondent Ralph Heinzen, "holds that the Reich would have been the victor of the [first] world war had it not been for the United States, and that our entry into the war would have been prevented if the Imperial German government would have conducted a stronger propaganda campaign in this country."[15]

Soon after taking office in January 1933, the führer created the Reich Ministry of Public Enlightenment and Propaganda and appointed his friend Joseph Goebbels as its head, a position that gave him oversight of all media: press, radio, art, music, publishing, and motion pictures. "For the first time in the history of political administration," Heinzen noted, "there is a Ministry of Propaganda that serves as a fundamental organ of government, enjoying not merely the same rank as a War Department or State Department, but often, indeed, dominating them both in authority and policy."[16]

Like Hitler, Goebbels, a failed novelist and playwright who received a PhD in literature from Heidelberg University, enjoyed watching movies and socializing with filmmakers. While Hitler believed movies should offer straightforward propaganda, Goebbels believed films were far more effective if they presented propaganda in an entertaining manner. "Even entertainment can be politically of special value," he explained, "because the moment a person is conscious of propaganda, propaganda becomes ineffective." Only when propaganda "remains in the background" does it become "effective in every respect."[17]

Hitler and Goebbels believed they could use film to sway world opinion in favor of Germany. "We are convinced that the film is one of the most modern and far-reaching means for influencing the masses," the propaganda minister wrote in March 1933. "A government can therefore not possibly leave the film to the world itself." For Goebbels, that meant exerting strict control over the ways in which Hollywood productions dealt with the Hitler regime. If studios vilified the Hitler regime as effectively as they vilified the Kaiser during World War I, it would mean trouble for the führer's world ambitions. Although World War I brought devastation to millions, it proved a boon to American filmmakers. With European filmmaking shut down by war, American studios moved west to sunny Los Angeles and cranked out movies over 300 days a year. By end of war, American films accounted for 90 percent of world's market, and Hollywood provided 80 percent of all productions.[18]

Determined to make sure that Jewish producers did not turn their powerful propaganda machine against Germany during his rule, Goebbels pursued a two-pronged cinematic strategy. With 350,000 German nationals living in the United States, as well as 23 million Americans of German ancestry, he wanted to use film first to "win our country fellowmen in the United States to the ideology of the Nazis," and secondly, to "create understanding and recognition for the Third Reich" among Americans. Goebbels's third but unstated goal was to use German film and newsreels to pave the way for a potential Nazi fifth column in the United States.[19] To do all that required exporting Nazi-made movies to America and sending a tough-minded representative who could pressure Hollywood studios to remain neutral when dealing with German themes.

Goebbels began his campaign against Jewish control of motion pictures in March 1933 by ordering Universum Film AG (UFA), the leading German production company, to fire all its Jewish employees; a month later, he ordered American film companies operating in Germany to expel their Jewish employees. On June 30 Goebbels announced a new law that excluded Jews from taking part in the making of German films. The law also applied to American companies producing films in Germany and included a provision forbidding the importation of any film that featured Jewish characters or cheerful aspects of Jewish life. With the exception of Warner Brothers, the moguls complied and transferred their Jewish employees to other European cities. Unwilling to abide by the new edicts, the Warners closed their offices in Berlin.[20]

With Jews purged from the Reich's film industry, Goebbels set out to impose his will on Hollywood and on American movie screens. Acting in concert with Ambassador Luther and the Foreign Office, Goebbels had sent Georg Gyssling to Los Angeles in the spring of 1933 to monitor the American film industry. His charge: stop the production of any film that defamed Germany or its Nazi leaders or that featured Jewish actors or characters. His weapon: the possibility of invoking the German film quota law passed in the summer of 1932. Intended to rebuild the German film industry, the law limited the importation of American films and contained a clause, Article 15, that denied import permits for any studio "which, in spite of warnings issued by competent German authorities, continue to distribute on the world market films, the tendency or effect of which is detrimental to German prestige."[21]

Although he succeeded in charming Los Angeles society, when it came to carrying out his official duties regarding Hollywood, Georg Gyssling proved the toughest foe the moguls had ever encountered. Invited to give his opinion on an American film for the first time in June 1933, the vice consul immediately filed a protest against Warner Brothers' *Captured*. After screening the film, which was set in a World War I German prisoner-of-war camp and starred Leslie Howard and Douglas Fairbanks Jr., Gyssling objected to its portrayal of the brutal treatment of American prisoners by German officers. He demanded massive cuts and threatened to invoke Article 15 if they were not made. When Warners released the film in August, it contained none of the demanded changes. Showing they meant business, Goebbels's propaganda ministry sent letters to German embassies and consulates throughout the world, announcing that they had banned *Captured*.[22]

Columbia studio heads proved far more compliant when Gyssling asked for cuts in *Below the Sea* (1933). Featuring Ralph Bellamy as the captain of a World War I German U-boat who kills an insubordinate sailor, Gyssling condemned the film as "highly detrimental to German prestige" because it portrayed the German submarine captain "in a most hideous way."[23] Columbia caved in to Gyssling's "requests" and revised the film accordingly.

Gyssling's initial success provoked an immediate response from Hollywood's most openly anti-Nazi studio. Angry at the consul's costly interference in their business, Warner Brothers' executives sought help from Frederick Herron, the foreign manager of the Motion Picture Producers and Distributors Association (MPPDA). Founded in 1922 to forestall growing calls for federal censorship, the MPPDA—popularly known as the Hays Office—served as the industry's self-censorship body. Headed by former postmaster general Will Hays, it served as Hollywood's political buffer against any outside interference in industry matters. Herron despised Gyssling. "You probably have gathered that this Consul out there is looking for trouble," he complained to the MPPDA's director of studio relations. "He is narrow minded and you will always find in any dealings you have with him that there will be trouble."[24]

Seeking to overturn the ban on Warners' films, Herron arranged for *Captured* to be seen by Gustav Müller, the far more accommodating German consul in New York. Following a screening on January 12, 1934, all parties agreed to a compromise: Warners would adhere to several but not all of the cuts demanded by Gyssling. In return, the German government agreed to lift its ban on *Captured* and all other Warner Brothers films. "This is just an example," a pleased Herron observed, "of what can be done if you deal with intelligent people, rather than obstructionists of the type of Dr. Gyssling."[25]

This was the last time Herron trumped Gyssling. Over the next several years, the "obstructionist" consul cost the moguls money by halting productions or forcing cuts in the films portraying aspects of German life. In addition to the specter of invoking Article 15, Gyssling's tools of persuasion included threats to seize any property in Germany owned by foreign-born moguls. He also sent letters on official government stationery to Hollywood's considerable number of German screenwriters and actors, warning them of potential reprisals against anyone participating in pictures that defamed the German government or people. Those reprisals included punishing family members still living in the Reich.[26]

Why would the moguls listen to a foreign government that told them what they could or could not make? Money! Studios were first and foremost in the moneymaking business, not the consciousness-raising business. The Great Depression had exacted a harsh toll on the movie industry and made its leaders far more compliant than they might otherwise have been. With domestic attendance declining from 90 million in 1930 to 60 million in 1933, only two of eight major studios—MGM and Columbia—turned a profit every year during the 1930s. However much they may have hated the German consul and the Hitler regime, the moguls had to cooperate with both if they wished to remain in the German market, where studios had more theaters than anywhere on the continent. After complying with Gyssling, Hollywood studios sold sixty-five films to Germany in 1933, as compared to fifty-four in 1932.[27]

Gyssling found his ability to censor American films aided by two additional developments: internal divisions among Jews, and the creation of the Production Code Administration by the Hays Office. As businessmen, the moguls appeased Hitler as much as possible; as Jews, they remained uncertain what to do. Many of the foreign-born studio heads feared that openly denouncing Hitler would increase anti-Semitism in Germany and at home. Consequently, they decided to keep overtly Jewish themes and critiques of Germany out of their films.

In July 1933, upon hearing that RKO intended to make *The Mad Dog of Europe*, screenwriter Herman Mankiewicz's proposed film about Hitler's persecution of Jews, Will Hays's public relations troubleshooter Joseph Breen asked Leon Lewis to head a new Anti-Defamation League advisory committee that would work with the MPPDA to monitor anti-Semitic images and pressure studios to abide by their decisions. Lewis agreed. Although he had been monitoring films on behalf of the ADL since before World War I, working with the new advisory committee gave him a closer look at Gyssling.[28]

The German vice consul had already approached the Hays Office, demanding that the project be scrapped. Taking Gyssling's side, Breen warned Lewis that *The Mad Dog of Europe* could spark an anti-Semitic backlash throughout the United States. ADL head Richard Gutstadt concurred. "This is an anti-Hitler film," he wrote Lewis, "but as we are given to understand, so fanatical in its treatment of the subject, that it is believed there may be a very unhappy kick-back from it."[29]

Working behind the scenes, Lewis convinced the studio to drop the project. When RKO abandoned it, independent producer Al Rosen secured the rights and asked Louis B. Mayer for help. Hollywood's most powerful mogul proved a most unpredictable figure. He hated the Nazis and hated their interference with his business. And yet, while privately leading the drive to finance Lewis's undercover operation, he neverthe-less placed the studio's interests ahead of his personal concerns as a Jew. He turned down Rosen's plea for help, explaining he would not make the anti-Hitler film "because we have interests in Germany; I represent the picture industry here in Hollywood; we have exchanges there; we have terrific income in Germany and, as far as I am concerned, this picture will never be made."[30] Not to be dissuaded, Rosen released the film a year later as an independent docudrama with a mix of newsreel footage and staged footage.

Concerns over potential anti-Semitic backlash in the United States led Lewis to side with Gyssling's attempts to halt the 1934 production of Twentieth Century Pictures' *The House of Rothschild*. Lewis thought the decision to make a film about the internationally famous Jewish banking family was a mistake. Although it vividly depicted anti-Semitism in Europe, Lewis argued that the film portrayed the Roths-childs in stereotypical ways that were potentially harmful to Jews. Its first reel depicted old man Rothschild as a rasping and devious ghetto moneylender. Pleading with Fox head Joseph Schenck to halt the produc-tion, Lewis explained that the "implications of international manipu-lations of finance and international politics by a family of Jewish international bankers may make this film one of the most dangerous presentations which could be released at this particular time." Lewis drew Schenck's attention to "the wave of organized anti-Semitic propa-ganda now sweeping through the country" that was "based very largely on the fiction of the 'international Jewish banker.'" From "this angle," Lewis concluded, "the film, no matter how fairly the subject matter is treated, may create a strong undercurrent of resentment among the Jewish public as well."[31] Unable to persuade the producers to drop the film, Lewis succeeded in watering down what he considered its offensive scenes.

Lewis and his ADL allies were not kowtowing to Gyssling, as one scholar has insisted. They wanted to avoid giving powerful anti-Semites such as Pennsylvania representative Louis McFadden more fuel for his diatribes against Jews. Lewis worried that the film "substantiates the fiction of the international Jew controlling governments and being able to make and stop wars," which was precisely what the Republican congressman had charged. In multiple speeches made on the floor of Congress, he insisted that the "money Jews of Wall Street and foreign parts" secretly controlled Roosevelt's financial policies. He also claimed that everything written in the anti-Semitic *Protocols of the Elders of Zion* was true, especially the perfidious role of Jewish moneylenders. Not wishing to give men such as McFadden any cause for celebration, *House of Rothschild* star Boris Karloff refused to read the line "I hate the Jews and all they stand for." The line was deleted from the film.[32]

The MPPDA's creation of the Production Code Administration in July 1934 made it far easier for Gyssling to halt or censor the production of any potentially anti-Nazi film. The Code, as it was known in Hollywood, was created to combat attacks on what conservative critics condemned as a licentious and uncontrolled industry. Promising to clean up American films, Hays appointed his assistant Joe Breen to head the self-censoring body. Gyssling could not have been more pleased either by the Code or the man chosen to enforce it. Breen, a former journalist and highly influential figure in the Roman Catholic community, held the moguls in low regard. In his private correspondence, Breen did little to hide his antipathy for the Jewish studio heads, whom he characterized as a "rotten bunch of vile people with no respect for anything beyond the making of money . . . Ninety-five percent of these folks are Jews of an Eastern European lineage. They are, probably, the scum of the earth."[33]

Gyssling's ability to limit the damage Hollywood could cause the Nazi regime was strengthened by Section 10 of the Code, which governed "National Feelings" and stipulated, "The history, institutions, prominent people and citizenry of all nations shall be represented fairly." Studios were now prohibited from making any films depicting "in an unfavorable light" another country or its people.[34] Gyssling was delighted, for the new Code meant there could be no explicit cinematic attacks on Hitler or Nazi Germany. The Hays Office made his ability to impose the will of the Nazi government on the moguls a great deal easier.

THE CONSUL AND THE GERMANS

As the official representative of Hitler's government, Gyssling presented a positive image of Germany to the American public and to the German community. Ironically, the latter proved more difficult to deal with than the Jewish moguls. Gyssling found the city's German population easy to please. All he had to do was conduct the usual ceremonial duties: appear at German American celebrations, give speeches that proclaimed the glory of the fatherland, shake hands and converse in German with gathered crowds, and defend the regime against all critics.

Gyssling tried to stay out of internal squabbles within the German American community, but that was not always possible. During the course of the German-American Alliance trial in January 1934, he responded to the damning testimony of Lewis's spies by denying that the German regime was spreading Nazi propaganda or encouraging the growth of the Nazi Party in the United States. "I want to state that neither the German government nor the German National Socialistic party has any connections whatsoever, official or unofficial, with said organization [the German-American Alliance] or the Friends of New Germany." Hitler had made it clear that he "not only disapproves of the spreading of any propaganda for National Socialism in foreign countries on the part of German citizens, but that he will immediately have members of the German National Socialistic party excluded from his movement as soon as he hears of them being involved in such activities."[35]

Gyssling lied. He knew Schwinn and Pape regularly drove to the San Pedro docks to receive illegal propaganda and money smuggled in on German vessels, material that was then sold in the Aryan Bookstore. He also received orders from Berlin that all propaganda should be secretly distributed to the FNG through the consulate offices.[36]

The consul was again called upon to defend the German government during the House Un-American Activities Committee's local hearings in August 1934. Refusing to testify on instruction by the German embassy in Washington, D.C., Gyssling denied secretly funding John Riemer's Nazi-run American Labor Party. To gain sympathy among his many Los Angeles friends, he told reporters he had received at least twelve anonymous telephone threats promising to bomb the consular offices and kidnap or kill his family. Once again, he lied. He had made up the bomb and death threats to turn attention away from the hearings. In truth, he received only three anonymous phone calls, none of which he took seriously.[37]

Gyssling's troubles with HUAC were nothing compared to the problems he encountered with Friends of New Germany leaders. The German consul discovered that American Nazis were just as deeply divided in their strategy for winning over Americans as Jews were in deciding the best path for opposing Hitler. Some FNG members believed the most effective way to bring National Socialism to America was by appealing to German immigrants, while others stressed the need to adapt Nazism to the American situation by recruiting more native-born followers. Militant FNG leaders such as Dr. Konrad Burchardi and his cohort welcomed open attacks on the Jews, whom they blamed for communism and the world's economic problems. Hermann Schwinn and his followers favored a more moderate approach that emphasized anticommunism and a less aggressive anti-Semitism. Schwinn argued that Germans living in America might respond to Burchardi's style of Nazism, but Americans would not. While many disliked Jews, they did not want a foreign government openly attacking any group of American citizens.

Los Angeles Nazis were divided in their approach to building a Nazi stronghold in America, but united in their contempt for the German consul. They believed they had a better sense of American public opinion than bureaucrats in Germany or Gyssling, who seemingly preferred hobnobbing with the city's elites to serving the needs of his countrymen. Whatever their internal disagreements, they wanted the FNG, and not some ineffective diplomat, to serve as Hitler's vanguard in America. They were furious at Gyssling's refusal to provide enough money to fund their effort to displace the despised "Jew-president" Franklin D. Roosevelt. Nor did they find him militant enough in attacking the Jews. "The Hitlerites do not think he is sufficiently sold on their program," John Schmidt wrote Lewis. They found him "too cautious" and predicted "he will shortly be removed and a real Hitlerite put in his place." Gyssling's credibility was further diminished by rumors that one of his grandparents had Jewish blood, which if true would bar him from membership in the Nazi Party.[38]

Peter Petsch, a strident National Socialist and instructor in UCLA's German department, had no hesitation condemning the German vice consul. He wrote letters to military authorities in Germany calling for the "immediate replacement and removal from office and disciplining of the not sufficiently national-socialistic Consul Dr. Gyssling who has done untold damage to the new Germany through his behavior." Petsch asked Berlin to send "a completely unblemished national-socialistic personality who will join the battle" against the Jews.[39]

Nazi leaders on all sides of the divide wondered about Gyssling's true loyalties. His "fellow Germans" accused him of inactivity at best, and traitorous actions at worst. Count Ernst Ulrich von Bülow, the secret Nazi operative who maintained a home near the San Diego naval base, thought there was something suspicious about the new vice consul. He accused Gyssling of being "a communist agent" who reported to Soviet dictator Joseph Stalin.[40]

Leon Lewis knew Gyssling was no Russian agent, but he did wonder whether he was setting up an espionage ring along the West Coast. Police captain William "Red" Hynes certainly thought so. When Lewis's agent William Conley visited him in September 1933, Hynes confessed that his men had discovered that the German vice consul was running "an espionage service between this country and Germany."[41]

Lewis never fully believed anything Hynes said, and he knew that military vessels docking in Los Angeles and ships belonging to the German-owned Hamburg-American Line all had Gestapo agents aboard, a fact uncovered by HUAC investigators. Gestapo agents passed on orders and information to Schwinn and Gyssling. After the war, Ernst Wilhelm Bohle, who headed the Auslands Office, the foreign branch of the Nazi Party in charge of overseeing the activities of Germans abroad, confessed to running "active agents" in the United States. Even if Gyssling was not a spy, he may well have been sending the "active agents" reports back to Germany via the diplomatic pouch.[42]

Who *was* Georg Gyssling? This was a question that puzzled Lewis and local Nazis alike. No one was completely correct in assessing his true character, for the consul was a man with secrets—a man who led two lives.

THE SECRET LIFE OF GEORG GYSSLING

Georg Gyssling lived a life of deception. The man so hated by local Nazis and moguls—and the archvillain of decades of subsequent histories of Nazi involvement with Hollywood—was not who he appeared to be. As his daughter Angelica explained, he was a man who "lived a two-sided life." Only three people knew the real Georg Gyssling: Angelica, his "housekeeper," Christina Boone, and, most surprising of all, his trusted Jewish confidant Julius Klein.[43]

When Ingrid Gyssling told the *Los Angeles Times* she was an orthopedist with a medical degree from Heidelberg University, she lied. She and her husband continually fed the press a series of lies, which reporters accepted at face value. Ever the skilled diplomat, Georg Gyssling hid his true domestic situation from almost everyone except his daughter. "My mother was a party girl," remarked Angelica. Ingrid was the spoiled, fun-loving daughter of Henry Horn, a wealthy shipping magnate whose Horn Line freighters ran from Hamburg to the Caribbean. The couple apparently met at a coming-out ball in Vienna or Berlin and married in May 1925. The marriage proved troubled from the start. Ingrid had neither the interest nor the talent to be the wife of a Foreign Service officer. Nor was she interested in being the mother of a brain-damaged son and difficult daughter. "She was a stranger to me, a total stranger," her daughter recounted. Instead of hosting diplomatic events, Ingrid fled Los Angeles and took her father's freighters to the Caribbean, where she could party to her heart's content.[44]

With Ingrid gone for months at a time, Georg entrusted care of his son to his wife's parents in Hamburg. Angelica, a self-confessed "terrible brat, a terror, terror, terror," was looked after by Christine Boone, an Austrian divorcée listed in German records as a housekeeper and nanny. She was in fact Gyssling's mistress, a secret he and Angelica kept from polite society. "I considered Tissy," as the young girl called her, "my mother. She was living with us in Los Angeles and acted as a hostess, but my father never married her. He was not a conventional man. Diplomats didn't usually do that kind of thing." Their affair was looked down upon by "members of the staff who disapproved of my father's lifestyle and her."[45] But they all kept their mouths shut and said nothing to the press.

Georg Gyssling was no ordinary diplomat, nor did he have much in common with American Nazi leaders. "My father was very quixotic, eccentric, unconventional in every way," Angelica explained. "He could put on a top hat and do the conventional, but he wasn't that way. He spent time attending séances and seeing Aimee Semple McPherson at the Foursquare Church." When his socially conscious mother Johanna came to visit from Germany, her son would let his beard grow and look "like a hippy just to annoy her." Gossip columnists shared Angelica's appreciation for her father's eccentricities. "He loves to wear a big sombrero, blue jeans and high-heeled boots . . . yippee!"[46]

Georg Gyssling joined the Nazi Party in 1931, two years before Hitler became Reich chancellor. But he was not a hard-core National Socialist. In Gyssling's mind, he was first and foremost a German nationalist whose main loyalty was to his nation and its peoples. To the extent he could, he placed the interests of his homeland ahead of the interests of the Nazi Party.

When it came to following government orders to stop Hollywood studios from making anti-Nazi films, Gyssling excelled at his job. Yet, like many colleagues in the Foreign Office, he felt trapped by a set of leaders he loathed. "He thought Hitler was a disaster," his daughter recalled. When the precocious preteen asked him, "How could so many intelligent people like you and other people, perfectly educated to the hilt, let somebody like that run your country?" Gyssling had no answer other than to suggest, "The Germans were the kind of people who did what they were told." When the young schoolgirl wanted to know whether she, as the daughter of the German consul, should pledge allegiance to the American flag, he replied, "You do as you like. You should choose."[47]

As a devout German nationalist, Gyssling often wondered when to support Hitler and when to support the fatherland, even if that meant going against the führer and the Nazi cause. FNG leaders were correct when they accused Gyssling of being far too passive in promoting the Reich and attacking Jews. Gyssling, in turn, had nothing but contempt for the Nazi diehards in the Friends of New Germany. He found their uniforms, parades, and anti-Semitic ravings likely to antagonize Americans and turn public opinion against the Nazi regime. FNG leaders, he wrote his San Francisco counterpart in December 1934, were all "unemployed" and used their "propaganda activity, supposed to be in German interest," as a way to justify not finding regular work. "Instead they are expecting the other working or wealthy pro-German persons to finance them."[48]

Gyssling carried his life of deception into his dealing with the city's Jewish community. His critics, most notably *B'nai B'rith Messenger* columnist Nayer Tomid, denounced him as an anti-Semite and were dumbstruck by the sheer stupidity of Jews who thought otherwise. "Gyssling is a Nazi," Tomid warned his readers, "which means that he is a Hun, the same as the rest of them."[49]

Gyssling was a Nazi, but not an anti-Semite. He made statements in the press about the fine treatment of Jews in Germany that he knew were false. Yet during his eight-year tenure in Los Angeles, he never uttered an anti-Semitic statement to reporters; nor did Leon Lewis's operatives ever suggest that the consul was an anti-Semite. Tomid got it right when he said, "If you want a Nazi speaker . . . it seems that Vice-Consul Gyssling is the man to whom you must apply."[50] But the German diplomat was not the same kind of militant Nazi as Hermann Schwinn.

The German Jewish émigrés who invited Gyssling into their home were not delusional. Gyssling cared little about religion or religious loyalties and never took his daughter to church. When she asked him one day, "Do we have a religion?" Gyssling replied, "When you grow up and learn something, you can choose your own religion." She remembered him adding, "'You might marry an Arab and then you might become a Muslim. It's your business.' It was always 'choose yourself.'" Rumors of Jews in Gyssling's background were true. "One of our relatives, Aunt Eda Mayer, married a Jewish man," Angelica noted, although the family kept that secret.[51]

As a dedicated nationalist, Gyssling felt it his obligation to represent *all* Germans in Los Angeles, regardless of their religion. He knew the "Jewish émigrés were in a hot spot," his daughter recounted. "They were not American citizens; they certainly didn't want to have anything to do with a Nazi official." They may not have trusted him, but Gyssling considered German Jewish immigrants as Germans, and as such, "he would do what he could for them." The savvy diplomat understood he could not be overtly friendly to Jewish émigrés if he wished to keep his position. "We had to be careful about who could come to the house," Angelica recalled. So Gyssling devised an elaborate code by which Jews could reach him by telephone. "He used the name 'Ginsberg' as a cover name for his German Jewish émigrés. If somebody got on the phone and asked for 'Dr. Ginsberg,' we knew it was from Jewish émigrés."[52]

Leon Lewis discovered that what Gyssling said in public and what he believed in private was often quite different. In December 1933 the Jewish attorney learned the consul had initiated secret "informal discussions through an intermediary, a certain German Baron [von Reichenberg] who lives in Los Angeles, with a friend of mine who is keeping in constant contact with me." The friend was apparently Jacob Marcus, an American-born rabbi who had studied in Berlin and taught at Hebrew Union College in Cincinnati. Marcus, von Reichenberg, and Gyssling were discussing the parameters of an agreement that might lead to "peace between Hitler and the much hated Jews" through "a gradual liberalization of the legal enactments effecting the status of Jews in Germany." If successful, Gyssling promised to take the proposal to German ambassador Hans Luther, who would then forward it to the Foreign Office in Berlin. Like many in the Foreign Office, Luther and Gyssling had "been in constant disagreement with Hitler and his internal policy against the Jews."[53]

Gyssling wanted his government to tone down its persecution of Jews for two reasons, both of which centered on practical considerations rather than sympathy for Jews. As he wrote von Reichenberg, the "very great danger exists" that Jews might realize they could gain far more support in the United States by critiquing the Hitler regime for its lack of basic democratic rights. Such a shift in strategy, he warned, "would be much more dangerous for us."[54]

Gyssling's quest to ease his government's persecution of Jews was also motivated by economic reasons. In 1933 the German economy was in shambles; nearly 30 percent of the population remained unemployed. Despite official denials, the international boycott of German products initiated by New York attorney Samuel Untermyer that spring had taken a toll on the nation's fragile economy. Easing restrictions and anti-Semitic attacks on Jews would gain sympathy for the regime among Americans and provide a shot in the arm for the German economy once the boycott was lifted. Gyssling ended his letter to the baron with a caution: "The entire matter has to be treated with the greatest discretion as even the slightest publicity would eliminate all chance of success."[55]

Despite Gyssling's tough stance with the moguls, he worried about the economic hardships that would occur if Hollywood studios ceased doing business with Germany. When Goebbels's Ministry of Propaganda threatened to ban MGM's 1933 film *The Prize Fighter and the Lady* because its Jewish star, former heavyweight champion Max Baer, was a "non-Aryan," the Foreign Office feared that the studio might pull out of Germany, which would mean the loss of needed jobs. Worse yet, a continued government ban on films with Jewish actors might lead all Hollywood studios to close their offices in Berlin; if they did, "5000 local Germans could lose their jobs."[56]

The hoped-for agreement never materialized. Gyssling and Luther discussed the matter by phone, but decided not to send any recommendations to Germany.[57]

Gyssling had one last secret that he did not share with anyone. The consul hated the FNG so much that he was secretly passing "valuable information . . . against the members of the Bund" to National Guard officer Julius Klein, a Jew, and continued to do so throughout his time in Los Angeles. As a dedicated nationalist, he also shared any information he could that would hasten the demise of the Hitler regime. Klein forwarded what he learned to General George C. Marshall at the War Department. While stationed in Chicago in 1933, Marshall had authorized Klein, then a lieutenant in the Illinois National Guard, to conduct the first officially sanctioned army investigation of subversion in America.[58]

Born in Chicago in 1901, Julius Klein was the son of Austrian parents who moved to Berlin while he was still a child. Interned in Germany with his family during World War I, Julius escaped to France, where he joined the U.S. Army and returned to Berlin in 1918 to spy for the American forces. After spending time as a reporter in Berlin between 1922 and 1923, he traveled back to the United States and settled in Chicago. Whether Klein met Gyssling while living in Berlin or when he moved to Los Angeles in 1934 is unclear. But by the end of 1934 the two men had become friends, joined together by a love of German culture, contempt for the FNG, and a mutual loathing of the Hitler regime. Gyssling, Klein would later write, was the only German official he met "who was willing, at all times, to cooperate for the rebirth of a German Democracy."[59]

Klein was a frequent guest at the Gyssling home. "They were an odd couple to look at," Angelica recalled. "My father was very tall, 6'4". Julius Klein was about 5'6" 5'7". We always called him the 'Little General.' It was well meant. They were evidently very close. My father didn't put up with idiots."[60]

Both men were careful to keep the true nature of their relationship a closely guarded secret, even from Gyssling's daughter. Klein was never invited to any of the dinners or cocktail parties the consul hosted at his home. Instead, "Mr. Klein arrived on foot and my father conducted him into the study and closed the sliding door between the room and the entry hall. This was quite unusual; the door was always open otherwise." The two men spent hours locked away in private conversation and had dinner served to them in the study. Angelica "never looked at Mr. Klein as though he was Jewish." He was simply another one of her father's odd friends.[61]

When Klein moved to Los Angeles in the spring of 1934 to begin a hoped-for career in the movie business, he met with Leon Lewis. The two spymasters shared information about Nazi activities in Chicago and Los Angeles, but it is unclear whether Klein ever told Lewis, whom he hired as his attorney, about his relationship with Gyssling. But he did the Los Angeles spymaster an enormous favor: he introduced him to his nephew Joseph Roos, who had assisted him in investigating Chicago Nazis and was willing to assist Lewis on a part-time basis.

The grateful attorney needed all the help he could get, especially after learning that the mutual antipathy between the consul and the FNG had reached a breaking point. Schwinn had written Nazi officials in Berlin, bringing "charges against Dr. Giessling [sic], because the Consul wasn't active enough against the Jews, and that Dr. Giessling was going to be fired." If that happened, Lewis heard rumors that "Mr. Schwinn would be the Consul."[62]

Lewis recognized an opportunity. If he could continue fueling the rivalry between Gyssling and Schwinn, he could weaken, if not destroy, the Nazi movement in Los Angeles. To do that, he needed to recruit new undercover operatives who could penetrate the FNG, gain the confidence of its leaders, and foment further discord between them and the hated consul. Lewis knew he also needed someone better equipped than himself to train the spies. Joseph Roos, Neil Ness, and Charles Slocombe proved the answer to his prayers.

III

NEW THREATS, NEW SPIES, 1935–1939

10.

Spy and Divide

On a cloudy Sunday morning in late September 1935, Leon Lewis and thousands of Angelenos opened their *Los Angeles Times* to discover that an anti-Semitic flyer had been inserted inside their newspapers. The "Proclamation" issued by the American Nationalist Party (ANP) boldly declared that "whenever a People or a Nation discovers existing within its body politic any factors or elements of a nature inimical to its welfare and to its very life, it is a right inherent in such a People or Nation, and indeed a duty if means are available to such an end, to curb and to eliminate all such injurious elements." Jews, "through their closely unified banking interests . . . have constituted themselves a menace to our free institutions, our Christian civilization and our Aryan culture." The bright red and blue ANP flyer called upon citizens "to prepare the way for an ultimate solution of the 'Jewish Problem,' now unattainable through any legislative enactment." The document ended by asking all "Gentile working people" to boycott Jewish merchants and their perfidious movie industry.[1]

The fascist American National Party, with close ties to Nazis and the Ku Klux Klan, had penetrated the city's most prominent newspaper. Lewis feared that the anti-Semitic fervor spreading across Europe was seeping into the fabric of daily life in Los Angeles and along the Pacific Coast, where 40,000 copies of the proclamation had been posted in cities from Pasadena to as far north as Portland. The spymaster knew that the timing of the proclamation was not coincidental. Two weeks earlier the German government had issued the Nuremberg Laws, which made it difficult for Jews to obtain citizenship and prohibited them from marrying or having sexual relations with Germans.[2]

Lewis was equally worried about the rapid revival of the Friends of New Germany and the Silver Shirts. In the months leading up to the House Un-American Activities Committee hearings of August 1934, both groups had reduced their public presence. Yet afterward, with the Red-focused hearings doing little to stem the growth of right-wing activism, Nazis and fascists succeeded in attracting new members to their cause.

Lewis no longer had any agents inside Nazi headquarters. Still, all was not gloomy. Community Committee chairman Mendel Silberberg used his considerable political influence to convince *Los Angeles Times* publisher Norman Chandler to print a formal apology on October 1, 1935. He also persuaded the police to investigate the matter. Within a short time, detectives discovered the man responsible was Ingram Hughes, a failed attorney who worked at the *Los Angeles Times* as a linotype operator from 1930 to 1933 and "had close friends who assisted him in placing the proclamation in the *Times*."[3]

There was even more reason for optimism. By the end of 1935, Lewis succeeded in recruiting an assistant spymaster and two new undercover agents. Their orders: spy upon and divide the Nazi and fascist enemy in Los Angeles.

JOE ROOS, NAZI HUNTER

Born in Vienna on December 10, 1908, Joseph Roos moved to Berlin while still a baby. As they settled into the German capital, Roos's parents joined the Social Democratic Party and continued the left-wing activism begun by his great-grandfather, who fled to the United States with his friend Carl Schurz after the failed German revolutions of 1848. Although Roos came from a long line of distinguished rabbis, dating back to fourteenth-century Padua, he rejected Orthodox traditions, preferring to remain a secular Jew.

In 1927, with Hitler's Brownshirt movement growing, the nineteen-year-old youth left Germany and moved to be near family in Chicago. Roos soon found a job working for the *Illinois Staats-Zeitung*, a German-language newspaper. In August 1929 the newspaper's publisher sent the young reporter to Berlin to cover an international advertising convention for his midwestern chain of German-language periodicals. Arriving in the German capital on the tenth anniversary of the Weimar Constitution, Roos stood on the wide expanse of the tree-lined Unter den

Julius Klein regards cartoon depicting 1929 *Chicagoer Harold* press tour to Berlin (Klein on far left in cartoon, Joe Roos second from left)
Courtesy Leonard Roos

Linden, the city's main boulevard, and watched a "tremendous" parade by the Brownshirts. The fervor of the marchers and onlookers made him realize how powerful National Socialism had grown in the two and a half years since he had left Germany. During his stay in Berlin, Roos met Colonel Frank Knox, publisher of the *Chicago Daily News*, and convinced him that the paper needed a reporter who could cover the concerns of the city's large German American community. Roos returned home with a job working for Knox. He did so well that he moved to the more prominent *Chicago Herald-Examiner*, the Hearst chain's morning newspaper.[4]

Frightened by what he saw in Berlin, Roos began a second career: spying on Nazi groups in Chicago. "I did not know when I arrived in Chicago in January 1927," Roos recounted in his unpublished autobiography, "that three years earlier the first Nazi organization in the United States had been started in Chicago bearing the name Teutonia" and was spreading "Nazi propaganda poison" among the city's German community. Before going to work for the Hearst chain, Roos and his uncle Julius Klein published their own newspaper, the *National Free Press*, a weekly periodical that aimed to "offset the pro-Nazi propaganda reaching German-Americans all over the country." The uncle-and-nephew team also organized the Reichsbanner, an anti-Nazi organization composed of German immigrants and their offspring that monitored the activities of Hitler's American supporters.[5]

Reporting for the *Herald-Examiner* during the day, Roos and Klein spent their nights and weekends keeping close tabs on local Nazis and

Joseph Roos ca. 1931
Courtesy Leonard Roos

gathering information from people coming back from Germany and Czechoslovakia. A sex scandal provided the journalist-spy with his first big break. After a local Nazi learned that his girlfriend had an affair with Hermann Schwinn while he attended FNG meetings in Chicago in 1933, the lovesick German got his revenge by handing Roos a series of documents describing how Hitler had spies and saboteurs trained to attack public utilities throughout United States. "That incident," Roos reflected, "determined the rest of my life."[6]

After reading a memo about his reporter's investigative work, *Chicago Herald-Examiner* publisher Roy D. Keehn, who also served as commanding officer of the Thirty-Third Division of the Illinois National Guard, called Roos into his office. Listening to the nervous, soft-spoken immigrant with a thick accent describe the pro-Nazi sentiments of many local Germans, Keehn ordered his reporter to meet with a U.S. Army colonel temporarily stationed in Chicago. "Do whatever he asks you to do!" Keehn told him. "And that has top priority over any assignment from the City Desk."[7] The colonel was George C. Marshall, future U.S. Army chief of staff, secretary of state, and author of the Marshall Plan, which aimed to rebuild postwar Europe.

Meeting secretly at the Bismarck Hotel in 1933, Marshall explained how he saw the growth of an American-based Nazi movement as a security threat to the United States. The colonel asked Roos and Klein, who was a lieutenant in the National Guard under Keehn, to collect information about the local Nazis for army intelligence (G-2, as it was known). To improve Roos's effectiveness, Marshall ordered his men to train him in espionage and counterespionage techniques. Over the next several weeks, Marshall's army intelligence operatives told their Jewish pupil to "keep your eyes wide open, never get into any arguments with anybody, talk as though you are in agreement with them, don't egg them on in order to have a better story to tell." His instructors also took him out on night maneuvers and taught him how to evade detection.[8]

Although he received his main training with army intelligence, Roos also learned a great deal about spycraft from his uncle Julius Klein. Returning to Chicago after his wartime stint spying for the American forces in Germany, Klein worked as a reporter for the German-language *Staats-Herold* and then the *Chicago Herald-Examiner* while also publishing the *National Free Press*.[9]

After receiving authorization from Henry Horner, Illinois's first Jewish governor, Klein and Roos conducted "the first [officially sanctioned] investigation of the activities of the Nazis and their American soul-brothers." Between 1933 and 1934, the duo, aided by several American and German American operatives assigned to them by Colonel Marshall, provided army intelligence and the War Department with 100 reports detailing Nazi activity in Chicago and across the nation. Unfortunately, not all G-2 officers shared Marshall's enthusiasm for the work being done by the two Chicago Jews. In a memo accompanying several of Klein's reports, Lieutenant Colonel Joseph Hattie urged his superiors

Spy Team of Joe Roos (l) and Julius Klein (r) ca. 1933
Courtesy Leonard Roos

to discount some of the findings because the operative "is strongly anti-Nazi and, therefore, inclined to be prejudiced in any conclusion he may draw."[10]

Klein also sent his reports to the Chicago-based Anti-Defamation League, which forwarded them to Los Angeles, where they were read with great interest by Leon Lewis.[11]

Joe Roos first heard about Lewis in May 1933, when one of his Chicago operatives reported that Hermann Schwinn had given a speech in which he "mentioned that a 'Jew son-of-a-bitch lawyer by the name of Leon Lewis was giving him and his people trouble in Los Angeles.'" Roos contacted Los Angeles rabbi Edgar Magnin to find out more about the attorney; after hearing back, he began corresponding with Lewis and exchanging information. The two men finally met in the spring of 1934, when Roos was sent to Los Angeles by the *Herald-Examiner* to investigate the murder of a German resident. This was his opportunity to talk to Lewis face-to-face. Traveling to the Roosevelt Building by bus, for Roos had never learned to drive, he was struck by the simplicity of Lewis's operation. His fourth-floor office door simply said "Leon L. Lewis, Attorney," and his staff consisted of a single secretary.[12] Roos returned to Chicago determined to relocate to Los Angeles and help Lewis with his undercover operation.

Uncle Julius paved Roos's path to the City of Angels. Klein had moved there in May 1934 to work as a special assistant to Universal Studio head Carl Laemmle. After signing a two-book deal with Haskell-Travers Publishers, Klein hired Roos as his research assistant and Lewis as his attorney to handle his business affairs. Roos quit his newspaper job and moved to Los Angeles sometime in the late fall of 1934 and, after a short stint in his uncle's employ, proceeded to work as a story editor, first for Carl Laemmle and then for Jesse Lasky and Mary Pickford. The Roos-Pickford relationship was undoubtedly an unhappy one. One of Hollywood's most die-hard conservatives, "America's Sweetheart," as Pickford was popularly known, was a longtime admirer of Italy fascist dictator Benito Mussolini. As she cheerily told a reporter in March 1934, "Italy has always produced great men and when she needed one most Mussolini was there. Viva Fascismo! Viva Il Duce!"[13]

Roos earned a good living in the movie business, but the work left him unsatisfied. The twenty-five-year-old writer began spending evenings and weekends assisting Lewis. "Before I knew it, I was his one and only volunteer who trained his under-cover people, taught them how to watch even for the smallest details, how to write reports, etc."[14]

A quiet man who stood just over five feet tall, with thinning hair and glasses with thick bottle-like lenses, Joe Roos preferred to work behind the scenes, taking quiet pleasure in knowing what he achieved. As one friend observed, "He could make things happen without calling attention to himself. He was a smart guy, a crafty guy." When asked what in his personality made Roos so successful at undercover work, one colleague explained, "If you're born in Vienna and raised in Berlin, and your mom is Czech and your dad Hungarian, if you're Jew, you hide it. That helps you develop the kind of skills you need to fight the enemy."[15]

Roos's working relationship with Lewis proved similar to his relationship with Klein. "Lewis was the lieutenant and Roos the sergeant who did the footwork," explained historian Leonard Pitt, who helped Roos write his unpublished autobiography. "He was the one who did the daily work. I don't know if there was a personal friendship," Pitt added, "but I thought they got along very well."[16]

Far more knowledgeable about espionage than Lewis, Roos immediately began professionalizing the Community Committee's spy operation. Until then, Roos observed, everyone was "identified by [code] number, and you had to figure out who is this and who is that. It was terrible. Well, I sort of took over. I was the guy who did the inside work. My job was to work with the investigators." Over the next several years, he taught Lewis's undercover agents lessons he had learned from George Marshall's men: "primarily to be careful, how not to take chances, and to understand what the Nazis were like in order to be able to act like a Nazi, and also to be able to discover what is important and what is not important." To protect his spies' identities, he ran all operations on a strictly need-to-know basis and cautioned his agents, "If you're involved in espionage, in spying, keep your mouth shut."[17]

In the fall of 1935, Roos made one of his most important contributions: he introduced Lewis to the man who would become one of the Community Committee's most important spies, the man who, more than anyone else, drove a wedge between Friends of New Germany leader Hermann Schwinn and German consul Georg Gyssling.

NEIL NESS: THE MAKING OF A SPY

Like any good spy, Neil Howard Ness kept parts of his life shrouded in mystery. The engineer turned journalist turned spy told different stories about his past to different people. He told Leon Lewis he was born in Chicago and received a degree in mechanical engineering from Berkeley. Several years later, he told House Un-American Activities Committee investigators he was born in San Francisco and educated after the war at the University of Berlin, where he earned degrees in engineering. What we know for certain is that Ness was born in Chicago on September 9, 1897. His father was a Norwegian-born baker and his mother a housewife who emigrated from Sweden. Sometime in the spring of 1918, Ness enlisted in the U.S. Army and joined the American Expeditionary Forces in France, serving in an artillery unit where he rose to the rank of corporal.[18]

Ness's career after leaving the military remains equally unclear. After working a number of engineering jobs in the 1920s, he developed an expertise in air-conditioning that brought him to Los Angeles, where he spent six years installing cooling equipment for movie theaters. In 1930, a visiting delegation of Soviet engineers hired Ness as a technical adviser. Pleased with his work, they invited him to the USSR to serve as a consultant for air-conditioning units. He proved so successful that in September 1931 he was elected as the Moscow District's representative to the All-Russian Technical Congress; several months later, Ness claimed to have been made a member of the Supreme Economic Council of the USSR. What he really wanted, however, was to be a journalist. During his time abroad, he interviewed numerous Soviet leaders, including a number of high-ranking officers in the OGPU, the Soviet secret police. In May 1932, after suffering an illness, he left Russia and spent several months recuperating in Germany.[19]

In a partially written autobiography, Ness told of his harrowing encounters with Nazis while visiting Berlin. One afternoon, he was sitting with friends in a café watching 300 Brownshirts marching in the streets when someone threw bricks at the Nazis. Enraged Brownshirts charged into the café where Ness was seated and hit him in the face with a rubber truncheon: "The impact made me stagger back a little and blood flowed instantly and profusely from my nose." A police officer came dashing up and demanded to know "why I had started the fight." Ness was arrested and taken to the police station, where a sympathetic commanding officer, who was not a Brownshirt, released him. Discussing the day's events with his anti-Nazi friends, he learned "that the Jewish question had been fabricated by Hitler from lies, forgeries, and wide-spread confusion." He left the country convinced of "the inevitability of Nazism in Germany" and determined to "better serve my country and my fellowmen."[20]

The last part of the story was true. No longer interested in engineering, Ness sailed from Germany in May 1932 and upon returning to Chicago began publishing the *Resolute*, "a literary journal which predicated its beliefs on the theories of genuine American liberalism." Determined to alert Americans to the dangers he had witnessed in Berlin, Ness also began working on a book that would "unearth the machinations of Nazi Agents in America."[21]

Ness first came to Joe Roos's attention while investigating Nazi and fascist groups in Chicago. "There was a screwy engineer," Roos recounted, "who published some magazines for a couple of months, and then he went out of business." Screwy or not, Roos recognized a kindred spirit and asked Ness to join his undercover operation. In December 1933, Anti-Defamation League secretary Miles Goldberg sent Leon Lewis a copy of the *Resolute*. In a piece entitled "The American Entente," Ness called for the right of Jews "to complete economic and social freedom" and observed how "for the first time in history a Christian

Neil Ness Testifying at HUAC, October 1939
USC Libraries Special Collection

army rises to fight shoulder to shoulder with our fellow-man the Jew and in unity stands determined to protect him from the atrocious onslaught of insane persecutors."[22]

Unemployed and in search of work, Ness moved to Los Angeles late in 1935 and contacted the one person he knew from Chicago, Joe Roos. "At that time, I was still working in the motion picture studio," Roos recalled. "I sent him to Leon Lewis and he became an undercover man."[23] Ness could not have approached Lewis at a better time.

INSIDE DEUTSCHES HAUS

Leon Lewis was thrilled at the prospect of placing a new undercover agent inside Nazi headquarters. When the two men met in early December 1935, Lewis briefed Ness on what had transpired in Los Angeles over the past two years and asked him to penetrate the inner circle of the Friends of New Germany. Once he achieved that, Ness was "to collect, if possible, documentary and conclusive evidence of a definite subordination among the Nazi front leaders here to a High-Command in Germany." At the same time, Joe Roos urged caution. "I never tried to talk him into doing any violence or preach hate; preach the wonderful Fatherland, the great Goethe, the great Schiller."[24]

Before entrusting Ness with too much responsibility, Lewis wrote Richard Gutstadt, the Anti-Defamation League leader who had known Ness in Chicago, asking for a frank assessment of his "'reliability, integrity, intelligence, etc.' How safe is he on investigation work? I have had him do a few little jobs but am somewhat in doubt as to how far I can go with him." Gutstadt telegrammed: "Believe Ness thoroughly reliable and intelligent STOP Cooperated considerably with us for some time STOP His economic status is unfortunate but believe he may be trusted."[25] After being offered a modest salary, the unemployed writer now known as Agent N2 began working for the spy duo.

Spying is a creative enterprise, especially for a writer with a vivid imagination. Ness planned on turning his espionage work for Lewis into a bestselling book when the operation was over. The greater the danger, the better the story.

Like Schmidt before him, Ness made his initial contacts with the Nazi community over food and conversation. On December 15, 1935, he accompanied his friend Harry Wenger to Max Tank's bakery-restaurant in El Monte, a popular eating spot for local Nazis. Introducing himself as a former magazine publisher who was "interested in political structures," Ness talked about his experiences in the Soviet Union. When his companions discovered that his "opinions of the Soviet regime were not favorable," they invited him to visit FNG headquarters to learn "the truth of the conditions in Germany." Ness attended his first meeting a week later and was introduced to FNG secretary-treasurer Albert Paehler, who was in charge while Hermann Schwinn attended meetings in New York. When Ness returned with his wife, Esther, several days later and told Paehler he wanted to publish a "magazine appealing to American youth," the excited Nazi leader urged the journalist to meet Schwinn when he returned at the end of the month. In the meantime, the couple accepted Paehler's invitation to join the festive Christmas Eve celebration at Deutsches Haus.[26]

Having been expelled from Turnverein Hall because of a rift between the German community's pro- and anti-Nazi groups, Schwinn and his outfit had moved to a large building on West Fifteenth Street near Figueroa Street. Attending his first FNG meeting, Ness was "surprised at the extent of the Nazi display of swastikas and literature that was available."[27]

Ness's rapid entry into the inner circle of Los Angeles Nazidom was facilitated by two propitious developments in the FNG's national organization: their determination to recruit more native-born Americans, and their desire to inaugurate a national youth movement. Hitler wanted to keep the United States neutral for as long as possible and did not want the FNG to turn public opinion against the Nazi regime. At a national gathering held in Pennsylvania in July 1935, Fritz Kuhn, who hoped to supplant Fritz Gissibl as head of the FNG, argued that the group could become a powerful political force in the United States only if its membership was confined to American citizens, including Germans who had taken out citizenship papers as well as native-born Americans. Kuhn, a chemist who had worked for Henry Ford, insisted that no German national be allowed to belong; otherwise it would look as if the FNG was a foreign-run organization serving foreign interests. Agreeing with Kuhn, Hermann Schwinn estimated that only 25 percent of his members were native-born Americans.[28]

In October 1935, under instructions from Adolf Hitler, Rudolf Hess had ordered German nationals living in the United States to cease all political activity, including membership in the FNG. When German leaders discovered that many local organizations had failed to obey their command, the government issued a second edict on Christmas Day, demanding "unconditional compliance with this order."[29] A final change came in March 1936, when the Friends of New Germany was dissolved and replaced by the German American Bund. Fritz Kuhn was appointed the new national führer, replacing Fritz Gissibl, who returned to Germany to work for the government.

Ness arrived at a perfect moment to infiltrate the Nazi organization. The FNG hoped to build a cadre of young Nazis who could carry on Hitler's work in America for decades to come. In July 1935, encouraged by the success of a similar movement in Germany, Nazis in New York opened Camp Siegfried. The first of many Nazi summer camps aimed at infusing American boys and girls with "the spirit of the new Germany," Camp Siegfried offered picnic grounds, hiking trials, swimming ponds, a mini-resort for family gatherings, and a children's summer camp.[30] Schwinn wanted to launch his own youth movement and hoped to open a summer camp in Hindenburg Park. Consequently, when Albert Paehler told the West Coast führer that an experienced American journalist was interested in starting a youth magazine, Schwinn arranged to meet him.

On Tuesday, December 31, two days after Schwinn held a special meeting to announce the expulsion of "alien members" from the organization, Neil Ness traveled to Deutsches Haus to meet the local leader. Walking into Schwinn's private office, Ness was taken aback by a bold red-lettered fourteen-by-eight-inch sign posted on his door: NO ADMITTANCE TO JEWS. As they sat down to talk, he saw a photograph of the young Schwinn dressed in a storm trooper uniform. The picture, the Nazi boasted, was taken in 1924, when he belonged to the old Sturmabteilung in Germany. Sitting alongside the Nazi leader was his vicious German shepherd, Lump. The two men spent an hour and a half discussing plans to publish a new magazine for German American youth. The proposed *Young Statesmen* would be modeled after similar periodicals circulating in Germany and Italy. Its purpose was "to rally youth to save the country as it did in the other countries."[31] After finishing their conversation, Schwinn handed Ness a slew of anti-Semitic literature to acquaint him with National Socialist ideals.

Schwinn walked away from the meeting hoping to make Neil Ness the American face of his organization. The well-built five-foot-nine, 170-pound former soldier with wavy dark hair, a friendly face, and a penchant for smoking a pipe looked like the kind of wholesome American the Nazis wanted to attract to their cause. Delighted with their conversation, Schwinn promised to introduce Ness to two other

Arno Risse (l) and Hermann Schwinn (r) in Uniform, 1936
Jewish Federation Council of Greater Los Angeles, Community Relations Committee Collection, Part 2,
Special Collections and Archives, Oviatt Library, California State University, Northridge

Americans working with the Bund: Ingram Hughes, author of the recent anti-Semitic proclamation, and his assistant, Charles Slocombe.[32]

Over the next week, Ness and his wife, Esther, visited Deutsches Haus on a daily basis. Like John and Alice Schmidt, the Nesses were a husband-and-wife spy team. Born in Copenhagen, Esther moved to the United States as a child and became a citizen in 1922. She married Neil two years later and moved to Los Angeles in 1927, where her husband was installing air-conditioning units in movie theaters. Assisting Ness throughout his undercover operation, the mother of two young children regularly accompanied him to FNG meetings, where she sat in the back of the hall taking careful notes of all speeches, notes that Ness used for his daily reports. Not surprisingly, the aspiring writer displayed the greatest literary flair of any of Lewis's spies. His reports were filled with vivid descriptions of people and places, and often reproduced dialogues of his conversations with Nazis and fascists.

The affable Ness so impressed Nazi leaders with his proposed youth magazine that Schwinn assigned him a desk at Deutsches Haus and permission "to move around freely throughout the various offices." He also asked Reinhold Kusche, one of his most trusted lieutenants, to help Ness refurbish his German so that he could translate German propaganda material into English. Ness understood the language when spoken slowly, but his writing and speaking skills had grown rusty. Anxious to have the American play a more visible role in the organization, Schwinn gave him two additional tasks: to lecture about his experiences in the Soviet Union, and to help the FNG establish friendly relations with like-minded American groups. Schwinn promised to pay Ness "in the near future," but until then he would labor for the love of Germany.[33]

Working evenings on the youth magazine at his home, Ness and Kusche struck up a friendship. The stocky six-foot-tall, forty-three-year-old tailor impressed the former engineer as "the heavy solid labor-type Pole . . . His education has been somewhat limited although he is well read. His English vocabulary is confined to a very common terminology and is marked by a decided foreign accent which at times makes his speech almost incoherent." Kusche had served five years with the German infantry during World War I, a year of which was spent in a French POW camp. The "rabidly anti-Semitic" tailor, Ness explained, was a "devout believer in Hitlerism and labors diligently for National Socialism in the United States."[34] Kusche's hatred of Jews intensified after suffering financial losses because of the Jewish boycott of local German businesses.

Having received glowing reports from Kusche about the progress they were making, Schwinn invited Ness to join him, Dr. Konrad Burchardi, and several others for lunch in mid-January. As the men spoke rapidly in German, Ness missed a lot of the specifics but understood enough to know they were discussing "initiating me into the inner circle." Taking Ness into his confidence, Schwinn told him how Nazis received secret shipments of propaganda materials every ten days from German boats docking in Los Angeles. He asked Ness to drive Kusche to the docks to pick up the next shipment.[35]

Ness further ingratiated himself with the FNG cohort by helping Ingram Hughes make the political platform of his American Nationalist Party more appealing to voters. Schwinn envisioned the propagandist as leading an American fascist front that would be secretly headed by the FNG. Meeting with Ness for the first time in February 1936,

Hughes insisted the time was right for action, but he needed more help. Ness agreed to assist in whatever way he could.

Delighted with the work he had done on behalf of the cause, Kusche told Ness how he and Schwinn "look upon you as a coming leader in an American youth movement that should really amount to something." The flattery was welcome, but Ness was even more pleased by Kusche's subsequent revelation of a growing rift within the organization over Schwinn's leadership of the Friends of New Germany's western division (which included the entire western United States). Kusche headed the forty-two man *Ordnungsdienst* (OD, or uniformed service, but more popularly known as storm troopers), the paramilitary Nazi security unit charged with protecting leaders and enforcing discipline among members. The OD leader complained that Schwinn had grown far too timid since the HUAC hearings. Kusche wanted the *California Weckruf*, the FNG's newspaper, to adopt "a more drastic anti-Semitic campaign."[36] Schwinn, however, favored downplaying anti-Semitism in favor of a more balanced approach aimed at attracting greater support among Americans.

This was the moment Ness, Lewis, and Roos had hoped for: a chance to foment discord among the Nazi cohort. The disgruntled Kusche invited Ness to attend an OD meeting in mid-February. The undercover operative came away impressed, and frightened, by what he saw. The OD unit functioned as a well-disciplined squad, ready to thwart any attack on the FNG or launch one against the enemy if needed. "Every action," Ness reported, "is carried out in a very militaristic basis."[37] Weekly drills and target practice ended with the OD commander ordering everyone to sing the "Horst-Wessel-Lied" ("Horst Wessel Song," the Nazi national anthem) and "Die Wacht am Rhein" while facing the swastika flag and giving the Nazi salute.

After attending several OD sessions, Ness warned Lewis that Willi Sachse, the OD's second in command, was "a confessed killer of two members of the Communist party in Germany" who fled to the United States in 1923 to escape being tried for the murders. The stocky German tailor boasted of "his record as a national socialist" and "one of the first brown-shirts."[38] These men had killed, and were willing to kill again. Worse yet, they knew the identity of their main persecutor, Leon Lewis.

Spending considerable time at Deutsche Haus, Ness grew friendly with Rafael Demmler, another dangerous Nazi "of the criminal type." Proclaiming himself "Jew-baiter number 1 in Los Angeles," the Bureau of Water and Power employee warned Ness to be wary of Lewis, "the most dangerous Jew in Los Angeles" and "the ring-leader of all Jews

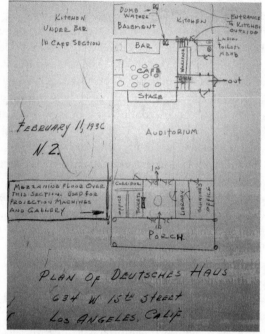

Neil Ness Sketch of "Plan of Deutches Haus"
Jewish Federation Council of Greater Los Angeles, Community Relations Committee Collection, Part 2, Special Collections and Archives, Oviatt Library, California State University, Northridge

here." No one knew "much of this fellow since he worked mostly under cover," Demmler explained. He swore his information came "from very reliable and authoritative sources." A penciled-in note in Ness's report suggested that the reliable source was Georg Gyssling. Just as Lewis was aware of the consul's activities, so, too, was the consul aware of Lewis's position as spymaster-in-chief.[39]

AGENT PROVOCATEUR

All was not well inside Deutsches Haus. Not only had Ness discovered deep internal divisions, but he also learned about the bitter tension between FNG leaders and German consul Gyssling. The diplomat had repeatedly complained to the Foreign Office that the FNG was causing the Reich more harm than good. In early February 1936, the German government responded to his complaints by dispatching "special agent" Hans Meyerhoffer to Los Angeles. A close friend of Rudolf Hess, Meyerhoffer was sent to "instruct the leadership here in new lines of action necessitated by the recent dictum from Berlin which pertains to the political activities of German citizens residing in America." He provided Schwinn with Berlin's plan to reorganize the western division of the FNG so as to put the nearly bankrupt organization on a more sound financial footing.[40]

When Meyerhoffer entered Deutsches Haus for the first time in mid-February, Ness immediately knew he was a man of considerable importance, for FNG leaders treated him with great respect and deference. Dining with Meyerhoffer and Schwinn a week later, Ness reported that Hess's friend was "a very militant personage for all of his 5' 3" of height. On the platform he speaks as one swept away by his emotions and his devotion to Hitler and the Nazi cause seems almost beyond fanaticism."[41]

A Steuben Society celebration of George Washington's birthday at Deutsches Haus provided Ness, Lewis, and Roos with an opportunity to drive a wedge between the Nazis and the German American community. When the spy and spymasters discovered Demmler had invited conservative film director and screenwriter Rupert Hughes (who Demmler wrongly assumed was an anti-Semite) to deliver the keynote address, they devised a plan that would backfire on the Nazi organization. Upon learning that Hughes was a good friend of Julius Klein, Ness drafted a letter that Klein signed and sent to Hughes, explaining how the Steuben Society "acted as a front for various organizations inspired by Mr. Goebbels' local representatives." Hughes's audience would be "90% confirmed Nazis." The letter asked Hughes to "give them a rip-roaring talk of the type you gave in introducing [outspoken British anti-Nazi] Lord Listowe."[42]

Phoning Ness the morning before the talk, Hughes promised to "do some missionary work with the heathen." The Hollywood writer devoted most of his forty-minute speech to praising the considerable service Jews such as Haym Solomon provided George Washington during the bleakest days of the American Revolution. He closed with a jibe at the Nazi faithful by insisting that "as an American he was as Goddamn good as any man and so he had to recognize that any other man was as Goddamn good as he was."[43]

Outraged at the speaker's betrayal, Demmler and Schwinn asked Ness to "save the day" by making a few impromptu remarks to the crowd of 250. Ness "gave them what they wanted," a passionate five-minute talk criticizing Hughes and urging the closest relationship between the people of America and Germany. When he finished, Schwinn was so appreciative, he made Ness an editor of the *California Weckruf* and promised "that from now on we would surely work more closely than ever."[44] Over the next several months, Ness rose to the task and turned out a series of militantly pro-Nazi, anti-Communist articles under the pen name Emeric Hutton von Cromstead.

Ness's standing in Deutsches Haus rose even higher after he and Demmler confronted the editor of the *Jewish Community Press* over his coverage of Hughes's speech ("Rupert Hughes Teaches Local Nazis Lesson in Americanism") and the paper's bold accusations that the Steuben Society was a Nazi front. Unbeknownst to Demmler and Schwinn, Ness phoned the editor in advance, warning him of the upcoming visit and suggesting he play along with whatever he might say. When the two men arrived at the newspaper's office, Demmler was duly impressed by Ness's fervor in demanding a retraction. Although the forewarned editor naturally refused, Ness was rewarded several days later by being made a member of a new secret Nazi committee.[45]

Meeting in early March to discuss the best ways to combat the "renewed and successful activities of the Jews against the Nazi front," FNG leaders formed a secret committee "for the purpose of camouflaging Nazi activities." The Camouflage Committee, Schwinn explained, made up of the FNG's elite "inner circle," would "act as a patriotic American front for all affairs of the Nazi organization which may arouse public criticism if the real organization in back of it were known." Schwinn asked Ness to serve as the group's secretary. Franz Ferenz, who replaced Hans Winterhalder as the Nazi's chief propagandist, also invited the American to serve as secretary of a second new organization. The Deutsches Buehne, he explained, was an association of artists that would operate under the auspices of the German American artists' guild while secretly advancing the Nazi cause.[46] No Lewis agent had ever penetrated so deeply into the inner sanctum of local Nazidom.

After learning his agent was slated to give his first speech in mid-March, Lewis asked Joe Roos to attend the FNG gathering "in order to see how really well Ness was doing." Roos decided to take his new wife along. Three months earlier, the twenty-seven-year-old offspring of generations of Orthodox rabbis had married Alvina Fontaine, a Christian nurse from Wisconsin, a coupling that did not please his family. "Even after they were married," their son remarked, "the family tried to break it up." Ever protective of his agents' identities, Roos did not tell his wife why they were going. His need-to-know policy applied even to Alvina. As they sat in the large auditorium, the couple heard Ness denounce France and urge Americans to embrace a strong leader such as Adolf Hitler. Leaving Deutsches Haus, Alvina "tore this guy Ness apart" and told her husband how upset she was by his rabidly pro-Nazi stance. Roos listened but never disclosed that Ness was his operative or that he had written Ness's speech.[47]

On March 6, 1936, Ness sent Lewis a "Mission and Personal Progress Report." As per orders, he had succeeded in penetrating "the alien Nazi front" and gaining the "esteem and respect" of its leaders. They had asked him to edit their newspaper, write propaganda articles favorable to Hitler, join their secret committees, and promote their cause among Americans. Despite his progress, Ness understood that his was a highly dangerous mission: "Here is a game deep with subterfuge, heavy with bait, infested with traps, poisonous with the fumes and stenches of the rats that slink forth from the filth of polluted sewers." Consequently, he had "found it necessary to employ tactics at times that under any other circumstance would nauseate me." He closed by reflecting, "How long it will be before these evils are destroyed at their roots I wish I could say."[48]

Ness had good reason to be afraid. In late March Charles Slocombe, Ingram Hughes's assistant, showed Hermann Schwinn an article in the *Jewish Community Press* that revealed far too much inside knowledge of FNG operations. After reading the piece, the furious Nazi leader warned, "We have a leak here someplace in our group; I suspect two people: one was a stranger that looked Jewish . . . and the other is one of our members, but I won't give any names until I'm sure."[49] Ness knew he was under suspicion.

For the next several months Neil Ness played a most dangerous game, fomenting discord among rival Deutsches Haus factions as well as between the German American Bund—the FNG's successor—and German general consul Georg Gyssling. As Ness worked to divide the Nazi cohort, Leon Lewis and Joe Roos confronted an even greater threat.

11.

The Plots to Kill the Jews

The year 1936 started off with troubling news for an already burdened Leon Lewis. On New Year's Eve, he received a disconcerting report that, on a designated night, twenty targeted men—Jews and politicians who supported them—would be kidnapped and hanged in a grove selected by Ingram Hughes. His assassins would begin with District Attorney Buron Fitts and end by lynching Lewis and Mendel Silberberg.[1]

Nazis and Silver Shirts knew Lewis was running a spy service out of his office in the Roosevelt Building, just minutes from Deutsches Haus. Every time he stepped onto the street, he faced the possibility of being attacked by some crazed Nazi or fascist determined to make his name by assassinating the city's most dangerous Jew. Lewis could feel the noose tighten around his neck, and prayed it would only be a proverbial one.

Fortunately, Lewis's spy Neil Ness was now working inside the American National Party (ANP) and reporting on Hughes's every move. A second spy, Charles P. Slocombe, would penetrate even deeper and emerge as Ingram Hughes's right-hand man. With Lewis and Roos operating on a need-to-know basis, neither spy realized that the other worked for the Jews. Ness thought Slocombe was a dedicated fascist, while Slocombe believed Ness was an ardent Nazi.

AGENT C19

After hearing about Hughes's plot to pave "the way for an ultimate solution of the 'Jewish Problem,'" Lewis contacted friends at naval intelligence, who owed him a favor after he'd tipped them off about the illegal sale of military weapons in San Diego the previous year. When he told them about Hughes's plot and asked for help, they directed him to Owen Murphy. The Long Beach police captain had been monitoring the local Ku Klux Klan for years and had recruited Slocombe—who joined the Klan in 1928—to work as an undercover agent. In a display of goodwill, Lewis, who had also been following Klan activities, sent the captain a copy of their Long Beach membership roster and a complete run of their minutes from January 1, 1934, onward. When Lewis asked Murphy to recommend someone who could burrow inside Ingram Hughes's operation, the grateful police captain introduced him to the man who would be known as Agent C19.[2]

Charles P. Slocombe was the most unlikely of Lewis's recruits: a Ku Klux Klan member who spurned his past beliefs but remained active in the Klan to maintain a front while helping the Jews. The six-foot-one, "distinctly German"–looking Californian with a "baby face" and light complexion was precisely the kind of handsome American fascists and Nazis wanted to recruit.[3]

Born in Oakland, California, in 1907, Slocombe moved to Long Beach with his parents and ten siblings in 1928. After finishing junior college, Chuck, as he was known, worked as a deckhand on the city's docks. By the time he met Lewis in October 1935, the hardworking Slocombe owned the City Water Taxi Company, which had an exclusive franchise to run seven boats from Long Beach to Catalina Island, where pleasure seekers could dance to the sounds of the Jimmy Dorsey and Glenn Miller orchestras. On weekends, he taught Sunday school at Emmanuel Presbyterian Church.[4]

Although it is unclear how Murphy and Slocombe first met, by 1935 KKK member No. 31712 was providing the police captain with information about local Silver Shirts as well as the Long Beach Klan.[5] When he started working for Lewis in October 1935, Slocombe was already well versed in leading a double life. But it came at a cost. Many of his friends became ex-friends because they could not understand why Chuck remained active in the Klan.

Why *would* a former Klan member agree to work for the Jews? Although Slocombe left no documents explaining his decision, it is likely he did so for three reasons. First, he was initially drawn to the Klan for its rabid stance against communism. Slocombe envisioned himself a writer and had published a pamphlet accusing *Scholastic*, a popular children's magazine, of Communist propaganda. Yet despite his Klan membership, Slocombe never showed any prejudice toward

Charles Slocombe
Courtesy Sherry Slocombe

Jews. As he wrote Lewis, "I'll defy anyone to show me anything that connects the Jewish people with fostering the Communist movement."[6] Second, Lewis presented his investigation as one focused on exposing un-American activities and not as an operation solely to protect the city's Jews.

Finally, there was the matter of money. Slocombe's relationship to Lewis was never purely altruistic. With seven boats and never enough business, he was often overextended and short of cash. The modest stipend Lewis paid him proved a godsend, especially when Slocombe fell behind on rent. When the cash-strapped entrepreneur married Martha Helen Ann Wells in January 1936, the couple was forced to live with his parents until sometime in 1937.[7]

GOING UNDERCOVER

Slocombe was experienced enough to know that a direct approach to Hughes would be foolish; he needed to meet the man through trusted intermediaries. To that end, Slocombe began visiting Ku Klux Klan headquarters at Seventh and Spring Streets in downtown Los Angeles, where he was well known to Gus W. Price, the Grand Dragon of California, and Robert Flournoy, his chief of staff. The water taxi owner's plan was simple: he would praise the proclamation sent to him from the Klan's downtown office and request more copies to post in Long Beach. When he asked Price and Flournoy where he might find the American

Nationalist Party's headquarters, neither seemed to know. "Rather than having anyone get suspicious of any of the questions I might ask," he told Lewis, "I dropped the matter altogether."[8] But he would soon find an answer at the Aryan Bookstore, just a mile and a half away.

As the newcomer browsed among the bookstore's various publications, storeowner Paul Themlitz approached and asked if he could help. When Slocombe requested copies of the *Silver Ranger*, Themlitz told him the Silver Shirts had disbanded and it was no longer possible to get their literature. When the water taxi owner mentioned he was a friend of Count Ernst Ulrich von Bülow, the San Diego Nazi who was providing Schwinn with money, Themlitz invited him into his private office. During the course of their conversation, Slocombe casually asked if he knew anything about the ANP. Themlitz played dumb and said nothing, but urged Slocombe to visit again.[9]

Slocombe returned several days later to a warm welcome. Always on the alert for Lewis's spies, Themlitz had undoubtedly made phone calls to verify that the Long Beach Klan member was who he claimed to be. Seeing the possibility of a new American recruit, Themlitz invited Slocombe to a screening of Nazi films at Deutsches Haus. After attending the show with his fiancée and another couple, Slocombe adjourned with his group to the building's beer garden to drink and socialize with their new Nazi acquaintances.[10]

After paying several more visits to the FNG and the Aryan Bookstore, Slocombe learned that Ingram Hughes had written the now-infamous proclamation, and the FNG was responsible for the printing and distribution. Hoping to burrow further inside the Nazi organization, he attended his first Nazi meeting in early November, where a hundred of the faithful, including a cadre of "two dozen men dressed in black storm troop outfits," heard speakers praise Hughes and his close ally Henry Allen for their wonderful work.[11]

After learning the address of the shop that printed the proclamation, Slocombe drove there, hoping to meet Hughes. Introducing himself as an anti-Red author, he asked shopowner Joseph Landthaler if he would print his latest pamphlet warning American youth about the dangers of communism. While discussing their mutual interest in anti-Communist literature, the German-born printer mentioned that Hughes had heard about him from friends in the KKK and FNG and wanted to meet.[12] The next three weeks resembled a Keystone Kops comedy, with the two men just missing each other at Landthaler's shop, KKK headquarters, and Deutsches Haus.

After a great deal of frustration, Slocombe and Hughes finally met. Hughes gushed over Slocombe's anti-Communist pamphlet "and said that I could be of use to them." Hughes was not the only one interested in Slocombe. Hermann Schwinn also wanted to discuss a matter of mutual interest.[13]

Driving the considerable distance from Long Beach to downtown Los Angeles, breathing in the toxic fumes emanating from the area's oil wells, a tired Chuck Slocombe returned to Los Angeles the next evening wondering what Schwinn wanted. Like Neil Ness's, Slocombe's timing was perfect. Schwinn envisioned recruiting another American to help launch his Nazi-inspired American youth movement. The Nazi leader had done his homework. He knew all about Slocombe's longtime involvement with the Klan and his considerable expertise on Communist infiltration of American youth literature. Impressed by their conversation that evening, Schwinn asked Slocombe to work on the FNG's new program for young Americans.

Despite the flattery he received from the Nazis, Slocombe knew that his main mission was to attach himself to Ingram Hughes and discover his plans. On a Thursday evening in late November, amid news of anti-Semitic riots in Budapest, the two men held their first prolonged meeting at Hughes's apartment on Fourth Street and Grand Avenue. Knowing his outspoken desire to "destroy the Jewish influence in America" would not sit well in powerful Jewish quarters, the ANP leader had left his wife and two sons in their San Fernando Valley home and rented a small downtown apartment so as not to place them in jeopardy. "Hughes is a man of about 50 years, heavy set, has grey hair, slightly bald, wears glasses, and uses excellent grammar," Slocombe reported. "He has a degree in law, and has been a journalist for many years. He has written many books, all anti-Semitic; each one more damaging than the last."[14] As for the proclamation, Hughes claimed he received requests from across the country and had mailed out 44,000 copies at a personal cost of $5,000.

Ingram Hughes, Slocombe quickly discovered, was a self-proclaimed patriot who believed he was saving the nation from the Jewish menace. Born in Whitman, Washington, in 1875, Hughes had been educated at the University of Washington and was admitted to practice law before the California Supreme Court in 1914. He soon abandoned the law and spent most of his adult life working as a linotype operator and writing anti-Semitic literature. In 1933, while employed as a printer at the *Los Angeles Times*, he founded the American National Party and turned out two self-published books: *Rational Purpose in Government: Expressed in the Doctrine of the American Nationalist Party* (1933) and *Anti-Semitism: Organized Anti-Jewish Sentiment; A World-Survey* (1934). Attacking Jews for their unwavering "contempt for our morality or ethical standards of conduct," the latter work savaged Jewish Hollywood for producing "the vilest stream of filth, indecencies and vulgarities, degradation and perversion, with ever increasing emphasis on sex and crime, that has been known in all the world's history." The Jews, he concluded, "must go."[15]

Talking late into the evening at his apartment, Hughes bluntly asked Slocombe why he wanted to work with him. "I told him that the groups I had worked for were not militant enough, that I wanted to have action and not a lot of talk."[16] Pleased with the response, Hughes confided that his FNG friends had "given high compliments on my work on Communism" and wanted him to serve on their new youth council. But Hughes had other plans. Trusting his new recruit more than he should, the ANP leader laid out his ambitious vision for the future. While Hitler used the Nuremberg Laws to restrict Jewish rights, Hughes planned to go a step further; he would rid America of the Jewish menace by building the ANP into a national organization with five regional leaders: himself, William Dudley Pelley, Ohio fascist Robert Edward Edmondson, Texas anti-Semite C. J. Wright, and a Mr. Tellian, who would handle party activities in the Northwest. Collectively, they would purge the United States of its unwanted Jewish population.

After breaking for dinner, the two men returned to Hughes's apartment, where Henry Allen joined them. Slocombe had heard much about Allen from Hughes and his FNG acquaintances, but nothing prepared him for the man's militancy or brazen self-confidence. Born in Massachusetts in 1879, Allen had been active in anti-Semitic organizations since 1911. His criminal activities dated back even further. In 1910 he was charged with passing fictitious checks, for which he received a three-year suspended sentence. Two years later, after violating parole, Allen was remanded to San Quentin Prison, where he remained until May 1913. Unable to stay out of trouble, he was convicted on forgery charges in 1915 and sent to Folsom Prison for sixteen months. As deeply crooked as he was prejudiced, Allen was arrested in 1919 on suspicion of felony, in 1924 for passing bad checks in San Francisco, and in 1925 for doing the same in Los Angeles. When Allen was arrested yet again in the mid-1930s, Hughes, despite rarely practicing, defended him in court and won the case.[17]

By 1934 the Allen household reigned as the first family of fascist Los Angeles. Henry's wife, Pearl, whose parents had emigrated from Italy, served as an investigator for the American White Guard and an important member of the local Silver Shirts. His twelve-year-old son Warren got in trouble for trying to recruit schoolmates into the Silver Shirts. As for Henry, he proved a far more dangerous foe than Ingram Hughes. The militant fascist spoke Spanish fluently and had spent years working as a metallurgical engineer in Mazatlán, smuggling money and anti-Semitic literature to Mexican Gold Shirts and acting as their liaison with Los Angeles Nazis. Henry told friends he had an engineering degree from MIT, but a local relief worker reported he "had only an 8th grade education." She also noted that his impoverished family of five received $64 a month from the State Relief Association.[18]

Despite his long history of right-wing activism, Allen insisted he had been a devoted Democrat until President Franklin Roosevelt began acting like a "Dictator." Denouncing the "Jewish Vampires" in his administration, Allen called for Roosevelt's impeachment and the creation of an "American" party that was openly anti-alien and anti-Semitic.[19]

Upon first glance, it is unlikely anyone would suspect Allen of being one of the most ruthless fascists in Southern California. A physically unimposing figure with a face resembling an emaciated death mask, Allen was a middle-aged man whom one of Lewis's later agents described as "wear[ing] glasses, iron gray hair, thin, about 145 lbs., wiry, small mustache, sunken cheeks, sticks out his jaw when speaking, rather pugnacious type." "Pugnacious" was an apt description. Allen gleefully instructed Slocombe on the most effective way to beat a Jew in a fight: always throw the first punch, something he had learned during the course of nineteen successful brawls.[20]

The first time the three men met, Allen surprised Slocombe by revealing he knew all about Jewish efforts to spy on their operation. He knew that Mark White was working for Mendel Silberberg and Leon Lewis. Hughes said he would ignore Lewis's activities until the time for exposing the Jew was right, "and then he would give him all the publicity he needs and none of it is very favorable." Allen reassured Slocombe they could literally get away with murder; his friends in the police department would cover for him. Following his arrest for illegally posting Hughes's proclamation, the police had released him and then asked "for some of his literature and wished him good luck." Turning to his two companions, Allen boasted, "No one will ever get any spies into the group."[21]

The next day Slocombe sent Lewis a diagram of Hughes's apartment, including where he hid his "confidential matter," and noted that the fascist had given him a key to come and go at will. "He is making me a sort of right hand man."[22] Suspecting that Leon Lewis was probably spying on him, Hughes taught his new assistant some basic spycraft: how to exit the apartment without being detected and the importance of always drawing the shades and leaving a light burning before leaving.[23]

As Hughes's trust in his new right-hand man grew, he clued Slocombe in to his next major project: the American National Party would forge an anti-Semitic organization called the United Front that would include the FNG, Klan, American White Guard, Silver Shirts, and Russian National Revolutionary Party. What separated Hughes's plan from similar past efforts was the number of prominent Angelenos he expected to be on his plenary council. In addition to the usual suspects— Hughes, Allen, Mrs. Allen, Slocombe, Schwinn, Ferenz, and Bülow of San Diego—the list of inner circle members included highly reputable figures such as former Los Angeles mayor and Klan leader John Porter, a California state senator, the Pasadena city prosecutor, and a Pasadena real estate agent who later served in Congress. Bülow and Dr. Crutcher, Hughes's wealthy local financial backer, promised to fund the group.[24]

Slocombe's rapid ascension within fascist circles pleased Lewis enormously. In addition to organizing the ANP's Nationalist Youth Society, the Long Beach operative served on the United Front's finance committee; he also worked as Hughes's point man with the Russian National Revolutionary Party, another violent anti-Semitic group.[25]

Ingram Hughes was not just another fascist crackpot with wild fantasies. By the end of 1935, he had set up ANP branches in California, Florida, Illinois, Maine, Utah, and Ohio. When Hermann Schwinn traveled to Chicago in December to attend the FNG's reorganization meeting, he took copies of the proclamation with him and promised to help organize a chapter there. Several weeks later, Hughes established a working relationship with Reverend Gerald B. Winrod, the far-right Kansas evangelist who was secretly working with the Reich Ministry of Public Enlightenment and Propaganda. He also forged an alliance with prominent fascists James True in Washington, D.C., Robert Edmondson in New York, and Colonel Eugene Sanctuary, whom the Jewish Telegraphic Agency referred to as the "Grand Old Man of Anti-Semitism."[26]

By mid-December, confident that the ANP was creating a national base, Hughes began planning a series of deadly actions against the Jews.

THE PLOTS

Ingram Hughes knew he needed allies in his fight against the Jews, men who would not hesitate to shed blood on behalf of the cause. Not surprisingly, he found his strongest support among the city's Nazi cohort. During the United Front's first plenary meeting on November 29, 1935, Dr. Bruno Schmidt, a former German officer, suggested they raise military units "that could handle every situation that may arise." Many of the Nazis Slocombe met at FNG meetings proved even more extreme, demanding "a new form of government, and they are in favor of Fascism."[27]

Prospects of help increased when Schwinn returned from Chicago more solidly entrenched in the Nazi hierarchy than ever. Disappointed that Fritz Kuhn, and not he, had been appointed the new American führer, Schwinn nevertheless cemented his position as one of the party's top four men, serving as *Gauleiter* (district leader) for the entire western quarter of the United States. More importantly, Nazi officials in Berlin felt their activities were too closely monitored in New York and let it be known "that the west is the place for all activity and the place to start things going." Schwinn's news was music to Hughes's often tone-deaf ears, for he had plans "that would rock America from one end to the other."[28]

Over the next two months, Hughes, Allen, and Slocombe devised a plan to end the "Jew Deal" and restore Christian America to its rightful prominence through a series of violent actions against the city's Jews and their supporters.

As millions of Americans prepared to welcome in the New Year on December 31, Hughes planned to have twenty trusted men—working in teams of four—kidnap and hang twenty prominent Angelenos. "Each man we hang will be an example of a specific case, and what a representative group it will be too." The targeted Jews included film director and choreographer Busby Berkeley, attorneys Milton Cohen and Jerry Giesler, Superior Court judge Henry M. Willis, Mendel Silberberg, and Leon Lewis. "Busby Berkeley will look good dangling on a rope's end," the ANP leader quipped. Sending a stark warning to Christians who proved too friendly to Jews, his hit list also included district attorney Buron Fitts and longtime political boss Kent Parrott. "The sooner we get these Jew sons of bitches and their Gentile fronts on ropes the better."[29]

Hughes planned the operation with the precision of a lawyer. To prevent the police from identifying them, he ordered the kidnappers to wear cotton gloves and heavy wool socks over their shoes. To emphasize Hughes's contempt for Jews and Jew lovers, after all the men were hanged, "they will be given a hail of lead." Those participating in the pogrom included Nazi propagandist Franz Ferenz, four members of the FNG, and several other trusted accomplices. The police, Hughes's friends on the force had assured him, "will not interfere but will give a sigh of relief."[30]

This was no hasty killing fantasy but a carefully planned terrorist attack in which none of the perpetrators would be caught. "Every man will have a perfect alibi," Hughes explained, and "several weeks will be spent in developing the minutest details to the nth degree." As for the plot's mastermind, "I will be out of sight when it all happens, that is the actual hanging, but I will be close enough to direct it all."[31]

The ANP leader hoped the hangings would spark a nationwide uprising against Jews. "My philosophy is one of action," he explained to Slocombe. The only way "to curb the Jews" is through violence. "What we need is a real sensationalism with a warranted program." Violent assault would follow violent assault until Jews would eventually leave the country for Palestine. To hasten that day, Hughes and his accomplices would get "automatic shotguns and drive up and down Boyle Heights [the Jewish district], and let the Jews have it." And "Believe me," he assured Slocombe, "the custom will be taken up all over the country and will take action like wild fire."[32]

Hughes's vision was not as far-fetched as one might believe. Leon Lewis certainly took him seriously. The ADL representative knew that anti-Semitism was tolerated if not widely accepted in many quarters of the nation. An estimated 14 million Americans listened to Father Charles Coughlin spew anti-Semitic venom on his weekly radio show. Angelenos heard equally vitriolic sermons on local radio from Reverend Martin Luther Thomas, a close friend of Hermann Schwinn. When a January 1936 *Fortune* magazine survey asked if "Germany will be better or worse off if it drives out the Jews," 55 percent of those polled said worse off, while 32 percent said they did not know. But the "highest numbers of incertitude came from the American West, where nearly half the people interviewed expressed ambivalence when asked the question." Two years later, a Gallup poll revealed that 35 percent of Americans believed that European Jews were largely responsible for their own oppression. Little wonder, then, that the February 1936 issue of *Fortune* spoke of the rising "apprehensiveness of American Jews."[33]

Hughes prepared for his Jewish pogroms by recruiting a cadre of supporters "militant enough to go through with anything." Killing Jews, he promised, would purify the nation. "When the Jew is eliminated, crime is eliminated; liquor will be eliminated, lawlessness will be eliminated, Communism will be eliminated." All his supporters needed to do was "hang a few in each part of the country and that will finish the Jews and their Gentile front crooks. Action brought results in Germany, not theories."[34]

The ANP leader expected armed support from the Klan, FNG, and Silver Shirts. Schwinn promised Hughes that he would provide "a handpicked group to help." He warned the fascist that not everyone could be trusted, "so that we must all be very tight lipped." Discretion, however, was never one of Schwinn's strong points. Unable to contain his enthusiasm for the proposed killings, the loose-lipped German told Neil Ness how he and his friends were "going after the K's [Kikes] who are most important . . . We are going after Louis B. Mayer next and when we get through with him he will know he got the works."[35]

Hughes was pleased by Schwinn's support and remained confident he could outsmart his enemies. "They'll not get anything on me . . . I'm a lawyer and I know the ropes; I'm too foxy for them." He urged his partners to stay the course, "and one of these days we'll rock the country into realization that the ANP does things in a big way; and a new way too."[36]

In the meantime, Slocombe continued working on youth material for Hughes while visiting Deutsches Haus on a regular basis. He also attended downtown Klan meetings, where he was viewed as a rising star and asked to join the group's state committee. During one of Slocombe's visits to Nazi headquarters, Schwinn told him about the youth magazine Ness was designing and suggested the two men meet and exchange ideas. "He also told me that Ness was a very good man and was well versed in international affairs and would be of use to all of us." Schwinn believed that having the two Americans work together would help get "a militant youth group started here like we had in Germany."[37]

Charles Slocombe seemingly enjoyed his double life, but his inexperience as a spy led him to spread himself too thin. The almost daily twenty-four-mile drive from Long Beach to Los Angeles and the need to tend to his boat fleet had exhausted him to the point that his energy for long hours of fascist activity flagged. Hughes had begun to wonder about his new recruit. Was his drop-off in enthusiasm fatigue or something more sinister: a spy with cold feet? When Hughes and Ness met to discuss the ANP's political platform in late January 1936, Ness asked the fascist if he knew anything about the excellent anti-Communist pamphlet he just read, "Whither American Youth." Hughes responded that it was written by "one of his young organizers." Chuck Slocombe, he confided, "was all right but was becoming too much of a pest." The "time was getting right for action," but "Slocum [sic] took up too much of his time without producing any results." Pretending to be sympathetic, Ness volunteered his services. Hughes promised to call him as soon as he was ready "for definite action."[38]

Hughes's slaughtering of Jews did not proceed as planned. In early spring 1936, he decided to postpone the hangings until after the November presidential elections. William Dudley Pelley was running for president, and while Hughes never expected him to win, he believed the Silver Shirt leader would enflame anti-Semitic hatred by exposing Roosevelt as the tool of manipulative Jews such as Bernard Baruch and Felix Frankfurter. "There will be a lot of disgruntled people after the election," Hughes told Slocombe and Allen, and disgruntled people "will act quicker than all others." Until then, Hughes instructed his East Coast allies "to carry on the organizing and await further instruction."[39]

When it came to dealing with Hermann Schwinn, Hughes's patience had worn thin. Schwinn's promised handpicked group never materialized. The Nazi crowd "are wanting to back us," Hughes complained, but "they are afraid to do anything. I told them that they were too contented with their beer and memories of Hitler's coming to power to do anything in this country."[40]

Hughes misread the cause for Schwinn's reluctance. It was not cowardice that stopped him and his men from participating in the assassination plot. Rather they—and Hughes—suspected that Leon Lewis's spies had penetrated their operation; they just did not know who was spying for the Jews and did not wish to risk being arrested for murder until the identity of the traitors could be discovered. "There are still spies in some organizations," Hughes told Slocombe and Allen in early February, "but thank God there are none in ours." Cautioning against overconfidence, Allen warned, "We must watch our step as we proceed, and leave no loopholes to get caught in."[41] Yet, fearing Lewis's reach, they decided to postpone the killings.

Unhappy with the dissolution of his assassination plot, Hughes turned his anger on his most recent recruit. Neil Ness, he told Slocombe, was full of "hot air." Although Ness claimed to have $26,000 in funds, "he hasn't done a thing. If I had that much to work with I'd have every Jew in the country afraid to go out after sundown." Ness "is a dreamer-theorizer like the rest" of the FNG. Hughes boasted that his proclamation drive cost less than $1,000 and "stirred up the biggest smell in this country yet."[42]

Slocombe was not the only one spreading himself too thin. Distracted by a court case and illness, Henry Allen found himself unable to devote his full attention to the Jewish death plots. On December 27, 1935, Allen and his son went to return a shirt at a store owned by Jewish merchant Louis Brinnig. When Mrs. Brinnig explained the shirt had been worn and could not be exchanged, Allen began cursing and was about to slap her when her brother-in-law rushed in to intervene. Allen stumbled and hit his head; his son immediately called an ambulance and had his father taken to a hospital. Although Allen suffered no real injuries, he filed a battery complaint against the Brinnigs, who believed Allen had planned the incident in advance.[43]

Allen turned the case into a national cause célèbre, writing articles in the *Christian Free Press* and *New Gentile* claiming that four Jewish thugs had assaulted him and his son, causing the boy to lose an eye. Only later was it revealed that his son had lost his eye while playing with a sling-shot. Facts aside, Allen received sympathetic notes from Reverend Gerald Winrod and Pennsylvania representative Louis McFadden, the House's leading anti-Semite. That would be his only satisfaction. On February 5, the case of *People v. Brinnig* went to trial in Pasadena Police Court. After listening to all the testimony, the Brinnigs were found not guilty. Unwilling to let matters rest, Allen spent the next three months filing unsuccessful civil damage suits.[44]

The court cases took a toll on Allen's health. In April 1936, while lunching with Schwinn and Ness at Deutsches Haus, Hughes reported that the former San Quentin inmate lay critically ill with blood poisoning at the Pasadena Hospital and had already received three blood transfusions. A month later, Allen was back in the hospital with a diagnosis of tuberculosis of the bone. Hughes suspended all murder plans. Not until Allen began recovering in July did the ANP leader announce his intentions to move forward against the Jews.[45]

With Allen waylaid by illness, Ingram Hughes relied more heavily than ever on Chuck Slocombe. Despite the ANP leader's earlier suspicions, the Long Beach operative proved himself a hard worker and a dedicated fascist willing to get up at 2:00 a.m. to post copies of the proclamation around the city. When Schwinn asked about Slocombe that summer, Hughes reassured him that the Long Beach man was a trustworthy addition to the cause. "A nice fine tall young fellow that Slocum [*sic*]," Hughes gushed. "He's big and husky; an ex-college athlete. And he is one of the best workers in the party. One of the finest men I have."[46]

His confidence in Slocombe restored, Hughes revealed a new wrinkle in his planned pogroms that summer. In addition to the hangings, he would form a fake fumigation and rat removal company. Instead of using the normal chemicals, his fake firm would drop cyanide into an acid solution and, using hoses and portable blowers, inject the poisonous gas into Jewish homes and synagogues. This would "kill them instantly," and thousands would be "strangled to death at once . . . women . . . children Jews of all sorts . . . Exterminated like rats, that is the way to get rid of them."[47]

A month later, while discussing possible leaks concerning the pogroms, a reinvigorated Henry Allen, out of the hospital and back to action, turned to Slocombe and confessed, "I suspect everyone at first. I even suspected you until I investigated your Klan record . . . and when I conferred with Hughes I knew you were alright. I even investigated where you have the boat business and found you were a regular."[48]

Slocombe had passed the test. Neil Ness was not so lucky. He had been playing a far more dangerous game, quietly pitting Nazi rivals against one another. But he had overplayed his hand. When Hughes met Slocombe at his apartment in late August, he told him that Allen and Schwinn were convinced Ness was part of the "Jew secret service."[49] A traitor was in their midst. Something had to be done to send a message. Ness was in danger. The Nazi cohort had warned him that any traitors discovered at Deutsches Haus would meet the same fate: instant death.

12.

Nazi versus Nazi

While attending a weekly drilling in March, Neil Ness overheard storm troopers discussing plans to "clean out the Jews in America." He approached Dr. Konrad Burchardi and casually mentioned what he had overheard. "I didn't know you were planning any new attack upon the Jews." Burchardi looked at him, laughed, and replied, "That will be fun, won't it?"[1]

Ness needed to act quickly to protect himself and the city's Jews. He had observed a growing desire for action among local Nazis ever since Hitler had violated the Treaty of Versailles agreement by marching his troops into the previously demilitarized Rhineland earlier that month. As the only American moderately trusted by Hermann Schwinn and Georg Gyssling, Ness set out to destroy the local Hitler movement by turning the Bund against the German consul, and then turning rival factions within the Bund against each other. But Ness was playing a dangerous game. He knew storm troopers such as Willi Kendzia and Willi Sachse would carry out their threat to execute anyone who betrayed them.

Having spent considerable time at Deutsches Haus talking to a wide variety of Bund members, Ness learned they were still bitterly divided over the best ways to attract Americans to National Socialism. Ness used those divisions to his advantage. "For the past few weeks," Agent N2 wrote Lewis in late March, "I have been working on widening the breach between the self-styled bosses at the Haus." On one side stood militants who advocated a more aggressive anti-Semitic course of action and were disgusted with Schwinn's seeming passivity. They were led by Camouflage Committee chair Rafael Demmler and included Reinhold

Kusche, the storm trooper leader who worked with Ness on the *California Weckruf*; Willi Sachse, deputy storm trooper head who fled Germany after killing two Communists in 1923; Franz Ferenz, the Bund's chief propagandist; Dr. Konrad Burchardi, known as "Scarface" because of the livid slash across his cheek; and "several members of the storm troop that Kusche can influence."[2]

On the other side of the increasingly bitter divide were Hermann Schwinn and those who counseled a more moderate anti-Semitic policy: *California Weckruf* editor Paul Lehman and a number of other Deutsches Haus players.

Both sides, however, remained united in their hatred of Georg Gyssling. Bund leaders regularly sent blistering letters to party officials in Berlin, insisting the new consul was neither sufficiently militant in his anti-Semitism nor duly respectful of their efforts on behalf of the Reich. Burchardi, Gyssling's personal physician, was "one of the main agitators against the local German Consul, hoping that the Consul would be recalled and that he would be appointed in his stead." Before returning to Germany in 1937 to take a government post, Burchardi complained to Ernst Bohle, who oversaw the Nazi Party's Auslands-Organisation, that Gyssling "may be doing things correctly as per old diplomatic usage, but what he needs is two years service in the German Storm Troop organization in order to teach him honest and real national socialism." Like Burchardi, Hermann Schwinn believed he would make a far better consul and "intrigued against Gyssling to accomplish that objective."[3]

No one was better positioned to act as an agent provocateur than Neil Ness, for he worked more closely with Schwinn and Gyssling than any of Lewis's previous spies. Equally importantly, he understood Schwinn's true nature. The West Coast führer appeared genial in public, but at Deutsches Haus his authoritarian nature and vicious lust for power struck many as ineffective leadership, turning former friends into enemies.

By the mid-1930s, as news of Hitler's militaristic intentions and mounting persecution of Jews spread throughout the world, the city's German community was divided over the Bund's efforts to import National Socialism to the United States. The same people who rallied around *Deutschtum* during the German-American Alliance trial in February 1934 turned against the Nazi cohort two years later after Rafael Demmler, the Steuben Society's president, began purging the organization of "all Jews and those German-Americans with liberal tendencies."[4] Disdainful of the Nazi cohort, Turnverein leaders expelled them from their hall in February 1936, forcing them to move to far more costly quarters in a rundown neighborhood on West Fifteenth Street known as Automobile Row. Schwinn converted part of the massive multi-use building into a huge auditorium that could seat 700 people for meetings or to watch Nazi films and newsreels that Franz Ferenz imported from Germany. The front of the building housed the Aryan Bookstore, and the rear contained offices for Bund officials.

Despite their initial disappointment, moving to their own facility offered the Bund an opportunity to attract new members by providing the city's Germans with a festive place where they could drink, dine, and dance in Deutsches Haus's main attraction: a carefully reconstructed German *Gast Stube* (restaurant) and old-fashioned *Bierwirtschaft* (beer pub) where waitresses dressed in brightly colored German costumes rushed about, bringing patrons their orders. The room's wooden tables were covered with red-and-blue-checked cloths, and its walls were adorned with large travel posters advertising Germany's

Hermann Schwinn Standing Outside Deutches Haus, July 1936
USC Libraries Special Collection

scenic beauties. And calmly watching over everything, standing by the bar or sitting at a table in the rear, was Hermann Schwinn.[5]

The restaurant and beer hall were an instant success, except for one thing. Schwinn's visions of grandeur had led him to overspend on construction; incoming revenues were not enough to offset the growing debt. Ness hoped to use the financial crisis at Deutsches Haus to bring down the local Nazi apparatus. Sales from the Deutsches Haus bar and restaurant averaged $50 ($855 in 2015 dollars) a day, but due to poor management and the refusal of anti-Nazi German societies to rent space in their building, the Haus quickly ran up a debt of $2,000 ($34,200 in 2015 dollars). Several Bund diehards suspected the debt was not entirely due to mismanagement or a lack of revenue-producing activities.

Catching a ride home with Neil Ness after a late-night meeting in mid-March, Deutsches Haus bartender Peter Klein warned the American to stay away from the Nazis: "I know you are a good fellow and I don't want to see you get in trouble but take it from me these Nazis are no good." Surprised by the unexpected outburst, Ness drove them to the Circle Café on Fifth Street, where over drinks Klein startled him again by revealing that despite receiving $60 a month for running Deutsches Haus operations, Schwinn was "pilfering the cash register and had been cheating on the Haus right along."[6]

Inside Deutsches Haus: Deutsches Haus Restaurant
Jewish Federation Council of Greater Los Angeles, Community Relations Committee Collection, Part 2, Special Collections and Archives, Oviatt Library, California State University, Northridge

Christmas Ball at Deutsches Haus Auditorium
National Archives, College Park, MD.

Several days later, Peter Klein went to Ness's home and told him he had been fired for complaining about the bounced checks Schwinn had given him. This was precisely the kind of information Ness could use to stoke greater outrage among Schwinn's opponents. At the same time, he hoped to earn Schwinn's loyalty by alerting him to the various plots to remove him from office.

THE ART OF THE DOUBLE CROSS

Ness began his double-cross operation by urging Rafael Demmler to wrest control of the Bund from Schwinn. A former chauffeur who boasted of seducing clients' wives, Demmler believed he could revitalize the Nazi movement in Los Angeles. "We have counted those whom we could feel sure would stand by us loyally . . . toward a revolutionary coup," Ness reported in mid-March. To steel Demmler for battle, Ness revealed he had discussed a palace coup with the German consul. "Dr. Gyssling promises us support financially and morally but he would remain in the background."[7]

Gyssling was willing to help Demmler and Ness because he loathed Schwinn and because Ness came to him with the best of references. While living on the East Coast, Ness had become friendly with German ambassador Hans Luther. When the diplomat learned that the American engineer was moving to Los Angeles, he asked him to visit his "very dear friend," Dr. Georg Gyssling. Ness did, "and through Dr. Gyssling I became acquainted with the German House."[8] As far as Gyssling was concerned, any friend of Luther's was at least a potential friend of his.

In early April, with Schwinn in Buffalo attending the Bund's first national convention, Ness met Demmler at Gyssling's office to plot the local führer's removal. Wasting no time, Ness told Gyssling he needed $200 cash to buy the Deutsches Haus lease from the landlord and fire Schwinn as its manager. Gyssling was intrigued: "I would like to have the Deutsches Haus [under my control] and see the present element out of there." Yet the consul was worried that if the money was ever traced back to him, it would get him into trouble with American and German authorities. Ness suggested the diplomat could avoid any potential blowback by giving them "a personal loan." When Ness assured Gyssling that he could obtain the lease and keep the loan a secret, Gyssling agreed to help: "You can count on me. But we must keep it confidential."[9]

As any good spy knows, even the most careful plans can go awry. Later that evening, when Ness telephoned Gyssling at home, the consul told him he had changed his mind. "You probably did not know," he explained, "that if you take over the *Haus*, Schwinn will undoubtedly go to jail." Many people had loaned Schwinn money from their personal accounts, and if he failed to pay them back, they would "charge him with receiving money under false pretenses" and Schwinn would wind up in jail.[10] If that happened, and the German community imploded on his watch, the consul would undoubtedly be recalled, especially given the number of complaints that had been sent to Berlin. Despite his loathing of Schwinn, Gyssling had to be careful.

Uncertain what to do after Gyssling's change of heart, Ness contacted Lewis, "who advised me to drop the whole matter and proceed to Schwinn with the information as though I was being used for some inside politics." Following Lewis's suggestion, Ness informed the Bund head that a group was trying to take Deutsches Haus away from him. "I was invited in," he said, "but managed to break it up." The grateful but suspicious leader responded, "O.K. N—— I can't tell you how glad I am that you came but tell me why do you believe I am right and they are wrong?" Thinking quickly, the undercover operative explained that his "adherence to the *Führerprinzip*" (unquestioning obedience to the leader) convinced him that anyone working "for their own aggrandizement was not working for the good of the organization."[11] Ness's answer and actions won him Schwinn's gratitude and, for the moment, eased any suspicions that he was a spy.

Worried about his own career, Gyssling tried brokering a peace between the city's warring German communities. He convinced Schwinn and German American League leader Philip Lenhardt, one of the plaintiffs in the German-American Alliance trial, to "bury the hatchet" and work together for the good of Germany. Meeting at a downtown hotel, Bund and Alliance leaders eased longstanding tensions by drinking "a lot of beer" and offering numerous toasts "to the Fatherland and to unity of *Deutschtum* in America." By the end of the evening, Schwinn and Lenhardt had struck an accord. In exchange for the German American League agreeing to move into Deutsches Haus and provide much-needed funds, Schwinn "promised to go slow on the Jew-baiting part of their program in order not to offend some of the more conservative members of the other German organizations." When the Bund leader made this promise, Ness noted, "he snickered, and most of the others laughed out loud."[12]

UNDOING THE PEACE

Gyssling's brokered peace revived the Bund's fortunes. By the end of April 1936, Deutsches Haus attendance had increased 150 percent, and its financial health had improved considerably. In an arrangement of convenience rather than conviction, "Schwinn and the Consul reached a new accord in their relationship." Insisting he was acting "for the benefit of the Third Reich," Gyssling agreed to recognize Schwinn "as the real leader of the German-Americans in this district" and acknowledged that the Bund "had done more for the New Germany than any other German Society here." At the end of the month, the two men met at the consulate and publicly proclaimed themselves "the best of friends."[13]

In private, however, both Germans maintained their mutual dislike. During a reception aboard the German battleship *Karlsruhe*, Gyssling treated Schwinn "with a marked degree of reserve," but was "more than cordial" to Neil Ness and his wife, Esther. He invited the couple on board the ship but left Schwinn standing on the dock, an affront that "much displeased" the Bund leader. Schwinn returned the snub the next week at a celebration of Hitler's birthday, when he left the consul standing in the auditorium wings for thirty minutes and then walked off the stage without introducing him, a slight that "very much chagrined" the diplomat.[14]

Spies need luck as well as skill. Due to Hermann Schwinn's cheapness, Ness became his driver, confidant, and, as much as any American could be, his right-hand man. From March until the fall of 1936, the two men spent practically every day together, largely because the perpetually impoverished Nazi complained that his car never worked. "I had a new car," Ness recounted, "and I would drive him about, and he would use my car whenever he wanted to go places."[15] Anytime a German ship came into the harbor at Los Angeles, Ness drove Schwinn to the docks. Along the way, the loose-tongued Bund leader would update him on the various rivalries within the Haus, as well as his continued loathing for Gyssling.

Schwinn saw Ness as a soft touch. Believing him a man of means—for how else could he afford to drive a car and work for no pay?—he constantly hit him up for small "loans" that were never repaid. When Schwinn felt a need to vacation at Mammoth Lake, he borrowed $25 ($428 in 2015 dollars) from his good friend Ness.[16] Grateful for the money, Schwinn left orders that the American be given the run of Deutsches Haus and that all visitors should be referred to him. No Lewis spy had ever been so trusted.

Ness and Lewis considered the loans and frequent trips to the docks an excellent investment. During his many chauffeuring forays, Ness witnessed massive amounts of propaganda and money being funneled through Los Angeles ports and then distributed by the Bund across the entire country. Like John Schmidt before him, Ness observed vessel captains handing Schwinn sealed packages with orders from Berlin, and saw the Bund head slip documents covered in red sealing wax to captains, exclaiming, "Here are the reports." And, on more than one occasion, he watched his seeming friend get so drunk while exchanging toasts onboard ship that "I had to carry Schwinn and he slept on my shoulder all of the trip in from the harbor to the Deutsches Haus."[17]

That April, Ness also discovered that party officials in Berlin were unhappy with the Los Angeles Bund. During one trip to the docks, Prince Kurt zur Lippe, the German-born undergraduate who recruited Nazi supporters at the University of Southern California, informed him that every German ship carried several officers who were members of the Nazi Party. The officers Lippe talked to "were entirely dissatisfied with the behavior of the Swastika leaders here" and intended to file an unfavorable report that would go "direct to the party headquarters in Germany and it is expected that the party will discipline the leaders of the western division of the friends of new Germany here."[18]

Ness's efforts at sowing discord had proven fruitful; news of tensions in Los Angeles had made their way to Berlin. A month later, Nazi officials ordered Tony Kerner, Paul Kendzia, and Hans Diebel, rumored to be a member of the German secret service, to return to Germany on "official business," undoubtedly to explain the local situation to unhappy party leaders.[19]

Lippe also delivered news that was not so welcome. Schwinn had recently complained to him "that N—— is a fine fellow but full of bunk." Ness assured Lewis he did not believe it and thought Lippe was jealous of his friendship with Schwinn. Yet Ness was not naive. "If Schwinn actually feels about me as Lippe says, it is quite probable that my effectiveness at the Deutsches Haus will be diminished greatly on that account."[20]

Ness was not the only member of his family under suspicion. Neil and Esther Ness were attending a dinner for the *Karlsruhe* crew at Deutsches Haus when Nazi sympathizer and bishop Albert Dunston Bell turned to her and asked, "I noticed Mrs. N—— that you were taking notes during my last lecture here. I wonder if you would be so kind as to furnish me with a copy of the notes you took." Quick on her feet, Esther explained that she "took notes only so that Mr. N—— could review them after your lecture." Apologizing, she explained, "I'm afraid that I may have put them in with other papers that have since been thrown away."[21] Bell was unconvinced.

Knowing that Ness's days as an effective spy might be numbered, Lewis began laying the groundwork for government action against Schwinn and his minions. They hoped to defeat the Nazis by revoking the citizenship papers of their leaders and deporting them to Germany. On Friday, July 10, 1936, Ness traveled to the downtown office of an old friend, Walter E. Carr, the district director of naturalization and immigration. The two had known each other for eight years, and Ness believed Carr a man "devoted to the duties of his office." During the course of their two-hour conversation, Ness explained that he had been tracking the activities of local Bund leaders, and "at least half of these Nazis are in the United States illegally." After listening to Ness, Carr responded, "Sounds like they want to bring Hitler over here," to which his friend answered, "They would like nothing better. But the thing that aggravates me so much is their allegiance to Germany and their contempt for everything American while at the same time they proclaim American citizenship."[22]

When Carr asked if he had come across any threats of violence, Ness snapped back, "I should say I have and on innumerable occasions." He described in vivid detail many threats and plots by Schwinn and his allies. Unlike other government officials Lewis had contacted, Carr immediately promised to assign one of his men "on an undercover basis." The immigration official then suggested something Lewis and Ness had hoped for: "You know if these fellows aren't careful we can take their citizenship away from them." Carr asked Ness to provide him with as much written information about Bund members as he could.[23]

Ness promised to stay in touch and left the office. Two weeks later, he was back. After reading through the documents Ness brought him, Carr concluded that "the activities of Hermann Schwinn and others at the Haus are such as to warrant the revoking of their citizenship papers which eventually will lead to their deportation." In addition to assigning his own agent, Carr promised to notify the Justice Department so "he could have their cooperation in his investigation" and ensure that everything outside of his department's jurisdiction would be covered. He also promised to persuade Justice officials to assign an undercover operative to the case.[24]

In the meantime, Ness continued working closely with local Nazis, acting as though nothing had happened. At Lewis's request, Ness also succeeded in ingratiating himself with Ingram Hughes and Henry Allen. Ness visited Hughes's apartment several times that July, volunteering his services to work on the latest proclamation while discreetly looking around for incriminating evidence. When he spotted two official-looking letters with German postmarks, Ness said casually, "I didn't know you had definite connections with the Nazi party there." Without revealing too much, Hughes replied, "Well they supply me with information from time to time."[25]

Whatever suspicions they may have harbored, the Nazis still considered Ness one of their own. At a special meeting in early July, Neil Howard Ness and four other men were formally initiated into the Bund. After beginning the ceremony in German, Schwinn repeated his initiation speech in English. Welcoming the new members, the Nazi *Gauleiter* reminded them of their two key obligations: "First to fight for the cause of our Fatherland in all its relations with other nations; Second to work for a close union between our Fatherland and our adopted country, the United States." As de facto members of the Third Reich, they were expected "to give all that you can in this cause." When the time for action arrived, "we expect you to give all. Your blood or your life whichever may be necessary."[26]

After a round of Heil Hitlers, an excited Schwinn read "personal greetings from Adolph [sic] Hitler" thanking them "for the work being carried on by the Western Division" of the Bund. "At this point," Ness recounted, "there was an outburst of applause from the fifty-six members present."[27]

CRISES AND SUBTERFUGE

By the end of July 1936, Ness's efforts at pitting Nazi against Nazi appeared to be for naught. Schwinn gained much-needed revenues by convincing the German American League, Silver Shirts, Black Legion, and several smaller fascist groups to meet and dine at Deutsches Haus. Los Angeles primary elections slated for late August offered Schwinn an opportunity to garner greater legitimacy and additional funds for the Bund. Fourteen political hopefuls, assured by Schwinn that "there is no such thing as a Nazi in America," spoke to a gathering of 300 men and women at Deutsches Haus and praised the German community for their fight against communism. Anxious for their votes, they also professed their love for Germany and admiration for the Bund. With the formal part of the evening over, the crowd remained in Deutsches Haus drinking and dancing until the early-morning hours.[28]

By speaking at Bund headquarters, politicians solidified Schwinn's position as leader of the city's German community. Two months later, pleased GOP officials asked Schwinn to chair the German American section of the Southern California Campaign Committee. They promised to give him a well-paying patronage job if he could deliver the German vote.[29]

The GOP's courting of Schwinn proved far less troubling to Leon Lewis than the fact that several Bund members were working in government agencies. That summer, deputy storm trooper leader Willi Sachse, rumored to be a member of the German secret service, took a job with the U.S. Secret Service in San Francisco. Equally troubling, Rafael Demmler, the man Ness hoped would replace Schwinn, had just returned from two weeks' training at a California National Guard camp and told Ness he wanted to obtain a full-time military commission. In the meantime, his position with the 251st Coast Artillery, Battery F, allowed him to gather information about Pacific Coast military defenses. Anticipating what they would do in case of war between Germany and the United States, Bundists were preparing "various methods of sabotaging any war effort by the destruction of municipal water works, industrial water systems and other things."[30]

Schwinn's fortunes and those of the city's Nazis appeared to be on the upswing. But suddenly everything changed, and the Bund seemed to be disintegrating. In late July, Schwinn called an emergency meeting to discuss the renewed financial crisis. Despite the influx of cash from new tenants, Deutsches Haus had a cash balance of $3.47, and creditors were pressuring Schwinn to pay long-overdue bills.[31] Attendance at the restaurant and beer hall had dropped after neighbors complained about "disorderly conduct" by patrons who "got drunk and would sing all hours of the night."[32]

As finances worsened, Schwinn again came under attack for mismanagement. "It looks fishy to me," Reinhold Kusche complained. "For the past three months every man in this outfit has been shelling out only to find that someway every cent we take in is spent in some mysterious fashion." When storm trooper John Tippre accused him of managing the Haus in a "lousy way," Schwinn lost his temper. "You can have this damn job and the $60 [$1,035 in 2015 dollars] a month it pays. I'm through with the whole bunch of you, good night." As Schwinn stalked out of the room in a huff, a disgusted Tippre cried out, "He can kiss my ass until he is a damn sight madder."[33]

Following Schwinn's abrupt exit, Hans Meyerhoffer, the tough Berlin agent sent four months earlier to get the Nazis into order, delivered the evening's most blistering criticisms and threats. "I will try once more to straighten you up and if it does not work this time then we will transfer the Western headquarters to San Francisco," he said. Insisting that he "had too much trouble with this bunch here already," Meyerhoffer went on to deride the city's German community: "Half of the people you call German in this town are not Germans at all; they are simply a bunch of Jew lovers and lackeys to a system and we don't want that kind of people." Before sitting down, the Berlin Nazi issued a final warning: "One more meeting like this and you are all through."[34]

Much to Ness's delight, the fragile truce between Schwinn, Gyssling, and the German community unraveled even more over the summer. Hitler had spent years planning to use the 1936 Berlin Olympics to show the world the magnificence of the Third Reich. But when the Bund delegation went to the Los Angeles Coliseum on August 1 to attend ceremonies honoring the opening of the Berlin games, they were infuriated to discover the Olympic Committee was flying the old German flag of black, red, and gold instead of the swastika flag. "Dr. Gyssling was cursed vilely and roundly" by Schwinn and his entourage for not protesting the swastika's absence. Schwinn, Meyerhoffer, and Willi Kendzia filed a formal complaint with Nazi headquarters in Berlin, insisting that Gyssling's failure to ensure the flying of the swastika was "a direct insult to the German nation."[35] Although a grievance from Schwinn might elicit only a modest response, one signed by Meyerhoffer would certainly attract attention.

Paranoia struck the Deutsches Haus that summer when Schwinn's inner circle met to discuss the presence of five suspected Jewish spies within their organization. Ness suggested they "keep them under observation and learn their business"; he volunteered to question all suspects. What Ness did not know was that he, too, was under suspicion. During a meeting at Henry Allen's Pasadena home in mid-August, Chuck Slocombe listened to the ex-convict denounce "this fellow Ness that is the official hand-shaker and information seeker at the Friends." Ness "always wants to know what is going on," and asked so many questions that "Schwinn and Hughes are suspicious of him."[36]

Suspicious or not, Schwinn asked Ness to drive him and their recently arrived Austrian guest Willi Schneeberger to San Diego in late August 1936 for a special meeting at the home of Count Ernst Ulrich von Bülow, a Nazi operative suspected of passing information to German and Japanese spies. Stopping in Los Angeles on his way to Japan, Schneeberger held a number of "very secret conferences" at the home of Dr. Burchardi, the city's most militant Nazi. A short time later, during a Bund meeting, Schwinn introduced the "very conceited and arrogant" visitor as one of the leaders of the Nazi party in the Austrian Tyrol.[37] After meeting privately with Schneeberger and Schwinn, Ness suspected that the youthful Austrian was a Nazi spy, but remained uncertain of his mission—until the next day.

With numerous military installations and aircraft production facilities located throughout Southern California, Lewis's ace spy kept his eyes open for potential espionage along the vulnerable West Coast. Schneeberger arrived in Los Angeles at a moment when rumors circulated of an upcoming alliance between Germany and Japan. On July 3, 1936, Henry Thomas Thompson, a thirty-year-old former navy yeoman, was convicted in a Los Angeles U.S. district court of stealing "vital secret tactical documents from aboard ships of the U.S. Fleet" and passing them to Toshio Miyasaki, an officer in the Imperial Japanese Navy. Thompson was sentenced to fifteen years in jail. In an editorial chastising military leaders and local defense contractors, the *Los Angeles Times* warned that the spy trial "served as a lesson to a nation whose disregard for ordinary precautions in protecting its military and naval plans and developments has amazed other governments."[38]

Sitting in the backseat of his car and talking with Schneeberger while Schwinn drove, Ness grew increasingly suspicious of the visitor. Convinced the camera-toting Austrian had been sent to investigate defense preparedness along the West Coast, Ness manufactured the most plausible lies he could. When they were ten miles south of Long Beach, he pointed out an area he claimed "was a new coast artillery fort and that the U.S. War Department was putting in some very new and modern high caliber coast artillery disappearing guns."[39]

In fact, Ness knew the land was being developed for a potential golf course. "After I had finished imparting this bit of imagination to Schneeberger he became quite excited and spoke to Schwinn very rapidly and in German." After hearing the Berlin agent mention something "about photographs," Ness knew he had fallen for the trap. When Schneeberger asked where he had received the information, Ness explained that a friend in the War Department was supervising the building of a string of new forts up and down the Pacific Coast. This was another lie.[40]

Convinced they had made a discovery that would thrill their superiors in Germany, Schwinn pulled off onto the shoulder of the highway and let Schneeberger get out to photograph the area. After taking shots looking out to sea, he "turned his camera on the clump of trees and very carefully took three exposures of the 'fort.'"[41]

When they arrived at Bülow's San Diego home, the German count welcomed the Austrian visitor "as one would greet a friend of long standing." Lewis knew Bülow conferred with every important Nazi and fascist leader who traveled through Southern California, and that he was funding Ingram Hughes's operation. He also suspected that the mysterious German who met with Nazi Party officials in Berlin every year was operating a spy ring from his San Diego base. Chuck Slocombe, who visited the place months earlier, had warned that Bülow's hilltop home enabled him to "see every move made by the Navy, the Marines, the fleet and the air base. He has the most strategic location in Southern

California." The count, Slocombe concluded, "is in the pay of the German government."[42]

Following an exchange of pleasantries with his host, Schneeberger asked to see the navy destroyer base in San Diego Harbor. After receiving permission to enter the base, the three men spent half an hour going through the yards; Schneeberger was able to take several pictures without being questioned. Afterward, as they drove along the shoreline, the Nazi "took several additional pictures of Naval vessels lying out in the harbor." Later that night Ness chauffeured the two men to the grounds of the California Exposition, where they spent the evening watching "a bevy of beautiful women who performed in the nude. This attracted Schneeberger's finer and more spiritual senses."[43]

By the time they headed back to Los Angeles, Ness was convinced the Nazi visitor was "connected with a German Espionage System if not an outright member of such an organization." In fact, he hoped Schneeberger was a spy. Believing he had obtained vital information about Pacific Coast defenses, the youthful Austrian cut short his trip and headed straight to Japan, taking his photographs with him.[44] The Lewis-Ness operation had momentarily foiled Nazi and Japanese plans for intelligence gathering.

NESS EXPOSED

Ness's triumph was short-lived. Henry Allen's charge that Ness was a member of the "Jew secret service" gained greater credibility in mid-September after *California Weckruf* editor Paul Lehman published "A Letter to My Good Friend 'Philo,'" accusing Ness of writing articles for the *Jewish Community Press* under the pen name Philo.[45] The undercover operative had been too clever for his own good. During the spring of 1936, he wrote a regular column for the *Weckruf* under the pseudonym "Ina Sniggle." As he explained to Leon Lewis, he chose the pen name because "when interpreted means in a trap . . . The column was written only because I had been trapped into writing it."[46]

Ness had greatly underestimated the intelligence of the Nazi leadership. Several days earlier, he published an article, "Mr. Pelley Comes to Town," in the *Jewish Community Press* recounting the Silver Shirt leader's recent speech at Deutsches Haus. Ness switched pseudonyms for Jewish and Nazi publications, but he never altered his style. Lehman was certain Ness wrote the Pelley piece because he employed the same unusual phrases, such as "waxes forth," that he used in his *Weckruf* articles. Schwinn agreed and remarked that the column contained information "that only three or four of us knew about and naturally that made us wonder where that came from."[47]

Rather than become defensive, Ness tried bluffing his way out of the situation. Two days after Lehman's accusatory piece, the undercover spy returned to Deutsches Haus to confront Schwinn about the scurrilous attack on his loyalty. Schwinn tried placating the angry American. "Well I hope there won't be any hard feelings. I'm sure everything will come out all right." To which Ness responded, "It better come out all right because I'm going to see that it does." Suspecting the end was near, Ness lined up as many allies among the anti-Schwinn contingent as possible. When he visited Reinhold Kusche that evening to explain what had happened, the surprised storm trooper leader promised to "stand by me to see that I was given a square deal."[48]

Confronting Lehman and Schwinn the following afternoon, Ness denied being Philo and vowed to "make so much noise" about their false accusations "that it will bounce up to Berlin." When he returned to Deutsches Haus two days later, Ness found the pair, who "seemed a bit chagrined over my presence," deep in conversation. After Ness demanded to be cleared of all charges, Schwinn again tried to mollify the journalist: "I'm satisfied that you are not Philo and I will make a public statement to that effect." When Ness asked why he was so certain, Schwinn explained how, after further investigation, he concluded the articles were "the work of some very well organized group," and named Leon Lewis as "the brains behind everything that is going on here." When Ness asked who Leon Lewis was, Schwinn spat out, "Well he has been a pain in our neck ever since we were first organized here. He is the one who has carried on the activities against us." Ness replied, "Do you believe that I am a member of that group?" and the Nazi answered, "No I do not . . . I am satisfied to take your word for that."[49]

Ness, however, was not satisfied. "You want me to drop the entire matter, but you are not willing to erase the stigma that you have placed me under," he said, feigning outrage, and volunteered to clear his name by finding out Philo's true identity.[50] Schwinn and Meyerhoffer accepted his offer.

Despite Schwinn's apology, Ness knew he was no longer trusted: "Insofar as my status at the *Haus* is concerned, I believe that as long as Schwinn and Lehman are the leaders they will do everything in their power to keep me out." Determined to foment as much discord as possible, he spent several hours discussing the Philo matter with storm troopers Joe Schnuck, John Ericksen, John Tippre, and John Haas. "Each stated emphatically that they believed in me." A furious Schnuck denounced Schwinn, claiming he "was lazy and working for his own gain rather than for the good of the organizing." Tippre and Haas "took this same stand against Schwinn."[51]

The men were true to their word. When Ness arrived at the Haus the following week, Haas, an "ex-heavyweight pugilist," pulled him aside and confided overhearing fellow storm troopers planning to jump Ness in the parking lot and beat the hell out of him—or worse. Haas would not reveal their names, but promised that if anyone tried to harm Ness, "he would be on hand to assist me in the fight." The steely-nerved spy went through his normal Haus routine and, though expecting a fight, soon realized it would not happen that day.[52]

Although fearing for his life, Ness refused to back down. Acting as an agent provocateur yet again, he drove with Glenn Duke to Rafael Demmler's home to discuss the best way to unseat Schwinn. After composing a list of Bund members they trusted, Duke bid adieu and returned home. This gave Ness the opportunity to prod Demmler into action. As they sat around planning the next move, Demmler explained that his Mondays were now taken with National Guard duty. Sensing a change in the Nazi since they first met, Ness seized the opportunity to appeal to Demmler's recently discovered sense of Americanism:

NESS: I've always felt very close to you on account of your patriotism for the U.S. Now Rafael I think you are more American
than German; isn't that so?

DEMMLER: That's correct my friend.

NESS: Still you are a German also; yet you don't get along with
Schwinn or Burchardi or anyone of the leading Nazis.

DEMMLER: Listen Neil, the only thing that gang has against me is
because I'm against the swastika flag waving. I came here to
the States when I was pretty much a kid. I played with American kids; I went to American schools and I believe first in
America but Schwinn and Burchardi and the rest of that gang
don't feel that way about it, so they claim I am not a German.
All right then I'm an American and they can go to hell . . .

NESS: Then you feel as I do; that is, that the 'Friends' is not an
American organization.

DEMMLER: They most certainly are not American. You know Neil, the more I think of it the more I believe that [Rep. Samuel] Dickstein was right. Why if I was a member of Military Intelligence I would investigate those—myself.

NESS: Well, isn't that quite a change in your viewpoint? You always were so much against Jews.

DEMMLER: Perhaps it is a change in my viewpoint. But I was never against any Jew like Schwinn or the rest of those guys are. That's all they can think of but I believe that any Jew has as much a right to love and enjoy the pursuit of happiness as I have. But I am against any group that wants to control the world.

NESS: Then you would be against any group, Jewish or non-Jewish, that could be considered exploiters of men?

DEMMLER: That's it exactly.[53]

This was an unexpected opportunity. Instead of pitting two groups of militant Nazis against each other, Ness now had a chance to unseat Schwinn and replace him with the self-professed American patriot. When Demmler confessed that his military service was "all I live for," Ness promised to use his influence to secure him a commission in the regular army. "If you can help me get an appointment," Demmler said, "I'll be your slave for life."[54]

Having set Nazi against Nazi, Ness continued his efforts to initiate government action against their leaders. The day after Lehman's accusatory column, Ness visited Walter Carr. The immigration official explained that his department had now listed the Bund as a subversive group. He wanted to "put the Deutsches Haus and its leaders completely out of business," but under present laws "he could do nothing about the matter whatsoever."[55] Unable to do more at the moment, Carr promised to look into Schwinn's citizenship status, a request that would pay off months later.

On October 20, 1936, Ness paid his final visit to Deutsches Haus to confront Schwinn and the Bund leadership about the Philo matter. After announcing he had discovered Philo's true identity, Ness refused to reveal anything more. "It would be foolish for me to give you fellows any information whatever. I feel quite positively that you fellows here haven't enough intelligence to use it properly . . . When you are dumb enough to pull the stunt that you did in the Philo matter you are dumb enough to use my good information to a disadvantage." In a final effort to generate more paranoia, Ness suggested that the real culprits are "three little dyed-in-the-wool and made-in-Germany boys in your own organization." When a worried Schwinn asked who they were, Ness responded, "You go to Hell . . . I'm a busy man. So I'll be on my way fellows and see you sometime in the far future."[56] And then he left.

Ness was not the only one to leave the Bund on an angry note. That same day, after a heated argument with Schwinn, John Tippre, who had pledged to stand at Ness's side in case of violence, resigned his position and withdrew from the Haus, as did his sons.[57] Having a well-respected family quit the Bund was a small but significant victory for Lewis's agent.

Ness's time as a favored American member of the Bund had ended, but his spying did not. Knowing how effective his agent had been, Leon Lewis asked him to infiltrate several of the city's most prominent anti-Semitic fascist groups: the American Warriors, the National Protective Order of Gentiles, the Civilian Army of American Bluecoats, and the Immigration Restriction League. Within two months of joining the American Warriors, a militant organization that was building "an army of men who can handle a rifle to actively fight communism" and the Jewish menace, the smooth-talking Ness was appointed its national director of Americanization. After Carl Kron, the group's leader, confided that Hitlerites "have a right to be against the Jews" and that it would "not be long before Jew-baiting will be a national pastime in America," Ness decided it was time to bring the group to its knees. He accumulated evidence of their illegal schemes and racketeering operations and sent it to the U.S. collector of internal revenue and to the Los Angeles Department of Social Service. The American Warriors soon folded.[58]

Lewis wished Neil Ness could have remained an active member of the Bund's inner circle, but he was delighted with his achievements. Within a year, Ness had widened the divisions within the Bund, as well as between Schwinn and Gyssling. He fed the German and Japanese governments false information about West Coast defense installations. He succeeded in getting the U.S. Department of Immigration and Naturalization and the Justice Department to investigate Schwinn and his Nazi cohort. He put the American Warriors out of business. And, in a final act, he alerted government officials to the various plots being planned by Ingram Hughes and Henry Allen.

A week before his final fallout with Schwinn, Ness had lunch with Allen's probation officer and told him all about Allen and Hughes's "plots to inflict physical violence on certain public officials including District Attorney Buron Fitts." He warned the probation officer that Allen, Hughes, and their latest recruit, Silver Shirt leader Kenneth Alexander, planned "to throw stench bombs and other gas bombs into certain courtrooms and offices where-ever any protagonist of democracy and opponent of Hilterism might be located." Allen's probation officer asked Ness to prepare a full report that could be used against the trio.[59]

Ness's actions succeeded in foiling the stench-bomb plan. But Chuck Slocombe soon uncovered a far more frightening plot for mass murder. Hughes, Allen, and Alexander had devised yet another plan to execute Hollywood Jews. If they succeeded, many of the movie industry's most prominent leaders would die. Studio heads had provided Lewis with a budget of $15,000 ($257,000 in 2015 dollars) for 1936.[60] The spymaster understood there could be no greater proof of the value of his operation than to foil a death plot against the moguls who funded him. Leon Lewis needed to act and act fast, for his name was also on the hit list.

13.

Silver Shirts, Nazis, and Movie Stars

On Saturday night, July 18, 1936, 500 excited Silver Shirts, German American Bundists, and fascists packed into Deutsches Haus to hear Christian Party presidential candidate William Dudley Pelley describe his vision for a new America. Marching to the stage dressed in "leather boots, blue breeches, a revolver belt, gray soft shirt with a red letter 'L' over the left breast, a brownish gray goatee under a weak mouth, and the red rimmed eyes of the chronic imbiber," Pelley opened his speech by proclaiming, "I am for Adolf Hitler and I claim to be the Adolf Hitler of America." Strutting around the platform "like a peacock," the Silver Shirt leader launched into an hour-and-a-half-long anti-Semitic tirade in which he promised that the destructive Jewish influence on American government would end under a Pelley presidency. Once elected, Pelley would "march up the steps at Washington and show them [Jews] that this is still a Christian nation."[1]

As they left Deutsches Haus, few of the enthusiastic audience knew their presidential hopeful had been pleasantly inebriated. Prior to the meeting, he'd spent thirty minutes talking with Neil Ness in Hermann Schwinn's private office. "Pelley had a pint bottle of Old Quaker whiskey which he took from his hip pocket and offered me a drink." Ness declined, but the fascist leader "took three hefty swigs" and promised to "return to Los Angeles with about 2000 Silver Shirts" ready to take whatever action necessary. As they walked onto the stage, Pelley turned the meeting over to his running mate, Willard Kemp, who told the gathered faithful, "The Jews in this country are facing the direst event of their lives. They are on the eve of a pogrom. Do you know what 'pogrom' means? It means—open season on Jews!"[2]

Reflecting on the evening's events, Ness, writing as "Philo" in the *Jewish Community Press*, asked how any sensible person could "be influenced by this man who has no presence, a weasel personality, and little oratorical skill. His speech was a flow of meaningless rhetoric. No two consecutive thoughts. No reason, no truths." But Ness knew the answer. Rationality is not what sways disgruntled voters. Pelley realized he needed to "make but one appeal, give but one cause for every evil, suggest but one cure: The Jew, and finish the Jew."[3]

National and international events of 1936 and 1937, combined with the often-frightening reports he received from Ness and Charles Slocombe, left Leon Lewis with a palpable sense of dread. In May 1936, two months after 30,000 German soldiers marched into the Rhineland, Italy's invading army occupied Ethiopia. On July 17, 1936, General Francisco Franco and his Nationalist army, with support from Hitler and Mussolini, launched a military coup against Spain's democratically elected leftist Republican government; the bloody civil war ended three years later with a fascist victory. Nazi and fascist military aggression was accompanied by outbreaks of deadly violence against Jews throughout Europe, especially in Germany, Poland, and Romania.

Attacks against Jews abroad led to increased calls to murder Jews by Nazis and fascists in Los Angeles and by anti-Semites south of the border. Lewis had learned that Henry Allen and Hermann Schwinn were smuggling guns and propaganda to anti-Semitic Gold Shirts in Mexico. Locally, Pelley's presidential run led Silver Shirts to reopen a branch dedicated to militant action against the Jewish menace.

But there was a ray of hope. Chuck Slocombe had burrowed deep within the city's fascist hierarchy and into the very center of a plot to murder two dozen of Hollywood's most powerful Jews and their supporters. Lewis also received help from a new ally significant enough to draw worldwide attention to the Nazi-fascist threat: the Hollywood Anti-Nazi League. But the stronger the Hollywood activists grew, the more determined their enemies were to do whatever it took to thwart their effectiveness, including murder.

THE REVIVAL OF THE SILVER SHIRTS

Henry Allen was tired of Ingram Hughes's big talk and no action. Early in the summer of 1936, having recovered from his illnesses and hungering for more drastic measures against the Jews, Allen joined with Ken Alexander, the newly appointed head of the California Silver Shirts, in reviving Silver Shirt posts throughout the region. When Chuck Slocombe visited the new Silver Shirts office in early August, Allen invited his trusted ally to join their inner circle. "I've told Alexander all about you so he has no fear to tell you anything or to give you freedom of the office." Before leaving to attend a meeting, Allen introduced Slocombe to Alexander, who immediately "began to rehash the old cry of the perils of Judaism."[4]

Kenneth Alexander seemed a most unlikely man to head the California Silver Shirts. Like William Dudley Pelley, he made a good living from the movie industry but hated the Jewish moguls who employed him. Born Alexander Kenneth Alexander in England in 1887, he apprenticed in a London photographic studio and then trained with prominent portrait photographer Ernest Walter Histed when his family moved to New York in 1903. Tall and slender with blue eyes and light brown hair, Kenneth, as he preferred to be called, gained fame photographing famous actresses. When MGM hired Lillian Gish to star in *La Bohème* (1926), she insisted on bringing him along to shoot publicity stills. Alexander moved to Los Angeles in 1925, and over the next decade worked as a general studio photographer, taking stills, portraits, and costume shots for Samuel Goldwyn, Paramount, Twentieth Century Pictures, United Artists, and MGM. By May 1935 the man the *Los Angeles Times* referred to as "Twentieth Century's ace" cameraman reigned as "one of the highest-paid photographers in the business."[5]

No single event drew Alexander to the Silver Shirts. When the young photographer took out his citizenship papers in 1914, he was enthusiastic about America. But sometime later, as he told Slocombe, he "learned that America was rotten through and through, just as much as England was."[6] While working in Hollywood during the 1930s, the disgruntled photographer became attracted to former screenwriter William Dudley Pelley. By the summer of 1936, he served as Pelley's right-hand man, often traveling from Los Angeles to Asheville, North Carolina, to confer with his boss.

Both men shared a hated for Jews and especially the Hollywood moguls. In their speeches, publications, and flyers, Alexander and Pelley branded Hollywood films as demoralizing and pornographic, and its Jewish studio heads as Communists, rapists, and sexual perverts who defiled Christian women. In an article for the Silver Shirt magazine *Liberation*, "Who's Who in Hollywood—Find the Gentile," Alexander complained that Jewish studio bosses packed "their casts with Yiddish ham actors and female Yidds who thus take jobs away from Gentile performers." He called for "an avalanche of Gentile wrath and intelligent determination" to confront the "Jewish problem in America."[7]

Looking for important allies in his battle against Jews, Alexander found Schwinn to be a like-minded soul; Schwinn thought well enough of the British-born photographer to make him a regular speaker at Deutsches Haus. Confident their two groups could work together, Alexander revived the militant "actionists," the armed wing of the Silver Shirts, composed of well-drilled men prepared to kill Jews if necessary.[8]

While Communists attempted to infiltrate Hollywood unions, Silver Shirts and Nazis pursued a different tack: they set out to purge all Jews working in blue-collar positions in studio lots. Alexander found the city's studios fertile ground for recruiting, especially among studio guards and craftsmen who resented their Jewish bosses, a fact that did not surprise Lewis. In October 1933, Dietrich Gefken, the Nazi who plotted to take over National Guard armories, bragged to Lewis's spies of working at First National and Universal, where he discovered "plenty of sympathizers and Nazis in both studios."[9]

Over the next several years, Lewis's operatives warned him that Nazis and Silver Shirts recruited laborers at First National, Universal, MGM, Paramount, Twentieth Century, and Technicolor. As Paramount watchman and Bund member L. Albert Brown told Ness in April 1936, "there is a great deal of anti-Semitic feeling" within the city's studios. Brown boasted how Christian foremen at Paramount "have weeded out most of the Jews." A month later, Lewis learned that the only Jew working in one MGM department had been let go because studio supervisors wanted "to keep certain departments one hundred percent Aryan." Paramount even hired Hermann Schwinn to do translating work that summer, where the starstruck Nazi was introduced to Gary Cooper.[10]

With anti-Semitism rife among below-the-line Hollywood employees, Alexander had little trouble reviving the Silver Shirts' secret Hollywood studio post. Having toiled in the industry for nearly a decade, he heard many Christian employees voice antipathy for their "Yid" bosses. Fascists were so entrenched at Louis B. Mayer's studio that when Alexander left to work for Pelley, MGM unwittingly hired another Silver Shirt to replace him and, as Allen boasted to Slocombe, "no one is the wiser." Alexander and militant ex-servicemen such as Paramount's

Albert Brown hoped to recruit studio anti-Semites into their campaign to bring about an America free from Jews.[11]

Los Angeles Jews also found themselves threatened by armed anti-Semitic groups in Mexico. In 1933, shortly after Hitler's rise to power, Allen, Schwinn, and two Nazi comrades traveled to Mexicali to help Mexican general Nicolás Rodríguez organize the Gold Shirts, a group modeled after Germany's Brownshirts. Their goal: a fascist takeover of the Mexican government. Hoping to hide any direct link between the Nazis and Gold Shirts, the Spanish-speaking Allen agreed to serve as liaison between the Silver Shirts, the Los Angeles Bund, and Rodríguez's organization. The ex-con and the ex-general shared a mutual fantasy of raising a large army that would, among other things, take care of the Jewish menace.[12]

Allen admired Rodríguez for being a man of action. On March 20, 1935, hoping to become führer of Mexico, the former general marched his Gold Shirts to the president's palace in Mexico City. During an ensuing riot, five Gold Shirts were killed, seventy people wounded, and Rodríguez was stabbed and taken to a hospital. Exiled for his attempted coup, the general moved to Texas but often visited Los Angeles to speak at Deutsches Haus. While there, he plotted his return to power with a small cadre of Nazis and Silver Shirts that included Schwinn, Allen, Alexander, and Slocombe.[13]

Leon Lewis knew all about their activities and passed on whatever information he had to government authorities. But with so many local authorities turning a blind eye to their activities, Silver Shirt chaplain Robert Bruce remained confident that "things will be popping before very long."[14]

Guns did not pop as Bruce had hoped, but that November fascists and Nazis undoubtedly popped open bottles of champagne to celebrate simultaneous visits by their two national leaders, William Pelley and Fritz Kuhn. The presidential election of 1936 had not gone as they had hoped. Franklin Roosevelt scored an overwhelming victory over Alf Landon, carrying all but two states and crushing his rival in the Electoral College by a margin of 523 to 8. Pelley, on the ballot only in Washington State, received fewer than 2,000 votes. In the wake of Roosevelt's victory, the two men arranged to hold "a very secret meeting" in Schwinn's office to discuss a common strategy for moving forward.[15]

On Sunday, November 15, as they waited in Deutsches Haus for Kuhn to arrive, Alexander pulled Pelley aside and introduced him to Chuck Slocombe. Pelley told Slocombe how grateful he was that

Alexander had "someone he could trust to take care of things whenever he was out of town." Later that night, several hundred Nazis, Silver Shirts, and White Russians packed Deutsches Haus to hear Fritz Kuhn give his first Los Angeles address. Speaking with a heavy German accent, the Bund leader exhorted the crowd to join "to build an America along the pattern created by our great Führer Adolf Hitler" and battle "until the country is purged" of Communists and Jews.[16]

As Kuhn sat down, Slocombe took the stage and delivered a fierce attack on *Scholastic Magazine* for its communistic efforts to "discredit Nazism and Fascism in the eyes of the school children." Americans, he told the crowd, "would be better off under Fascism than under democracy."[17] As far as Schwinn and Alexander were concerned, the evening could not have gone better. Sitting in the back of the room, taking meticulous notes on everything being said, was Neil Ness, who still did not know Slocombe was working for Lewis.

Poised for even greater success, Alexander and Allen faced a new enemy that threatened fascists and Nazis alike: the Hollywood Anti-Nazi League.

HOLLYWOOD FIGHTS BACK

Hitler recognized the political power of Hollywood in the 1920s, but the vast majority of Hollywood actors, writers, and directors did not become fully politicized until the early 1930s. The one exception was Louis B. Mayer, who turned MGM into a publicity wing of the Republican Party in the late 1920s and served as vice chair (1930) and chair (1932) of the California GOP. That singular situation changed during the presidential election of 1932 when, inspired by the charismatic Franklin D. Roosevelt, previously complacent movie stars entered the political arena en masse. As *Little Caesar* star Edward G. Robinson remarked, FDR made politics "no longer a politician's 'job'—he made it the concern of every human being . . . and in doing so he left the artist with no excuse to remain aloof from it."[18]

Although domestic issues proved important to Hollywood's new activists, events in Europe ignited their greatest political passions. Between 1933 and 1941, 200,000 refugees fled from Germany and Austria to the United States, with 10,000—half of them Jews—settling in Los Angeles. Given the large numbers of Jewish movie industry personnel and European émigrés who populated the city in the 1930s, it is not surprising that anti-Nazism emerged as a focal point of political action. Of the 1,500 film professionals who left Germany after 1933 and Austria after 1938, over half settled in Hollywood, where they told their stories of Hitler's horrors to anyone who would listen.[19]

Given the city's large émigré population, it is hardly surprising that Hollywood activists were at the forefront of internationalist politics at a time when most Americans were still isolationists, a situation that led many citizens to see the movie capital as a bastion of liberalism and, worse yet, liberalism on behalf of Jews. Anti-Semitism was a fact of life in much of America, and few people were willing to risk war to aid European Jews; 95 percent of those polled in November 1936 opposed U.S. participation in any potential European conflict.[20]

Hatred of Nazism led Hollywood liberals, Communists, and some conservatives to join a wide range of Popular Front groups such as the Motion Picture Artists Committee to Aid Republican Spain (which had 15,000 members at its peak), the Joint Anti-Fascist Refugee Committee, and, most notably, the Hollywood Anti-Nazi League (HANL). Forged by the Communist International in 1935, the Popular Front represented a broad coalition of groups and individuals on the left, center, and right who put aside sectarian differences and united in a common effort to fight the spread of Nazism and fascism. Whether these organizations contained Communists or not seemed irrelevant at the time; political causes trumped political labels.

No group proved more important or visible than the HANL. An offshoot of the New York Non-Sectarian Anti-Nazi League founded by Samuel Untermyer in 1933, the Los Angeles group gained widespread attention after movie stars got involved in April 1936. Far from being a dilettante celebrity group, the HANL used the popularity of its members to "keep the public informed about the true nature of the Nazi regime in Germany," to "fight Nazism and Nazi agents in this country," and to "maintain a constant fight for justice to political prisoners in Germany."[21]

Leon Lewis was delighted to have a new ally in what often seemed a lonely battle. Movie stars could draw the kind of national and international attention that he and Jewish organizations could not. When stars spoke out, observed Leo Rosten, who conducted a sociological study of the movie industry between 1937 and 1940, their pronouncements were "reported to the world in greater detail than any other single group in the world, with the possible exception of Washingtonists . . . People would know Clark Gable or Greta Garbo in parts of the world where they didn't know the name of their own prime minister or the mayor of their own little town."[22]

Led by writer Donald Ogden Stewart, the group included an amalgam of liberals such as Edward G. Robinson, Melvyn Douglas, Sylvia Sidney, Eddie Cantor, and Gloria Stuart, along with prominent conservatives such as John Ford, Bruce Cabot, Joan Bennett, and Dick Powell. Taking office space at 6912 Hollywood Boulevard, conveniently located between Graumann's Chinese Theater and two popular bars frequented by screenwriters, Musso & Franks and Rose's Bookstore, the HANL proceeded to mount star-studded anti-Nazi demonstrations, photographs of which appeared on the front pages of the nation's newspapers. The group also organized talks on topics such as "Hitlerism in America," sponsored two weekly radio shows, published the biweekly newspaper *Hollywood Anti-Nazi News*, and called for boycotts of German and Japanese products. Bolstered by its celebrity presence, HANL membership swelled to over 4,000.[23]

Perceiving the neophyte group as "babes in the woods," Lewis agreed to serve as liaison between the Hollywood Anti-Nazi League and the Community Committee; he attended executive meetings and informed the CC's executive board of their plans during regular Friday luncheons. Over the next several months, the HANL held talks and readings aimed at alerting citizens to the fact that "one hundred and ninety-five organizations are openly issuing anti-racial and anti-religious propaganda to the American people."[24] The group also began planning their first major anti-Nazi rally at the Shrine Auditorium in late October.

Recognizing the threat posed by the HANL, Alexander, Allen, Schwinn, and Hughes met to discuss the best ways to disrupt the forthcoming rally. Hughes suggested they fill the auditorium with cyanide fumes and then fire "automatic rifles, [and] sawed off shotguns" into the audience. When the group decided that would not work, the ever-creative Hughes came up with the idea of making a hypodermic gun inside a fountain pen that could shoot poisoned needles at Jews. That idea was also abandoned, as was Allen's suggestion that they send a gang of thugs to provoke a fight. The only thing they agreed upon was the need to hold a special meeting at Deutsches Haus to plan a collective response by Bundists and Silver Shirts.[25]

Despite the threats of violence, the Shrine rally proved a tremendous success. Over 7,500 people—including a large contingent "of famous screen personalities" such as Fredric March, Eddie Cantor, Gloria Stuart, Florence Eldridge, and composer Oscar Hammerstein—turned out to protest the "invasion of Nazism in America" and listen to speakers denounce the activities of Nazi agents in the United States. Two thousand more Angelenos patiently waited outside the exotic Moorish Shrine Auditorium, hoping to catch a glimpse of their favorite movie star.[26]

Over the next year, the HANL staged well-publicized celebrity events featuring Viennese-born director Fritz Lang, black scholar and activist W. E. B. Du Bois, and actors Ray Bolger, Fanny Brice, Bing Crosby, Joan Crawford, Fred MacMurray, and Sophie Tucker. Studio moguls were so worried about the negative effect movie-star activism might have on box-office returns that they considered inaugurating "a squelch campaign against anything savoring of political activities, even incorporating a clause in contracts covering this, like the famous morals clause."[27] Knowing the blowback would be too great, the moguls backed off.

HANL members drew worldwide attention to their cause by boycotting Hollywood visits by Benito Mussolini's son Vittorio in September 1937 and by Hitler's favorite filmmaker, Leni Riefenstahl, in December 1938. "There is no room in Hollywood for Leni Riefenstahl," the group declared. "In this moment when hundreds of thousands of our brethren await certain death, close your doors to all Nazi agents."[28]

Nazis and fascists responded to the rise of the Hollywood Anti-Nazi League with an aggressive campaign to stem the growth of Jewish resistance. In early January 1937, worried that the "Jewish situation is getting pretty tense," Ku Klux Klan leaders told Chuck Slocombe of their intention to "declare open season" on the Jews. They asked him to help secure allies for their anticipated attack on Jews by working with the Civilian Army of American Bluecoats, a new group that was raising a "Christian Army."[29]

As a palpable sense of militancy spread among the city's many hate groups, Schwinn and two dozen Bundists marched to the Shrine Auditorium to disrupt a speech by exiled Communist and anti-Nazi playwright Ernst Toller. Hoping for a fight, Schwinn got his wish. Earlier that morning, when he alerted William Hynes of his plans, the Red Squad leader told him there would be only two policemen at the door, so "just go ahead and do whatever you please." Sitting patiently among the crowd, the Nazis waited until Toller got up to speak, at which point Schwinn stood up and yelled, "We don't want to hear from this Communist murderer." A fight broke out. Outnumbered four to one, the Nazis wound up on the losing end of the melee. The bloody battle lasted fifteen minutes, until Hynes's two cops finally escorted Schwinn's thugs out of the building. Reinhold Kusche was so badly beaten that he was bedridden for several days.[30]

For Hermann Schwinn the worst was yet to come. On Sunday, March 7, 1937, the Communist periodical *Sunday Worker* ran the first in a series of articles by investigative reporter John L. Spivak revealing how the Nazi government had sent "secret agents" to "interfere actively and directly in the internal affairs of the United States government and the American people." Spivak described the full scope of Nazi activism, including $2.5 million spent annually on propaganda sent through the nation's seaports. But the writer's most spectacular exposé centered on the secret workings of the Los Angeles Bund. "In Hollywood," he wrote, "motion picture producers pay fabulous prices to imaginative writers who concoct stories to thrill the countless movie fans throughout the world. Yet—a few miles away, in Los Angeles, are far more thrilling scenes than Hollywood can imagine—an amazing story of international intrigue, espionage and activities designed not to amuse and thrill but undermine a democratic government and place the American people under a fascist heel. I referred to activities directed from the Nazi head-quarters on the West Coast, located in the Deutsche Haus, 634 W. 15th St., Los Angeles."[31]

Knowing he needed help in gathering information, Spivak had traveled to Los Angeles a year earlier to meet with Leon Lewis and Mendel Silberberg. Always anxious to alert Americans to the Nazi threat, Lewis opened his files to the reporter, asking only that his name be kept out of the press and that Spivak share any new information he uncovered. After reading months of reports by Lewis's operatives, Spivak approached Schwinn and requested to interview him for a story he was writing about the Bund. Of course, he never mentioned that he was writing the piece for a Communist newspaper. Schwinn believed he could put a favorable spin on the article, but within minutes of their interview, Spivak noted how the "little Fuehrer" with "a thin, quivering mustache on his upper lip" turned pale when the writer described in precise detail how the Bund leader regularly traveled to the docks to receive secret orders, money, and propaganda from Germany; and how he drove to San Diego with Nazi spy Schneeberger, who photographed military installations and then left to turn over his findings to the Japanese government.[32]

Schwinn was again taken aback when Spivak told him he knew that Rudolf Hess had sent Hans Meyerhoffer to reorganize the Bund. He also knew that German consul Georg Gyssling had provided the Bund with money, and that the two men despised each other. But these revelations were nothing compared to the "look of actual fear" that spread over his face when Spivak asked Schwinn about his connection to Count von Bülow, the man who seemed to be running a Nazi spy operation in Southern California. No longer smiling, Schwinn responded with a dazed look, "I know nothing."[33]

Leon Lewis and the Community Committee hoped Spivak's spectacular revelations would incite government officials to action. Although few in power paid attention to the findings of a Communist newspaper, local Nazis and Silver Shirts did. When the articles came out, it was no mystery who had provided Spivak with background information. "Ness had taken Schwinn in completely," a furious Kenneth Alexander complained to Chuck Slocombe. No longer trusting the Nazi leader to keep his mouth shut, Alexander put Slocombe in charge of investigating how many more spies had infiltrated the Bund. He also asked him to "train fellows to bore into these other [Jewish] organizations," just as they had "always bored into us."[34]

On the morning of April 16, 1937, embattled Nazis and fascists learned that the Hollywood Boulevard office of the Anti-Nazi League had been trashed and burglarized the previous evening by unknown parties. The HANL periodical *Hollywood Now* blamed the vandalism on the followers of Adolf Hitler, who were "desperately trying to cover their activities in our country." As in the past, little could be expected from local law enforcement. Hollywood Detective Bureau captain J. J. Jones refused to investigate the break-in. "You are a political organization," he told upset HANL leaders, "and if another political organization doesn't like you—so what?"[35]

The joy Nazis and Silver Shirts took from the burglary was short-lived. On July 27, 1937, Samuel Dickstein took to the floor of Congress and named forty-six Nazis and fascists working in the United States as "expert spies and agitators," among them Hermann Schwinn and Ingram Hughes. Dickstein warned colleagues about the rapid growth of Nazi summer camps, including one slated to open in Los Angeles, where young boys could be seen "drilling in uniform, goose-stepping, clicking of heels and boots, and they swear allegiance to Mr. Hitler, and at the same time downing Americans." Four months later, armed with information from Leon Lewis, the congressman returned to the House floor to read the names of 116 Southern Californians who were leaders of the "Hitler movement" on the West Coast.[36] The time had come to launch a new congressional investigation of Nazism in America.

Frustrated by a growing local anti-Nazi movement that threatened to stop their successful recruiting efforts, Alexander, Allen, and Schwinn came up with their most diabolical plot to date. They would send a message of hope to anti-Semites throughout the United States by murdering Hollywood movie stars and the Jewish moguls who employed them, including the most famous man in the world, Charlie Chaplin, and the industry's most powerful studio head, Louis B. Mayer.

14.

Slaughter the Hollywood Jews

In September 1937 Adolf Hitler sent his "personal deputy," Captain Fritz Wiedemann, to Los Angeles on a dual mission: to assess the extent of Nazi sympathies in Southern California and to deliver orders to Consul Gyssling and local Bund leaders.[1] Los Angeles had assumed new importance to the führer after Germany and Japan signed an anti-Soviet treaty in November 1936. Not only was the city strategically positioned halfway between Berlin and Tokyo but it also served as a major center of American defense production, turning out vast numbers of airplanes and warships. With the ports of Los Angeles and San Pedro relatively unmonitored, German and Japanese spies found it easy to slip into the country and send back information to their masters.

Following his return to Berlin, Wiedemann told Hitler that he found strong sympathy for Germany among leading businessmen, and pronounced "fascist leanings" among the coast's financial oligarchy.[2] Wiedemann assured his former World War I corporal that Nazis had powerful allies in Southern California.

That same September, former FBI agent James J. Metcalfe alerted readers of Hitler's intentions for America in a series of articles in the *Chicago Times* recounting the results of his six-month undercover investigation. Among his many frightening disclosures, Metcalfe warned that "an army of 20,000 American Nazis is preparing to seize control of the United States."[3] Although the coup d'état never happened, Lewis and Slocombe uncovered a plot closer to home, one far more likely to happen than 20,000 armed Nazis marching through the streets of America.

On a beautiful Sunday afternoon on September 12, 1937, 3,000 men, women, and children journeyed to the Nazi-controlled Hindenburg

Park, seventeen miles northeast of downtown Los Angeles, where they paid thirty-five cents to attend the annual German Day celebration. As Chuck Slocombe and Kenneth Alexander entered the park, they heard bands playing popular German songs, saw booths selling Nazi books and German merchandise, and spotted a large stage decorated with swastika flags and a sole American standard. Following a festive parade of Bundists wearing their Nazi uniforms, everyone crowded around the stage to hear the day's speakers. Seated on the platform were honored guests Baron Manfred von Killinger, Georg Gyssling, and representatives sent by the mayor and sheriff. Standing at attention just below the stage were a cadre of storm troopers led by Reinhold Kusche, Rafael Demmler, and Arno Risse, head of the San Gabriel Bund and a rising star in the local movement.

The main speaker was San Francisco's recently appointed German consul general, Baron Manfred von Killinger. He was the former death squad leader who in 1921 masterminded the assassination of Matthias Erzberger, the pro-peace minister who negotiated Germany's surrender in World War I. Gyssling and Schwinn would now take their orders from the militant San Francisco consul.[4]

As Killinger began addressing the gathering, a plane hired by the Hollywood Anti-Nazi League dropped hundreds of flyers on the crowd.

Raising the Swastika at German Day Celebration, Hindenburg Park
Jewish Federation Council of Greater Los Angeles, Community Relations Committee Collection, Part 2, Special Collections and Archives, Oviatt Library, California State University, Northridge

To make sure everyone got one, the pilot turned around and dropped a second round. The HANL leaflet was an act of revenge for the earlier trashing and burglarizing of their offices. As the leaflets floated into the park, celebrants expressed their indignation at the "Jew Communist" movie people who had disrupted their festivities. An unfazed Killinger merely smiled and finished his speech.[5]

As the honored guests left the platform, Henry Allen introduced Alexander and Slocombe to his English fascist friend Leopold McLaglan. They were soon joined by White Russian leader George Doombadze (who went by the name Samsonov) and Dr. Konrad Burchardi, who introduced them all to Killinger. After discussing the state of the Hitler movement in America, the new consul thanked his fellow anti-Semites and suggested they meet at a later date to "talk things over in more detail." Slocombe knew little about the Nazi leader, but Alexander and Allen told him "Killinger was one of Hitler's best friends and his right-hand man."[6] They felt honored he took the time to speak to them.

The only important figure missing from the day's celebration was Hermann Schwinn. In yet another sign of Germany's greater focus on the Pacific Coast, Nazi officials had invited the Bund's western region leader to attend the National Socialist Party convention in Nuremberg and the annual Deutsches Ausland-Institut (Folk-Union for Germandom Abroad) convention in Stuttgart over the summer. Leaving Los Angeles on July 10 and returning September 29, Schwinn spent much of his time conferring with Nazi Party officials in Berlin, including Deputy Führer Rudolf Hess and his protégé, Ernst Bohle, the man he placed in charge of the Ausland Institute. German ambassador to the United States Hans-Heinrich Dieckhoff did not think much of the Bund, but his government found the Los Angeles group useful in smuggling in spies, money, and propaganda. Schwinn received a joyous reception upon his return to Los Angeles and traveled to San Diego, accompanied by Killinger, to deliver the keynote address at their German Day celebration.[7]

Schwinn's trip to Germany and the presence of Killinger were just two of the many pieces of disturbing news Lewis received that summer and fall. Neil Ness had been exposed, and Chuck Slocombe, emotionally exhausted and fearing for his life, took a two-month break from undercover work. He returned in August to resume spying on Allen and Alexander. Lewis was glad he did, for he found himself confronted by yet another man determined to make his mark by killing the city's most prominent Jews.

CON GAMES AND DOUBLE CROSSES

Leopold McLaglan was intelligent, dangerous, and delusional. He was a combat veteran and martial arts expert who knew how to kill and had taught others to do so with precision. Sydney Temple Leopold McLaglen (he would later change the spelling to McLaglan to differentiate himself from his brothers) was born in London in 1884. The second of ten siblings, Leopold, as he called himself, was a towering six-six (some reports say six-eight) and 226 pounds. An early expert in jiu-jitsu, he won the world's championship in 1907, beating the reigning Japanese titleholder.

A skilled military veteran, McLaglan had fought for the British in the Boer War and in World War I, done intelligence work for the military, and ended his service with the rank of captain. Upon leaving the army, he taught jiu-jitsu to police and military forces throughout the world, including Scotland Yard and the French Sûreté. He also published four books instructing readers in jiu-jitsu, bayonet warfare, and hand-to-hand combat.[8]

In 1920, Leopold wound up in Los Angeles and co-starred in the film *Bars of Iron* (1920). After leaving the city for a decade of police instruction and jiu-jitsu barnstorming, he returned in 1930 with the intention of following in the footsteps of his five movie-star brothers, the most famous of whom was Victor McLaglen, recipient of a best actor Oscar for his performance in *The Informer* (1935). A first-class con man, Leopold often passed himself off as his famous brother, which infuriated Victor. After Victor spread the word that his brother was "unreliable and should be watched," Leopold filed a $900,000 lawsuit charging him with slander and defamation of character. The case was thrown out of court.[9]

Chuck Slocombe knew little of McLaglan's background when they met that September afternoon at Hindenburg Park, but he gladly accepted his invitation to join him, Henry Allen, Kenneth Alexander, and several storm troopers to dine in a private room where they could talk without being overheard. Schwinn's crowd loved McLaglan; not only had he built a fascist organization in England, but he was currently teaching Nazis and White Russians "how to kill through Jiu Jitsu."[10]

When the group convened at the House of O'Sullivan, a popular restaurant on Sunset and Vine that prided itself on serving "Real Irish Food" and whiskey, McLaglan, elegantly dressed in a white linen suit and flush with funds, told them a story of betrayal, duplicity, and espionage that he would spin out in bits and pieces over the next two weeks— all of which he cloaked in half-truths. He began by expressing his desire to seek revenge against Jews, especially Hollywood Jews, whom he loathed. McLaglan told his dining companions how after King Edward VIII's abdication, he overheard a group of British movie industry Jews gloat, "We at last have England in our power." He also told them about his unpleasant encounters with obnoxious Jews at Wilshire Boulevard Temple, synagogue to the Hollywood moguls. He knew that Leon Lewis was spying on honest Americans and needed to be stopped.[11]

Having intrigued his fellow anti-Semites, McLaglan met with the three men several times over the next two weeks to discuss what might be done. Much to their surprise, McLaglan repeatedly grilled Slocombe about his knowledge of Japanese vessels operating in Long Beach Harbor. Wondering what to do, Slocombe contacted Lewis, who, anxious to discover McLaglan's intentions, ordered him to play along. Slocombe provided the former British soldier with "certain matters of common knowledge . . . which might be considered as evidence of Japanese espionage." McLaglan was delighted, but a suspicious Alexander wanted to know why he needed information about Japanese vessels "inasmuch as we were all pro-Japanese."[12]

Hoping to string the wary men along so they would help in a deadly plot he soon planned to reveal, McLaglan told them a partially true tale of how he had been betrayed by Santa Barbara millionaire Philip Chancellor, the thirty-year-old heir to the Elgin Watch Company fortune.

Unable to earn a living in the movie business because of his vindictive brother Victor, Leopold was forced to fall back on his skills as an intelligence operative. The previous April, he had approached Chancellor, who claimed to be a high-ranking officer in naval intelligence, and promised to get him information he needed about local Nazi, Japanese, and Russian espionage activities, for which McLaglan would be paid $20,000. Chancellor, who served in the U.S. Navy Reserve, handed McLaglan a letter addressed to the head of naval intelligence in San Diego "stating that if I were picked up by any other Intelligence officers or the police" it "would clear me of anything I might do." McLaglan then hired Bishop Albert Bell, an ally of Hermann Schwinn, to help gather evidence of espionage in the Los Angeles area. Bell, he told his three companions, was also working with deputy sheriff Frank Gompert to help naval intelligence monitor activity among Japanese vessels in Los Angeles Harbor.[13] This was the reason McLaglan had pumped Slocombe for information about Japanese goings-on in San Pedro.

McLaglan told his companions he had completed his end of the bargain by providing Chancellor with reports on local Japanese espionage. However, when he asked for his money, the millionaire refused to pay, insisting that McLaglan "had not fulfilled my contract." McLaglan then threatened to blow the lid off Chancellor's operation unless he was paid the money owed him.[14]

Sensing his companions cared little about his conflict with Chancellor, McLaglan piqued their interest by promising to provide them with documents "showing that certain Jews have their finger in the Naval Intelligence organization." This time the con man was telling the truth. Leon Lewis had been providing naval intelligence with information since 1934. Visibly excited by the embarrassment such documents

Leopold McLaglan (far left, first row) at the home of Bishop Albert Bell (middle, first row), September 1937

Jewish Federation Council of Greater Los Angeles, Community Relations Committee Collection, Part 2, Special Collections and Archives, Oviatt Library, California State University, Northridge

would cause, Alexander exclaimed, "We have been looking for an opening wedge to blow this whole Jewish situation wide open and with this evidence we can swing the army and navy officers to our side showing who some of the double crossers are and their Jew dupes and the naval officers who are selling out to the Jews."[15]

Thrilled at the prospect of exposing Jewish interference with the military, Alexander and Allen offered their help. Suspecting McLaglan was lying, Slocombe went to see Long Beach Police captain Owen Murphy, hoping to learn the truth. Murphy told his longtime under-cover operative (whom he now shared with Leon Lewis) a very different story about McLaglan's activities. Private detective Edwin Crumplar and deputy James Foze, the sheriff's liaison with naval intelligence, had recently contacted him about an operation that had gone bad. Hoping to earn a regular commission as a naval intelligence officer (rather than a naval reservist), Philip Chancellor launched his own undercover opera-tion and hired the two men to discover whether the Japanese were building a West Coast spy network or relying on German operatives for information. The millionaire planned to pass his findings to naval intel-ligence. With a paying client in place, Crumplar hired McLaglan—who had taught Chancellor jiu-jitsu the past two years—and Bishop Bell as his investigators. When Chancellor realized Bell and McLaglan were milking him "for tremendous sums for expenses and salaries" but providing few results, he ordered Crumplar to fire the pair and "get the goods" on McLaglan, in case he proved difficult.[16]

Crumplar confessed to Murphy that he had bungled the operation. McLaglan had gone rogue and persuaded Chancellor to break into the offices of the Hollywood Anti-Nazi League, looking for evidence of their ties to Communist espionage, knowing that he could blackmail his employer for the illegal break-in if their relationship went south. When Chancellor fired him for failing to deliver any information of value, McLaglan did precisely that: he demanded $20,000 to keep quiet about their illegal activities.[17]

The two detectives now feared Bell and McLaglan would "spill the beans" and get them into trouble. Anxious to avoid embarrassing naval intelligence and the Los Angeles sheriff's office, Murphy advised Foze to have McLaglan arrested for extortion and to keep the full story of the botched spy operation quiet.[18]

As Murphy concluded his account, he told Slocombe that McLaglan had been honest about one thing: he hated Jews and wanted them dead. Several weeks earlier, the former British captain gave "a very rabid anti-Semitic speech" at a Long Beach Motor Police Association meeting. He urged the officers "to organize a reserve armed [unit] with machine guns and wipe these cursed Jews off the face of the earth," a call that received widespread approval from the audience.[19] After leaving Murphy's office, Slocombe contacted Lewis and, at his urging, agreed to play along and see what McLaglan's end game might be. What he learned shocked them all.

DEATH PLOT

Several days after revealing his plans to expose Jewish interference in the military, McLaglan invited Alexander, Allen, and Slocombe to celebrate at his favorite restaurant, the House of O'Sullivan. While sitting at their "usual table" drinking Tom Collinses and scotch and soda, McLaglan presented the three men with a "bloody good idea." And bloody it was! To garner "worldwide publicity, we are going to have to do a wholesale slaughtering here in the city of plenty of the leading Jews." That meant targeting the leaders of the Jew-infested movie industry, the Hollywood Anti-Nazi League, and the Christians who aided both. "I can get the Nazi boys and the White Russians who would do this for us," McLaglan promised. Doombadze, he added, has a "psycho" fellow "who does this stuff for him all the time." None of them would have to do the actual killing.[20]

Promising to use the money he received from Chancellor to pay for the hit men, McLaglan began compiling, with his friends, a list of people they would kill. Allen wrote down the agreed-upon names and then handed the hit list to Alexander for safekeeping. The assassinations would occur on the same day McLaglan released his information about Jewish control of the navy, which he promised to do in the next six weeks. Later that night, Slocombe sent the following twenty-four names to Leon Lewis and Joe Roos, which included some of the most famous people in the world: Jack Benny, Herbert Biberman, James Cagney, Eddie Cantor, Charles Chaplin, Emanuel Cohen, Sam Goldwyn, Henry Herzbrun, Al Jolson, Leon Lewis, Fredric March, Louis B. Mayer, Paul Muni, Joseph Schenck, B. P. Schulberg, Mendel Silberberg, Franchon Simon, Donald Ogden Stewart, Gloria Stuart, Sylvia Sydney, Ernst Toller, Walter Winchell, Marco Wolff, and William Wyler.[21]

Allen and Alexander had been longing to take dramatic action against the Jews. This was their opportunity. Boasting that he "could get all the dynamite he needed through the police," McLaglan tasked Allen with getting pipes they would stuff with dynamite and shrapnel "to make it cause the most destruction." The ex-captain would provide two dozen Nazi and Russian assassins with the bombs and the names and addresses of their targets, all of whom would be murdered on the same night. Knowing that they would likely fall under suspicion, McLaglan suggested they spend the night of the killings in Santa Barbara to have "a perfect alibi."[22]

As they reviewed the final hit list, McLaglan revealed he had spoken to Hermann Schwinn about the assassination plot "many times." The Bund leader, in turn, discussed potential targets with San Francisco consul Manfred von Killinger. Anxious to destroy the troublesome Hollywood Anti-Nazi League, Schwinn told McLaglan that his Nazi allies "were particularly interested in eliminating" the key leaders of the Hollywood Anti-Nazi League. The assassinations, McLaglan promised, "will start a worldwide stink."[23]

McLaglan was right. Murdering Hollywood moguls and movie stars, especially Charlie Chaplin, then the most famous person in the world, would have attracted international attention. Lewis had foiled earlier plots, but this one worried him. Maybe McLaglan was just another big talker, but he had the expertise to carry out the massacre. Slocombe warned Lewis that "the Hermann Schwinn gang, and the White Russian Fascist gang" had forged a "united front" with McLaglan and were ready to take action against Jews. White Russian leader George Doombadze was a man to be feared. One of his uncles was "the inciter of pogroms in and about Odessa, where many Jews were tortured and killed." Another was "active in strikes . . . [where] workers were shot and tortured at his order." If given the opportunity, their "worthy nephew," who worked as a chemist at Columbia Pictures, would kill Jews just as easily as his brutal uncles.[24] Encouraged by the opening of concentration camps in Dachau, Sachsenhausen, and Buchenwald, and by the murdering of Jews by anti-Semites in Germany and Poland, McLaglan and his allies had every reason to believe their plot would succeed.

As they left the restaurant, an exuberant Kenneth Alexander turned to Slocombe and gushed, "Oh boy, this is fine. Exactly what we need. I think we can absolutely bank on McLaglan. There is no question now about our being with him 100%."[25]

The next day, McLaglan met Slocombe at the Long Beach docks and added a new twist to his murder scheme. "In Germany when the lid was blown off, the Jews took steamers, trains and automobiles to get out of the country. Naturally they will want to do that here, too." When they did, McLaglan would take one of Slocombe's fast boats, "catch the steamers as they go out, dynamite them and get rid of the whole damn bunch for all time." A friend of McLaglan's who owned a gravel business on Catalina Island promised to supply a "fleet of trucks" to catch anyone who escaped.[26] Everything was ready; all they needed to do was set a date.

FOILING THE DEATH PLOT

When McLaglan, Allen, and Slocombe met again at the House of O'Sullivan in early October, the troubled Englishman told the others that Chancellor was about to sail off to Mexico "until the whole thing blows over." Fearing the millionaire would implicate him in a series of crimes before fleeing the country, McLaglan suggested they all go to the U.S. district attorney and charge him with falsely "parading around as a Naval officer." They would also accuse him of breaking into HANL headquarters. After agreeing to confirm McLaglan's story, Allen suggested they confess to assistant U.S. district attorney Benjamin Harrison, a Christian, rather than to Jewish DA Palmer.[27]

Piling into McLaglan's Ford V-8 coupe, the trio, absent a nervous Alexander, drove to the Pacific Electric Building on Sixth and Main and met with Harrison. As rehearsed, McLaglan blamed Chancellor for ordering him to "do a lot of things that were dangerous and illegal." "I love this country," he told the assistant DA. He helped Chancellor because he believed the millionaire was working for naval intelligence. As proof, he handed Harrison a copy of Chancellor's introductory letter. Taken aback by the tale of espionage and intrigue, Harrison promised to investigate the matter.[28]

As they left the building, confident of having pulled the wool over Harrison's eyes, McLaglan asked Slocombe to run back in and tell the assistant DA that Chancellor was preparing to sail to Mexico and turn his reports over to "some foreign power." Slocombe did as he was told, but upon entering the office he pulled Jewish DA Palmer aside and confessed, "I am an inside man in this case, and the man you should contact is Captain Murphy of the Long Beach Police. He is in charge of this situation." The surprised DA promised to call him immediately.[29]

Despite their bravado, the conspirators were getting cold feet. As they stopped to eat at a nearby restaurant, a nervous Allen confessed, "I don't like this thing." Alexander had stayed at home because he was "scared out" of his mind. Even McLaglan wondered whether he should hire a lawyer.[30] Seeing an opportunity to blow the assassination plot out of the water, Slocombe drove to Alexander's apartment, hoping to turn the Silver Shirt leader against McLaglan. This time, he was not driving alone. Sitting alongside him was Leon Lewis. Unwilling to wait for a written report or telephone call, the spymaster debriefed his agent as they drove and then stepped out of the car before they reached Alexander's apartment and headed downtown to meet with assistant DA Harrison.

Once inside Alexander's apartment, Slocombe acted like a frightened schoolboy and accused McLaglan of being a double-crossing crook. He feared the scheming Englishman would tell authorities "the whole story of the bombing plot and try to hang it on them." To prevent that from happening, Slocombe planned to "make a clean breast of the whole situation" so that he would "not be held as an accomplice." He urged Alexander to join him, warning that if Allen got into a jam, he "would try to clear his skirts" by blaming everything on the others. Screaming "Henry is a God Damned fool," Alexander suggested they drive to Allen's Pasadena home and convince him to accompany them to the DA's office so "their stories jibe."[31]

When the trio gathered later that night, they agreed Bell and McLaglan "had connived in trapping" them to "serve their own purposes." Fearing McLaglan would betray them, Allen agreed to accompany his friends to the DA. When he suggested they warn Doombadze, a furious Alexander told Allen to shut up; if they implicated the White Russians, they, not the Jews, would wind up dead.[32]

Eager to accelerate matters, Slocombe returned to Alexander's apartment the next evening to warn that Allen was "backing down" on their agreement to join them at the DA's office. Slocombe explained that when he failed to reach Alexander that morning, he drove to DA Buron Fitts's office, gave a full statement, and promised his two companions would do the same. Alexander grew frantic when Slocombe explained the DA knew all about Bell and McLaglan's efforts at extortion and plans for mass murder. "Alexander agreed that we had gotten ourselves into a terrible mess," Slocombe told Lewis, and feared Allen "would try to clear himself by incriminating Alexander and me."[33]

To protect themselves, Alexander reached under his mattress, pulled out the original assassination list, cut it diagonally, kept half for himself, and gave half to Slocombe for safekeeping. "That's in Henry's handwriting and we can use it to make him keep his mouth shut." Alexander suggested they drive to Pasadena, "scare Henry to death," and agree upon a collective strategy. When they arrived, Alexander could not contain his fury. "Here you were yelling your head off about dynamiting and bombings and you can see what a mess we are in now." After they all calmed down, the three men agreed to visit the DA and claim McLaglan had dragged them into his plot.[34]

The district attorney's office knew about McLaglan's extortion and assassination plots because Lewis and Captain Murphy had contacted them and reported everything they had learned from Crumplar, Foze, and Slocombe. Chancellor had recently come to Murphy for help. He realized he had made a fool of himself "before the Navy people" and had resigned his reserve commission to save them further embarrassment. Not wishing to humiliate naval intelligence or the sheriff's office for their role in the bungled affair, Lewis and Murphy suggested that they keep Chancellor's undercover operation quiet. They advised the sheriff and DA to arrest the British fascist on charges of extortion and conspiracy to murder. Lewis hoped the case would "blow the lid completely off all of the anti-Semitic groups in Los Angeles" and break up "a very dangerous militant organization which has been formed in Long Beach under McLaglan's tutelage."[35]

THE ARREST, THE TRIAL, THE OUTCOME

On October 7, 1937, Charles Slocombe met with Los Angeles district attorney Buron Fitts and his staff and explained everything that had happened since first meeting Leopold McLaglan at the September 12 German Day celebration. The next afternoon, Slocombe returned with Kenneth Alexander and Henry Allen to swear out affidavits. A deal was struck. In return for their testimony, none of them would be charged as accomplices. Detective Seay knew precisely what questions to ask each man; he had received a lengthy memo from Leon Lewis outlining the "terrorist plot" and suggesting lines of inquiry the DA's office might pursue.[36]

In the meantime, the sheriff's office, embarrassed by their role in the affair, demoted Foze and set a trap for McLaglan. Several days earlier, the British fascist had telephoned Stanley Glimm, the millionaire's former secretary, and suggested they meet to discuss a matter of mutual interest. Glimm immediately contacted the sheriff's office, which sent Crumplar and two deputies to plant a Dictaphone in his office. The plan worked. They heard McLaglan offer Glimm $3,000 if he lied and testified that Chancellor had agreed to pay $20,000 for his investigative work. They also heard him boast that he threatened to tell the authorities that Chancellor had ordered him to break into HANL headquarters. With evidence in hand, deputy sheriff Tom Thomas arrested McLaglan as he left Glimm's office.[37]

Appearing at a packed press conference the next day, Captain William Penprase, head of the sheriff's bureau of investigation, announced that Leopold McLaglan had been arrested and charged with bribing a witness, soliciting the commission of perjury, attempted extortion, and preparing false evidence. Taking full credit, Penprase attributed the arrest to a six-week investigation by the sheriff's office. No mention was made of the murder plot or the role played by Lewis and Murphy.[38]

Given his own turn before reporters, the "giant former soldier," as the New York Times called him, denied committing any crime. "I have been doing U.S. intelligence work," he said, and "whatever I have done

Attorney Harry Sewell (l) and Leopold McLaglan (r) in Court, November 1937
Los Angeles Daily News Negatives, Collection 1387, UCLA Library Special Collections, Charles E. Young Research Library, UCLA

has been done under orders. The British Consul in Los Angeles is fully acquainted with my activities."[39] When contacted by the press, the consul refused to comment. Unable to come up with the $5,000 needed for bail, McLaglan remained in jail awaiting his trial in superior court.

Over the next two weeks, the DA's office succeeded in keeping the assassination plot out of the press. That changed on November 15, when a *Los Angeles Herald-Express* headline announced, "Plot to Massacre Rich L.A. Jews Probed." A "so-called plot for the wholesale massacre of a list of wealthy and prominent Jews, including Louis B. Mayer, Eddie Cantor, and others," the paper reported, "was revealed today to be under investigation by the district attorney and the sheriff's office." An "execution" list that contained the targeted names was currently in possession of the Anti-Defamation League. Attempting to cover up the full story, chief investigator Eugene Williams explained how a month earlier he learned of "secret Nazi meetings" held in Pasadena (Allen's home) at which an "execution list" had been drawn up. The homes of everyone on the list would be bombed and the men and women inside killed. After questioning "three leaders of local Nazi organizations" (Allen, Alexander, and Slocombe), the sheriff's office had succeeded in nipping "wholesale murder plots in the bud." No arrests were made because the "conspiracy never got beyond the conversational stage."[40]

Although the sheriff's office was happy to take all the credit, the *California Jewish Voice*, probably tipped off by Lewis, suggested that others were responsible for uncovering the planned assassinations. "The first indication of the plot," the newspaper reported on November 19, "was revealed when a group of Jewish leaders conferred with DA Fitts and revealed the threats made by Nazi sympathizers . . . to massacre a group of leading Jewish citizens."[41]

The full story of government incompetence never got out. Lewis was torn between exposing the murder plot as evidence of the depth of local anti-Semitism and his willingness to cover up the blunders made by naval intelligence and the sheriff's department. In the end, he decided to play the long game. He let the DA and sheriff take all the credit. They now owed him, as did naval intelligence, and hopefully would be more responsive to future cries for help. At the very least, by foiling the assassinations and saving lives, Lewis had proved his worth to the moguls. He would have no trouble getting money from them now.

On December 14, 1937, Leopold McLaglan, dressed in a dapper suit and sporting a monocle, pleaded not guilty to all charges. His trial was set for February 28, 1938. On the appointed day, appearing in superior court before Judge Thomas Ambrose, Chancellor and McLaglan took the stand and repeated the same story they had told the press over and over again. The millionaire testified that he had hired the ex-soldier to furnish information on "activities of Nazi, anti-Nazi, Communistic and anti-Semitic organizations in Southern California" for a book he was writing on international espionage. When he refused to pay him for shoddy information, McLaglan had demanded $20,000 or else he would tell the police that his employer was responsible for breaking into HANL headquarters. Testifying several days later, McLaglan denied all charges.[42]

On March 12, after a series of delays, jury foreman Grover Ross announced they had found McLaglan guilty of attempted extortion. Remarkably, given the Dictaphone recording in which the accused could be heard offering Glimm $3,000 to lie, Ross told Judge Ambrose they remained deadlocked on charges of bribery of a witness and soliciting perjury. The fourth charge of preparing false evidence was dismissed. McLaglan was remanded to custody in county jail; the judge refused his attorney's appeal to let him remain at liberty pending sentencing.[43]

On April 5, Judge Ambrose sentenced McLaglan to five years in prison but granted probation on the condition he take the first ship back to England and not set foot on American soil during that time. Not trusting McLaglan, Ambrose sentenced him to an additional year in county jail, which would be suspended the day he left for England. Probation came at the request of brother Victor, who, anxious to be rid of his troublesome sibling, agreed to pay his brother's $500 fine and his ocean-liner ticket to Liverpool.[44]

DÉNOUEMENT

When Williams told the press that no arrests had been made in the murder plot because his men had nipped it in the bud, he lied. It was not the sheriff or district attorney who had foiled the plot. Murder on a large scale had been plotted and thwarted not because of a failure of will on the part of the assassins but because of the actions taken by Slocombe and Lewis. This was a death plot that would have shaken the entire world. Moviegoers in cities around the globe flocked to see films starring Charlie Chaplin, Al Jolson, and James Cagney. A smart Jew with no official standing had foiled the plot, but Lewis understood he might not be so lucky the next time; there were many other Angelenos who believed the country would be better off without Jews. A week before the British fascist's sentencing, Dr. A. Earl Lee, pastor of the local Immanuel Temple, gave a sermon, "Shall We Kill the Jew in the United States," in which he openly sympathized with McLaglan's desire to eliminate the Jews who "have monopolized the basic industries of this nation."[45]

Anxious to stay out of jail, McLaglan returned to England, where he continued to profess his innocence. By 1940 the con man was serving as a commissioned officer in the Royal Air Force. In 1946 he asked the British War Office to reopen the case with the Americans and get the conviction reversed, insisting that he had spied on the Japanese at the behest of the British. The War Office did not believe him, nor did the Americans. McLaglan died in Devonshire, England, on January 4, 1951.

Kenneth Alexander moved to North Carolina after the trial to work with William Dudley Pelley. He returned to Los Angeles in August 1938, determined to revive the fallen Silver Shirt movement. Bishop Bell remained in Los Angeles and continued to work for the sheriff's office. The less-than-expert detective Edwin Crumplar wound up in San Quentin State Prison in 1942, sentenced to a five-to-life term for second-degree murder.[46]

Disappointed that the murder plot did not incite more national outrage, Lewis received a welcomed piece of news in December 1937. Based on the information Neil Ness had provided, Walter Carr of the Department of Immigration and Naturalization had persuaded federal officials to begin hearings aimed at revoking Hermann Schwinn's citizenship and deporting him back to Germany.

Having saved moguls and movie stars from murder, Lewis now turned his attention to saving them from the increasingly militant and costly actions of the hated German consul Georg Gyssling.

15.

The Most Hated Nazi in Hollywood

As Leopold McLaglan sat in jail awaiting his trial, a weary Leon Lewis read disheartening daily newspapers accounts of Nazi and fascist forces expanding across Europe and the Far East. A year earlier, Germany had signed separate treaties with Italy and Japan. When the three nations formed the Axis alliance in November 1937, four months after Japan invaded China, the Berlin-Rome-Tokyo partnership appeared poised to take on the rest of the world.

With the Reich on the move, propaganda minister Joseph Goebbels tightened his command over his government's image at home and abroad. In April 1937, he transferred control of all German film companies to the government and appointed himself as overseer of all productions. Henceforth, the content of domestic films would "fulfill with distinction the National Socialist idea." As Fritz Wiedemann, now vice president of the Reich Film Chamber, boasted, "There is no such thing as public taste; we can shape that as we will. We have determined political taste; we can do the same with artistic taste."[1]

Goebbels wanted to keep the United States neutral for as long as possible. That meant stopping Hollywood from producing films intended to sway American public opinion against the Hitler regime. The propaganda chief knew there were many kinds of battles to be fought during the course of war, and he considered the battle to control the mind among the greatest. Goebbels understood a basic truth about the power of cinema: movies matter the most about the things that people know the least. Many Americans got their first glimpse of what a Nazi rally or storm trooper looked like by watching movies or newsreels. Whether they thought of these people and their ideas as good or bad might well be determined by what they saw and heard on the screen.

By shaping the content of American films, Goebbels hoped to shape the ways in which Americans thought about Hitler and his policies.

With movies being seen by 88 million Americans a week in 1937, and by 150 million people throughout the world, Goebbels feared that a powerful anti-Nazi campaign by Hollywood studios could prove disastrous to German ambitions. Consequently, the propaganda minister turned to Georg Gyssling for help in manipulating the American psyche. Gyssling cajoled, threatened, and did everything in his power to ensure that the Jewish-dominated studios followed Production Code Administration regulations and made no film attacking Hitler or his government.

As Leopold McLaglan, Hermann Schwinn, and Henry Allen were concocting plots to kill Jews, Georg Gyssling was inflicting a different kind of pain, one that would hurt the moguls where it mattered the most: at the box office. By 1937 the motion picture business reigned as the nation's fourth largest industry, with over $2 billion in capital investments. Lavishly paid movie industry leaders accounted for forty of the sixty-three Americans earning more than $200,000 in 1937. Topping the list was Louis B. Mayer at $1.3 million, making him the highest paid employee in America. The MGM head earned more in salary that year than the entire U.S. Senate combined. As the number of American films shown in Germany steadily dropped from sixty-one in 1933–34 to thirty-six in 1936–37, the moguls were forced to deal with Gyssling if they wanted to protect their studios' bottom lines and their own high salaries.[2]

During his first three years as consul, Gyssling repeatedly used the threat of imposing Article 15, which refused permits for any film deemed "detrimental to German prestige," to hammer the moguls into compliance. As German military aggression increased after the 1936 Berlin Olympics, Gyssling became even more aggressive with Hollywood, intimidating individual actors and studio employees. When he heard that Malvina Pictures was preparing to release *I Was a Captive of Nazi Germany* in July 1936, Gyssling contacted the Motion Picture Producers and Distributors Association and demanded they stop the filming. Based on a true story, the movie recounts the harrowing experience of American journalist Isobel Steele, who was arrested and imprisoned by Nazi authorities on charges of espionage in August 1934. Steele spent four months in solitary confinement at Berlin's infamous Moabit prison and was deported only after the intervention of the U.S. State Department. Upon her return home, the celebrated journalist wrote numerous stories describing her experiences in Nazi Germany.

When MPPDA officials told Gyssling they had no jurisdiction over independent companies such as Malvina, the consul sent Isobel Steele a letter on German consulate stationery, threatening her for participating "in the making of a film allegedly dealing with certain experiences of yours in Germany."[3] He warned Steele that if the film were released, any future production in which she might appear would be banned. Similar threats were sent to every cast member, warning they too would be permanently banned in Germany if they appeared in the film.

Gyssling also summoned the movie's German actors and actresses to the consulate. Seated at his desk with a massive portrait of Hitler behind him and swastika flags throughout the office, the six-foot-three consul appeared a daunting figure to his nervous visitors. He let the actors know reprisals would be taken against family members living in Germany if they appeared in the film. The movie's cast took Gyssling's threats seriously. Following their meeting, a number of actors quit, while others agreed to continue under the condition that their names did not appear in the credits.[4]

When producer Alfred Mannon approached industry censor Joseph Breen about getting the seal of approval needed to book *I Was a Captive of Nazi Germany* into first-run theaters, the Production Code Administration head agreed with Gyssling and rejected the movie on the grounds that it violated the Code provision "which directs that 'the history, institutions, prominent people and citizenry of other nations shall be represented fairly.'" The PCA's board of directors in New York overruled Breen; however, without a major studio backing it, the film soon disappeared from circulation.[5]

Although he ultimately lost this battle, Gyssling won a larger war by letting Hollywood's German community know they could not escape the long arm of Adolf Hitler. The PCA might have defied Gyssling, but who would protect their relatives in Germany if actors and actresses dared do likewise?

Gyssling had considerably more success in forcing changes in two major films that promised to be far more critical of the Nazi regime, *The Road Back* (1937) and *Three Comrades* (1938). Both were based on novels by German writer Erich Maria Remarque, the fervent anti-Nazi who lived in exile and had published *All Quiet on the Western Front* in 1929. Hitler hated Remarque's antiwar novel so much that he banned the author and his books from Germany. Although *Three Comrades* was released after *The Road Back*, it was the first of the two productions to catch Georg Gyssling's attention. Set in late-1920s Germany, the novel told the story of three disillusioned German World War I veterans, Robert, Otto, and Gottfried, fighting to survive in an economically devastated nation. In the film, which is filled with critiques of the German government, the left-wing hero Gottfried is eventually killed in a street clash with Nazi thugs.

One of the qualities that made Gyssling so effective was his ability to find out about potential film projects long before most people in Hollywood. That was because he had his own spy, the handsome, fun-loving, and very popular Werner Plack. Gyssling hired the Berlin-born actor and wine salesman, his daughter Angelica recounted, "to go around to the nightspots and the bars and pick up Hollywood gossip" and information about the latest productions. "He kept an eye on all of the émigrés, all of those creative people who came over from Berlin."[6] Dividing his time between film sets and swanky Los Angeles nightspots such as the Swing Club on North Las Palmas Avenue, the jovial Plack plied his informants with enough alcohol to loosen any inhibitions.

Little surprise, then, that in the fall of 1936, well before the film went into production, Joseph Breen received several letters from the German consul, undoubtedly tipped off by Plack, expressing his country's concern that MGM was turning *Three Comrades* into a film. When the studio sent the PCA a highly polemical script written by F. Scott Fitzgerald and Ted Paramore, Breen responded to Gyssling's earlier threats by meeting with Louis B. Mayer and producer Joseph Mankiewicz. The MGM pair agreed to eliminate content deemed offensive to the Nazi regime. The subsequent draft they sent the PCA contained no references to the threatened status of democracy in post–World War I Germany, no images of swastikas, and no references to Brownshirts or Jews. After the film was completed in May 1938, Breen arranged a special screening for the German consul, who convinced the studio in his subtly threatening manner to cut three scenes. MGM agreed they would do "nothing to indicate in any way that the story is a reflection on the Nazi government." The only resistance came when Mankiewicz refused to turn the film's Nazi villains into Communist villains. The movie opened in June 1938.[7]

Gyssling succeeded in turning Remarque's anti-Nazi critique into a harmless love story stripped of its dissident political edge. As the opening page of the film's press book declared, "*3 Comrades* IS NOT A PROPAGANDA PICTURE. The locale might be any large Central European city and the time is the present. It is not political or controversial and its turbulent scenes could happen in any country."[8] Americans would learn nothing about the Nazi threat from this film, which was precisely what Gyssling wanted.

The able representative of the Nazi government also fought to depoliticize *The Road Back*, Remarque's sequel to *All Quiet on the Western Front*. The 1931 novel told the story of a shell-shocked squad of German veterans forced to deal with the economic and political chaos of postwar Germany. When Gyssling learned that Universal Pictures was turning the book into a film, he contacted Breen with his usual objections: "It would beyond all doubts lead to controversies and opposition on the part of the German government as the story gives an untrue and distorted picture of the German people." He urged Breen to use his influence to kill the project.[9]

Breen did not kill the film, but he did ask director James Whale to meet with Gyssling. Sitting in the German's office, surrounded by portraits of Hitler and Nazi flags, Whale recalled how "Consul Gyssling was, characteristically, never openly threatening in his attitude . . . He simply insinuated 'he'd be sorry to have to take counter measures.'" Whale told Gyssling that the story took place immediately after World War I and said nothing about Hitler or the Nazi government. Their conversation ended with the consul again warning that "he would be very sorry to have to be forced to report to his government that the picture was unsatisfactory." Several weeks later, Gyssling visited the Universal studio lot, watched an early version of the film, and then sent Breen his suggested cuts.[10]

When Universal Pictures refused to comply with the consul's requested changes, he sent registered letters to sixty actors working on the film. Adopting the same language as in the past, he warned: "With reference to the picture, *The Road Back*, in which you are said to play a part, I have been instructed by my government to issue you a warning, in accordance with Article 15 of the German decree of June 28, 1932, regulating the exhibit of foreign motion pictures." Gyssling threatened to refuse permits for any future film featuring any actor who participated in *The Road Back*.[11]

This would be one of the few times when Gyssling's threats met with outrage from the Hollywood community. A copy of his letter was reproduced in the Hollywood trade press, in the Hollywood Anti-Nazi League's *News of the World*, and in newspapers across the nation. Calling Gyssling's missive "one of the most insidious examples of Nazi interference in the lives of American citizens," HANL leaders sent a telegram to secretary of state Cordell Hull condemning the consul's intimidation tactics and calling for his immediate deportation.[12]

For once, the notoriously anti-Semitic State Department agreed with the protestors and lodged a formal complaint with the German Foreign Office. It was one thing for a foreign government to threaten studios with a loss of business, but quite another to threaten individual actors, many of whom were American citizens. Concerned about potential backlash, German ambassador Hans-Heinrich Dieckhoff issued a formal apology and promised that Gyssling's strong-arm tactics would not be repeated. The consul, he explained, had been following orders from former ambassador Hans Luther. A not-so-contrite Gyssling told a *Los Angeles Times* reporter, "I did just what I was advised to do in an order originating in Berlin." Reports that he received a rebuke from his government, he added, were "just fiction and fabrications not based on any facts."[13]

The Nazi consul had the last laugh. Whatever Universal officials may have said publicly, they ultimately caved in to German demands. The final version of *The Road Back* was a neutered rendering of the polemical novel. As *New York Times* film critic Frank Nugent complained, "the spirit of the book has been lost, its meaning changed"; the novel's "tragic impact has been vitiated by a meandering conclusion."[14] Berlin had little to fear from this production.

Gyssling also achieved a number of smaller victories along the way. After news leaked out that Warner Brothers was planning to make *The Life of Emile Zola* (1937), a film about Alfred Dreyfus, the Jewish officer wrongly convicted by anti-Semitic officials of transmitting French military secrets to the German government in 1894, Gyssling called the studio and spoke to the film's associate producer. Several days later, Jack Warner ordered several lines cut in which Dreyfus was referred to as a Jew. The word "Jew" was never spoken in the film.[15]

Gyssling's power over Hollywood was clear. More often than not, the German diplomat succeeded in convincing studios to delete scenes his government would find offensive. The moguls hated Gyssling but understood that the cost of ignoring his demands went far beyond any one film; he had the power to keep their productions out of every theater in the rapidly expanding German empire. Despite their bitterness, most movie executives just shrugged and chalked it up to the cost of doing business.

THE LOCAL ATTACK ON HOLLYWOOD

While Georg Gyssling was busily criticizing individual films, anti-Semites in Los Angeles were organizing boycotts against any Hollywood film featuring Jewish actors. In September 1938, Hermann Schwinn published a compilation of "Objectionable Motion Picture People" in the local *Deutscher Weckruf und Beobachter.* Silver Shirt leader Ken Alexander offered a similar list of "Who's Who in Hollywood— Find the Gentile!" in the *Liberator.* Both articles divulged the birth names that revealed actors' Jewish origins, such as Emanuel Goldenberg (Edward G. Robinson), Asa Yoelson (Al Jolson), and Israel Iskowitz (Eddie Cantor). German audiences could now easily identify Hollywood's Hebraic population.[16]

Ingram Hughes and Henry Allen went a step further and joined national Bund leader Fritz Kuhn's call for a total boycott of the Jewish-dominated industry. Vilifying Hollywood as the "Sodom and Gomorrha" [*sic*] of "International Jewry" where "Young Gentile girls are raped by Jewish Producers, Directors, and Casting Directors who go unpunished," Hughes's infamous proclamation called upon the nation's Christians to "Boycott the Movies!" Allen and his fascist friends spent many afternoons over the years standing high atop downtown buildings throwing thousands of stickers and handbills onto the city streets—"snow storming," as he called it. Those walking below picked up flyers urging them to "Destroy Jew-Monopoly of the Motion Picture Industry with its Sex Filth Films and Jew Communist Propaganda."[17]

Like Hitler and Goebbels, Los Angeles Nazis loved watching movies; they just did not want to see films made by Jewish Hollywood. Instead, they flocked to Deutsches Haus or Franz Ferenz's Continental Theater, where they could watch a steady stream of German-made films. Ferenz served as primary distributor of Nazi films and newsreels along the West Coast. In addition to operating the Continental Book Store on West Seventh Street near MacArthur Park, the Austrian-born American citizen opened the Continental Theater on West Twenty-Fourth Street, conveniently located just a mile south of Deutsches Haus. Charging a modest thirty-five cents for adults and ten cents for children, Ferenz's movie theater was a place where Nazi admirers felt comfortable watching Aryan-made films and newsreels of Hitler's latest triumphs.

Men and women entering the Continental Theater often gave Ferenz the Nazi salute, which he returned in like manner. As they walked to their seats, patrons admired the portraits and bronze plaques of the führer hanging on the walls. Moviegoing in this Nazi social center was an exuberant participatory experience. Each night's program began with Ferenz displaying a picture of Hitler on the screen and the audience rising to sing the "Horst Wessel Song," the Nazis' unofficial anthem. Extending their arms in a Nazi salute, the enthusiastic crowd ended the song with rounds of "Heil Hitler!" and "Sieg Heil!" Audiences loved hearing their mother tongue spoken on the screen and enjoyed cheering newsreel scenes of Hitler's army marching into the Sudetenland, Austria, and Czechoslovakia. The Continental Theater was also one of the few places where audiences felt comfortable unleashing their anti-Semitic feelings. Following a scene in *Kosher Schächten* (*Kosher Slaughter*, 1938) that depicted a Jew slaughtering a steer, several patrons screamed out, "Let's do the same thing to the Jews!"[18]

Ironically, Georg Gyssling secretly loved watching Hollywood movies with his daughter. Sometimes Georg and Angelica went to the movies together; other times the consul would sneak into the back of a theater to watch the latest Hollywood hit undetected. "He enjoyed films like *Ninotchka*," she recounted. "He thought the scene when Ninotchka [Greta Garbo] arrives in Paris was hilarious and the men giving the Nazi salute was a hoot." Unlike his masters in Germany, whom he felt "never had a sense of humor," Gyssling was especially fond of the actor most hated by Hitler: "He liked Charlie Chaplin," and despite his official protests to Breen, "thought *The Great Dictator* was hilarious."[19] The German consul was smart enough to know that he had to keep his enjoyment of Hollywood films a closely guarded secret.

GYSSLING UNDER ATTACK

At the same time the German consul stepped up pressure on the studios, he found himself attacked on several fronts: from studio heads and trade press columnists who objected to a foreign nation interfering with their business; from government authorities who accused him of running a spy ring; and most of all from local Bundists who simply hated his guts.

The uproar surrounding *The Road Back* brought Gyssling out of the shadows of screening rooms and into the limelight. *Motion Picture Daily* editor Red Kahn blasted the German diplomat and his "crackpot and irrational government" for their "unwarranted interference in matters which are none of its business." The *Hollywood Reporter* denounced Gyssling and insisted that his threats had "aroused American film interests to a high state of resentment against Nazi policies." Anger at the consul and his government grew so intense that *Hollywood Spectator* editor Welford Beaton published a widely circulated letter to the Jewish moguls urging them to use "one mighty voice" to help "your persecuted blood-brothers."[20]

The unwanted attention the Nazi consul received in Washington, D.C., proved far more disturbing than editorials in Hollywood periodicals. In July 1937, Samuel Dickstein accused the German government of running a "well organized subversive, un-American spy system in this country." Georg Gyssling responded to Dickstein's charges with "hearty laughter" and insisted "Nazism is not an exportable commodity. This is all too laughable. It doesn't sound like the assertion of a man in his right mind." Four months later, Dickstein named 116 suspected West Coast spies who answered to San Francisco consul Manfred von Killinger, who in turn was aided by Gyssling.[21]

Dickstein singled out Hermann Schwinn as the city's most prominent Nazi, but many believed Gyssling to be in charge of local espionage activities. Never a formal spymaster like Lewis, Gyssling had been ordered by Berlin to assist secret agents sent to the United States if they needed money or help.[22]

Gyssling may not have run an espionage ring with spies sent from Berlin, but he did have his own local agents, men like Werner Plack who kept him abreast of news about "important film personages" and general Hollywood developments. Plack left Los Angeles in 1940 under suspicion of being a secret agent and returned to Germany, where he went to work for the Foreign Office. Gyssling also obtained information from his close friend Hans Wolfram, editor of the Los Angeles *Staats Zeitung*. According to Lewis's operatives, Wolfram served as the consul's "go-between for the German American Bund and the more respectable elements in Los Angeles who were sympathetic to German Fascism." Wolfram's girlfriend, Jo Alderman, the city's social leader and frequent guest at Gyssling's home, proved a valuable source of information about elite attitudes to Germany. Given the consul's knowledge of the goings-on at Deutsches Haus, it is likely he had other men reporting to him.[23]

To Schwinn and Konrad Burchardi, the consul was the most hated Nazi in Los Angeles. Gyssling knew it and informed the Foreign Office in the summer of 1936 that he had lost the confidence of many German Americans who no longer regarded him as the "appointed representative" of the National Socialist government.[24]

When Burchardi returned to Germany in 1937 to take over as head of the general hospital in Bremen, he sent Auslands head Ernst Bohle a 22-page report denouncing Gyssling and laying out his vision of how Nazi activities in America should be conducted. The consul's former physician also sent a copy to Schwinn, who read the entire report at one of his staff meetings. Burchardi blamed Gyssling for the Bund's failure to attract more followers. Had he given them more help, the Bund could have "grown into an organization of 200,000 to 300,000 members, powerful enough to defeat all the bolshevist and Jewish machinations against Germany." The fact that the doctor had well-placed friends in Berlin only made matters worse for Gyssling. There was "a rumor in this city," one Lewis agent reported, that "Bohle feels that Burchardi's work has been so valuable that he will be sent back to Los Angeles to continue his activities."[25]

Hostilities between the consul and the Nazis never improved. Contemptuous of the diplomat's authority, Bund leaders refused Gyssling's order, sent to him by the Foreign Office in March 1938, to expel all German citizens from the Bund and to cease open displays of Nazi emblems. When the consul learned that Paul Kendzia, a noncitizen and active member of the Nazi Party, was still in the Bund, Gyssling ordered him to resign immediately. The fanatical Nazi ignored him.[26]

Fritz Kuhn, the Bund's American führer, was equally unimpressed with the Los Angeles consul. When investigative reporter John C. Metcalfe interviewed Kuhn, pretending he was writing a favorable story about the group, the Bund head told him about the constant friction between Gyssling and the Los Angeles group and confided that the consul might soon be replaced by a more militant figure, someone like San Francisco's fearsome Manfred von Killinger.[27]

Gyssling was as contemptuous of the Bund as they were of him. The consul complained to the Foreign Office about Schwinn's failure to dismiss German citizens and how Deutsches Haus had turned into an "amusement strip, with wild things going on."[28] Their bumbling efforts were hurting Germany's reputation among Americans and German Americans alike.

Schwinn and Burchardi were right about one thing: if the consul had been a more militant Nazi, he could have helped them forge an effective fifth-column movement in Los Angeles, one that could not have been so easily penetrated by a small amateur Jewish spy ring. However, there was a reason Gyssling was considered a rising star in the diplomatic corps. The savvy diplomat knew it was more important to please his masters in Berlin by keeping Hollywood neutral than to win the approval of local Bundists. His superiors in the Foreign Office ignored complaints from Los Angeles Nazis because they considered Gyssling "very efficient" at his job.[29]

Georg Gyssling understood something his Bund critics did not. For him to gain their loyalty, he would need to become a more outspoken anti-Semite. Yet doing so would have undermined the main reason he was sent to Los Angeles: to stop Hollywood from making any film that damaged Germany's image in America or abroad. Everything else was secondary. Gyssling could not fulfill his primary mission if he was as openly anti-Semitic as men like Burchardi demanded. It is hard to imagine the moguls cooperating, even begrudgingly, with the likes of Schwinn or Burchardi.

Fortunately, the Foreign Office shared Gyssling's views about the Bund. In January 1938, frustrated by the increased fragmentation of the German American community often brought on by the Bund's activities, the Foreign Office ordered its American consuls to concentrate "on cultural issues" and halt any effort to exert political influence on the local Germanic community.[30] This policy made Gyssling's position on the cultural front of Hollywood more important than ever. So long as he succeeded in thwarting the moguls, his superiors in Berlin were willing to overlook all complaints.

ANSCHLUSS

Hostilities between Gyssling and the Bund were momentarily suspended on the morning of March 12, 1938, as German troops marched into Austria, where they were greeted with cheers, flowers, and Nazi salutes by adoring crowds. Three days later, 200,000 cheering German Austrians gathered in Vienna's Heldenplatz (Heroes' Square) to hear Hitler boldly proclaim, "The oldest eastern province of the German people shall be, from this point on, the newest bastion of the German Reich." Over the next several weeks, 70,000 Jews, Social Democrats, Communists, and political dissidents were arrested or sent to concentration camps. Those Jews remaining behind were beaten and humiliated by angry mobs that plundered their homes and shops. Newspaper wire photos showed Viennese Jews on their hands and knees, forced to clean the streets under the eyes of gleeful Brownshirts. "The

Jewish district looked as though it had just been through a locust plague," reported NBC radio correspondent Max Jordan.[31]

Los Angeles Nazis and fascists greeted the Anschluss with joyous celebration. Hundreds of proud Reich supporters gathered at Deutsches Haus to watch newsreels of Hitler's triumphant entry into Vienna. They saw cheering Austrians greeting the führer and his storm troopers with outstretched arms and faces as rapturous as if the Messiah had arrived. On April 10, 1938, just five days after Leopold McLaglan sailed for home, 450 Bundists, Silver Shirts, White Russians, and Italian and Spanish fascists flocked to Nazi headquarters for an evening of speeches and celebration. Surrounded by uniformed guards and walls decorated with swastika flags, the ubiquitous Henry Allen strode to the stage, thrust his arm upward, and told the crowd, "I salute you, Adolf Hitler, and you, Greater Germany, and what you have done in five short years." The führer, Allen went on to say, "is the great Christian of our era, and his great deeds will inspire other Christians to follow his steps and not rest until the entire Judeo-Bolshevist brood is wiped from the surface of the earth. Yes, fellow Christians, we must not rest until the public is roused to revolution against the [American] government."[32] Following speeches by Franz Ferenz and others, the crowd adjourned to the building's restaurant, where they spent the rest of the evening dining, drinking, and dancing.

The Anschluss changed the course of Joe Roos's life. Deciding he needed "a more solid knowledge of the goings on at the German House," the Viennese-born Roos attended the celebration with his wife, Alvina. For several years, Community Committee members had urged Lewis's part-time assistant to quit his screenwriting job and work full-time for the group. Roos had resisted until that evening. "I felt it wasn't fair for me to continue thinking up nice boy-meets-girl stories for the movies, because I understood what Nazism stood for." Encouraged by Alvina, "who understood what was in his heart," Roos, who considered himself a deeply "political animal," gave up his cushy job at United Artists to work for Lewis and the Jewish community. For her part, Alvina, a nurse turned housewife, returned to work to make up for the family's loss in income.[33]

Although the Anschluss proved a peak moment of German pride, it evoked outrage among American citizens across the nation. In Los Angeles, Gyssling, who now also served as the Austrian consul, found himself enmeshed in a round of unprecedented public criticism. After going on KMTR radio to defend his government, he accepted an invitation to discuss the German occupation at a town hall luncheon held at the luxurious Biltmore Hotel. Gyssling justified the invasion, explaining that "residents of post-war Austria were 98% Germanic in language, culture and sympathies." When asked about Nazi persecution of Austrian Jews, he insisted that "Jews in Austria would not be deprived of property rights any more than German Jews had been." This last comment, a reporter noted, "brought laughter from the audience, but the Consul doggedly kept on talking." Gyssling proved such a smooth speaker that he deflected all criticism; when the meeting ended, the "German Consul was given considerable applause."[34]

No applause was heard that June, when 500 protestors assembled at the German Consulate on West Ninth Street and spent two hours marching in picket lines with banners and posters that read "Hitler Persecutes the Catholics in Germany and Murders Catholics and Jews" and "Stop Bombardment of Spanish Towns." This was only the second time Gyssling had come under public assault. A year earlier, 175 picketers had marched outside his office to protest the bombing of Almeria during the Spanish Civil War. In both instances, the crowd was told that Gyssling was not in his office. He was; he simply refused to confront the angry group.[35]

With the House Un-American Activities Committee preparing for a new round of hearings under the leadership of Texas Democrat Martin Dies, Leon Lewis and his now full-time assistant Joe Roos used the growing national anger at the Nazi regime to renew the support of veterans' groups. That June, the Veterans of Foreign Wars and the Disabled American Veterans passed unanimous resolutions at their county and state conventions urging the Dies Committee to "make a most exhaustive study of the Nazi menace in America and on the Coast." Singling out the Bund as a particularly dangerous un-American group, the veterans promised to aid congressional investigators in any way they could. National Bund leader Fritz Kuhn insisted his organization had nothing to fear from such an investigation, but he secretly ordered Schwinn to destroy all important papers and documents.[36]

As summer drew to a close, the ever-cautious Lewis found himself uncharacteristically optimistic. Opposition to the Nazi regime in Los Angeles and across the nation was growing. In response, Gyssling was ordered back to Berlin in mid-August for six weeks to meet with Adolf Hitler and Foreign Office officials. Schwinn also found himself on the defensive. In addition to facing deportation hearings, he now had to deal with anti-Nazi groups in New York who accused him of being a propagandist for the Hitler regime and demanded that the Justice Department force him to register as a foreign agent.[37]

With the Bund under attack and HUAC set to begin hearings in Washington, D.C., and Los Angeles within the next year, Lewis believed he was finally making headway in thwarting the Nazi threat to America. The far more experienced Joe Roos was running his operatives, and they had just recruited a highly placed Bundist to spy for them.

16.

The Three Most Dangerous
Enemies List

Meeting at their Temple Street offices following Leopold McLaglan's arrest, Leon Lewis, Mendel Silberberg, and the Community Committee's executive board began planning a quiet revenge against the plotters and their allies. They started by drawing up a list of their three most dangerous enemies in Los Angeles: Henry Allen, Hermann Schwinn, and the recently arrived Mrs. Leslie Fry, the suspected money and brains behind both men. Lewis promised everything would be done in accordance with the law, but that "no stone will be left unturned to find the Achilles heel in the case of each individual involved."[1]

Fortunately, Lewis had taken on Joe Roos as his full-time assistant in March. Over the next several months, the two men set out to discover each of their three enemies' weaknesses and use that knowledge to undermine their power.

Driving to San Diego in his dark blue Studebaker Commander on the morning of April 22, 1938, Henry Allen was invigorated by the militant speech he'd given several days earlier at the Deutsches Haus celebration of the Anschluss. He and three other men were driving down to disrupt a talk that Judge Henry Hollzer planned to give to San Diego Jews. They intended to "snowstorm" Hollzer's event with thousands of anti-Semitic flyers written by himself, Hermann Schwinn, and their latest patron, Mrs. Leslie Fry.[2]

Allen was especially pleased to have Chuck Slocombe sitting beside him. His erstwhile fellow plotter had left town after Leopold McLaglan's arrest. He'd told Allen it was because of the slow winter water taxi business in San Pedro, but in truth he was sick and frightened. Fearing revenge by White Russians, Slocombe had left Lewis and taken a job that December running tourist excursions in Boulder City, Nevada. Following a fight with his employer, he returned to his water taxi business in Long Beach, and back into Lewis's service.[3]

Slocombe had another goal as they drove down the Pacific Coast Highway. He, Lewis, and Roos had devised a plan to get ahold of Henry Allen's leather briefcase, the one that contained documents even his most trusted friends had not seen—documents Roos believed would be "of importance to our intelligence agencies." Allen guarded his treasure with his beloved "Kike killer," an eighteen-inch-long, two-and-a-half-inch-wide oak club with a leather thong that could be wrapped around the wrist. During a stop along the way, Allen took the club out of the car and showed Slocombe how to use it: "You wrap it around your wrist and then poke it in the man's stomach, and when he bends over, come down on top of his head with the flat side."[4]

Allen had called Slocombe several days earlier, asking him along, but was coy about the date; he did not want to take a chance that Lewis's spies might discover his plans. Slocombe immediately called Lewis, who in turn telephoned the San Diego district attorney to warn him about Allen's intended "snowstorming" visit to his city. When they arrived in San Diego, Allen left the car with a parking lot attendant and the four men looked for tall buildings to drop flyers from. While pretending to check a nearby roof, Slocombe slipped into the office of a Jewish attorney, tipped him off about the snowstorm operation, and asked him to call the police and district attorney.[5]

Slocombe returned to the attorney's office thirty minutes later. Sergeant Whitney and the local district attorney were already there. They had talked with Lewis and agreed upon a plan: the moment Allen and his accomplices started tossing their anti-Semitic handbills from rooftops, the police would pick them up for illegal posting.

Everything went off as expected. The police seized the four men and took them to jail, along with Allen's briefcase, which they removed from his car. Sergeant Whitney knew about the setup, but not his men. They believed they were arresting Communists. After reading the anti-Semitic flyer, one officer apologized to Slocombe. "This is a hell of a note that we have to pinch a guy that's fightin' the Communists. I wish I had read that before I brought you to the station. This is good and I am going to put one of those in my pocket." He handed copies to the jailor. "Hell, they ought to give him a medal."[6] Nodding in agreement, the police then passed handbills to one another.

Slocombe and Allen's two other assistants paid a $3 fine and were given a six-month suspended sentence. After the police found Allen's "Kike killer," the two-time felon was charged with possession of a "deadly weapon" and held over in jail.[7]

Early the next morning, Lewis jumped in his car and drove to San Diego to inspect the contents of the briefcase. As soon as Lewis, the sheriff, and the DA opened the bag and realized what it contained, they called in FBI agents from San Diego and Los Angeles. Several hours later, as the five men examined Allen's prized possession, they were astounded to find the names and addresses of nearly a hundred Nazi, Japanese, and Italian secret agents working in the United States and the addresses of their contacts in Germany. Mixed in among the files were maps, diaries, and reports of Allen's secret meetings with foreign spies and embassy officials from Germany, Austria, Hungary, Egypt, and Mexico. They also found a notebook containing the code names of his various correspondents. Allen used the name Rosenthal; Schwinn went by Laura, Big Fellow, Peter George, or Arthur George; Leslie Fry was Auntie; Nazis were referred to as Arabs, Japan as Alaska, and Jews as Garlics.[8]

As they dug through the files, the group was shocked when they came across correspondence among American Nationalist Confederation leaders—a coalition of several militant Christian groups—describing their plot to overthrow the government after the 1940 elections. Earlier that January, Clayton F. Ingalls, husband of famed aviatrix and Nazi spy Laura Ingalls, had sent George Deatherage the blueprint for a fascist military organization and the names and addresses of hundreds of coup leaders and subleaders scattered across the country. They were organizing their military cadre into "cells of thirteen each, consisting of four Nazis from the German Bund, Italians with Fascist connections, White Russians and three Americans who 'believe in the Cause.'"[9]

Ingalls planned to equip each cell with weapons obtained through the National Rifle Association in Washington, D.C. After the government takeover, citizens who refused to surrender peacefully—most likely Jews and Communists—would be shot on the spot. Coup leaders, Ingalls insisted, must not "flinch from issuing orders to field officers to mow down without hesitation the great Communist front. The ranks of big-breasted women carrying babies while behind them the Communist contingents dare our men to fire. They must fire and kill even those if we would save our own. To hell with public opinion once again."[10]

Ingalls and Deatherage believed they had the money and connections to mount a coup that would rid the nation of "Jewish Imperialism and Judeo-Communism." Ingalls was in direct touch with San Francisco consul Manfred von Killinger, while Deatherage, "a former Nazi agent in the Bay area," had raised $25,000 for weapons—and received promises of more to come from Leslie Fry. Henry Allen suggested they could obtain additional guns from their mutual acquaintance James True. "If your friends want some peashooters," True wrote Allen that February, "I have connections now for any quantity at the right price." At the bottom of the typed letter, True added a handwritten sentence: "But be very careful about controlling this information and destroy this letter."[11]

Here was a group of Americans plotting treason against their own government, and Nazis and fascists were assisting them. Lewis pleaded with the sheriff and FBI agents to photostat the briefcase's contents. When they refused, explaining that Lewis had no official standing, he had them call his friend Commander Ellis Zacharias, the district naval intelligence officer and a fellow Jew. Zacharias was out of town, but his replacement brought Lewis and Slocombe to naval headquarters that night, where they stayed until 3:00 a.m., getting Allen's "disorganized mass" ready for photostatting.[12]

Lewis's timely actions provided the FBI and naval intelligence with concrete evidence of espionage and treason by Nazis and fascists that they had been unable to obtain on their own. The State Department was even further behind in tracking Nazi activities. Three months earlier, secretary of state Cordell Hull denied reports that Nazis were arming fascist Gold Shirts in Mexico, but documented proof of arms dealings were found in Allen's briefcase. When Zacharias returned, he forwarded Allen's list of foreign agents to intelligence agencies in Washington, D.C., where it proved extremely useful in identifying potential enemies.[13]

Henry Allen was released from jail the next day after posting bail and immediately drove back to Los Angeles. He promised the court he would return to San Diego to face a felony weapons charge. The police returned Allen's briefcase, but only after Lewis had copied everything at naval intelligence headquarters.

Now that Joe Roos was working for Leon Lewis full-time, the pair devised a two-part strategy for taking Allen out of action. The first step was to entangle him in so many court cases that he would be too busy to work on Ingalls's coup d'état. Roos discovered that Allen had registered to vote in the 1936 presidential election, so he filed charges against him: the penal code made it illegal for a felon to register to vote. Allen would have to go to trial and, if convicted, faced a minimum sentence of twenty years under the Habitual Criminal Act. As anticipated, the San Diego and Los Angeles court cases tied Allen up into the next year. To make his life even more difficult, Lewis and Roos supplied the state comptroller's office with evidence that Allen had been receiving relief funds through fraud. They hoped it would lead to more criminal proceedings.[14]

The second part of the spymasters' strategy involved using Allen's Achilles' heel against him. Allen was a perpetual lieutenant—the kind of man who always preferred being second in command, especially if paid to do so. He had served as right-hand man to Ingram Hughes, Kenneth Alexander, Leopold McLaglen, and now Leslie Fry. Lewis and Roos turned to Chuck Slocombe to drive a wedge between Allen and the mysterious Mrs. Fry.

Born in 1882 to American parents living in Paris, Louise Chandor married Russian aristocrat and Imperial Navy officer Feodor Ivanovich Shishmarev, who was murdered by Bolsheviks during the Russian Revolution. Fleeing Russia, Paquita Louise de Shishmareff, as she called herself, lived in Britain, Canada, and New York before settling in Los Angeles under the name Leslie Fry. Her experiences in Russia left her with a profound hatred of Jews and Communists. Upon arriving in Los Angeles, the woman Lewis and Roos considered "the chief Fascist propagandist in Southern California" founded the Militant Christian Patriots and the *Christian Free Press*, an anti-Semitic newspaper modeled after Germany's infamous *Der Stürmer*. The short, dark-haired fascist, who enjoyed wearing expensive furs and gloves, used money from Pasadena heiress Mrs. W. K. Jewett to become the main financier of fascist and Nazi activities in Los Angeles. As one of Lewis's agents warned, "she is very well informed; has great intelligence, don't underestimate her. She has the brains of the outfit."[15]

When Allen drove back to Los Angeles after his release from the San Diego jail, he was too deep in thought to notice that several cars behind him were Leon Lewis and Chuck Slocombe. Allen led them straight to Fry. She and Allen agreed that he had been set up, but disagreed over who had tipped off the police. Fry suspected Slocombe, suggesting that he was the leak in both the McLaglen case and the San Diego fiasco, but Allen vehemently disagreed. He suspected Fry because she was the only one who knew the precise date of his San Diego snowstorm expedition.[16]

Having put Allen out of commission for the near future, Lewis and Roos turned their attention to the second name on the enemies list, Hermann Schwinn. This time they needed to proceed with caution:

Mrs. Leslie Fry (l) and Henry Allen (r)
Jewish Federation Council of Greater Los Angeles, Community Relations Committee Collection, Part 2,
Special Collections and Archives, Oviatt Library, California State University, Northridge

over the past several months Schwinn had grown more powerful and dangerous. Nazi sympathizers at the courthouse warned Schwinn that a Jew named Joe Roos had brought charges against Allen. In retaliation, one evening shortly after Allen's arrest for voter fraud, Roos was jumped just steps from his house. "I was beaten up, and I suppose they would have beaten me much more than they did, but they ran when they saw a car coming. My wife doesn't know about that. My glasses were pulled off, so I told my wife that I fell."[17]

The spymasters never found out who attacked Roos, but they suspected Nazi storm troopers, who now called themselves the Ordnungsdienst (Order Service), the name Hitler gave his armed forces in the 1920s before changing it to Sturmabteilung. Two months before Roos's beating, OD leader Michael Drey told his men, "If ever an attempt is made to disrupt our affairs, we will fight, and if necessary we will not stop fighting until the last of the *OD* lies dead on the floor." Drey handled the Bund's "strong-arm tactics" and ordered his men to carry hand-size rubber hoses wrapped in newspaper and hidden inside their pants, hard rubber hoses that could smash a skull with one blow.[18]

THE TRANSFORMATION OF HERMANN SCHWINN

On Monday, May 30, 1938, 1,500 delegates, many dressed in Nazi uniforms, settled into their seats inside San Francisco's California Hall to hear Hermann Schwinn deliver the keynote address at the Bund's first Western Regional Conference. As several hundred anti-Nazi demonstrators stood outside the hall chanting "Down with Hitler" and waving placards that read DRIVE THE NAZIS OUT OF TOWN, the western führer strode to the podium and presented a "Five Point Americaniza-tion Program" that would "help the United States back on its feet." Insisting "our fight is against Communism in this country," he demanded that Franklin Roosevelt sever all ties with Russia, fire his Jewish advisers, and fill all high government positions with Gentiles. Schwinn ended by calling on Nazis and fascists "to unite and put their shoulders to the wheel to lead this country and to rid it of Jews and Communists." He sat down to "tremendous applause."[19] With the main part of the meeting over, delegates spent the rest of the evening dancing and drinking until the hall closed at 2:00 a.m.

The convention received the national publicity Schwinn had long desired. Reporters from sixteen newspapers covered the two-day gath-ering, while newsreel teams set up cameras, hoping to record fights between Nazis and demonstrators.[20]

The next morning, Schwinn's cohorts greeted their leader with much backslapping and congratulations. Despite considerable opposition from hotel owners who refused to house Nazis and kitchen staffs that refused to serve them, Schwinn had pulled off a successful event.

William Bockhacker, Schwinn's new right-hand man, noticed dramatic changes in his leadership style. Since returning from Germany in late September 1937, where he had met with "men of high Party standing," Schwinn had showed considerable skill as a regional leader, dazzling the San Francisco crowd by proposing more statesmanlike solutions to the nation's problems. He made delegates feel as if *they* were the true Americans, not the riffraff heckling them outside California Hall. Following the convention, Schwinn traveled across the western

United States, weaving local Bunds into a unified body with a common strategy for success. He also strengthened alliances with Italian, Japanese, and Mexican fascists, inviting their leaders to speak at Deutsches Haus and cooperating with Japanese secret service agents.[21]

Fortunately, Lewis and Roos had a new man inside Deutsches Haus: William August Bockhacker, Agent W2. In early December 1937 the thirty-five-year-old Bockhacker, who had spent four years working for the Burns Detective Agency, agreed to join the Bund as an undercover operative working for Lewis and the Disabled American Veterans' Americanism Committee. His charge: to report on subversive activities within the Bund and discover instances of "possible espionage and sabotage." In return, Lewis agreed to pay the unemployed former investigator a salary of $35 a week.[22]

Bockhacker entered the Bund when Schwinn needed to recruit more Americans if he wished to be taken seriously by Reich officials. He seemed a perfect candidate to groom for Schwinn's new American leadership core. Born in Colorado in 1902 to a Swiss father and a German mother, he was married to a German woman who preferred speaking her native tongue in their home. Too young to fight in World War I, Bockhacker spent the war years and early 1920s living in Germany, where he became active in the Free Corps movement, the precursor to Hitler's Brownshirts. After moving back to Denver in the late 1920s, he helped organize the Colorado War Veterans' Association. Unable to find work, he moved his family to Los Angeles.[23]

When the German-speaking spy visited Deutsches Haus for the first time on December 6, 1937, he told Hermann Schwinn he wanted to help with his German Radio Hour, a thirty-minute program of German music and news the Bund leader hosted every Friday night on KRKD from 7:45 to 8:15, with replays on Sunday. Much to Bockhacker's surprise, Schwinn "knew all about me and my work in Denver [with war veterans], and in a short while we were sitting with beer and cigars, talking about Germany, the Party, and the present situation here in the States."[24]

Schwinn was still suspicious. Having been deceived by Ness, he asked OD head Michael Drey and *Weckruf* editor Arno Risse to be on high alert for new spies sent by the Jews. When Bockhacker returned three days later, Schwinn "inspected my papers, family tree and records of the Denver World War Veteran organization." He passed the test. Later that night, Risse introduced Bockhacker to the OD unit and hailed him as "a member in good standing."[25] Being unemployed, Bockhacker volunteered to do whatever work needed to be done, which often kept him in

Deutsches Haus until 3:00 a.m. and gave him plenty of time to snoop around.

The hardworking Bockhacker soon emerged as the Bund leader's new confidant and chauffeur. By April 1938 he was attending Deutsches Haus staff meetings, driving his boss to the docks, doing propaganda work, and hosting the German Radio Hour when Schwinn was out of town. Bockhacker rose high enough to become a trusted member of the OD, standing guard at meetings and working closely with Michael Drey.

Bockhacker proved so effective in passing confidential information to Roos and Lewis that Bundists were convinced the Jews had placed another spy inside Deutsches Haus. "Drey asked me who I thought 'could be blowing off to the Jews.' He said that he was not supposed to tell me but that every time we decide on something there is action against us at the particular point."[26] The lingering presence of an undetected spy began turning Bundists against one another and against Schwinn, who many felt was not paying attention to local problems.

Schwinn was in fact more concerned with bigger issues. His meeting with party leaders in Germany did more than flatter his ego. He finally understood what he needed to do to attract a following powerful enough to take over the government either by the ballot or the bullet. He ignored orders to expel German citizens from the Bund, but hoped to please officials in Berlin by attracting more Americans members and removing its taint as a "foreign" organization. At meetings throughout the spring and summer, Schwinn stressed the need for everyone to become citizens so they could flex their collective power at the ballot box: "As citizens we have the right to open our mouths and demand equality of rights." Like Hitler, Schwinn believed that a neutral America was a soft America. If he could convince substantial numbers of German American voters to pressure Congress to maintain neutrality, he had an excellent chance of replacing the Bund's national leader, Fritz Kuhn, a man held in low esteem by the Foreign Office and by Auslands head Ernst Bohle.[27]

Schwinn created an American "Sympathizer's Group" that April and asked Marius Mannik to forge its men into a military unit that would complement the OD. By June the group had 22 volunteers who met at Deutsches Haus every Friday night. Schwinn asked Bockhacker to mentor the Americans and instruct them in the Bund's ideological background and purposes.[28]

Michael Drey was more concerned with the Sympathizers' military training. Since the Anschluss, Bund leaders had been gripped by a new sense of militancy. Drey and Schwinn appealed to the Sympathizers not as National Socialists but as patriotic anti-Communists. A heavily armed and well-drilled Bund was the only group capable of saving America from the anticipated Red effort to seize control of the government. Once Communists started their killing spree, Drey predicted, "the public will open their arms to the Bund" and "jump into the fight against the Jews and the Communists." Seeking experienced military men to join them, Schwinn and Drey regularly brought U.S. Navy sailors to Bund meetings, where they were wined and dined by OD troops.[29]

The Bund's fascist allies offered an equally violent vision of the near future. Speaking at Deutsches Haus that spring, Silver Shirt field marshal Roy Zachary promised Bund members that if no one else volunteered to kill President Roosevelt, he would shoot the "dictator" and "blow the entire Jew Deal sky-high." Zachary's call to assassinate a sitting president was greeted with enthusiasm by the Bund's rapidly expanding audience. In the months following the Anschluss, meetings drew upward of 350–400 people, among them disgruntled high school students like Charles Bukowski, a future novelist/poet who was attracted to the Nazi cause.[30]

Growing increasingly confident in his abilities to lead Nazis, fascists, and Americans alike, Schwinn mounted the first Western Conference of the Anti-Communist Federation at Deutsches Haus from August 6 to 8, 1938. He saw this as an opportunity to win over middle-class and patriotic organizations by presenting the Bund as champions of anticommunism.

As 150 delegates gathered inside Nazi headquarters for Saturday night's opening session, 3,000 pickets—organized by the Hollywood Anti-Nazi League and a consortium of labor unions—flooded the streets outside the building, shouting "Down with Nazism" and "Down with Fascism," while Captain Red Hynes and thirty police kept order. When the pickets finally dispersed, Leslie Fry, who had funded the event, thanked the Red Squad leader for his good work, while Schwinn ordered free beer for the tired police.

What none of them knew was that Joe Roos had arranged to have a truck parked outside Deutsches Haus, where newly recruited operatives took photographs of everyone entering and leaving the building; several other volunteers stood across the street, photographing anyone their companions may have missed. Roos posted another man on the rooftop of the nearby Chevrolet Building, taking photographs and writing down the license plate numbers of all arrivals. Roos and Lewis used

Anti-Nazi Protest outside Deutches Haus, August 1938
Jewish Federation Council of Greater Los Angeles, Community Relations Committee Collection, Part 2,
Special Collections and Archives, Oviatt Library, California State University, Northridge

their extensive network of contacts to recruit several out-of-town delegates and newspaper correspondents, who agreed to report back on
events inside. To ensure that none of the operatives would be caught,
Bockhacker volunteered to inspect the credentials of every delegate and
reporter. By the end of the convention, Roos and Lewis had photographs
of all participants and knew everything that happened in the meetings,
information they forwarded to government intelligence agencies.[31]

Over the next two days, delegates heard Italian Blackshirt Joseph
Ferri call on all fascists to fight their "common enemy shoulder to
shoulder." They listened to a variety of Nazi and fascist speakers lavish
praise on Germany and Japan while denouncing the United States and
the Soviet Union. The fifteen resolutions passed by delegates listed the
expected array of anti-Red, anti-Semitic demands, including passage of
a law that would allow only Christians to hold high positions in the
military and the government.[32]

What was not expected was the huge painted sign on the wall of the
auditorium: "The Jewish Agents for the persecution of Christian

Patriots are The Jewish Anti-Defamation League of the B'nai B'rith, 660 Roosevelt Building and The Hollywood Anti-Nazi League, 6912 Hollywood Blvd." The sign contained the names of the Nazis' two most dangerous enemies, Leon Lewis and Mendel Silberberg. The message was clear: these men needed to be dealt with one way or another. Showing they were not afraid of initiating violence, Michael Drey and fifty of his OD men marched to the German American League's anti-Nazi counterdemonstration and beat their delegates with rubber truncheons. Open warfare within the city's German community had broken out. A month later, after someone fired two bullets at Bund leader Arno Risse, Drey warned his men, "This, I assure you, is only the beginning. We will experience violence just as the early followers of Hitler did."[33]

Initially, Schwinn did not openly countenance violence. His first ambition was to supplant Kuhn as the Nazi leader in America. Traveling to New York for the Bund's national convention in early September, the ambitious western führer led a floor fight calling for its complete Americanization. Schwinn told the 632 delegates that, since beginning his Americanization program in Los Angeles, applications for membership had been "pouring" in. With 28 million people of German descent living in the United States, he predicted the Bund could become a powerful political force, but only if it adopted a more American appearance. He demanded that all meetings and public events be conducted in English; that greetings of "Heil Hitler" be changed to "Free America"; and that Bund newspapers print a majority of their articles in English. Schwinn's plan met with strong opposition from older members who wanted more National Socialism, not less. "After a bitter and hard fight," Schwinn won.[34]

Kuhn was unanimously reelected as the Bund national leader, but Schwinn emerged from the meetings as its rising star. His self-confidence, and that of Bundists across the nation, grew stronger over the next several months as Hitler achieved a series of political and territorial victories against a seemingly complacent Europe. On September 30, 1938, representatives from Germany, Italy, France, and the United Kingdom signed the Munich Agreement, which allowed Hitler to annex portions of Czechoslovakia inhabited by German-speaking residents. Several days after British prime minister Neville Chamberlain declared he had achieved "peace for our time," Nazi forces marched into the Sudetenland and absorbed it into Germany's expanding Reich.[35]

Los Angeles Bundists greeted news of the territorial seizure with a week of celebrations that culminated on Monday night, October 10, when 600 people filled every seat at Deutsches Haus. They listened to Schwinn's report on the Bund conference and his usual denunciations of the "Jew United States." The crowd also heard Italian fascist Ferri deliver an uncharacteristically anti-Semitic speech. "For the first time," Bockhacker reported, "he really opened up and declared war on our enemies, the Jews, now that Mussolini has announced his new policy." Until the Munich capitulation, Bockhacker observed, Italian "anti-Semitism was officially very luke warm." But after being pressured by Hitler, Mussolini enacted racial policies toward Jews similar to Germany's.[36] Lewis had new enemies to worry about.

Following Munich, few could doubt that Germany was preparing for war. Two weeks earlier, Schwinn's lieutenant Arno Risse received a letter from Dr. Konrad Burchardi explaining that the Bund would soon get a request from the city's administrator to send 10,000 skilled laborers to Bremen; all travel expenses would be paid for by the government. German authorities sent similar requests to Bundists throughout the United States. Stopping in Cleveland on his way home from New York, Schwinn discovered that 75 percent of the city's Bundists had already packed their bags and returned to the fatherland.[37]

Nazis in America were also gearing up for war at home. Hans Diebel, now in charge of the Aryan Bookstore, boasted of the coming day when a domestic revolution launched by Reds would ultimately lead

Hans Diebel Leading Pistol Practice
Jewish Federation Council of Greater Los Angeles, Community Relations Committee Collection, Part 2, Special Collections and Archives, Oviatt Library, California State University, Northridge

to a Nazi seizure of the government. To prepare for "Der Tag" (The Day), Bockhacker began recruiting men within the police and sheriff's departments, the National Guard, and army and navy soldiers stationed in Los Angeles. That fall, the Bund's national headquarters ordered all OD units to train in the use of firearms, but cautioned that practices must be camouflaged and hidden from American eyes. Bundists were told that any citizen who joined the National Rifle Association could purchase new guns from them for $14 or used pistols for $7.50.[38]

"THE TERRORIZATION OF LEON L. LEWIS"

Leon Lewis's worries about Nazi activities at home and abroad were nothing compared to facing the moment he had dreaded since starting his spy operation. Lewis considered Leslie Fry his third most dangerous enemy, but she judged him her worst foe. Just as Lewis knew Fry's weakness was her dependence upon Allen and Schwinn to carry out her orders, she knew Lewis's Achilles' heel was his children.[39]

Despite their falling-out after the San Diego arrest, Allen and Fry forged a truce that summer when she agreed to pay his considerable legal fees. Fry also held another weapon to force Allen's compliance: she threatened to tell his wife about an affair he had had in Mexico. In return for her silence and financial largesse, Fry asked him to help her plot the "terrorization of Leon L. Lewis."[40]

After scouting out Lewis's neighborhood, Fry had Allen accompany her to the ADL leader's home. She had purchased rubber gloves and an oilcloth to wrap around their shoes so that no footprints would be left. The two walked around the house several times, carefully noting where Lewis's car was parked and locating the best escape routes. Allen had no idea why they were there, but after leaving, he reported, Fry "informed me that it was her desire to 'terrorize' Lewis in every way possible before my trial." Fry suggested that they "arrange to get what men were necessary, change the license plates on my car, pass by Lewis's house late at night, heave rocks upon which might be tied suitable messages, through the big plate-glass window in front of the house—and speed away." The rocks would contain a message warning Lewis that his daughters Rosemary (fifteen) and Clare (ten) would be kidnapped if he did not halt his investigations.[41]

This was no hastily planned plot. Fry bought a small rubber printing press to write the notes so their handwriting could not be traced. The purpose of her afternoon scouting mission was to acquaint Allen with the layout of Lewis's home and neighborhood so there would be no surprise on the night of the rock throwing. If Lewis chose to ignore the warning, Allen was convinced Fry's next step was an actual kidnapping—or worse.

The terrorization plot was never carried out for two reasons. First, as Allen explained to James True, the friend who offered to supply weapons for the Ingalls-Deatherage coup, "I am not so dumb that I failed to realize that an act of this nature would have but one result, namely, criminal prosecution." Allen still suspected Fry had set him up in San Diego and thought the kidnapping was another effort to frame him. As a twice-convicted felon, he would be put "behind bars forever" if she turned him in.[42]

Uncertain that Allen and Fry would not reconcile and fearing for his children's safety, Lewis had Slocombe pit the two against each other. "The strategy decided upon by Li [Lewis] is to impress Allen with the idea that I am sore at Mrs. Fry and would stop at nothing until she gets what is coming to her."[43] Throughout the summer and fall, Slocombe and Allen compared notes on how Fry had betrayed them both.

Multiple court cases and constant worry took its toll on the already sickly Allen. When Slocombe ran into him in mid-September, he was surprised at how ill Allen looked. "I hardly recognized him. He did not look as prosperous as he did several months ago." As they stood on the corner of Sixth Street and Hill, Allen confessed, "I am through with her." Despite Fry's efforts to convince him that Slocombe was working for the Jews, Allen continued to defend his Long Beach ally. "Mrs. Fry still throws the whole burden on you, and blames you for everything but I still don't believe that you are the guilty one." He believed Slocombe was telling the truth because sympathetic San Diego police had told him they had been tipped off four days before Allen's trip. "That clears you," he told Lewis's spy, because only Leslie Fry knew the precise date of the snowstorm operation.[44] Allen forgot that while he had never given Slocombe a set date, he'd asked him to be ready to travel to San Diego several days earlier, which led Lewis to call the city's police.

By pitting Allen against Fry, Lewis and Roos succeeded in raising Nazi suspicions about their benefactress. Fry had been a regular visitor to Deutsches Haus, meeting with Schwinn behind closed doors and providing financial assistance to the perpetually cash-strapped Bund. As

Allen's relationship with Fry soured, he tried turning his Nazi friends against her. When he visited Deutsches Haus in early October, Allen told storm trooper leader Arno Risse and William Bockhacker that Fry was working for Lewis. "You should have heard how she spoke about the Bund and Schwinn and Risse," he told the pair. "She absolutely had no use for you people here."[45]

Allen's court cases dragged out well into 1939, but Lewis succeeded in creating a permanent split between his number-one and number-three enemies long before then. In October, Fry ran an article in her *Christian Free Press* denouncing Allen and portraying him as an easily deceived fool. Feeling double-crossed by Fry and hoping to cut a deal in his voter fraud case, Allen provided Hollywood Anti-Nazi League attorney Charles Katz with a statement concerning the various illegal activities engaged in by Fry. A month later, he posted circulars throughout Los Angeles accusing Fry of being a Russian agent working for the Russian secret police.[46]

Lewis's plan worked. With Slocombe's help, he had succeeded in neutralizing Allen, weakening Fry, and tying them both up in more court cases. After their final break, Fry stopped paying Allen's legal fees, which led his attorney Henry Elder to file suit against Allen, Fry, and her money source, Pasadena millionaire Mrs. W. K. Jewett. By the time the case came to court in January 1940, Fry had fled the country for Rome.[47]

To ensure that Allen would not resume his activities, the spymasters involved him in yet another court case. On September 8, 1938, *Ken* magazine published an article, "Exposing Native U.S. Plotters," based upon documents found in Allen's briefcase. Lewis apparently gave them the information. In January 1939, the litigious fascist filed suit against the magazine, asking for $330,000 in damages.[48]

SCHWINN'S ACHILLES' HEELS

Having taken Allen out of action and minimized Fry's effectiveness, Lewis and Roos began exploiting the first of Schwinn's two Achilles' heels: the long-standing internal divisions between militants such as OD leader Michael Drey, who wanted to pursue a more aggressive National Socialist course of action, and those who favored Schwinn's more accommodationist Americanization plan. Drey considered

Schwinn "a slacker and a poor organizer." He told Bockhacker earlier that May he would only "co-operate with Schwinn on matters which he himself approves of."[49]

Bockhacker informed Lewis that local Bundists had grown disillusioned with the leadership cadre of Schwinn, Drey, and Hans Diebel. Members accused the warring leaders of being too arrogant and insufficiently *kameradachaftlich* (comradelike). Worse yet, they suspected Schwinn was still pocketing money belonging to the Bund because Deutsches Haus was always in the red. Resentment against Schwinn grew so great that the Bund leader kept his home address secret from all but trusted confidants Diebel and Bockhacker. Only obedience to the *Führerprinzip* (unquestioning loyalty to the leader) prevented opponents from ousting him.[50]

Bockhacker ingratiated himself with leaders on both sides of the divide. When Drey bitterly complained about Schwinn's inability to stop Jewish spies from penetrating Deutsches Haus, Bockhacker agreed to track them down. But he was playing a very dangerous game. Drey promised that when they caught the spy, "he would have nothing to laugh at."[51]

Paranoia gripped Deutsches Haus that summer and fall as Bockhacker did his best to inflame the climate of mutual suspicion. Things got so bad that Nazis started spying on each other. When Bockhacker found out that Schwinn had "put a tail on him," he confronted the Bund leader and offered to withdraw from all activities if they doubted him. They did not. During the course of the operative's subsequent "investigation" of potential spies, he discovered that Hans Diebel, still a German citizen, was either a Gestapo agent or an informer reporting to their headquarters in Germany. Even Schwinn was not above suspicion. During his visit to Germany, he had been shown copies of every order he had issued while serving as the Bund's western regional leader.[52] The revelation unnerved him. Someone inside the Bund was spying on him.

While Bockhacker did his best to heighten ongoing rivalries, Lewis and Roos increased Schwinn's legal troubles. In September 1938, acting on information Neil Ness had provided Walter Carr, the Department of Immigration and Naturalization began taking steps to revoke Schwinn's citizenship. When Schwinn signed his naturalization papers in July 1932, he perjured himself by swearing he had been in Los Angeles since October 1926; in fact, he had moved to Los Angeles in October 1927, which left him three months shy of the required five years' residency in the same city. The Bund leader also failed to disclose his Nazi activities in Germany and the United States when he filed his papers, an oversight that provided a second reason for denial of citizenship.[53]

On December 14, 1938, acting on the recommendation of the chief of the U.S. Immigration Service, the U.S. attorney general began proceedings to revoke Schwinn's citizenship. A week later, assistant U.S. district attorney Ira Brett filed formal charges in Los Angeles federal court claiming that Schwinn's citizenship had been "illegally procured." The flustered Nazi downplayed the charges, explaining, "It was merely a mistake which I made while filling out my application of citizenship papers."[54] Simple mistake or not, Schwinn now had to shift his attention away from Bund activities and focus on remaining in the United States.

Lewis and Roos received more good news that fall. Following a recall election in which reformer Fletcher Bowron replaced corrupt mayor Frank Shaw, the Red Squad was disbanded and Captain William "Red" Hynes demoted to patrolman. Schwinn and Fry considered Hynes a close ally and had flooded the city with handbills opposing the recall. "The Jew-Radical-Methodist gang that chose him [Bowron] have but one real object, to fire Chief Davis and disband the Red Squad" and replace Hynes with a Jewish police captain. "If you want the same wholesale massacre of Gentiles, the same wholesale rape of Gentile women by Jews and Negroes, that took place in Russia and Spain, elect FLETCHER BOWRON."[55] Their candidate lost; Hynes could no longer protect them.

Bundists could rejoice at their own piece of good news. On November 9 and 10, 1938, Nazi storm troopers and citizens in Germany, Austria, and the Sudetenland responded to the pretext of the assassination of a Nazi diplomat in Paris by a young Polish Jew by launching the most deadly pogrom in the region's history. Attackers armed with sledgehammers systematically demolished Jewish homes, hospitals, synagogues, schools, and businesses while beating, raping, and murdering anyone who got in the way. By the time order was restored, the Kristallnacht (Night of Broken Glass) massacre left at least 91 dead, 7,000 Jewish businesses destroyed, and hundreds of synagogues burned to the ground; 30,000 Jews were arrested and sent to Nazi concentration camps.[56]

Blaming the victims for instigating the violence, the Nazi government imposed a $400 million fine upon the German Jewish community. Joseph Goebbels defended the attacks to the press. "The German people are an anti-Semitic people, and will not tolerate having their rights curtailed or being provoked by the parasitic Jewish race."

Newspapers reported that new laws would soon be issued "with the object of a 'final solution' of the Jewish question."[57]

Kristallnacht marked a turning point in American public opinion against the Hitler regime. Politicians, clergy, and civic leaders throughout the nation denounced the pogroms, and a Gallup poll taken that November revealed 94 percent of respondents disapproved of the Nazi treatment of Jews. Although Americans denounced anti-Semitism abroad, they remained more ambivalent in their attitude about Jews at home. A Roper poll taken after Kristallnacht revealed only 39 percent believed Jews should be treated like everyone else; 53 percent believed Jews were different and should be restricted; and 10 percent believed Jews should be deported.[58]

There was no ambiguity in the Bund's response to Kristallnacht. At a Deutsches Haus celebration in mid-November, Hermann Schwinn blamed Jews for sparking the events that led to his nation's rightful response. The Bund leader also sent a telegram to President Roosevelt opposing Jewish migration to the United States and reminding FDR of George Washington's warning "to keep aloof of foreign entanglements."[59]

The combination of Kristallnacht and the Munich Agreement led Americans and Bundists alike to see war as inevitable. When asked by Gallup pollsters following the Munich accord whether they believed Hitler when he said he had "no more territorial ambitions in Europe," 92 percent replied no, and 8 percent yes. When asked if they believed that the Sudetenland settlement would lead to war, 74 percent said yes. No formal poll was taken in Deutsches Haus, but after receiving a 21-page set of military instructions from national headquarters in New York, OD member Reinhold Kusche told his brethren, "It seems we are in the Army now."[60]

Despite the horrors of Kristallnacht, the year ended well for Leon Lewis and Joe Roos. They had created an irrevocable breach between Henry Allen and Leslie Fry, and had forced Hermann Schwinn to focus on preserving his citizenship rather than strengthening the Bund. The enemy was finally in retreat.

17.

The Race Is On

On January 15, 1939, while newspaper headlines reported France's efforts to stop Italian incursions in North Africa, Los Angeles Bundists hosted an elaborate costume ball at Deutsches Haus. Tables lit by candlelight in the spacious auditorium were pushed close to the stage to make room for a night of celebration. The evening was a great success until the early-morning hours, when twelve police detectives, tipped off by Leon Lewis's inside man, William Bockhacker, raided Deutsches Haus, seized 10,000 anti-Semitic circulars that had been prepared for a new snowstorming operation, and arrested Schwinn and four of his chief aides. Releasing the group the next day, police chief John Klein warned the men that any future attempts to distribute hate-filled circulars would lead to prosecution under the California State Syndicalism Act.[1]

The arrests were among the few pieces of good news that January. Lewis and Roos had weakened the Bund by putting Schwinn, Allen, and Fry on the defensive, but not the German government or their loyal American diehards. Emboldened by the capitulation of European leaders at Munich, Hitler and Mussolini were moving across Europe and North Africa relatively unchecked. Less than two weeks after the Los Angeles costume ball, Generalissimo Francisco Franco's troops seized Barcelona and with it control of Spain. Closer to home, German and Japanese spies were infiltrating the United States in unprecedented numbers and had already obtained blueprints of every type of destroyer built in the United States from 1933 to 1937.[2]

Still, American Nazis needed to be careful. A revived House Un-American Activities Committee had begun questioning the Bund's national officers the previous summer and planned to hold hearings in

Los Angeles the following year. Bundists were also worried when the FBI arrested eighteen suspected Nazi spies who were then indicted in a New York federal court in June 1938 and charged with violating U.S. espionage laws. The trial began in October and ended with the conviction of four spies in November and their sentencing a month later.

The busting of a Nazi spy ring could have marked a major triumph for the FBI, except for one thing. FBI head J. Edgar Hoover held a press conference announcing the dismantling of a Nazi spy operation that included members of the German American Bund. But there was a problem. Hoping to take all the credit, Hoover made his revelation before Leon Tourrou, the FBI agent who had uncovered the espionage ring, had time to arrest all the suspects. Forewarned by Hoover's egotistical blunder, the fourteen main leaders managed to flee the country.[3]

Concerned about the woeful state of American counterespionage and the lack of cooperation among government agencies, President Franklin D. Roosevelt ordered the FBI, naval intelligence, and the U.S. Army's Military Intelligence Division to launch a counteroffensive against foreign espionage and to share all information. Roosevelt allocated $50,000 for the FBI to conduct espionage investigations, which Congress soon raised to $300,000. Yet even after its increased funding, the Bureau remained woefully understaffed; as late as 1940, it had a scant 898 agents covering the entire United States.[4]

Following Kristallnacht, Lewis and Roos found themselves involved in a deadly race between two opposing forces: Nazis who called for eliminating the dual threats posed by Communists and Jews, and Jews who worked to stop them. Herman Schwinn was getting smarter by "Americanizing" the Bund and expanding its membership to include greater numbers of native-born citizens. Berlin also increased its operations on American soil, sending well-trained espionage agents to assess the nation's readiness for war and to begin planning for possible sabotage. With the FBI still dragging its feet, it was up to Lewis and Roos to stop the Nazi assault on Los Angeles.

As news of Nazi militancy increased, Roos expanded the scope of the Community Committee's undercover operation by bringing in several new full-time spies as well as a number of trusted informants. By January 1939, he succeeded in placing three undercover operatives inside Deutsches Haus. In addition to William Bockhacker (Agent W2), now Schwinn's right-hand American, Roos recruited Charles Young (Agent Y9), a German-born naturalized citizen and financial investigator who deplored the bad name Germans were getting because of Hitler. The underemployed father of three was grateful to serve his new nation and receive a modest stipend of $50 a month for so doing.[5] Roy Arnold (Agent R3) did not need the money. The Maine-born life insurance salesman loathed the city's Nazi cohort and was happy to feign being one of Schwinn's desired American followers.

Roos recruited four other informants who worked for him on a sporadic basis: Mrs. Anna Friedman (Agent Mrs. F), a German American who sent back important information gleaned from mingling with Bund women; Harwood E. Park (Agent P8), an American-born aircraft mechanic who alerted the spymasters to potential sabotage at local aircraft factories; Walter Hadel, who investigated incidents of anti-Semitism and tracked Nazis and fascists working in the movie studios; and Jimmy Frost, an investigator who acted as a go-between with a number of local and federal officials.

With Schwinn's inner circle on high alert for Jewish spies, Roos continued to refine the counterespionage techniques he had learned from General Marshall's operatives. Since the Nazis knew where Lewis worked, Roos made sure his spies never came to the office. Instead, he debriefed his agents in a rented room in a "flea hotel" on Main Street not far from Deutsches Haus. Despite its run-down state, the hotel had one advantage: three different ways spies could enter and leave. "We had understandings, how to meet, when to meet, how to reach each other, and so forth" and "how to detect whether they were being followed, in and out, in and out." Once in the room, the operatives dictated their reports to Roos or Lewis's secretary, who took notes in shorthand and then typed them up. Roos encouraged his spies "to get materials but never take a chance of getting caught."[6]

With his spies in place, Roos began reorganizing the office's chaotic filing system. "Everybody was identified by [code] number, and you had to figure out who is this and who is that. It was terrible." Roos also created separate index cards with the names and addresses of hundreds of Nazi and fascist individuals, along with other information about them, as well as separate cards for the many organizations they had investigated. Immersing himself in the details of operations past and present, Roos turned himself into a "walking encyclopedia" who knew the name of every Nazi and what he or she looked like.[7] More importantly, he made his list of Nazis, fascists, and suspected spies readily available to government agencies at a moment's notice.

Yet despite his work professionalizing spycraft and systematizing his operatives' reports, Roos was frustrated by the lack of national attention to their findings. "From the very beginning, I pressed for a new policy, namely to publicize what the Nazis and their American sympathizers were doing." As he told Lewis, "What's the use of having all these files? . . . The world ought to know about them." Joe Roos understood the vital importance of public relations and the need to disseminate information that would awaken an American public that was becoming increasingly hostile toward Jews. A Gallup poll conducted in August 1937 found that 38 percent of respondents believed anti-Jewish feelings were increasing in the United States. By March 1939, as Hitler continued his march across Europe, the figure had risen to 45 percent.[8]

Roos moved to counter growing domestic anti-Semitism by taking a page from Joseph Goebbels, a man he considered the "most clever, ablest propaganda operator in the world." The Austrian-born Jew began his own propaganda campaign by launching the News Research Service in January 1939. Drawing upon his considerable skills as a former newspaperman and Hollywood story editor, Roos published the weekly *News Letter*, which turned his spy reports into a read as gripping as any detective thriller. Over the next three years he sent copies to government agencies, newspapers, popular magazines, and influential political columnists. Roos slowly transformed Leon Lewis's local spy ring into a successful national operation whose *News Letter* "reached millions practically every week because of the 'pickup'" by popular syndicated columnists such as Walter Winchell and the team of Robert Allen and Drew Pearson.[9]

Lewis and Roos would now fight their enemies on two fronts: a private undercover operation and a more open public relations campaign aimed at alerting Americans to the growing threats to democracy.

SECRET CELLS AND *DER TAG*

In late 1938 Hans Diebel, Schwinn's closest lieutenant and a likely Gestapo agent, was secretly preparing his men for the time when "physical violence will be the order of the day" and "Nazis will take over the government." Bundists began laying the groundwork for *Der Tag* by creating a network of cells, each no larger than ten men, spread across the country. Modeled on the cell system used by Hitler in the 1920s, all meetings were held in secret and no cell knew of the existence of the other. Los Angeles already had eighteen such cells and anticipated more. Fortunately for Lewis and Roos, Bockhacker had gained Diebel's confidence. The Nazi leader asked the operative to raise money for new cells among wealthy Americans and to draw up a list of dependable men who could be "relied upon in an uprising."[10]

Knowing the importance of swaying public opinion to their cause, Schwinn and Diebel began organizing "private discussion groups" in the homes of sympathetic Americans who were secretly supporting the Nazis. Bund meetings were attracting 250 to 300 people, but Schwinn wanted to build a support network that ran into the thousands. By early 1939, Diebel had succeeded in organizing a hundred discussion groups throughout Los Angeles and nearby Pasadena and Glendale. Much to the Bund's delight, the leaders of these groups included prominent members of the city's social register, such as wealthy Beverly Hills socialite Mrs. Preston Harris Fisher, who recruited like-minded people from the city's Women's Club.[11]

Roos received news about other private meetings from his latest recruit, Anna Friedman. Her first attempt to meet Herman Schwinn failed because he was "on the [Deutsches Haus] roof taking a sun bath and didn't want to be disturbed." Unfazed, she soon established herself as a regular at Bund meetings, enough to learn about secret cells operating on Flower Street, not far from Lewis's offices. Other informants told of secret cells meeting in downtown homes and offices, in Pasadena, and, in a surprise report from Lewis's first spy, John Schmidt, in isolated Tujunga Canyon. Schmidt would have liked to get back into the spy game, but was too well known to be of much use. Earlier that fall, while walking downtown, a heavyset Bundist stopped him and warned with a snarl on his face, "I see they haven't got you yet. You better look out."[12]

Bundists were not the only ones preparing for violence. The American Patriots, Schwinn's American wing, had moved out of Deutsches Haus to attract American supporters who did not want to be openly associated with the Bund. Although operating independently of Schwinn, the American Patriots still shared the same goal: the creation of a fascist United States. Many of them, including their leader, Emil Lodahl, belonged to the National Guard and were well trained in military tactics and the use of weapons. Speaking at a Bund meeting that spring, Lodahl predicted that "blood will flow on the streets of the United States and the people of America will wake up and rid themselves of the 'Jewish pest.'"[13]

Emboldened by Hitler's relentless march across Europe, several new militant fascist groups—the American Rangers, Vindicators, American Vigilantes, and Actioneers—rose up during the winter and spring of

1939 and presented themselves as anti-Communist warriors determined to rid the nation of Reds and Jews. Luckily Lewis and Roos's agents had infiltrated each of these groups, and in a number of cases rose to leadership positions that gave them access to secret information.

The revived Ku Klux Klan wanted to do something that would attract national attention: they planned to assassinate Louis B. Mayer and a number of prominent Jews. In early February 1939, Charles Young met with Klan leader Jack Peyton, who was also running the American Rangers, a "militant and aggressive" group that he claimed had the support of mayor Frank Shaw and police chief James Davis. Hoping to recruit Young, Peyton revealed how he and his associates had "completed all arrangements to have Louis B. Mayer and several other Jews killed." The assassins had "purchased high powered rifles and plenty of ammunition to do the job," but at the last moment "the fellows who were to do the killing got yellow and nothing came of it."[14] Disappointed with the failure of one plot, Peyton told Young he still had the weapons and planned to use them when the right men could be found.

While rebellion, revolution, and murder were being plotted in secret, an undeterred Hermann Schwinn continued forging a powerful alliance among the city's growing number of Italian, Japanese, Russian, Mexican, and American fascists. He would not let his citizenship woes deter his desire to supplant Fritz Kuhn as the Bund's national leader. Early in 1939, he conferred with Anastase Vonsiatsky, national leader of the White Russians in America, the group Leopold McLaglan had recruited to carry out his assassination plot. Married to American millionaire Marion Stephens, the former czarist officer used his wife's wealth to fund his operations. Vonsiatsky was important enough that German, Japanese, and Italian functionaries regularly visited his headquarters in Thompson, Connecticut, to discuss, among other things, a fascist coup in the United States. He was now on his way to meet with government leaders in Tokyo and then Berlin and Rome. But beforehand, he stopped in Los Angeles to talk with Schwinn about plans "to unite all fascist movements."[15]

Following a lengthy meeting at Deutsches Haus, Chuck Slocombe accompanied the Nazi and Russian leaders to the docks. Once settled in his stateroom, Vonsiatsky ordered drinks for everyone and offered a toast to the day "when the Communists and International Jewry will be wiped from the face of the globe."[16]

That day seemed to grow considerably closer after March 15, when Nazi troops marched into Czechoslovakia and made it a protectorate of

Germany. Later that evening Hitler made his triumphant entry into Prague. Ever the diplomat, German consul Georg Gyssling downplayed the territorial seizure, referring to it as a mere family squabble. But Bundists knew better. Two weeks after Hitler's triumph, 350 people turned out at Deutsches Haus to welcome home Arno Risse and hear his firsthand account of the vibrant state of the German nation. The Bund's third most important leader, Risse left Los Angeles in late October 1938 and returned five months later, singing the praises of the New Germany. Sitting in the audience that evening was Anna Friedman, who listened to him speak for two and a half hours. Risse's message was clear: war was inevitable. "He said that all Germany looks like one great armament factory. People who are not working directly in armament productions are employed in road building and other construction work that is essential for the coming war."[17]

Risse reassured the audience that "Jews are no longer a problem in Germany," nor were political dissidents. They had all been thrown "into concentration camps."[18] With Jews and their allies out of the way, the German people now had plenty of work and plenty to eat. The only reason he had returned to the United States, Risse told galvanized listeners, was that after receiving his citizenship papers he'd sworn to fight the enemy within and without. And that meant doing in America what Hitler had done in Germany.

Anticipating the day that Hitler would conquer the United States, Norman Stephens, a wealthy engineer who made his money mining silver in Colorado, and his wife, Winona, daughter of a wealthy industrialist, began constructing a fifty-acre compound nestled in the Santa Monica Mountains just above Pacific Palisades that would serve as the western command center for a Nazi White House on the Pacific. The Stephenses, believers in the paranormal, had purchased the land from movie star Will Rogers in 1933 under the assumed name Jesse Murphy after their Svengali-like German mentor known only as Herr Schmidt prophesied Hitler's inevitable victory over America. During the next several years, the couple spent $4 million ($69 million in 2015 dollars) constructing a self-sustaining community that included a 395,000-gallon concrete water tank, a 20,000-gallon steel diesel fuel tank, and a power station with two generators large enough to serve a small town. Newly planted gardens and an enormous meat locker would provide sufficient food to feed compound inhabitants.[19]

The couple hired a series of architects, including Paul R. Williams, the city's most prominent African American architect, to draw up plans for a four-story mansion. The main floor included a grand central hall featuring multiple meeting rooms, libraries, and social rooms; the upper floors would contain twenty-two bedrooms and suites, enough to house the men needed to run Hitler's West Coast operations. They also envisioned the compound serving as a logical place for the triumphant führer to stay on his way to Japan. To keep prying eyes away, the Stephenses surrounded their property with a high fence topped by barbed wire; armed guards patrolled the area.[20]

Despite neighbors' reports of paramilitary maneuvers taking place on weekends, local authorities took no action. Not until June 1940 did the *Los Angeles Times* alert readers to suspicious Nazi activities in the Santa Monica Mountains. Lewis and Roos knew what was going on long before then. A year earlier, Jimmy Frost had warned them of a large home being built, intended to serve as "the headquarters of some Fascist movement." He promised to monitor the situation and report back on any new developments.[21]

FIGHTING BACK

There was nothing Leon Lewis and Joe Roos could do about events in Europe. But they could help thwart the unprecedented infiltration of German and Japanese spies and ensuing threat of sabotage along the Pacific Coast. Hoping to keep America neutral for as long as possible, Hitler sent the personable Fritz Wiedemann to San Francisco early in March 1939 to replace the much-loathed Nazi consul Manfred von Killinger. The handsome diplomat, whom Roos considered "an expert on advertising, propaganda and publicity," informed the press he had been dispatched by the führer to create "good will between our two countries." His main mission, one he did not tell the press, was to organize pro-German and anti-Jewish propaganda in the United States, encourage fascism in Mexico, and turn the San Francisco consulate into headquarters for German and Japanese espionage in the West. Wiedemann came to San Francisco with $5 million ($85.3 million in 2015 dollars) to spend on spying and propaganda.[22]

The new consul charmed the city's social elite and was a frequent topic of its society columns. Martha Dodd, daughter of former American ambassador to Germany William Dodd, had met Wiedemann in Berlin and knew the charm was a facade. Underneath the friendly smile, she wrote in her diary, lurked a Nazi with the "shrewdness and cunning of an animal. Wiedemann was a dangerous man to cross, for despite his social naiveté and beguiling clumsiness, he was as ruthless a fighter and schemer as some of his compatriots."[23]

Dodd underestimated the man's daring. Less than three months after his arrival, he met with Hermann Schwinn and Irish Republican Army leader Sean Russell to plot the assassinations of King George and Queen Elizabeth during their upcoming visit to San Francisco. No attempt was ever made to murder the closely guarded royal couple, but Wiedemann succeeded in turning the consulate into a forwarding point between the Berlin Foreign Office and German diplomatic stations in the western hemisphere. He also maintained close touch with Schwinn and the various spies and Gestapo officers passing through Los Angeles, a city he found gripped by "violent anti-Semitism."[24]

Hitler was sending spies and money into the United States in unprecedented quantities, and yet American intelligence seemed woefully behind in tracking any enemy other than Communists. With over 750 Nazi and fascist groups operating in America in 1939, and almost all cooperating with the Bund, Lewis and Roos must have felt overwhelmed by the enormous task of discovering and monitoring the spies pouring into the city. How could they possibly compete against a better-prepared and -funded enemy? German military intelligence and the Gestapo were training spies at espionage-sabotage schools in Berlin, Dresden, and Hamburg and funneling money for their American operations through consular offices. While the two Jewish spymasters received under $30,000 a year to fund their operations, Germany, Japan, and Italy spent more than $80 million in 1938 on espionage activities.[25]

Lewis and Roos had run a successful operation spying on local Nazis and fascists, but they now faced a threat that went far beyond anything they had encountered before. The spymasters continued doing what they did best, focusing the bulk of their undercover operations on the Bund and its leaders. Their agents filed regular reports describing meetings at Deutsches Haus and at various secret cells, and accompanied Schwinn to the docks, where he received money and instructions from visiting ship captains.

Knowing large numbers of spies were arriving each day, Lewis and Roos expanded the scope of their operations by recruiting and training more than half a dozen additional operatives and informants. William Bockhacker, who regularly chauffeured Schwinn and other Bund leaders, uncovered his first suspected spy that April, Erich Bruening. Driving the recent German arrival to the docks to visit the *Donau*,

Bockhacker saw Bruening taking photographs of boats in the harbor and then meeting privately with the ship's captain. At one point, hoping to impress Bockhacker, Bruening pulled out his wallet and showed him an official gold-plated emblem that had a black eagle and swastika on it. When Bockhacker later asked Diebel why the recently arrived German was not a member of the Bund, the Bund leader slyly replied, "You know sometimes people are more useful not being members."[26]

Roos's operatives also discovered that Helmuth Bollert, who claimed to be an economic envoy of the German government, was "a special agent of Goebbels" sent to Los Angeles to persuade fellow countrymen to oppose the city's anti-Nazi forces. Staying at the posh Ambassador Hotel, Bollert visited German residents involved with anti-Nazi groups and warned them to desist, or "strong counter measures" would be taken "against their friends and relatives in Germany." Bollert had one fatal weakness: he could not hold his liquor. One evening when he went to the Century Club to hear his mistress sing, he got sloppily drunk and was overheard by one of Roos's agents boasting of being a Nazi agent. Bollert's effectiveness was compromised.[27]

Roos's new cadre of operatives uncovered other Nazi agents such as Hans Schiller, an aviator who was flying arms to Gold Shirts in Mexico, and William Baxter, who was being paid by German agent Prince Kurt zur Lippe to serve as liaison between Wiedemann and American fifth columnists. Roos's spies reported that Nazi propagandists such as Dr. Ernst Wiese were organizing "private meeting" groups in Los Angeles and across the country and encouraging their support of Germany.[28]

As Japanese forces solidified their control of Asian territory, Lewis and Roos expanded their espionage activities to include spying on suspected Japanese agents. With the FBI and army and navy intelligence understaffed and inadequately trained in counterespionage, officials at all three agencies welcomed the spymasters' reports, but none more than their trusted friend Commander Ellis Zacharias. After several years stationed at sea and then in Washington, D.C., working for the Office of Naval Intelligence, the Jewish naval officer returned in 1938 to San Diego, the "very hub of the wheel of Japanese espionage," as head of naval intelligence for the entire Pacific Coast. His area had been overrun by Japanese agents who were "organized on a vast scale" and "became bolder as time passed."[29] With only a handful of agents, Zacharias was happy to receive reports from Lewis and Roos.

With the bulk of their spies tailing Nazis, the two spymasters assigned their most experienced agent, Chuck Slocombe, to assist Zacharias. In addition to working with the Jews, Slocombe had been sending reports on suspicious Japanese activities to Long Beach police captain and navy reservist Owen Murphy. Lewis and Murphy now asked the water taxi owner to keep close tabs on Japanese fishing vessels that were not necessarily looking for fish. Murphy was especially keen to learn more about activities around Terminal Island, home to 3,000 Japanese residents and a suspected haven of Japanese intelligence agents.[30]

Realizing the enormity of the task, Lewis assigned one of his latest recruits, navy veteran Harwood Park, to help Slocombe. Knowing Park's familiarity with a variety of vessels, Lewis asked him to assist the water taxi owner in monitoring suspicious Japanese activities in the harbors of Los Angeles and Long Beach. By the middle of July, Park presented Slocombe with a series of reports, which Lewis then forwarded to Zacharias.[31]

The spymasters also provided naval intelligence with detailed accounts of suspected Japanese agents such as Ralph Townsend, Mr. Akashi of the Japanese Chamber of Commerce, and the region's most active agent, Y. Hajaschi. Anna Friedman observed that the forty-year-old Hajaschi frequently met with Schwinn and storm trooper leaders in a room on the second floor of Deutsches Haus, a place the Bund head took "important" people who preferred not to be seen.[32]

By February 1939, Roos had completed the enormous task of systematizing the office files and began sending Zacharias the first of many updated reports on "Nazi Spies and Agents in the United States." His initial eighteen-page memorandum contained the names, addresses, and activities of 157 suspected Nazi and Japanese spies and their fascist allies scattered across the United States. Zacharias forwarded the report to naval intelligence headquarters in Washington, D.C., with a note explaining that the data he had received from a "private source" in Los Angeles contained valuable information "that has never reached this office." Following Roosevelt's orders to share information, naval intelligence sent the reports to army intelligence and to the FBI.[33]

Having established themselves as a small but effective unofficial wing of American intelligence, Roos and Lewis turned to uncovering potential sabotage. The spymasters were especially concerned about the vulnerability of American aircraft plants, over half of which were located along the West Coast.

Local Nazi leaders were also playing the long game, preparing for the day the United States might go to war against Germany. Shortly after the invasion of Czechoslovakia, OD head Michael Drey urged members who had citizenship papers to apply for jobs at the Lockheed plant in Burbank or "any other airplane factory." Although all applicants were being fingerprinted, Drey assured them they would be okay if they kept "their mouths shut about politics" and did not let anyone know they were connected to the Bund.[34]

That April, Anna Friedman provided a chilling account of what Nazis intended to do once inside the aircraft factories. Establishing herself as a regular patron at Charlie's T-Bone Steak House on Fifty-Fourth and Broadway, a popular haunt of Bundists, Friedman became friendly with a waitress who told her how a number of Germans got rip-roaring drunk one evening and "boasted about their sabotage activities at the Douglas Aircraft plant. It appears that they have taken bolts out of planes which will endanger the safety of the planes." Chuck Slocombe filed an equally disturbing report three weeks later, noting that Silver Shirts were securing positions at the Douglas factory. Lewis sent information to security officers at the airplane factories.[35]

TIGHTENING THE NOOSE

On April 28, 1939, Fritz Kuhn traveled to Los Angeles to meet with Schwinn and to speak at the Bund's May Day rally. Unlike his triumphant Washington's Birthday rally at Madison Square Garden three months earlier, when 22,000 of the Nazi faithful turned out to hear him denounce President Roosevelt and his Jewish allies as enemies of the United States, Kuhn now found himself and the Bund under attack. He told Schwinn and Diebel that after his home had been machine-gunned, he went into hiding with three full-time bodyguards. Fearing for his family's safety, he sent his son to Germany. His wife, believing her life to be in danger, had left him, though the fact that he was maintaining a mistress may have influenced her decision.[36]

The botched arrests of the Nazi spy ringleaders in New York had embarrassed the FBI, and Kuhn knew they were determined to make up for their mistakes by going after him and the Bund. Consequently, he issued orders that all Bund branches were "to remain undercover and are not to seek the limelight whatsoever."[37] The only exceptions were New York, Chicago, and Los Angeles, where he believed Bund leaders were trained well enough to cope with any situation that might arise.

Kuhn had reason to be concerned. On May 25, following an investigation ordered by New York City mayor Fiorello La Guardia, the Nazi

Fritz Kuhn at Hindenburg Park, April 1939
Jewish Federation Council of Greater Los Angeles, Community Relations Committee Collection, Part 2,
Special Collections and Archives, Oviatt Library, California State University, Northridge

leader was indicted on charges of embezzling $14,548 from Bund coffers,
a good deal of which he had spent on his mistress. Reaction at Deutsches
Haus was divided. Following the *Führerprinzip*, Schwinn and the leadership cadre maintained absolute silence; but ordinary members, Bockhacker reported, were "pretty sore," calling Kuhn a *Schweinehund* (pig)
and even suggesting he be shot for treason.[38]

By late spring 1939, Roos and Lewis had put emboldened local Nazis
on the defensive. Schwinn, Kuhn, and the Bund also came under attack
by a Hollywood studio determined to produce the nation's first openly
anti-Nazi film.

IV

ESPIONAGE, SABOTAGE, AND THE COMING OF WAR, 1938–1941

18.

Closing In

On April 27, 1939, Warner Brothers Studios declared war on Germany.

That evening, amid tightened security that included armed guards on the roof and plainclothesmen inside the Beverly Hills Theater, Harry and Jack Warner premiered the nation's first explicitly anti-Nazi film, *Confessions of a Nazi Spy*. The Warners' hard-fought victory came amid a series of threats and violence from diplomats, Bundists, and Silver Shirts.

For years the Warner brothers, sons of a Jewish cobbler who fled pogroms in Poland, had desperately wanted to make an anti-Nazi film. But they were repeatedly thwarted by the Production Code's prohibition against defaming any nation or its leader. The busting of the Nazi spy ring by FBI agent Leon Turrou provided the Warners with an opportunity to skirt the Code by making a film based on actual events. In the fall of 1938 they sent screenwriter Milton Krims to New York to cover the trial of the eighteen individuals charged with spying for Germany. Hiring Turrou as a consultant, the Warners asked Krims to turn the events surrounding the spy ring into a movie. The trial ended on December 2; a month later the studio submitted Krim's script to PCA head Joseph Breen, who approved it on January 28. Four days later, *Confessions* went into production.[1]

Hollywood was closing in on the Nazi threat by exposing their American spy operations to millions of citizens. Berlin did not like it. Propaganda minister Joseph Goebbels feared that *Confessions* would open the floodgates for other anti-Nazi films. As in the past, German general consul Georg Gyssling did his best to halt the production. From November until the film's release in late April, Gyssling sent numerous letters to movie industry leaders Will Hays and Joseph Breen, urging them to stop the offensive movie from being made or face a ban of all Hollywood films in Germany. For the first time in his career, Gyssling suffered a major defeat. Although PCA censors urged the Warner brothers not to make *Confessions*, Breen ruled that it was based upon true accounts and therefore did not defame any nation or leader. The brothers did have to make one concession. They could not explicitly mention the plight of German Jews or their sufferings at the hands of Hitler and his minions.[2]

Approval from the PCA was one thing; completing the film was another matter. Fearing retaliation against relatives in Germany, a number of German actors refused to take part in the production. Those who agreed to appear did so only after Warners promised to use fictitious names in the credits; just ten of the seventy-eight cast members were listed by their real names. Warners received so many anonymous threats that they closed the set and posted four uniformed guards to bar anyone not directly involved in the film from entering the sound stage. Copies of the script were locked up, and actors received only a few pages of dialogue each day.

During the course of production, the studio encountered several "accidents" that did not seem accidental: a boom holding a camera collapsed, narrowly missing director Anatole Litvak; a light falling from a catwalk nearly killed the film's star, Edward G. Robinson. Fortunately for the Warner brothers, Leon Lewis's agents tipped them off to several instances of potential sabotage. Chuck Slocombe learned that Silver Shirt leader Kenneth Alexander had two men working at the Warners studio who kept him posted "on the inside goings on" regarding the film. Alexander's informants provided him with the exact dates and places when scenes were to be shot outside the studio lot. Slocombe also warned Lewis that the studio's chief of police and assistant chief of police were Ku Klux Klan members and sympathetic to the Nazi cause.[3]

On the night of the premiere, the film arrived in an armored car under heavy police guard. Dozens of Los Angeles policemen, along with forty studio guards, patrolled the theater, looking for possible danger. Louis B. Mayer was so afraid of potential violence that he threw a "surprise" birthday party for Lionel Barrymore the night of the opening and ordered all MGM stars to attend.[4]

The Warner brothers' determination paid off. *Confessions* debuted to glowing reviews. "The evening of April 27, 1939," declared film critic Welford Beaton, "will go down in screen history as a memorable one. It marked the first time in the annals of screen entertainment that a picture ever really said something definite about current events, really took sides and argued for the side with which it sympathized." Not surprisingly, the movie received a very different reaction in Germany. Joseph Goebbels banned *Confessions* and ordered the German film industry to make a series of documentaries exposing the seamy side of American life: unemployment, gangsterism, and judicial corruption.[5]

Los Angeles Bundists hated the film and believed the Warners were the main financiers of "all the anti-Nazi 'persecutions.'" Seeking their revenge, Schwinn and local Nazi film exhibitor Franz Ferenz drew up 12,000 handbills that attacked both *Confessions* and the money-grasping Jewish industry "which is driving non-Jewish Americans to desperation."[6]

Schwinn wanted to do more than just issue handbills. The Jews had finally bested Georg Gyssling, and he saw an opportunity to wrest control of the city's Nazi leadership from the German consul. He began by drawing up a four-page list of actors, directors, and writers who would "be purged when 'der Tag' would dawn in America." The list took a more ominous tone when Mrs. Leslie Fry returned to town that June. Seeking her own revenge against Leon Lewis, Fry began to plan with the Bund leader the "means of liquidation of the objectionable individuals" on Schwinn's list.[7]

Fortunately, the room in which they discussed their assassination plans had been bugged. Joe Roos's spycraft had paid off. Either William Bockhacker or Charles Young had planted a recording device in Schwinn's office. When the recorded conversations were "played back to a number of people who were on the purged list," Roos recounted, "they were amazed to hear liquidation of themselves through murder discussed in a tone as if the would-be assassins were talking about a Sunday Church picnic."[8]

With the opening of *Confessions of a Nazi Spy*, the Warner brothers accomplished what Lewis and Roos had long hoped to do: they brought considerable attention to the dangers that Nazis—foreign and domestic—posed to national security. Hollywood seemed to be making greater inroads against the Nazi threat than the U.S. government.

EMBOLDENED NAZIS

Following the release of *Confessions of a Nazi Spy*, local Bundists received two pieces of news that in earlier years would have troubled them: embarrassed by Hoover's blunders, the FBI was increasing its surveillance of Nazi activities; and Martin Dies, chair of the House Un-American Activities Committee, announced that he would begin hearings in Los Angeles that May. Schwinn's cohort was concerned but not too worried. They were more afraid of Lewis and Roos than the FBI or HUAC, for the Jews knew more about their operations than any government agency.

FBI agents had interviewed Schwinn for two days in November 1937 but saw no reason to investigate any further. Several months later Hoover presented the Justice Department with a report concluding that the Bund had not violated any laws. Arno Risse, just back from his trip to Germany, was delighted that the FBI was whitewashing his organization: "Now the timid sympathizers of the Bund who were afraid to join will not hesitate to do so." The FBI report, he boasted to Young in April 1939, "shows that we are a patriotic American organization, and that we have no connections whatsoever with Germany."[9]

Silver Shirts proved even more disdainful of the FBI. That same April, a Bureau agent sent to question Kenneth Alexander confessed to the Silver Shirt leader his disgust that he had been ordered to investigate loyal American groups rather than Communists. Alexander was dumbfounded but pleased. FBI agents, he gloated to Charles Slocombe, were "the most stupid asses in the world . . . The secret service operatives of the most insignificant countries of the world could run circles around the F.B.I. men."[10]

Bund leaders were not especially troubled by the upcoming HUAC hearings because they knew its chair, Texas congressman Martin Dies, was far more focused on tracking down Reds than exposing Nazis and fascists. As Henry Allen gleefully told Slocombe, "We have three friends on the Dies Committee so we really have nothing to worry about."[11]

Dies's initial chief investigator, Edward Sullivan, was a convicted thief and an anti-Semite who maintained friendly relations with Nazi groups. While speaking at a Friends of New Germany meeting in June 1934, he urged the audience to "throw the Goddamn lousy Jews—all of them—into the Atlantic Ocean." Lewis discovered Sullivan's loathing of Jews when the two met on board a train traveling from Washington, D.C., to Los Angeles. After learning that HUAC had hired only five investigators, all assigned to the East Coast, Lewis had gone to Washington in an effort to have Chuck Slocombe appointed as the Committee's West Coast investigator. On his return home, he met Sullivan, who let loose with a series of anti-Semitic statements. Keeping quiet at the time, Lewis later responded by seeking the removal "of a Jew baiter of this type." In September 1938, after senator Robert LaFollette revealed that Sullivan had worked as a labor spy for the anti-Semitic Railway Audit and Inspection Company, Dies's chief investigator was fired.[12]

Despite Sullivan's dismissal, Dies's political leanings became evident when Lewis received a report in January 1939 that Mrs. Leslie Fry, now living in New Jersey, was attempting to get hired as "an investigator for the Dies Committee." The Reverend Martin Luther Thomas, an anti-Semite who was happy to help the Jews if paid enough, telephoned Lewis in February, warning that Fry was "dickering with Congressman Dies" to join the committee while at the same time "trying to frame Mr. Lewis."[13]

Whatever his unease, Lewis agreed to Dies's repeated requests for information, but with limits. Not trusting the discretion of the HUAC chair, Lewis refused to send him any report that might reveal the identity of "operatives who are still unexposed." He asked Joe Roos to cull their files and prepare a comprehensive report on the activities of Nazis and their sympathizers in Southern California. Lewis then sent the document to Dies in his capacity as chair of the American Legion's Americanism Committee. Roos's 400-page *Summary Report on Activities of Nazi Groups and Their Allies in Southern California*, which he updated annually, provided detailed accounts and photographs of every Nazi and fascist group and leader they had investigated. Uncertain whether his information would see the light of day, Lewis also sent Roos's report to naval intelligence and the FBI. "I doubt whether I will be given the results of their further check-up," he confessed to an Anti-Defamation League colleague, "but feel that that is not so important."[14]

When Hermann Schwinn received a subpoena to appear before HUAC investigators at a closed hearing on May 18, 1939, he felt confident that "the Dies Committee will find nothing on us." Schwinn expected the subpoena, which ordered him to bring copies of the Bund's membership list. What he did not expect was HUAC's knowledge of the precise location of the list; they knew the membership files were "contained in five wooden boxes, which boxes are kept in a wooden cabinet which is located in an office on the first floor, right hand side, of the Deutsches Haus at 634 W 15 Street."[15] Schwinn realized the information could only have been obtained from someone inside the Bund, someone working for Leon Lewis.

Believing he could hold his own against HUAC, Schwinn told investigators that the Bund had no formal membership list. In truth, the Bund maintained two lists: one of members and one of people friendly to the Bund who were sent notices of social events. Expressing his eagerness to cooperate with HUAC, he gladly turned over the latter list. Upon returning to Deutsches Haus, Schwinn boasted of his ability to hoodwink the investigators; before testifying, he had hidden or destroyed every important document. As for the mailing list, he assured everyone, "Don't worry, the Bund knows how to protect its members—somehow, for a reason which I cannot understand, the membership list disappeared and there is nothing to worry about."[16]

Subsequent testimonies by Bund treasurer Willi Kendzia, Aryan Bookstore owner Hans Diebel, and Ordnungsdienst leader Michael Drey proved equally unrevealing. Denying any direct connection to the Hitler regime, Kendzia explained that the Bund's goal "is to organize all fair-minded Gentiles" in America "to fight Communism and at the same time to enlighten people with the truth about New Germany." Likewise, Drey denied that the OD was a quasi-military storm trooper unit; they were simply a group of men who did "a lot of singing" and enjoyed discussing contemporary politics.[17]

Despite their bravado, the Nazis knew they had to be cautious; public opinion could easily turn against them with enough hard evidence. They worried that "agent provocateurs . . . sent to the German House continuously by our 'enemies'" were feeding information to HUAC investigators.[18] To make it more difficult for outsiders to penetrate the Bund, Schwinn decided that henceforth notification of subsequent meetings would be delivered by word of mouth only.

Schwinn emerged from the first round of local hearings convinced he had bamboozled the committee. His optimism also extended to his personal life. The perpetually cash-strapped Bund leader now earned a decent living by combining his modest salary for managing Deutsches Haus with his new position as head of the Western German Travel Center, a recently created travel agency funded by Bund headquarters in New York. Feeling confident he could now support a wife, the thirty-three-year-old bachelor married New York–born Thekla Therese Nagel on June 1. Thekla had wanted to get married months earlier, but other Bund leaders did not want Schwinn tied down by matrimony. For once, Schwinn chose love over duty and eloped with his twenty-eight-year-old fiancée to Las Vegas.[19]

ATTACKS AND COUNTERATTACKS

Schwinn's honeymoon did not last long. During the winter and spring of 1939, Lewis and Roos had expanded their spy network to combat the growing influx of outside espionage agents. But their primary focus remained on Deutsches Haus. Working closely with sympathetic officials at the Department of Immigration and Naturalization, they set out to disrupt the Nazi movement by deporting the city's two main leaders, Schwinn and Diebel.

On June 22, Schwinn and his bride, accompanied by Bockhacker and several Bundists, took their seats in the downtown federal building and waited for Judge Ralph Jenney to begin Schwinn's citizenship trial. Prosecutors argued for revoking the German's citizenship on two grounds: the witnesses signing his papers had made false statements about the length of his residency in Los Angeles (they were off by two months of the required five-year residency), and Schwinn was not of "good moral character."[20] To prove their case, prosecutors called several witnesses from the Department of Immigration and Naturalization to the stand. Armed with notes provided by Lewis and Roos, the witnesses described how Schwinn had repeatedly threatened violence against the city's Jewish residents.

Following their testimony, Schwinn took the stand. As Thekla dozed in the back of the courtroom, her husband, speaking in flawless English, told the judge he was a loyal, hardworking immigrant who had moved to Ohio as a sixteen-year-old and had been employed his whole time in America as a bank clerk, bookkeeper, insurance salesman, Deutsches Haus manager, and travel agent. The two-month error his witnesses had made was "an honest mistake."[21] He had earned the right to remain in his new homeland.

When the trial resumed after a lunch break, Judge Kenney delivered his verdict. Stating that there is no such thing as a right to citizenship, Kenney revoked Schwinn's citizenship, due to the defendant's admission that he had not fulfilled the five-year rule. Sitting in the back of the room, Bockhacker observed that the "Bundists took it hard." Two hours later, Lewis received a report from his informant Jimmy Frost that the Immigration and Naturalization Service was now preparing deportation proceedings against Schwinn.[22]

Returning to Deutsches Haus following the disappointing news, Bund leaders announced the creation of the Hermann Schwinn Legal

Defense Fund and swore to take his case to the Supreme Court. Speaking at a meeting several days later, an irate Schwinn told the faithful, "Today they prosecute us, but today I also predict that within less than five years, our enemies in this country and those who framed me, will dangle from the lantern posts and trees." There was no question as to the identity of their number-one enemy. As Young reported, everyone at Deutsches Haus knew the verdict was "due to the wire pulling of Leon Lewis of the B'nai B'rith ADL." Bundists hoped Schwinn's recent marriage to a native-born American would help reverse the decision in the court of appeals, but Schwinn confessed to Young that "he expected to lose the case."[23]

Schwinn was not the only one worried about deportation. The previous January, a troubled Diebel complained to the ever-present Young that he was supposed to have received his final citizenship eight months earlier. He needed those papers so he could "come out in the open with his propaganda campaign" and purchase weapons from the National Rifle Association, which required proof of citizenship. Unbeknownst to Diebel, Lewis and Roos were sending Immigration officials a steady stream of reports proving that the Aryan Bookstore owner was a propaganda agent of the German government engaged in subversive activities.[24]

Despite their troubles, Schwinn and Diebel went on the offensive that summer, opening their long-dreamed-of youth camp on July 2, 1939. Held at Hindenburg Park (which the Bund renamed La Crescenta Park to make it more appealing to American parents), Camp Sutter was one of many American Nazi summer camps designed to indoctrinate boys and girls from six to eighteen in the principles of National Socialism, camps that *Look* magazine referred to as "Germany in America." The Nazi government considered the summer camps so important they brought Bund youth leader William Sellin to Germany for several weeks of training in April 1938. At a special Youth Evening just prior to the camp opening, Sellin told the gathered offspring of the city's German, Italian, Spanish, and Japanese fascist communities of his hope to foster unity "among the children of our four nationalities and to prepare them for the day when the fate of our nation will lie in their hands."[25]

The forty girls and ten boys who attended Camp Sutter between July 2 and August 12 spent their days being molded into faithful National Socialists. They played, sang, and paraded in Nazi-like uniforms decorated with swastikas. Although the Bund promised the camp would be nonpolitical, storm troopers took the older boys under their wing to

"prepare them for their future duties as leaders of a new America."
William Sellin took the older girls under his own wing and into the
basement of German House for what informant Julius Sicius euphemis-
tically referred to as "certain purposes."[26]

Joy over the success of the summer camp paled in comparison to the
startling news that Hitler and Joseph Stalin had signed a German-
Soviet Nonaggression Pact on August 23, 1939. The two leaders pledged
to take no military action against each other for the next ten years. The
agreement shocked the world, but made sense for both sides. Stalin had
time to build up his military for what he knew would be an eventual
battle against Germany, while Hitler could now march eastward
without fear of Russian reprisal.

Los Angeles Nazis greeted the news with unrestrained delight.
"Everyone feels that Hitler has outsmarted all the diplomats of the
world and that soon Hitler will rule all of Europe," Young reported.
Schwinn and Diebel gloated over the führer's "great diplomatic coup"
and predicted that the pact would mean bad news for the world's Jews.
As they told fellow Bundists, "bloodshed will some day be the order of
the day in the United States."[27]

WAR

At 4:45 a.m. on September 1, 1939, 1.5 million Nazi troops marched into
Poland. Two days later, France and Great Britain declared war on
Germany. World War II had begun. American reaction was swift. On
September 1, General George C. Marshall, one of Joe Roos's few trusted
allies in the government, was sworn in as the army's chief of staff.
Five days later, President Roosevelt placed the FBI in charge "of investigative work in matters relating to espionage, sabotage, and violations of
the neutrality regulations." Roosevelt ordered all law enforcement agencies to send appropriate information to Hoover's office. Concerned
about the influx of foreign spies, the FBI launched a special program to
train its agents in counterespionage. By the end of September, the
Bureau had added 150 men to its Washington office to investigate threats
of sabotage and espionage, especially in the aircraft and shipbuilding
industries.[28]

The State Department went a step further. On September 23, they
invoked the 1917 wartime Espionage Act and demanded that all
employees of foreign embassies, legations, and consulates who engaged

in political activity register with the State Department as agents of a foreign government or face a possible $5,000 fine and five years in prison. Within a matter of days, 363 men and women notified the State Department of their work as foreign agents.[29]

Bundists were thrilled by the outbreak of war and what they saw as Germany's inevitable victory. The general attitude inside Deutsches Haus, Bockhacker observed, was that "Hitler can lick the whole world." During meetings that fall, Schwinn called for American neutrality and urged members to send letters and telegrams to Congress opposing entry into a war that would be fought on behalf of Britain and the "kikes." Speaking at a "peace rally" on September 3, Schwinn told the boisterous crowd of 300, many of whom wore "Keep U.S. Out of War" buttons, that the "Bund is a force for peace and wants nothing but American neutrality. The fault of the war is not Germany's."[30]

A week later 6,000 German men, women, and children, many dressed in traditional German costumes or Nazi uniforms, turned out to cele-brate German Day at La Crescenta Park. Emboldened once again by Hitler's military success, the Bund opened a recruiting booth with a large sign atop warning, "People who have Jewish blood or colored people do not apply." An array of speakers addressed the crowd in English and German, while twenty uniformed storm troopers guarded the stage. The day ended with everyone standing, giving the Nazi salute, and singing "Deutschland Über Alles" and the "Horst Wessel Song."[31] All of this was happening less than seventeen miles from downtown Los Angeles.

War fever gripped Deutsches Haus that fall as Bundists hung a map in the spacious restaurant bar showing the advance of German troops into Poland. Flags on the map representing troops from both nations were moved each day based on radio and newspaper reports received from Germany; any negative information gleaned from American media was dismissed as lies. Enthusiasm for Hitler's campaign ran so high that Georg Gyssling's consular office was flooded with offers to join the German war effort. The German consul general urged his countrymen to "keep calm, keep your jobs and wait until you hear from me."[32]

The momentum Lewis and Roos had gained after Schwinn's court hearing had shifted. To shift it back again, Lewis moved part of his operation into a larger space on Hollywood Boulevard between La Brea and Highland. He needed more room to accommodate Roos's expanding work organizing files and publishing his weekly *News Letter*. Their new office suite had enough space for Roos, a secretary, and, as one HUAC investigator noted, "a room filled with filing cabinets and card files which contain the information and data gathered through a system of informers and from magazines, newspapers, and other sources."[33]

Although the Los Angeles FBI office had been slow to investigate local Nazis, Lewis and Roos kept sending them reports and photographs throughout the spring and summer of 1939. They also sent copies of Roos's *News Letter*, documenting the activities of Nazi and fascist leaders and providing important leads about suspected espionage and sabotage. In mid-September Bureau agents, acting on a "tip" from sources in Los Angeles, announced they had discovered the existence, but not the location, of a munitions cache in San Francisco that included 100,000 German-made Mauser rifles, 20,000 other military rifles, 800 million rounds of rifle ammunition, and various quantities of trench mortar shells, small aerial bombs, and several lots of gas masks.[34]

Two weeks later, as newspaper headlines across the nation warned Americans to be alert for possible espionage and sabotage, the Los Angeles bureau, working in cooperation with "an attorney in Hollywood," told reporters they were compiling a "suspect" list of more than 1,000 people in Southern California. The G-men, as the press liked to call them, were especially interested in obtaining the names, addresses, and photographs of the Bund's storm troopers; they had been told that Los Angeles had an estimated fifty such men.[35]

Lewis and Roos were happy to let Hoover's men take all the credit. However, Chuck Slocombe warned them they could not trust all the local agents. Klan leader C. Earle Snelson had told his chief investigator about a recent meeting with FBI special agent in charge Richard Hood. After visiting Hood's office and speaking with a number of Bureau agents, Snelson determined that the FBI had five men "who are favorable to the Klan but there are a couple of Jews there who have to be watched."[36]

With government agencies suddenly showing far greater interest in their material, Joe Roos worked closely with a network of European contacts to expand the *News Letter*'s coverage to include events abroad. The former newspaperman also cultivated editors and reporters at the city's newspapers, sharing inside information that, in his words, might help "awaken the American public" to threats at home.[37]

Lewis and Roos sent copies of the *News Letter* to sympathetic contacts in the State and War Departments and to an array of senators and congresspeople. The spymasters also began cooperating with like-minded officials in the British embassy, Britain's Secret Intelligence Service, the British Ministry of Information, and the French Sûreté, providing them with information and copies of the *News Letter*. The British, in turn, gave them their list of suspected spies operating in Los Angeles.[38]

Without question, their most powerful media allies were Walter Winchell and the writing team of Drew Pearson and Robert Allen. The popular political columnists regularly used material from the *News Letter* to provide readers with an often frightening look at Nazi activity inside and outside the nation's borders. The normally modest Roos insisted that, as a result of these exposés, several "slow-moving government forces were compelled to take action against a number of Nazi propaganda agents who had failed to register as foreign agents with the State Department."[39]

THE RETURN OF NEIL NESS

During the course of its hearings in 1939, HUAC spent 75 percent of its time investigating Reds and only 25 percent focused on Nazis and fascists.[40] But the 25 percent it did spend proved enormously important in helping Leon Lewis convince Americans to take the Nazi threat seriously.

When Lewis learned that Neil Ness had been subpoenaed in June to testify at an upcoming HUAC hearing in Washington, D.C., he immediately contacted his former agent, who was living in Oakland. Unlike the 1934 Los Angeles HUAC hearings, when he worked behind the scenes with congressman Charles Kramer, Lewis had no close ally on the Dies Committee. Unwilling to expose any of his current operatives, he had to rely on Ness to convince HUAC that the Nazi threat was real and that revolution was their goal.

Knowing this was a chance for national publicity, Lewis sent the debt-ridden engineer money to travel to Los Angeles so he could review his earlier reports. The spymaster also took the unusual step of inviting Ness into his home. Since beginning his undercover operation in 1933, Lewis had been careful to separate his personal life from his work life. He did not socialize with his operatives and certainly never invited them to his house. But this was an exceptional opportunity unlikely to occur again. During the summer prior to Ness's appearance, the two men spent several weeks carefully rehearsing his testimony and orchestrating what they hoped would be theater on a grand scale.[41]

On Thursday, October 5, 1939, Neil Howard Ness began the first of his two-day testimony before Martin Dies's committee. Dressed in a double-breasted gray suit and light-colored tie, and holding a pipe that rarely left his hand, Ness looked more like a college professor than an undercover operative, a look intended to give his testimony a greater sense of gravitas. Ness opened by recounting how he had joined the Bund as an undercover agent late in 1935. He described how members "swore allegiance to National Socialism and to Adolf Hitler" and awaited the moment when they would be "called upon to give even our lifeblood in defense of the fatherland."[42] Ness described driving Hermann Schwinn to the docks where he received money, propaganda, and sealed orders from visiting German ship captains or Gestapo agents who traveled on board each vessel. He told of seeing Schwinn hand them confidential reports to take back to their masters in Germany.

The Bund, Ness warned the committee, was not just another American organization as its leaders claimed. It was "an arm of the German government." While working undercover, he learned that the Nazi government was secretly funneling funds through the local consulate. He testified that German consul Georg Gyssling had asked him to bring money to help the Bund, but warned he needed "to be very careful because they could not have it officially known that the money was coming from the consulate."[43]

Committee members had heard similar testimony before. What caught their attention was Ness's riveting description of Nazi plans for espionage, sabotage, and war with America. During his time in the Bund, Ness discovered that Nazi spies were pouring into the country through unguarded ports in Los Angeles and then traveling unobserved to the far corners of the United States. At Schwinn's request, he had driven a spy sent from Berlin to San Pedro, where he wanted to observe the American fleet, and then to San Diego, where he took photographs of the Navy's submarine and destroyer base.

The dapper engineer explained how on their drive down the coast, he had fooled the unnamed agent (though never mentioned by name, it was Willi Schneeberger) into believing that a golf course being built alongside the highway was in fact a proving ground for an army artillery unit. The Nazi spy "became quite excited and he wanted to stop and take some pictures" of the alleged military base as well as photographs of navy vessels stationed off the coast. Once in San Diego, Ness encountered the dangerous Count Ernst Ulrich von Bülow, whom he suspected "was the head of the German espionage" on the West Coast. Not only did the German agent live on a high hill in San Diego from which he could observe the Pacific Coast's main naval base, but he was also "a very close friend of the chief of the naval intelligence in that district."[44]

These revelations were merely a prelude. On the following afternoon, Ness shocked the committee and gathered reporters by revealing the Bund's plans for sabotage and armed revolt. "We always discussed what we would do toward helping Germany [in case of war], such as blowing up aviation works and munitions plants and docks." Pausing for dramatic effect, he added, "We had about a hundred members on the Pacific coast at one time that we could depend on to paralyze the defense on the Pacific coast."[45]

When the startled HUAC investigator asked whether the Bund had concrete plans for sabotage, Ness responded in the affirmative. "We planned on paralyzing the Pacific coast from Seattle to San Diego." The Nazi strategy included "blowing up the Hercules powder plant, where they make munitions, and also blowing up all of the docks and warehouses along the water front." The Bund had already placed a number of its skilled machinists and mechanics inside Douglas Aircraft and other airplane and munitions factories. Hitler's American forces were preparing for the day when sabotage would be followed by revolution. Max Egan, an "expert rifleman" who served as an instructor in the German army during World War I, was secretly training Los Angeles storm troopers for armed combat. When asked the purpose of their training, Ness shot back, "Taking over the government of the United States." Schwinn told him that once the Nazis were in control, they would follow the "same policy and program that Hitler had followed; that is, that we would commence with the attack upon the Jews and after we had beaten down the Jews we would go after the Catholics."[46]

Thanking him for his lengthy testimony, Martin Dies adjourned the hearings and dismissed Ness.

Media coverage of their operative's riveting testimony was everything Lewis and Roos had hoped for, and more. Playing up the threat of a hundred Nazis poised to blow up docks, aircraft factories, and waterworks, newspaper headlines across the United States and Canada reported Ness's warning about Nazi plans for espionage and sabotage. "Dies Witness Tells Bund's Plans to Paralyze Coast," read a *Los Angeles Times* headline on October 7. "Bund Sabotage Plan Told: Ex-Member of

California Unit Also Reveals Espionage Aid to Nazis at Defense Bases," screamed a *New York Times* story. The *Los Angeles Herald-Express* warned readers, "Bund members would be on the side of Germany in case of war between that country and the United States."[47]

Ness's testimony so captivated the public's attention that newspapers in Florida, Utah, Ohio, Kansas, Pennsylvania, Indiana, Michigan, Virginia, Kentucky, Texas, Missouri, and elsewhere continued running stories about his shocking tale of espionage and intrigue. Nazis were planning terrorism on American soil, and authorities had done little to stop it. On October 6, in a stroke of good fortune that lent greater credibility to Ness's claims, navy authorities in San Pedro reported discovering evidence of a plot to sabotage the 33,000-ton USS *Arizona*, one of the Pacific fleet's main battleships.[48]

Ness's dazzling testimony won over a number of previously hesitant members of the American intelligence community. During the course of his testimony, Ness never revealed that he was working as an undercover operative for Leon Lewis. But a number of government authorities, American and foreign, knew the identity of his boss, and many of them now flocked to the two Jews for more information. As Joe Roos wrote a close friend that October, "It seems like our office is the meeting places for the largest assortment of FBI, NI [naval intelligence], G2 [army intelligence], British Secret Service, etc. Too bad I can't tell you about it in this letter."[49]

Back on West Fifteenth Street, Bundists greeted news of Ness's testimony with anger and frustration. Ness was still "pulling the chestnuts out of the fire for the Jews," Hans Diebel complained to Chuck Slocombe. Calling Ness's accusations "a pipe dream," Hermann Schwinn told reporters that he had never received funds or exchanged sealed packages with German ship captains; nor was the Bund planning a campaign of sabotage. Despite his denials, Schwinn knew his cause had been badly damaged by the publicity surrounding Ness's testimony. "Many of the people who visited German House frequently," Bockhacker observed, "are now staying away."[50]

The momentum had shifted. Government authorities were finally closing in on the Nazi movement in America. The FBI was so impressed with Lewis and Roos's undercover operation that they asked the duo to let William Bockhacker work for them as their full-time informant. Pleased with the recognition, Lewis and Roos turned Bockhacker over to the FBI that December.

Despite Hitler's victories in Europe, by the end of 1939, American Nazis were on the defensive. Refusing to despair, the embattled Hermann Schwinn responded with a new strategy: he would take his movement underground and unite with a number of groups dedicated to maintaining American neutrality. Some isolationist organizations, such as America First, were genuinely opposed to foreign intervention and insisted on maintaining an arms embargo against the Allied powers. Yet many others secretly wanted to keep America weak until the moment the führer was ready to cross the Atlantic Ocean.

Always vigilant and fearing backsliding by government agencies, Lewis and Roos continued running their spy operation and turning out copies of the *News Letter*, warning the nation of the growing fifth column and danger from within.

19.

Sabotage, Secret Agents, and
Fifth Columnists

On October 11, 1939, five days after Neil Ness's dramatic testimony, Charles Young—Agent Y9—was dining at Deutsches Haus with fellow Bundists when Karl Jaeckel, a German aviator recently arrived from China, sat down at their table. The German-born Young sensed that this was no ordinary visitor: Jaeckel had "the manner of a typical German officer" and the furtiveness of a spy. Hoping to discover the man's true identity, Young volunteered to drive Jaeckel around Los Angeles during his visit and invited the Nazi and his wife to his home for dinner. During the course of their meals, Jaeckel expressed his utter contempt for Hermann Schwinn and the Bund. He had spent several hours talking with Schwinn and his inner circle behind locked doors. Their conversation left him unimpressed. "They are just a bunch of nobodies and they are not the type of people I can use, we need more reliable people who have good jobs like you have for instance." Jaeckel so despised Schwinn that he offered him $2,000 ($34,000 in 2015 dollars) to leave the country.[1]

After the two men had spent several weeks together driving around the city, inspecting aircraft manufacturing plants, Jaeckel revealed his mission. The Gestapo had sent him to Los Angeles to blow up aircraft factories that were about to ship planes to Canada and then on to Allied forces in Europe. Not trusting Schwinn, Jaeckel asked Young to recruit three or four Americans or assimilated Germans who had no accent. His masters in Berlin had given him $10,000 to spend on espionage in the United States, and he would pay each man $300 to $400 a month to help destroy the planes before they left Los Angeles.[2]

Jaeckel's plans might have succeeded except for two things: he was a morphine addict who revealed far too much when high, and everything he told Young went straight to Lewis and on to Commander Ellis Zacharias at naval intelligence. A grateful Zacharias told Lewis how the information Young uncovered "had opened up leads and avenues of the very greatest importance." Naval intelligence and the FBI tightened security at aircraft plants and succeeded in thwarting Jaeckel's plans. The Nazi saboteur had intended to stay in the United States for six months, but, suspecting he had been discovered, he fled the country in December, never to be seen again.[3]

Before he left, Jaeckel told Young that Berlin had secret agents in place in Los Angeles and throughout the United States; local diamond dealer H. A. Russell was in fact "the chief of the German Intelligence operatives in this area" and had twenty "very good operatives," all of whom owned or worked in respectable businesses. Russell and his agents were setting up "peace groups" aimed at keeping the United States out of war. Money was no problem. German spies received whatever they needed from Gustav Riedlin, Jaeckel's contact at the local Bank of America, who laundered money from Berlin and kept "a dossier on all German people living in this district."[4]

Jaeckel had been foiled, but Lewis and Roos suspected he was just one of many German secret agents operating among them. Yet they could not be sure if the Nazi spy ring was as widespread as Jaeckel claimed, or if morphine led him to exaggerate.

INSIDE THE "WASHINGTON CONFERENCE"

In early January 1940, German embassy chargé d'affaires Hans Thomsen ordered his most important consuls and military attachés to a secret meeting in Washington, D.C., to discuss the war's progress. Since September, Hitler had conquered Poland and massed troops on the French border. On December 30, the führer told the German people that 1940 would be the most important year in the nation's history.

As he walked to the meeting at the Mayflower Hotel, German general consul Georg Gyssling ran into his longtime friend Julius Klein, Joe Roos's uncle, who was staying at the Mayflower. The National Guard captain was in town to meet with army intelligence head General George C. Marshall; he had been sending Marshall reports on Nazi activities since 1933, including accounts of his early conversations with Gyssling. After Gyssling described the reason for his visit, Klein asked if they could meet to discuss the consuls' conversations about the war.

Explaining that he was "afraid to talk" in Washington because "everyone is watched by spies and counter-spies," Gyssling promised to meet his friend on the way back to Los Angeles.[5]

After three days of meetings, the consuls returned to their posts, except Gyssling, who made a brief detour, stopping in Chicago on January 15. He spent the morning locked in a room at the Lake Shore Hotel with Klein. In one of the most extraordinary events before the United States' entry into the war, a highly placed German official sat down with a Jew and revealed secret military information. He was willing to do so because, as a German nationalist, Gyssling believed his first obligation was to his nation and not the Hitler regime. Like many Foreign Office officials, he "thought Hitler was a disaster" and despised the men who surrounded him. The sooner his nation was rid of the führer, the sooner it could achieve a "rebirth of German Democracy."[6]

As they sat locked in Klein's hotel room, Gyssling recounted how consuls and embassy officials had discussed a range of war-related topics. Their most heated conversation centered on the wisdom of having Gestapo agents operating in the United States. They complained that with the exception of a few men in the "inner circle of the Nazi Party and Gestapo," consular and diplomatic officials were "kept in ignorance" about their activities. Outside agents, the assembled men agreed, were not needed to spy on American military and defense installations. Consuls were already monitoring the production and shipment of aircraft in their areas and sending reports to Berlin. Embassy military attachés scoffed at how naive American companies constructed their planes in plain sight. "Look here, there are dozens of planes on the open field of the airport in Los Angeles," naval air attaché Peter Riedel had pointed out. "Everybody can see them."[7]

Gyssling had argued that assistance from Berlin was unnecessary "because we get enough volunteers to aid us in securing this information." Hundreds of fifth columnists loyal to the führer were working in aircraft factories along the Pacific Coast and were prepared to stop the production of any weapons to be used against Germany.[8] The consuls used the term "fifth column," which came into popular usage during the Spanish Civil War in 1936, to describe fears of betrayal by disloyal forces living within a nation's borders. For them, American fifth columnists were not betrayers but heroes of the Reich.

Worried that Gestapo agents would attempt to sabotage American defense industries, the embassy's three military officials—military and air attaché Friedrich von Boetticher, his assistant Riedel, and German naval attaché Robert Witthoeft-Emden—had appealed to Hermann Goering to halt Gestapo activities. Hitler, they argued, needed at least a year before his armies would gain control of Europe. But for that to occur, Germany needed to keep the United States from entering the conflict. A majority of Americans were currently in favor of neutrality, but if they discovered German spies were committing sabotage on their soil, "it would poison the American mind" and lead to a victory by those calling for intervention. If America entered too soon, Boetticher warned, it would "probably turn the events of the war."[9]

After three hours of intense conversation, Gyssling returned to the train station, leaving Julius Klein to ponder the consul's extraordinary revelations. Los Angeles was in danger. Gestapo agents, consuls, and their fifth-column allies were spying on the city's aircraft industry. Sabotage was a real possibility. The consuls did not know what was being planned by Berlin, but they were concerned that any attack on American defense industries would be considered an act of war.

Wishing to keep their remarkable conversation fresh in his mind, Klein typed out a six-page single-spaced memo that he sent to two trusted people: George Marshall and Joe Roos. His informant, Klein wrote Marshall, had been providing him with details concerning "subversive activities of the Nazis" for nearly a decade, and his information had "always proven to be authentic."[10] The only thing Klein did not reveal was the consul's name. He trusted Marshall but was afraid that if Gyssling's name leaked out, the Gestapo would execute him before he could return to Berlin.

Klein was less circumspect with his nephew; Roos knew Gyssling was the man in question. Klein forwarded his report and an amended document from Roos to G-2 (army intelligence) headquarters. Several weeks later, Klein received a letter from Marshall asking Roos to provide army intelligence with any further information he might uncover. Washington insiders who received his weekly News Letter, Klein told his nephew, had "praised your work out in California."[11]

Gyssling's conversation with Klein confirmed several of the spymasters' worst fears. They were now dealing with an enemy far more dangerous than the likes of Henry Allen, Leslie Fry, or Hermann Schwinn. Trained Gestapo agents were spying in Los Angeles with an eye toward sabotaging local defense industries. With Douglas, Lockheed, Vultee, North American, and Consolidated Aircraft plants turning out the bulk of the nation's aircraft, and given Gyssling's warning about the presence of fifth columnists in their city, that meant Los Angeles was a prime target for Nazi violence.

Armed with Gyssling's information and a steady stream of reports from their own operatives, Lewis and Roos set out on three missions: uncover German secret agents operating in Los Angeles; discover the identity of fifth columnists before they could do any damage; and stop sabotage. They would start by focusing on the place where they were most likely to find the greatest number of fifth columnists: Deutsches Haus.

INSIDE THE TROJAN HORSE

In November 1939, a month before William Bockhacker went to work for the FBI, Lewis and Roos succeeded in recruiting Julius Sicius, one of the founding officers of the Friends of New Germany. The German-born accountant had served as secretary to its leader, Captain Robert Pape, and was responsible for bringing Hermann Schwinn into the organization. After falling on hard times, Sicius took a job working as a waiter at Deutsches Haus until he was fired in the fall of 1939. Unemployed, angry, and desperate, he approached Leon Lewis offering to work as an undercover operative for the Jews.[12]

Suspecting Sicius might be a Nazi plant, Lewis and Roos spent several days grilling the Bundist at their office before agreeing to hire him on a trial basis. They offered the impoverished German a modest stipend, but insisted he needed to work for them "not in the spirit of revenge" but "as a service to the country and to clear the name of the German American community, which has been besmirched through the activities of the German American Bund." Any information they found "suitable and valuable, would be turned over to the F. B. I."[13] They never told Sicius that William Bockhacker and Charles Young were also spying for them.

Sicius proved even more effective than Bockhacker in monitoring Bund activities and reporting on its connections to the growing number of groups calling for American neutrality. Within a matter of weeks, he supplied Lewis and Roos with the names and addresses of Bund members and sympathizers, along with detailed comments. As a long-time waiter, he overheard many secrets Bundists revealed after too many rounds of bock beer at the Deutsches Haus bar. Equally important, Sicius—referred to as Agent S4—knew Georg Gyssling well enough to be invited to small dinner parties where the consul and his deputies discussed the war's progress. Sicius sent Lewis reports of their conversations, which Lewis forwarded to naval intelligence and the FBI.[14]

Schwinn and Hans Diebel knew spies had penetrated the Bund and were reporting to the Jews. They just did not know who or how many. But Lewis soon suspected that the Nazis had followed through on their threat to kill anyone caught betraying them. In February 1940, a Bund Youth Group member spotted Sicius writing down license plate numbers at Deutsches Haus and reported him to Hans Diebel. A week later, Diebel warned Sicius "about what he would do to men who were caught taking down license numbers." Sicius thought he had bluffed his way out of a jam by explaining he had stopped in the parking lot to write a memo to himself. Three months later, he died of a "basal skull fracture and softening of the brain." The coroner ruled that the fatal blow had occurred after Sicius fell down on Sunset Boulevard due to an epileptic fit, a condition he had never mentioned to the spymasters. But Sicius had fallen in the company of a fellow Bundist; given Diebel's promise to murder anyone found working for the Jews, Lewis suspected foul play.[15]

While Bundists attempted to weed out spies in their midst, Hitler's armies blazed a path of destruction across Europe. By May 1940, the führer's troops had seized control of Denmark, Norway, Belgium, Luxembourg, and the Netherlands. A month later, triumphant German forces marched into Paris and raised the swastika flag. The human toll was enormous: tens of thousands lay dead and hundreds of thousands wounded.

After receiving Lewis and Roos's reports on suspected Nazi spies in the region, the Los Angeles bureau's special agent in charge sent J. Edgar Hoover a memo entitled "Herman Schwinn: Espionage." The chief G-man turned down his agent's urgent request to launch a further investigation of the Bund, explaining that Schwinn had not broken any federal laws. Preferring to have his understaffed office focus on Reds, Hoover ordered the Bureau "to place the case in a closed status." Local agents followed Hoover's order, but they asked Roos to teach them his elaborate system for systematizing all reports and creating a master file that could be accessed at a moment's notice.[16]

Acting with a greater sense of urgency than the FBI, Los Angeles district attorney Buron Fitts created an Anti-Fifth Column Department in May 1940, while police chief Arthur Hohmann launched a new Anti-Subversive Unit a month later. Neither proved effective. Charles Young knew the men who had been assigned to the district attorney's unit and warned Lewis that the "whole bunch in Fitts' Office were rotten and that included Fitts, himself." The spymaster needed no one to tell him that the two-man police unit would be of little help. Hohmann had appointed Frank Gompert, who had blown the investigation of the Leopold McLaglan plot, and the disgraced William "Red" Hynes, who had been demoted after he was discovered taking money from suspected German and Japanese agents.[17]

Lewis and Roos knew that eliminating Schwinn and Diebel could disrupt the Bund's rigid chain of command and inhibit the activities of fifth columnists. To ensure that happened, they continued working with allies at the Department of Immigration and Naturalization to rid the city of the two Nazi leaders. On May 10, the Ninth Circuit Court of Appeals ruled against Schwinn and upheld the cancellation of his citizenship. As the Bund head prepared his appeal to the Supreme Court, immigration authorities, armed with information from Lewis and Roos, began completing their case for deportation.[18] Government officials also began sifting through the material Lewis sent to be used against Hans Diebel at his upcoming citizenship hearings.

The Bund may have been in decline, but the nation's German American community remained a powerful political force. As *Fortune* magazine observed that fall, 7 million first- and second-generation German Americans belonged to German clubs and societies. Although most Germans were "more or less lukewarm about Nazism," the magazine estimated that 10,000 to 500,000 were "militantly pro-Nazi" and posed a distinct "threat to U.S. security." Hitler's sympathizers and the 800 "Fascist-minded groups" operating in the United States were growing in strength and gaining support "from well-to-do anti-Semites."[19]

Hoping to mobilize that potentially powerful voter bloc, Schwinn and Diebel began working with politicians and peace groups calling for American neutrality. Speaking at a May Day picnic that drew a thousand men, women, and children to La Crescenta Park (which Nazi faithful still referred to as Hindenburg Park), Schwinn called on all German Americans to write their representatives in Congress, urging them to "keep America out of the British war."[20] He also encouraged them to join isolationist organizations demanding American neutrality.

Not all groups calling for neutrality were fifth-column fronts. Many were composed of loyal citizens with lingering memories of the needless death and destruction caused by World War I. They were determined to prevent the United States from becoming entangled in

European affairs. Yet, unknown to most, noninterventionist groups also included agents provocateurs who hoped to keep America neutral until Hitler triumphed in Europe. They wanted peace now, but only until the right moment for war. Knowing he had to be cautious while his citizenship case made its way through the courts, Schwinn had let isolationists take the public lead while he and his allies worked behind the scenes, organizing secret cells led by Nazis or their paid American recruits. As the Bund's national führer, G. Wilhelm Kunze, told Charles Young, he wanted Nazis to work closely with America First, but wanted the public to "be kept unaware of this."[21]

Needing more American-born operatives to infiltrate American-dominated cells and peace groups, Lewis and Roos recruited two new spies that June, the mother-and-daughter team of Grace and Sylvia Comfort. Sent to them by a mutual friend at the Warner Brothers' studio, the Comforts met the attorney at his downtown office and recounted the troubling events that had led them there. Grace's recently deceased husband, Commander James Comfort, had spent twenty-six years as a career officer in the navy. A year after his death in April 1939, Grace and Sylvia left their home near the naval base in San Diego and moved to Los Angeles, where they began looking for work; her husband's military pension was not sufficient to support them.[22]

Jumping into the conversation, twenty-seven-year-old Sylvia explained that she was a stenographer who had attended San Diego College and hoped to find employment as a clerk or script reader in the movie business. Needing money to tide them over, she had taken a temporary job doing secretarial work for their next-door neighbor's brother, William Pierce Williams, and his Educational Service Bureau. She had assumed that the Texas-born army veteran was a loyal American, but after reading a number of his isolationist newsletters, mother and daughter were "so aghast at the viciousness of the anti-Semitic propaganda" that they decided "to see something done about it."[23]

Sylvia was convinced Williams wanted to do more than just turn out anti-Semitic propaganda. After working together for several weeks, she learned that the fifty-two-year-old high school teacher was organizing secret groups in Los Angeles, Santa Barbara, and San Diego dedicated to ridding the nation of the Jews. When Comfort suggested using the electoral system to solve problems, Williams shot back, "We won't do it that way. It will be more drastic."[24]

Eager to put a halt to Williams's activities, Grace reported him to the local FBI, but they "did not seem to be very much interested."[25] Grace hoped that she and her daughter could be of service to Lewis. After vetting the pair with Ellis Zacharias—who had been a good friend of Grace's husband—Lewis accepted their offer to join Williams's group and agreed to pay Sylvia a modest stipend. But he warned her that spying was a dangerous undertaking, even more dangerous since the outbreak of war and the suspicious death of Julius Sicius.

Mother and daughter would not be deterred. Over the next several months, Sylvia (Agent S3) joined Williams's movement and sent detailed reports of cell meetings to Lewis and Roos. Grace (Agent G2) soon realized that Williams wanted her to provide him with "entrée into Naval circles" where he could "spread his propaganda." When Sylvia warned Lewis that her employer was planning a recruiting trip to San Diego, he contacted Zacharias, who promised to arrange for a group of naval officers to be "subverted" by Williams.[26]

Even more troubling, Sylvia discovered that Williams was taking orders from suspected German agent Eugene Messerschmitt. A month after beginning their undercover work, mother and daughter learned the two men had organized at least one cell comprising commercial pilots, aircraft mechanics, and people involved with aviation. Williams knew them from his days as a pilot in the National Guard. When he told Sylvia he was taking his boat out to San Pedro Harbor, she feared he was not doing it for pleasure but intended to inspect defense facilities on Messerschmitt's behalf.[27]

Taking no chances, Lewis ordered Sylvia to establish contact with Messerschmitt, find out what he was up to, and "keep a careful record of any conversation you may have with him."[28] She did, and over the next several months Grace and Sylvia penetrated deeper into Williams and Messerschmitt's operation.

THE NAZI ATTACK ON AMERICA

Lewis's efforts to monitor fifth columnists and potential saboteurs assumed greater urgency that fall when the Hercules powder plant, identified by Neil Ness as a Nazi target, was blown up on September 12, 1940, killing fifty-two people and destroying twenty buildings and 123 million pounds of explosives. The only comforting news for Pacific Coast residents was that saboteurs blew up the plant in Kenvil, New Jersey, and not the one in Hercules, California. FBI investigators sent to the scene downplayed the possibility of sabotage, but HUAC chair

Martin Dies blamed the blast on Nazi agents. "Everyone laughed when a man named Van Hess"—he got Ness's name wrong—"testified before our committee . . . about plans to blow up the Hercules Company." When the plant blew up, Dies added, "it happened in the way Van Hess said it would."[29]

On November 12, a series of explosions occurring within twenty minutes of each other destroyed three defense plants engaged in the production of explosives, torpedoes, and signal flares in New Jersey and Pennsylvania, killing sixteen and wounding two dozen. Dies again chastised the FBI, insisting that the Bureau's "whole method of approach must be radically changed." Foreign agents needed to be exposed and stopped before they did more harm.[30] Dies was right. Hoover had been so busy preparing for his anticipated war with the Soviet Union that he underestimated Nazi preparations for war with the United States.

No explosion rocked the Pacific Coast in part because Lewis, Roos, and their agents had been carefully monitoring defense plants for potential saboteurs. Just days before the Hercules blast, their operatives discovered that San Francisco consul Fritz Wiedemann had several agents and a number of Germans sympathetic to the fatherland working inside the local Douglas Aircraft plant. Lewis immediately warned plant security agents, the FBI, and naval intelligence of potential sabotage.[31]

Lewis and Roos knew the Nazis had other spies and sympathizers working in the city's defense plants, and he feared what might happen if they were not stopped. Hoping to prompt Hoover into action, Roos sent political columnists Drew Pearson and Robert Allen information culled from his operatives' reports and an issue of the *News Letter* detailing the vulnerability of West Coast defense plants—with a caveat not to use his name in any article. On November 19, their "Washington Merry-Go-Round," the country's most widely read syndicated column, warned tens of thousands of readers that the nation's biggest "danger spot" was not along the eastern seaboard but in Los Angeles, which "contains one of the largest concentrations of defense work in the country." The columnists had obtained a copy (from the unnamed Lewis and Roos) of a secret mailing list of 2,500 loyal Los Angeles Nazis and had determined that "800 of them are employed in airplane plants, shipyards, oil refineries, auto factories, and other key defense industries." The leader of these potential saboteurs was Hermann Schwinn.[32]

Immediately after reading the column, an irate Hoover sent a memo to the Los Angeles bureau, demanding to know "what we have on

Hermann Schwinn. If we have anything was it sent to the Department? If not why?" In his obsession with tracking Communists, the director had apparently forgotten his previous memo ordering them to discontinue investigating the local Bund leader. Two days later the Bureau sent him a hastily compiled seven-page report that was filled with errors. The information they did get right came largely from documents sent to them by Lewis and Roos. Although Lewis had reservations about Hoover, local agents had been "very cooperative" and had followed through on the leads he and Roos had given them. Lacking a sufficient number of men to monitor the Bund, agents often took articles from Roos's *News Letter* and presented them to Hoover as "reports by the local FBI."[33]

As hoped, the Pearson-Allen column generated dozens of angry letters to Hoover wanting to know, as one Mississippi writer asked, "what is the U.S. Government waiting on any way? Why does the Government not take out this old Traitor [Schwinn] and shoot him at sunrise . . . Is the FBI absolutely doing every thing in its power to destroy this subversive activity?" A week later, Hoover ordered the Los Angeles bureau to check Schwinn's immigration status and report back to him as soon as possible.[34]

Schwinn was not the only local Nazi to come under FBI scrutiny after the explosions. Suspecting Georg Gyssling was involved, Bureau agents tapped the consulate phone lines. But they did so in the most amateurish manner. During a visit to Gyssling's office that November, Charles Young listened to the consul contemptuously refer to FBI agents as "nothing better than a bunch of school boys." Gyssling showed Young a clearly visible wire the agents had strung from his office window to their car parked below. Amused rather than annoyed, the consul told Young how the agents had such great "difficulty in disconnecting the wire" that before leaving his office, he "idled to give them enough time so they could get ready to follow him."[35]

Despite the horrors caused by the East Coast explosions, Lewis and Roos were making progress. On October 28 the Supreme Court, referring to Schwinn as the "Number 2 Bundist in America," upheld the lower court decision to revoke his citizenship on the grounds that it had been "illegally procured." A week later, obeying orders from Germany requiring all members to be citizens, Schwinn resigned from the Bund. Equally heartening, the FBI was taking the Jewish spymasters far more seriously. Their reports referred to Lewis and Roos, "Confidential Informants Nos. 21 and 22," as men "in a position to know" all about

Nazi operations in the Los Angeles region. The respect also extended to their agents. Impressed with Charles Young's investigative skills, both the FBI and naval intelligence asked him to work for them in November 1940. He declined the offer, preferring instead to work for Lewis and Roos.[36]

GOING UNDERGROUND

Despite his resignation, Schwinn remained in charge of Nazi activities, but he conducted them in a more covert manner. "Schwinn is active along new lines," Sylvia Comfort reported, "but with the same objective." That fall, Nazis and fifth columnists rallied around the newly created America First Committee, which soon established itself as the nation's leading isolationist organization. At its peak, America First attracted 800,000 dues-paying members in 450 chapters, among them Gerald Ford and John F. Kennedy, who sent the group $100. Disappointed that Republicans had selected interventionist Wendell Willkie to oppose Roosevelt in the 1940 election rather than isolationist senator Robert Taft or New York district attorney Thomas Dewey, America First loyalists called for strict enforcement of the 1939 Neutrality Act and hoped to persuade aviation hero and Hitler admirer Charles Lindbergh to run for president.[37]

Despite worrying about the influence of America First, Lewis was far more concerned by reports of the growing number of men and women meeting in secret cells, many of them led by Nazi spies or their paid American agents. Given recent incidents of sabotage and knowing the enormity of the threat that faced them, Lewis and Roos recruited an unprecedented number of operatives in an effort to uncover useful information: Charles Young, Anna Friedman, John Barr, Jimmy Frost, Roy Arnold, Chuck Slocombe, Grace and Sylvia Comfort, and Captain John Schmidt, who was so incensed at having his life threatened by Nazis in December 1938 that he resumed spying for Lewis and Roos in the summer of 1940. Zacharias considered their operation so far ahead of any intelligence agency in Southern California that he asked to make it part of naval intelligence. Like Charles Young, Lewis politely declined the offer. By the end of the year, the two Jews had established themselves as an unofficial branch of American intelligence, sending regular reports to naval intelligence, the FBI, the War Department, and the State Department.[38]

While Barr and the Comforts focused on secret cells, Slocombe alerted Lewis and Roos to a dangerous new enemy in their midst. On September 4, a week before the Hercules powder plant explosion, German-born Fred Heidenreich asked his longtime friend Chuck Slocombe to help organize secret cells in Orange County "to fight the Jews." As Slocombe soon learned, the cells were a cover for a major Nazi espionage operation. Heidenreich was a former member of the German navy who had served twelve years in the U.S. Navy and an additional stint as a lieutenant in the U.S. Coast Guard. A man familiar with warships and naval maneuvers, he had kept himself combat ready. He "carries himself erect, military type, 5'11" tall, gray hair, thin face, brown eyes, usually wears a gray suit, almost continuously smokes a pipe, always wears a brown hat."[39]

Stringing him along, Slocombe discovered that Heidenreich was a paid agent of Count Ernst Ulrich von Bülow. The shadowy German who had run Nazi spy operations in Southern California out of his hilltop home overlooking the naval base in San Diego—and hosted Schwinn, Neil Ness, and German spy Willi Schneeberger in August 1936—had reemerged from his new home in Mexico, accompanied by two German navy officers. Bülow wanted Heidenreich to recruit Americans to run his cells while also spying on naval movements and defense fortifications. After convincing Bülow that Slocombe was the man for the job, Heidenreich told his friend that the German leader would "make it worth while" if he "would be willing to follow him." Slocombe knew this was no amateur operation. Bülow had "contact men in practically every city" along the Pacific Coast and plenty of cash to recruit more agents.[40] After conferring with Lewis and Zacharias, Slocombe agreed to become Bülow's American front man.

John Barr (Agent J2) had been attending a number of secret cell meetings in Los Angeles that fall, and found their tone "distinctly Nazi from every point of view." After one particularly militant gathering of two dozen supporters, Barr warned Lewis that cell chairman Charles Slocombe was "a bad egg" who, he suspected, was planning to sabotage vessels in San Pedro. "He has contact with the clipper ships and has a contract to service them with gasoline . . . If anything happens to any of these clipper ships, Slocombe is the man who did it."[41]

Slocombe did so well at his job that Bülow appointed him *Kreis Führer* (district leader) and asked him to take command of new cells in Long Beach and Orange County. By the end of 1940, as word of Slocombe's success spread in Nazi and fascist circles, he was asked to join the five-man steering committee of the newly formed United Front. Led by Martin Meader, a former Nazi organizer in Germany, the group was coordinating activities among all fascist and pro-German groups in Southern California. Meader adopted the same organizational structure employed by Hitler's intelligence officers during the 1920s: he would use an elaborate array of leaders and subleaders to make it difficult for government agents to monitor their movements. Their core members included battle-scarred veterans and former government agents familiar with espionage and counterespionage, including two Justice Department investigators and a retired Secret Service agent.[42]

Only a small part of Slocombe's work for Bülow involved overseeing the expanding number of secret cells. The Nazi spy wanted him to spend most of his time gathering information about navy operations and fortifications around Los Angeles, San Pedro, Long Beach, and down the Pacific coast to the Naval base in San Diego.[43]

In mid-December, Bülow's chief aide, former German navy captain Kasselmann, brought Slocombe deeper into the world of Nazi espionage. He provided his American operative with a badge that would "open all doors to German Secret Agents in friendly circles." He cautioned Slocombe never to show it unless contacted by someone who would show him the same badge before engaging in conversation. Having proven himself an effective cell leader, Slocombe received a new set of instructions. Kasselmann would pay him and Heindenreich $5,000 ($84,500 in 2015 dollars) to find out whether mines were being laid around the new navy base on San Clemente Island.[44] Even more money was available if Slocombe could discover whether the San Pedro Harbor was mined and, if so, where. Kasselmann also wanted the precise location of power lines on Terminal Island (located in the harbor between San Pedro and Los Angeles), as well as information about what was being shipped in and out of the Long Beach docks.

Slocombe learned from Heidenreich that German submarines were hiding in Mexican waters just below the border. Their officers would come ashore at night for secret meetings with Bülow and his small inner circle in Tijuana. As Hitler's forces scored victory after victory, Bülow and Kasselmann asked Slocombe to provide even more detailed information about American preparedness along the Pacific Coast. They wanted nautical maps and data about the number of navy personnel stationed in the Los Angeles and San Pedro harbors, and precise information concerning fortifications at Fort MacArthur, the U.S. Army base at the tip of San Pedro Harbor.[45]

Hoping to thwart Bülow's plans, Lewis sent Slocombe's reports to the FBI and to the latest member of Zacharias's team, Owen Murphy, who had resigned his position as Long Beach police captain to work with naval intelligence.[46]

While Slocombe was busy with Bülow, the Comforts gathered information on Williams and Messerschmitt's expanding number of cells. The two men preferred small neighborhood units of eight to twenty-five people because a large organization "would be too easy for spies to infiltrate." By September 1940, Williams and Messerschmitt had attracted 800 "mostly German" members. Much of what they heard at meetings struck mother and daughter as just the usual anti-Semitic talk, but sometimes the discussion turned to murder. At one gathering in October 1940, a German American war veteran named Fischer told of his plans to assemble a group of men familiar with "rough stuff" who would go about "'liquidating' those Jews who hold important governmental offices." Anyone betraying them would also be "liquidated." A few weeks later, Silver Shirt head Kenneth Alexander promised that if "certain people within the government have to be done away with, I would do it, but it must be a cold calculated plan."[47]

Given the growing belief that Hitler might soon establish his promised thousand-year Reich across Europe, Lewis took the threats seriously. Even a single mistake would be too costly. Moreover, his life was in danger. Fifth columnists, Charles Young reported, feared Lewis "more than the entire FBI put together because of his tremendous ability" and were determined to rid the city of their most dangerous enemy. When the German citywide association met in early May 1941, Nazi film exhibitor Franz Ferenz denounced "that dirty Jew and kike Leon Lewis" and warned the group "we have a spy among us who reports to Mr. Lewis." The organization's president promised to have his men watch Lewis's office to see who brought him information.[48] The implied threat was clear.

Leon Lewis and Joe Roos wanted to do more than simply monitor groups and send reports to government agencies. They set out to break up the most dangerous cells before they could do any damage. And Sylvia Comfort helped them do that. As the only trained stenographer in most groups, Comfort was asked to serve as secretary on several executive committees and made privy to secret inner-circle meetings. She learned that a small number of men and women were planning to sabotage the city's water and electrical systems; they had already set up secret groups that could function "under cover if an emergency arises in this country."[49]

As per usual, Lewis and Roos sent Comfort's reports to the FBI, hoping they would act on the information. This time they did. A month after founding the United Party Movement in January 1941, a political party dedicated to ridding the country of Jewish power, Andrae Nordskog asked Sylvia Comfort to serve as its secretary. Comfort did more than take minutes; she used her shorthand skills to write exact accounts of every speech at their meetings. Six weeks later, Nordskog dissolved his anti-Semitic group because the FBI was harassing him and he wanted to get them "off his heels." Greatly appreciative of the information they had received, Los Angeles bureau chief Hood telephoned Roos and asked him to send Hoover copies of his weekly *News Letter*.[50]

Casting an ever-widening net of espionage, Comfort soon charmed her way into the Bund's inner circles. Williams considered Hermann Schwinn "a good friend" and introduced mother and daughter to the Bund leader and his wife while attending an America First meeting in December 1940.[51] After describing the ongoing citizenship woes he and Diebel had been forced to endure, Schwinn invited his seemingly sympathetic listeners to attend the Bund's usually closed meeting as his guests. Over the next year, Sylvia became a regular presence at Deutsches Haus, establishing friendships and socializing with Schwinn, Diebel, and the man who would supplant them as the city's most important Nazi, Franz Ferenz, chief distributor of German films on the West Coast.

Ferenz was taken with the young stenographer and invited her to his Continental Book Store on the corner of Seventh Street and South Coronado. Playing German records and showing her his array of Nazi propaganda, the Austrian-born Nazi told Comfort of the troubles he faced trying to rent a movie theater to screen the latest films from Berlin. Every time he was about to sign a lease, Jews had intervened and persuaded landlords not to do business with a known Nazi (the "Jews" were Lewis and Roos). He and Schwinn considered the latest newsreels important tools for persuading Germans and Americans alike of the invincibility of Hitler's armies and the führer's inevitable triumph over all enemies. Comfort agreed to help him screen films at Deutsches Haus.

After watching a series of newsreels, Comfort warned Lewis that Ferenz had not exaggerated. The newsreels were powerful weapons of propaganda. She described scenes from *Blitzkrieg im Westen* (*Rapid Attack in the West*) that showed the relentless Nazi war machine demolishing Allied tanks, trapping British troops at Dunkirk, and engaging in door-to-door combat in which no Germans were killed. Taken collectively, they were far more effective than Schwinn's speeches in steeling Axis supporters and frightening their enemies. Equally important, every time Ferenz screened films or newsreels, he attracted a crowd of 600 to 800, instead of the usual 60 or 70 Germans, to Deutsches Haus.[52]

Grateful for her efforts, Schwinn invited Comfort to a private dinner that May to honor the Bund's visiting national leader, G. Wilhelm Kunze, who had replaced the jailed Fritz Kuhn. During her time at Deutsches Haus, she discovered that Bund leaders had been tipped off to the fact that the FBI was tapping their phone lines, a piece of information Lewis reported to the Bureau and was "received with great appreciation."[53]

THE MEMORIAL WEEKEND SABOTAGE PLOT

After foiling Karl Jaeckel's plot to blow up airplanes bound for Canada in October 1939, Lewis and Roos asked Jimmy Frost and their wide network of informants to monitor aircraft factories and provide them with the names of all suspicious employees. Their information proved so useful that by the spring of 1940 FBI agents and security officers employed by Lockheed, Douglas, Vultee, and North American aircraft plants regularly came to their offices to check the names of suspected fifth columnists against Roos's large master card index of all foreign-born employees working in the region's aircraft industry.[54]

Those visits grew more frequent between June 1940 and March 1941, after the Navy and War Departments awarded $772 million in contracts to private defense industries along the West Coast, with the bulk of money for aircraft construction going to Los Angeles companies. On March 11, 1941, Congress abandoned all pretense of neutrality and passed the Lend-Lease Act. Officially known as "An Act to Promote the Defense of the United States," the bill gave American defense firms permission to send planes, ships, and weapons to Allied forces in Europe. Within weeks of its passage, Los Angeles County accounted for 60 percent of all war-related production. "Planes in all stages of construction," the *New York Times* reported, "fill every vacant space around the long, low factory buildings" in the Southern California city.[55]

With Congress allocating millions of dollars to American defense firms, Lewis's operatives were on high alert for sabotage. From June 1940 onward, their agents found twelve bottles of explosive chemicals in the apartment of a German airline official sent to inspect planes at the Lockheed plant. They uncovered submarine and "other war machine data" at the home of an ardent Nazi supporter whose son worked at North American Aviation. They also discovered more subtle forms of sabotage: pro-Hitler aircraft employees were slowing down plane production and "telling others to do the same."[56]

As the fear of sabotage grew, Roos's organizational genius endeared him to even greater numbers of government agencies and aircraft security personnel. Roos divided the hundreds of names he received from agents and informants into three lists: one for suspects known to be pro-Nazi, most of whom were associated with the Bund; a second for people working in aircraft plants who were not native-born Americans; and a third for suspicious people either born in Germany or the children of German parents. Roos filed each name on a separate index card and used pink cards for the most dangerous suspects to make them more easily identifiable.

On May 7, 1941, the FBI received a report from a woman "well known to the Los Angeles Field Office" that Hermann Schwinn had obtained secret orders from Berlin detailing plans to sabotage aircraft factories along the Pacific Coast. The operation was set to occur over Memorial Day weekend, when plants would be lightly manned. The attack would be accomplished in one of two ways. Trusted men working inside each facility would try to sabotage production without violence. If that failed, "a force of saboteurs using private planes" would start from Seattle on May 30 and work their way south, "destroying all aircraft industries enroute, while a second contingent, also using private airplanes, would start from Mexico and work north." In the event that both plans failed, Schwinn was to order Bundists working in local defense plants to "persuade at least five employees of any ammunition or aircraft factory to stop production in the event the U.S. Government continued its present policy of aid to England."[57]

Taking the threat seriously, the Los Angeles bureau notified FBI agents in San Francisco, Seattle, Portland, and San Diego, as well as naval and army intelligence. The Bureau also alerted officials at aircraft and munitions plants along the Pacific Coast and asked them to close their operations over the Memorial Day weekend, with a warning to keep the information top secret so as "to eliminate the possibility of publicity."[58]

Forewarned by government authorities, factory owners shut down production and increased security over Memorial Day Weekend. No sabotage occurred, and Hermann Schwinn was furious. The Bund leader was convinced that Berlin's plan was foiled because someone inside Deutsches Haus had "betrayed the Führer." He swore that "no matter what the cost the offender would be ferreted out and dealt with according to the rules of the Gestapo." Although Sylvia Comfort's name was never mentioned, she was the FBI's likely source. In a subsequent memo sent to Hoover, the Los Angeles bureau noted how a regular informant (probably Lewis) asked them "not to contact or interview [name blanked out by FBI] under any circumstances."[59] Warned by Slocombe that a number of local FBI agents were sympathetic to the Nazi cause, Lewis was unwilling to put his agent's life at risk.

Whatever joy Lewis and Roos may have felt over the thwarted sabotage plot soon evaporated. On June 22, 1941, Hitler's armies invaded the Soviet Union in the largest German military operation of World War II.

20.

Darkening Skies, New Dangers

O n the morning of June 28, 1941, Angelenos living near North
Curson and Mariposa Avenues awoke to darkened skies filled with
clouds of soot and ash. Beginning the previous evening and lasting
until long after dawn, German consul Georg Gyssling and his staff had
been sorting through massive amounts of material as they prepared to
close their office and return to Germany. By early morning the fireplace
in Gyssling's hilltop home, which also served as consulate headquarters, was clogged with the ashes of confidential files too risky to leave
behind. At noon on June 29 the consulate—technically German
territory—closed its doors and became American property once again.
All that remained was a soot-covered photograph of Hitler that hung
over the fireplace.[1]

Leon Lewis saw Gyssling's expulsion as another sign that the United
States was inching closer to war with Germany. Rumors had been circulating since March that President Roosevelt, angered at repeated instances
of subversive activities by German spies, was considering expelling their
nation's diplomats. Three months later, undersecretary of state Sumner
Welles ordered the German government to close their embassy and
consular offices and leave the United States by July 10. German officials,
Welles remarked, were engaged in "improper and unwarranted activities" inimical to American welfare. Welles's accusations, the *New York
Times* explained, were simply "another way of saying fifth column
activities."[2]

The usually unflappable Gyssling was "visibly affected" by Sumner's
orders. "I am very saddened," he told reporters. "I have been in the
United States fourteen years, eight years in Los Angeles. I have thousands of friends here. And my little daughter Angelica, she was born

here."[3] Gyssling denied knowing anything about sabotage and insisted he had always conducted himself along proper diplomatic lines.

Gyssling was telling the truth—at least partially. His daughter did not want to leave the only country she had known. When Georg told her they would be departing for Germany, she asked if they could remain in the United States. Gyssling made "discreet inquiries" about whether that was possible. His contact was undoubtedly Julius Klein, to whom he had been passing valuable information since 1933. The German consul was advised that if they stayed, father and daughter would be sent to an internment camp. Gyssling could not do that, Angelica explained, because he "felt he would be accused of being a traitor and said, 'I can't be a traitor.' So that was that."[4]

On July 9, after meeting with San Francisco consul Fritz Wiedemann and exchanging "secret information and documents," Georg and Angelica boarded a train to Washington, D.C., and then sailed to Germany. Four months later, after settling in Berlin, Gyssling sent the German Foreign Office a memo describing his work monitoring local defense plants. He had provided German embassy military attachés with reports about the region's considerable airplane and warship

Georg and Angelica Gyssling Return to Germany, July 1941
USC Libraries Special Collections

production. Information was easy to obtain because "almost the entire airplane production takes place in public." He regularly sent the embassy clippings from ten Southern California newspapers detailing local aircraft and military news he thought would interest Reich officials.[5]

Defense plant security in Southern California was abysmal, and Gyssling was astounded at the naiveté of some easily flattered industry executives. On one occasion, he called the president of Lockheed and asked if he and his daughter could take a tour of the factory. "And they said, 'Yes, we'd be delighted to have you,'" Angelica recalled. "Not only did they do that, they gave him a copy of their production schedule."[6]

Gyssling was gone, and the Bund was in retreat. Lewis and Roos were dismantling the Nazi apparatus in Los Angeles one by one. Hermann Schwinn no longer ruled over Deutsches Haus, Leslie Fry had fled the country, and Henry Allen had withdrawn from all activism. Nor did Hans Diebel pose a threat. Armed with evidence provided by the spymasters, the Department of Immigration had denied Diebel's application for citizenship the previous March. Like Schwinn, he now faced deportation.[7]

The fifth-column danger assumed a new dimension after June 22, 1941, when German military forces invaded the Soviet Union. Millions of Hitler's soldiers crossed the border, determined to conquer the Communist nation and murder the Jews whom they claimed ran its government. Following that, Hitler expected to vanquish Great Britain and then turn his attention to the United States.

Three weeks after the invasion, President Roosevelt readied the nation for war by asking Congress to appropriate $4.8 million for military defense programs. He did so in the face of considerable opposition from the American public. Americans today like to wax nostalgic about World War II as the "Good War," a war where "good" and "evil" were easy to identify. However, as late as July 1941, 79 percent of those polled opposed America entering the war.[8] The desire for peace was understandable, but many of those calling for nonintervention were not really pro-peace; they were pro-Hitler.

As the isolationist cry gathered greater support, Lewis and Roos hoped to change public opinion by sending copies of their News Letter to "researchers, editors, authors, scenario writers, public speakers and others engaged in defense of American Democracy against the encroachments of totalitarian ideologies."[9] Roos's News Letter distilled operative reports and coverage of the international press into a series of lively articles accompanied by photographs and illustrations bound to catch the reader's eye. He reported on Nazi and fascist threats not only in Los Angeles and the United States but also throughout Europe, Asia, Mexico, and Latin America.

Lewis and Roos knew that their service to governmental agencies more than justified the painstaking "drudgery entailed in systematizing and making readily available the mass of data assembled."[10] Nearly a dozen government agencies were regularly requesting information or coming to their modest office on Hollywood Boulevard to check their extensive lists of suspected spies and fifth columnists.

Fortunately for the FBI, the two men had perfected their filing system at the moment it was most needed. On June 17, 1941, the day after Roosevelt announced he would expel German diplomats, J. Edgar Hoover ordered the Los Angeles bureau to conduct a thorough investigation of Hermann Schwinn, whom he described as "a German agent or connected with German espionage." After consulting Roos's files, local agents reported that Schwinn "was active in a conspiracy" to encourage men to evade the recently passed draft. Receiving further instructions from Hoover, the Bureau finally assigned an agent to monitor the former Bund head on a full-time basis. Hoover's order, however, did not come until November 28, 1941.[11]

The FBI's delay in investigating the Nazis had put the city in danger. Even though Schwinn had lost the support of most Bundists, German authorities were using him as a conduit for secret operations. After working together with Schwinn on the anti-Semitic isolationist newspaper the *American Gentile*, undercover agent John Barr warned Lewis that the former Bund head was taking orders from some "higher up" German official.[12] It made sense. If Schwinn launched an operation that went wrong, Berlin could pin the blame on an overzealous American supporter. Barr knew Schwinn was planning some dangerous action, but had no idea what it might be.

Fearing the worst, Lewis and Roos continued feeding information to naval and army intelligence about Nazi and fifth-column espionage at the region's ports, military bases, and defense plants. That fall, Lewis told Ellis Zacharias that Count Ernst Ulrich von Bülow and his agents had disappeared from the scene. Chuck Slocombe suspected they had left Southern California, but could not be certain. The Gestapo leader might have grown suspicious and cut off all contact with him.

Bülow's disappearance did not signal an end to the threat of Nazi espionage and sabotage. Sylvia Comfort warned Roos that William Pierce Williams was working with Schwinn to bring aviation employees into his secret cells. That September, Williams visited March Airfield Base, hoping to enlist more officers. The Army Air Corps bomber base in nearby Riverside County housed the military's latest bombers and fighter planes. After learning about Williams's visit, Roos contacted Captain Ralph Riordan, the army intelligence officer in charge of harbor defense for Los Angeles. "One of the most active Nazi propagandists in this section of the country," Roos warned, was attempting to recruit his pilots.[13] Riordan made sure Williams would have no luck.

In October 1941, Lewis and Roos provided Riordan and naval intelligence with one of their greatest espionage coups to date. Charles Young, their German-born operative and trusted Bund insider, had gone through the wastepaper basket of a suspected Nazi spy and discovered ten pages of secret German naval codes marked "Complete Chart," "Numerical Code," "Mexican Code," and "Ship Code." Reading through the documents in Roos's office, Riordan confirmed that Young's information was "definitely a code" and promised to forward it to the War Department in Washington, D.C. Riordan was so pleased, he sent Captain James Hughes, who headed antiaircraft intelligence at Camp Haan, to work with them on counterespionage surveillance.[14]

Over the next few months, as word of their work spread to other federal agencies, Lewis and Roos received requests for information and copies of their *News Letter* from an expanding number of officials in the Justice Department, State Department, War Department, Secret Service, Department of Immigration and Naturalization, and many more departments and agencies.[15]

As military orders for new planes kept coming in, Lewis and Roos continued working with army and navy intelligence and security chiefs at the region's numerous aircraft factories, answering nearly daily requests for information about foreign-born employees in their plants. The spymasters warned them about Bundists and Nazi sympathizers working as mechanics and engineers at the Douglas plant in Santa Monica and the Lockheed factory in Glendale, men such as Mark Infield, part of the armament group at Lockheed assigned to the army's latest plane, the XP38. Due to their reports, suspicious individuals such as Ku Klux Klan Grand Dragon and Lockheed employee C. Earle Snelson were fired before they could do any damage.[16]

Roos also sent reports to his contacts at army intelligence, warning them about dangerous men and women such as Julius Gipkins, a "snappy dresser" and reported "payoff man for German espionage group"; longtime Bundist Paul Kendzia, who they now believed was the Nazi's "ranking secret agent on the West Coast"; and Marie Wolff, suspected of carrying secret government orders between Hamburg and Los Angeles. Perhaps most frightening, they alerted military authorities to Kurt Schlueter, who had "twenty-five incendiary bombs" in his possession.[17]

THREATS FROM WITHIN

Espionage and sabotage were only two of the mounting dangers Lewis and Roos faced that summer and fall. As they learned more about the pro-Nazi rhetoric of many local isolationists, the spymasters asked Young, Slocombe, Barr, Roy Arnold, and the Comforts to infiltrate as many groups as possible. As usual, none of the operatives knew the others were working for the same bosses. In addition to keeping track of familiar foes such as Schwinn, Diebel, and Franz Ferenz, they wanted their spies to gather information about dangerous fifth columnists such as Williams, Martin Meader, T. W. Hughes, Ellis Jones, and Robert Noble—all of whom worked closely with the city's Nazi leadership.

Slocombe was the first to warn that some isolationist groups were openly calling for violence against Jews. The Royal Order of American Defenders, an organization restricted to "Protestant Americans of Anglo-Saxon descent," was determined to achieve peace by removing the Jewish menace. Slocombe heard guest speaker Colonel H. A. Horton, head of the Americanism Committee of the American Legion's Hollywood Post, blame Jews for the nation's chaotic conditions. Horton urged fellow Christians "to strike now to maintain our American standards and wrest from these people the powers they have usurped, and by 'these people' I mean the kikes. We have to do it even if we have to go to the synagogues to get them."[18]

Sylvia Comfort warned Lewis that American Rangers founder Jack Peyton was also calling for a campaign of terror. Peyton was working closely with Bundists and the Japanese consulate, all of whom shared a loathing for FDR and his "Jew Deal." Comfort had attended Ranger meetings filled with calls to save America from Jewish interference in foreign policy, even if that meant spilling Jewish blood and the blood of "some of the higher ups" in government. If Jews managed to involve the United States in the European conflict, Peyton warned, they "will be liquidated the moment they succeed in getting America to declare war."[19] The former military officer was gathering men among the Rangers who would assist him in seeking revenge.

Fortunately, Lewis and Roos were tracking the activities of the most dangerous groups calling for violence. By summer, Sylvia Comfort was deeply embedded in the city's noninterventionist movement and trusted by most "peace leaders" who turned to her for secretarial support. Comfort still spent the bulk of her time with Williams, helping organize his secret cells and a new America First chapter in North Hollywood. At Lewis's urging, she also became a familiar figure in pro-German isolationist groups that maintained close relations with Schwinn and the Bund: Ellis Jones's National Copperheads, T. W. Hughes's League to Save America First, and the Friends of Progress, led by Jones, Noble, and Ferenz, the alleged brains behind the operation.

By August, Comfort had succeeded in getting herself appointed as secretary to several secret executive boards and to a leadership position in America First, which now had dozens of chapters and thousands of members. Jones and Noble, Lewis's American Legion Americanism Committee warned, were poisoning American minds with "Hitler's three hatreds (hatred of Britain, hatred of Jews and hatred of the American Way of Life)." Anyone attending the meetings "may unwittingly be transformed into a Nazi sympathizer, and even into a potential traitor to his country."[20]

Comfort spent several nights each week attending meetings of different peace groups throughout the area: from private homes in the mid-Wilshire and Pasadena areas that drew 40 people to downtown gatherings of 400 at Embassy Auditorium to meetings of a thousand at Glendale's Masonic Hall to America First rallies at the Hollywood Bowl that attracted tens of thousands of men and women. Whenever possible, Comfort took copious notes, sending them to Lewis along with the names of dozens of suspicious people she met, all of which made their way onto Roos's mushrooming list of potential fifth columnists and into the feature-story section of the *News Letter*.

Comfort penetrated so deeply into the right wing of the isolationist movement that she drew the attention of Secret Service agent Fred Wasson. The Secret Service had traced a series of anonymous letters threatening President Roosevelt to Williams. They suspected Comfort of complicity not only because she was his secretary but also because her name appeared on a list of prominent anti-Semites circulated among Hollywood studio heads. Before approaching mother and daughter,

Wasson interviewed Williams about the letters and queried him about Comfort's involvement. After denying any knowledge of the missives, which he did in fact write, Williams went to the Comfort home to warn Sylvia that the Secret Service had questioned him and would undoubtedly visit her next. He thought Wasson had believed him because he asked Williams to compile "a list of subversivists" and warned him not to tell Comfort "that he contacted me."[21]

Two weeks later, at Lewis's urging, Comfort went to see Wasson at his office in the downtown federal building. She told the Secret Service agent that she was working undercover for Lewis and Roos, investigating Williams and his pro-German isolationist allies. Williams had already set up 500 small secret cells and was working closely with former Nazi organizer Martin Meader, organizing cells "based upon the plan used in Germany" by Brownshirts. They kept the cells small, three to seven people, to prevent infiltration by outside spies. Only Williams and Meader knew the identities of all cell members. Comfort warned Wasson that anti-Semitism was widespread among isolationists and that men like Meader and Williams were plotting violent action.[22]

Convinced she was telling the truth, Wasson warned Comfort she was in danger. Williams had betrayed her during their interview, blaming her for writing the threatening letters to Roosevelt. After promising that he would alert the local FBI to Williams's activities, Wasson asked Sylvia and Grace Comfort to take part in a sting operation. To give mother and daughter greater credibility within the fascist community, he would arrange to have them both picked up and taken in for questioning in the presence of Williams or one of his Nazi allies. Sylvia agreed to become Wasson's unofficial agent and report to him on Williams and his inner circle. He, in turn, promised to share information with Lewis and Roos.[23]

The next day, Secret Service agents arrested mother and daughter at a post office in front of Williams's pro-Nazi friend Edith Shol, who had long been "very suspicious" of the pair. Shol and Williams spread the news that Sylvia and Grace had been taken in by the Secret Service. When Sylvia saw Williams the next evening at an America First meeting, she followed Wasson's "instructions to the 'T'" and told of her harrowing detention and subsequent release.[24] Neither Williams nor Shol doubted her again.

Sylvia Comfort's leadership in America First groups calling for a united Europe under Hitler brought her into close contact with famed aviatrix and outspoken Nazi supporter Laura Ingalls. Ingalls created a national stir in September 1939 when she flew her plane over the White House, dropping hundreds of pamphlets calling for appeasement. Ingalls was now a featured speaker at America First meetings, second in popularity only to Charles Lindbergh. After attending many of the same meetings, Comfort and Ingalls became friendly and started socializing during the summer of 1941. Dining at Carl's Restaurant on Crenshaw Boulevard that July, Ingalls told Comfort how a German mother and nanny had raised her, and how she now worked for the betterment of Hitler and the Reich. Ingalls wanted Comfort to accompany her to Germany, where "there is much work to be done by Americans over there, especially by people who know how to type and have a good command of English."[25]

Ingalls's most valuable disclosure came at the end of the meal. Over the years, she had become close friends with Fritz Wiedemann and Hans Borchers, the powerful German consul general in New York. They had confided that Gestapo agents were in America, preparing for the day Hitler would cross the Atlantic, and had already compiled "a complete list of all the big men in every big city of the United States, what their vices are, whether they can be bought and what their price would be."[26] Comfort sent reports of their conversations straight to Lewis and Wasson, who forwarded them to the FBI. She also warned them that Ferenz was working closely with Williams and Ingalls and had supplanted Schwinn as the city's leading Nazi.

Comfort confirmed what Roos already knew: Ferenz was one of the city's brightest and most dangerous Nazis. He could cause serious trouble if he found the right men to carry out his plans. The arrogant Viennese-born immigrant who came to the United States in 1914 "considered himself better than Hitler." His father had served as "right-hand man" to Karl Lueger, the former anti-Semitic mayor of Vienna, to whom Hitler referred in *Mein Kampf* as his teacher. During a court dispute over a canceled movie theater lease in 1940, a local judge lambasted the heavily accented Nazi for "fomenting hatred, criticism and enmity" against Jews.[27] While Ferenz was unlikely to lead a physical assault, he worked with men who would not hesitate to do so.

Equipped with information from Comfort sent via the spymasters, three FBI agents paid a surprise visit to Ferenz's Continental Book Store in early September. During a previous visit, Ferenz told FBI agents "I have nothing to hide" and invited them to search his store at any time. After receiving Comfort's report, they did, and spent four hours looking around the bookstore for incriminating evidence. This time Ferenz was not so cooperative. If the FBI wished to search his store again, they needed a search warrant. Several days later, the agents returned with warrant in hand.[28]

Ferenz was furious. The Jews had prevented him from obtaining a lease for a movie theater to show German films, and he suspected they were behind the FBI visits. There had been too much talk by isolationists and not enough action. "The time would come," he promised Comfort, when he "would no longer need to remain in the background." Like his friends Robert Noble and Ellis Jones, he would use the America First movement as a front for helping "Mr. Hitler."[29]

THE ATTACK ON HOLLYWOOD AND IMPEACHMENT
OF FRANKLIN ROOSEVELT

Lewis was used to dealing with local threats to Jews. However, by the fall of 1941, he and the city's Jews faced an unprecedented threat from a national isolationist movement, many of whose members advocated anti-Semitic and pro-German policies. When Chicago businessman General Robert E. Wood founded America First in September 1940, he publicly stated his willingness to hand Europe over to Adolf Hitler. What made groups such as America First especially dangerous is that many of their most prominent supporters were not Nazi or fascist extremists but widely admired Americans and anti-Semites, such as Charles Lindbergh, Henry Ford, U.S. Olympic head Avery Brundage, and U.S. senators Burton Wheeler and Gerald Nye.[30]

Berlin admired the isolationist group. "The America First Committee," the Reich Ministry of Public Enlightenment and Propaganda proclaimed in January 1941, "is truly American and truly patriotic!" Several months later the *Deutscher Weckruf und Beobachter*, the Bund's official newspaper, urged its members to "join the America First Committee and continue to bombard your representatives in Congress with letters and telegrams in protest against President Roosevelt's foreign policy."[31] Ferenz promoted their cause by serving as the main distributor of America First literature in California.

America First enabled previously disreputable hate groups to move from the margins to the mainstream of American life and politics. With local meetings drawing several hundred to several thousand supporters, Lewis worried that Americans who had held no prior grudge against Jews would start listening to Lindbergh and anti-Semitic politicians. By associating Jews with treachery bordering on treason, America First speakers implicitly, and sometimes explicitly, invited extremists to do whatever was necessary to stop the Jewish threat to American security. Lewis and Roos feared that such statements might embolden violent extremist groups such as American Rangers and Royal Order of American Defenders to carry out their calls for death to Jews.

Men such as Lindbergh would never resort to violence, but local extremists such as Noble, Jones, and Ferenz would. As a report by Lewis's Americanism Committee noted, groups such as the Friends of Progress used the America First movement as a front for "sponsoring the indiscriminate spread of hatred, confusion, dissension, defeatism, and various other elements of the propaganda line set down by the Nazi government for its agents in the United States." Worse yet, Noble and Jones tried to turn "sincere California citizens against their government."[32]

Lewis knew most isolationists were genuinely committed to peace and did not welcome anti-Semitic rhetoric or death threats. But he needed to find out which "peace" groups were voicing a sincere opposition to government policies and which were attempting to swing American support to Hitler and Germany. Faced with a rapidly growing number of "hate disseminators," Lewis told his executive board they could not "afford to relax our vigilance."[33] Placing Sylvia Comfort in danger yet again, Lewis asked her to work with even more groups to determine the identities of their enemies.

The first major national attack on Jews came in September 1941, when isolationist senators Gerald Nye of North Dakota and Bennett Clark of Missouri, both ardent supporters of America First, launched a Senate investigation into propaganda in motion pictures. In January 1940, Production Code Administration head Joseph Breen had reversed the ban on films attacking foreign nations or their leaders. Hollywood studios reacted by releasing a spate of anti-Nazi films, such as Charlie Chaplin's *Great Dictator* (1940), Fox Studio's *I Married a Nazi* (1940), and MGM's *Mortal Storm* (1940). The movies raised the ire of those sympathetic to Hitler and Germany. In a radio address given on the eve of the Senate hearings, Nye accused the Jewish-dominated industry of producing films "designed to rouse us to a state of war hysteria." As he slowly read aloud the names of each studio head—Louis B. Mayer, Adolph Zukor, Jack Warner—the anti-Semitic audience chanted "Jew" after each name. Nye denounced Hollywood as a "mighty engine of [pro-war] propaganda" and accused the moguls of exerting undue influence on Roosevelt.[34]

America First Anti-War Rally, Philharmonic Auditorium, September 3, 1941
Jewish Federation Council of Greater Los Angeles, Community Relations Committee Collection, Part 2,
Special Collections and Archives, Oviatt Library, California State University, Northridge

Clark opened the September Senate hearings by condemning the motion picture industry for glorifying "England's imperialism" and creating "hatred of the people of Germany." Nye joined the vilification campaign by calling Hollywood the "most potent and dangerous Fifth Column in our country." He identified twenty-five American films he considered prowar propaganda, but admitted that he had seen only two of them, which was two more than Clark had viewed. Both senators insisted that their investigation was driven by patriotism and not prejudice. "If anti-Semitism exists in America," Nye declared, "the Jews have themselves to blame."[35]

Although the hearings would be suspended later that month, following a successful backlash campaign, the damage had been done. U.S. senators had gone to war against Hollywood Jews and emboldened many who shared their views. Nye was already a well-known figure in Los Angeles, having spoken at local America First meetings. Sylvia Comfort had met the senator and did not trust him. Nor did she trust his ally, Senator Wheeler, or his son John, who headed the America First movement in Southern California. But Wheeler did have one notable admirer: Joseph Goebbels. He praised the senator for his attacks on Hollywood and heralded him and fellow isolationists as the sole "representatives of sanity in America."[36]

No one was more encouraged by the Senate hearings than Franz Ferenz. Convinced that a majority of Americans shared his views, Ferenz decided the moment for action was finally at hand. That October, angry that he had been called into the FBI offices yet again, he told Sylvia Comfort of his plans to organize an armed motorcycle brigade of thirty or more men who could respond to any emergency at a moment's notice. Once they received sufficient military training, his troops would "march down the street" and eliminate anyone who got in their way.[37]

Ferenz was not the only one emboldened by the Senate's anti-Semitic-tinged hearings. Speaking before 200 men and women assembled at the downtown Embassy Auditorium on Ninth Street and Grand Avenue in early October, Friends of Progress leaders Ellis Jones and Robert Noble professed their admiration for Germany and "hoped Hitler would win." Americans, the Yale-educated Jones declared, were strongly behind Charles Lindbergh, and "at a word they . . . would turn the [Jewish] ghetto of New York, Chicago, and other cities into a slaughter house." A week later, addressing a crowd of 400, Noble once again declared, "I am for Germany and for Hitler," and ended his speech by giving a Nazi salute and yelling "Heil Hitler" to the audience.[38]

Noble and Jones were not simply demanding a change in foreign policy. They were welcoming an American Kristallnacht.

Lewis and Roos experienced a glimmer of hope later that month when state assemblyman Jack Tenney's Fact-Finding Committee on Un-American Activities opened hearings to investigate un-American activities in Southern California. Over the course of several days, Tenney called the city's leading Communists, Nazis, and isolationists to the stand. Sitting in the back of the hearing room, taking down the testimony in shorthand, was Sylvia Comfort. Ferenz and Schwinn believed she was there to lend support and to provide them with an accurate transcript of the proceedings. As she listened to Tenney's questions, Comfort was appalled at his lack of preparation. Tenney knew a great deal about local Communist activity and spent most of the committee's time exposing their actions. He seemed far less interested in scrutinizing right-wing and anti-Semitic actions.

Comfort listened to Schwinn, Ferenz, and the others lie with impunity and present themselves as anti-Communist defenders of American democracy, claims Tenney did little to refute. She heard Schwinn deny knowing anything about Bund membership lists, deny conducting military drills at Deutsches Haus, and deny ever giving a Nazi salute at meetings. Not a single committee member challenged him. They heard

Robert Noble announce that he would like to become the American Hitler. No one challenged him. Sensing Tenney's sympathies, Ferenz did little to hide his political views. Hitler "has done the right thing for his people," he told the committee. "We need a leader in America who will do that, and we should and will develop such a leader."[39]

Hermann Schwinn was so delighted with the proceedings that he held a special celebratory dinner at Deutsches Haus. That evening, National Bund head G. Wilhelm Kunze, who had come to Los Angeles to instruct Bundists on what to say in their testimony, commended them and especially Ferenz for their courage in fighting communism and speaking "the truth to those from Kosher canyon."[40]

As the nation moved closer to war, isolationist speakers heightened their praise for Hitler and denunciation of the Jews who controlled FDR's administration. Speaking at a meeting of the Friends of Progress in late October, Ferenz told a crowd of 300 that "one of the four freedoms is disappearing from the United States, the freedom of speech." He laid blame for local persecution of pro-peace Americans at the feet of Lewis

Franz Ferenz Testifies at Tenney Hearings, October 1941
Jewish Federation Council of Greater Los Angeles, Community Relations Committee Collection, Part 2, Special Collections and Archives, Oviatt Library, California State University, Northridge

and his News Research Bureau. In case anyone wanted to pursue the matter further, he announced Lewis's office address to the crowd.[41]

This was precisely what Lewis had feared the most: that the new patina of respectability given to hate groups would lead them to issue death threats. He just did not expect it would be his life that was threatened. What might have sounded crazy a year earlier could now be justified as protecting the national interest against alien forces living among us—aliens who placed their religious loyalty above their national loyalty. Killing Lewis and Jews who wanted to take the United States to war would be not an act of murder but a patriotic effort. As Charles Young told Lewis, right-wing isolationists feared him "more than the entire FBI put together because of his tremendous ability." He was a ghostlike figure who no one ever saw, because "he always surrounds himself with such people who know how to keep quiet and he operates in darkest secrecy." As one anti-Semite told Young, the "only way that one can realize his racial origins is by watching his feet, he is supposed to be flat footed."[42]

Too impatient to merely wait and see if anyone would take up his not-so-subtle invitation to violence, Ferenz told Comfort of his plans to stake out the offices of the News Research Service. Lewis was the Jew most "responsible for all the trouble caused here," he said, and getting rid of him would be a blessing.[43] Williams told Comfort that he, too, was planning to take action, but would not reveal his targets until he was fully prepared, which he promised would be soon.

While Ferenz and Williams spent time planning, the recently organized National Minute Men and Women of America began their campaign of terror. In early November, their leader Larry Griffith boasted to Sylvia how "men with nerve went out with glass cutters and carved the word Jew on certain storefronts." If it were up to him, Los Angeles storefronts would look like those in Germany, with Stars of David painted or carved on all Jewish-run shops' windows. Griffith planned to have his men parade down city streets with banners and unloaded guns (so they would not be arrested) to send a clear message of intimidation to all Jews. Dr. Albert Carlson, the equally impatient head of the Christian American Guard, whose membership had grown to over 1,000, complained to Sylvia of his difficulty in controlling anti-Semitic members who "wanted action now."[44]

Lewis and Roos saw how the looming prospect of war exposed the deep thread of anti-Semitism that ran through the fabric of American life. And pollsters confirmed it. In April 1940, when asked whether

"Jews have too much power and influence in this country," a majority answered in the affirmative. The subsequent "Good War" did little to diminish anti-Semitism. As late as July 1945, the number of Americans responding yes to the same question rose to 67 percent.[45]

Roos used the News Letter to expose pro-Nazi peace groups that passed themselves off as anti-Communist Christian warriors. That fall he described the activities of forty-eight such anti-Semitic groups, from the Christian American Builders to the National Protective Order of Gentiles. Many of these groups comprised men and women who would deny being anti-Semites yet found themselves enthralled by America First's charismatic leader Charles Lindbergh. The nation's leading aviation hero insisted he was no anti-Semite, but he had accepted the Order of the German Eagle from Hermann Göring in October 1938 without a second thought. Following the outbreak of war, Lindbergh emerged as the isolationists' most popular speaker. In June 1941, 20,000 Angelenos packed into the Hollywood Bowl for an America First rally to hear "Lucky Lindy" deliver an impassioned call for nonintervention.[46]

As Los Angeles' pro-Nazi isolationists grew bolder in their verbal attacks on Jews, Lindbergh traveled to Des Moines, Iowa, to deliver what became his most famous speech, "Who Are the War Agitators?" Collusion among the British, Jews, and Roosevelt was forcing the nation into a war citizens did not want to fight, Lindbergh claimed. He understood why Jews opposed Hitler: "The persecution they suffered in Germany would be sufficient to make bitter enemies of any race." But Jewish interests, he warned, were not American interests. "We cannot allow the natural passions and prejudices of other peoples to lead our country to destruction." Citing a familiar anti-Semitic complaint, he insisted that the "greatest danger to this country" lies in Jewish "ownership and influence in our motion pictures, our press, our radio and our government." Instead of agitating for war, Jews should be opposing it, "for they will be among the first to feel its consequences." What those consequences might be were left vague.[47]

Lindbergh's speech helped legitimize the anti-Semitic rants of the most radical hate groups, groups such as Noble and Jones's Friends of Progress. On November 1, before a jammed auditorium of 350, Robert Noble announced plans to hold a mock impeachment of Franklin Roosevelt. If "Congress will not impeach the president, then the people will do it."[48] Three weeks later, 1,000 supporters piled into the Embassy Auditorium to hear Noble and Jones open "hearings" in which the

House of Representatives would debate and then vote on a bill of impeachment. Sitting in the back of the room, taking down all the speeches in shorthand, was Sylvia Comfort.

Assuming the role of a California congressman, Noble presented the prosecution's case against the president. Upon taking office in 1933, Roosevelt had promised to cut taxes, reduce unemployment, and make government more efficient. Since then, he had failed at all three. In contrast, "Germany has put her people to work" and "driven out the international Jewish bankers." Under Hitler, every adult was assured of a good job with decent pay and two weeks' vacation each year. In the United States, certain groups who control the media were pushing us closer to war and preventing "great Americans like Charles Lindbergh" from speaking out against such actions. Resting his case, Noble concluded, "We do not want to see our boys sent all over the world to fight for Britain." The only way to stop that was to remove Roosevelt from office.[49]

Several minutes later, after consulting offstage, the House "legal committee" returned its verdict: sixteen votes for impeachment, one against. The audience was invited back for a trial in which a mock Senate would vote on impeachment. Noble was delighted by the evening, except for one thing: he had narrowly avoided a potentially fatal "accident." While driving to the meeting, he discovered that someone had deliberately loosened the lug nuts on his tires, and the wheels had almost come off. Like Leon Lewis's, Noble's enemies wanted to see him dead.

One week later, 900 enthusiasts once again took their seats in the Embassy Auditorium to listen to the "Senate" impeachment hearing. A waxen-faced effigy of Franklin Roosevelt was brought onto the stage and kept there throughout the proceedings. With "Supreme Court Chief Justice" Ellis Jones presiding over the trial, Senate prosecutor Noble presented the case against the president. Charging Roosevelt with disregarding the "will of the people," Noble accused him of mental and intellectual incompetence, greed, and deliberate deceptions aimed at forcing the nation into war. Noble got so carried away that he spoke late into the evening and had to adjourn the meeting before a final impeachment vote was taken. He invited the disappointed crowd to meet again in another week.[50]

On December 6, 1941, at 8:00 p.m., a thousand men and women turned out for the third session of the impeachment hearings. Noble called a series of witnesses to testify to Roosevelt's many crimes. Wearing signs around their neck for easy identification, a "Bit Wiser, A. A. A. Farmer" complained of having his farm taken away by the Roosevelt administration; an "American Mother" wanted her sons to work and live at home rather than fight and die on foreign soil; a "Dole-less Pensioner" lamented the hardships faced by the elderly and the lack of support from the president. After several hours of speeches in which he repeatedly spoke of "our brother, Adolf Hitler" and referred to Japan as a "glorious nation," Noble apologized for the late hour and promised to take a final impeachment vote at the next meeting, set for Thursday night, December 11.[51]

That vote never happened. The following day, Japanese forces attacked the American naval base at Pearl Harbor. On December 8, when Los Angeles and the United States were at their most vulnerable, local and federal agents began arresting suspected Nazi and Japanese agents. But how did authorities know whom to arrest? They turned to Leon Lewis and Joe Roos, who were ready to use their extensive list of suspected spies and fifth columnists to help authorities round up all potential enemies and keep their city safe from harm.

21.

Pearl Harbor Roundup

O n Sunday, December 7, 1941, at 7:48 a.m. Hawaiian time, 353 Japanese planes attacked the U.S. naval base at Pearl Harbor, killing more than 2,400 Americans and damaging or destroying 8 navy battleships and 188 airplanes. Three hours later, the Japanese government declared war on the United States and Great Britain. The following day, after listening to President Franklin Delano Roosevelt call December 7 "a date which will live in infamy," Congress passed a declaration of war against Japan. Four days after Pearl Harbor, Germany and Italy declared war on the United States; Congress responded in kind later that day.

On the morning of December 8, as fire trucks were dousing smoldering ships and aircraft in Pearl Harbor, Angelenos prepared for a possible invasion by Japanese forces or sabotage by fifth columnists. Army trucks and jeeps filled with heavily armed soldiers barreled down Hollywood Boulevard on their way to set up military camps in Exposition Park, a block south of the University of Southern California. Farther north and slightly east, troops prepared to move into the Nazi picnic grounds at Hindenburg Park.[1]

With rumors of enemy air raids growing stronger each hour, the county board of supervisors declared a state of emergency. Antiaircraft crews and National Guard machine gun units raced to protect the area's airports and factories, while naval forces secured the city's harbor. All bridges, tunnels, airports, and gas, telephone, and power lines were placed under twenty-four-hour guard. Long Beach police ordered stores to close at 4:30 p.m. and warned citizens to prepare for a total blackout from evening until dawn.[2]

That same day, U.S. attorney general Francis Biddle authorized the FBI to apprehend people "believed by the Bureau to be dangerous." At

4:35 p.m., FBI Los Angeles special agent Richard Hood received a tele-type from J. Edgar Hoover with the names of people "recommended for custody." Four hours later, Hoover sent a second teletype ordering the arrest of all German and Italian aliens who posed a threat to the "Internal Security of this country."[3] Heading the "A" list of dangerous suspects were Hermann Schwinn and Hans Diebel.

In the days and weeks after Pearl Harbor, Hoover's men received nationwide acclaim for the speed and efficiency with which they rounded up suspected German, Italian, and Japanese spies and fifth columnists. Roos would later reflect that the Los Angeles FBI "had scant security information of their own."[4] Hoover had not ordered a thorough investigation of Schwinn until less than a month before Pearl Harbor. The FBI files on the West Coast Nazi leader contained virtually no important material generated by their own agents. The Bureau had even less material on Schwinn's lieutenants. What useful information they did have came largely from Lewis and Roos's operatives William Bockhacker and Charles Young.

Government lists and their priority ordering of suspicious men and women in Los Angeles came directly from the massive amounts of information and rankings provided by Lewis and Roos. The army, navy, and Justice Department lists were divided into three categories, ranging from the most dangerous men and women who were placed in category A to the merely suspicious placed in category C. Intelligence agents simply retyped the data sent by Lewis and Roos and claimed it as their own. The Jews' spy reports were put in the service of national security as Bureau agents began rounding up Los Angeles's most dangerous Nazis and fifth columnists.[5]

As 1,000 people gathered in downtown Pershing Square that evening to listen to radio bulletins broadcast over loudspeakers, FBI agents Howard Davis and Ira Kellogg drove to Deutsches Haus to arrest Schwinn and Diebel. Answering the expected knock at the door, a surprisingly cordial Schwinn greeted the duo. The agents explained that a presidential warrant had been issued for his arrest and asked if they could search the premises. "I have no objections," the former Bund leader responded, "and I will get the keys which will gain access to any part of the premises." The FBI men reported that Schwinn "treated the whole thing very lightly." At 9:20 p.m., after conducting a cursory search of the building, Agent Kellogg took Schwinn to the county jail, where he was booked on suspicion of violating federal laws and sent to the federal prison on Terminal Island in Los Angeles Harbor.[6]

While FBI agents were busy with Schwinn, Los Angeles police detective George Ingham and sergeant Floyd Fritzler staked out Hans Diebel's room at the Del Rio Hotel. The Bund's number-two leader never showed up. Fearing arrest, he had headed to Deutsches Haus. As he tried sneaking in through the building's rear entrance, FBI agents were there to greet him. Several hours after they dragged Schwinn away, Diebel was reunited with the former western region führer on Terminal Island. Two of their lieutenants, Max Assman and Reinhold Kusche, soon joined them in jail, as well as Hans Gebhardt, the longtime president of the German American League.[7]

After booking Schwinn and Diebel, agents Kellogg and Davis returned to Deutsches Haus to conduct a more thorough search of the premises and the adjacent Aryan Book Store. Schwinn had cooperated because he was certain he had hidden all incriminating evidence. Once again, he proved far less clever than he thought. Relying on information provided by Lewis and Roos, the agents confiscated two large trunks crammed with incriminating maps, motion picture and still cameras, shortwave radio broadcasting sets, photographs, reams of Nazi propaganda, and "large sums of ready cash." The city's Bundists were furious

Hermann Schwinn Arrested December 8, 1941
USC Libraries Special Collections

with Schwinn, Young reported, because the material in the captured suitcases "will get a lot of people into trouble."[8]

Back at the FBI's downtown office, Richard Hood was sending Hoover hourly updates on captured aliens. At a press conference held late on December 8, Hood reported that 325 Japanese, 52 Germans, and 9 Italians had been arrested and sent to county jail—and added, "there's plenty more to come." Sixty of the most dangerous suspects had already been transferred to Terminal Island.[9]

Franz Ferenz's arrest on Tuesday, December 9, was contentious and traumatic. Ferenz was awakened from a deep sleep in the early-morning hours by a loud banging at his front door. When he failed to respond, three policemen began yelling out his name, waking his neighbors and frightening the Nazi ideologue. Before letting them in, Ferenz called Robert Noble and left a message saying he was being arrested and asking Noble to bail him out of jail. When he finally opened his door, the infuriated officers began pushing him around. "They wanted my citizenship papers and were very ugly because I could not find them immediately."[10]

Handcuffed and sitting in the back of the police car, Ferenz shuddered as the officers drove him to the First Street Police station "because of the stories I heard of the things that go on there." Tired of listening to the Nazi complain the entire time he was being fingerprinted and photographed, an angry policeman kicked him. When Ferenz protested, another cop "hit me in the mouth with his fist and said what he would do to me if I would say anything further." The Continental Book Store owner was then placed on a bus and sent to Terminal Island, where he was deloused, given prison clothes, and thrown into a small, unventilated cell with forty other German suspects. "The way these men had been picked up was very bad," Ferenz noted. "Some were taken away from home with no way of communicating with their families. Others were taken right out of their business places. We were surprised to learn of the war with Germany. We were not allowed newspapers or the radio in the prison."[11]

Late Tuesday evening, FBI agent Hood notified Hoover that an additional two dozen Germans had been arrested. Thirty-six hours later, the Los Angeles Field Division had taken custody of 66 German aliens, 12 U.S. citizens of German sympathies, 14 Italians, and 326 Japanese. "Dangerous aliens" without citizenship papers were kept in jail, while detained Germans who could prove their citizenship were released within a few days.[12]

On Thursday evening, December 11, before an audience of 200, Robert Noble and Ellis Jones resumed their postponed meeting of the

Friends of Progress and voted to impeach President Roosevelt. Noble and Jones denied that Japan had attacked the United States, arguing that Hawaii was not a legitimate U.S. possession. "Japan has done a good job in the Pacific," Noble told the audience. "I believe this war is going to destroy America." He and Jones called on American forces to fight on the side of Germany. When the meeting ended, FBI agents arrested the "nationalist" leaders—a term now preferred by isolationists—and took them to the Hall of Justice. After being held overnight, the men were charged with "conspiracy to make false statements intended to interfere with operation of United States military and naval forces." Their stay in jail was short. On December 20, Attorney General Biddle dismissed all sedition charges, explaining that the isolationist leaders had been exercising their right to free speech. Following their release, Noble and Jones resumed their meetings.[13]

While Deutsches Haus was shutting its doors, the FBI office on Spring Street was a whirl of constant activity. Since the attack on Pearl Harbor, the Bureau's twenty-five agents had been working round the clock, picking up men and women suspected of being dangerous aliens or fifth columnists. Hood told Hoover that his agents "were in a very exhausted condition and were about to drop from overwork." Despite their fatigue, the Los Angeles bureau continued to arrest suspected subversives; their total arrests for the week after Pearl Harbor grew to 85 Germans, 348 Japanese, and 14 Italians. But more work remained; an additional 3,000 German Americans in Los Angeles were still under investigation.[14]

AN UNOFFICIAL WING OF AMERICAN INTELLIGENCE

The day after Pearl Harbor, Joe Roos handed the FBI a complete list of all Japanese agents in this country. "I didn't develop it," he confessed; "somebody developed it who had reason to do it." British intelligence had been running two spies in Los Angeles well before 1941, men Roos met when they came to get copies of his *News Letter*. When Hoover discovered foreign agents were operating on American soil without his permission, he had the State Department expel them. But before they left, the British operatives, "who knew every Japanese agent," gave their list to Roos. And Roos, in turn, gave it to Special Agent Hood, who thanked him for the valuable material. "It was really sad to see how poor our own intelligence operation was," Roos lamented. Two Jews working in a small office had gathered more information about Nazis than the entire Los Angeles bureau.[15]

In the weeks and months after Pearl Harbor, Roos described his office as "a pigeon coop. One FBI guy leaves and another Naval Intelligence man walks in, and it was continuous." Roos's pigeons were quite an array. On December 17 he and Lewis received a visit from Captain Ralph Riordan, the army intelligence officer in charge of harbor defense for Los Angeles, asking for information about suspected saboteurs. He was followed by Agent Furbush of the FBI, Mr. Tellner of the Immigration Department, Mr. Berenzweig, chief security officer at Douglas Aircraft, Officers Brown and Brower of the Police Subversive Squad, and a revolving array of local and federal intelligence men, not all of whom wished to share information with others. "I can tell you stories about one agency being jealous of the other," Roos recounted.[16]

As arrests and investigations continued into the early months of 1942, some of Roos's pigeons preferred phoning in their requests. Agents from the Treasury, Immigration, and Justice Departments, as well as Coast Guard Intelligence and the Office of War Information, all called asking for information about specific individuals, many of who worked in the region's defense plants.[17]

If they had ever felt slighted by the FBI, Lewis and Roos did not let it interfere with what they felt was their patriotic duty. In mid-December, after turning over dozens of reports, Lewis met with Hood to determine "in what way I can be of most help to the government in the present crisis."[18]

On January 24, 1942, Joe Roos achieved one of his greatest personal triumphs: J. Edgar Hoover asked him to serve as an unofficial agent for the FBI. Explaining that Walter Winchell recommended he contact Roos, Hoover wanted the Viennese-born Jew to "help to us in our work by bringing to our attention any information you deem of value in connection with subversive activities." The Bureau, he explained, could not officially investigate someone without showing cause. But if private citizens such as Roos and Lewis could "secure evidence," the FBI could then investigate and arrest suspects. Hoover asked Roos to send all information directly to him or to his representative in Los Angeles, Richard Hood. Flattered by the signal achievement, Roos provided Hoover and Hood with updated weekly summaries of their master index containing the names of all German, Japanese, and American suspects.[19]

While Roos was sending regular reports to the FBI, Lewis began "working up cases on approximately fifty individuals" belonging to the

Bund's storm trooper unit or radical isolationist groups. Agents were coming and going on a daily basis, Lewis reported, and the "FBI has kept us busier during the past weeks than ever before. Some sessions lasted all day." On one typical Saturday, three agents descended on his office at the same time, each asking for information on different individuals. The spymasters' weekends remained busy as they also prepared extensive files, photographs, and evidence for House Un-American Activities Committee chief investigator James Steedman and state assemblyman Jack Tenney in preparation for upcoming hearings in Washington, D.C., and Sacramento, respectively.[20]

LOCKUP

By early March the once lively Nazi headquarters on the corner of West Fifteenth Street and Figueroa had gone virtually dark. A large For Rent sign hung on the outside door of Deutsches Haus. The building only came alive on weekends, when the restaurant opened to serve Germans who wished to discuss the war's progress without being overheard. Karl Woeppleman, who replaced Schwinn as Bund leader, and Willi Kendzia, his number-two man, had dissolved the organization and stopped all formal meetings. "Many of the men who were very active in pro-Nazi groups until Pearl Harbor," Lewis observed, "have withdrawn from the field, in most cases, due to fear."[21]

The Los Angeles Bund was dead and its two main leaders in jail. Schwinn and Diebel spent December on Terminal Island, with only regular visits by Franz Ferenz and Sylvia Comfort to cheer them up. Following through on Hoover's request to work as an unofficial wing of the Bureau, Joe Roos asked Comfort to drive Ferenz to the federal prison to visit detained Germans, listen to their conversations, and report back to him and Agent Hood on what she discovered. Over the next several weeks, she and Ferenz brought Schwinn, Diebel, and their imprisoned friends cigars, cigarettes, games, and cards. The bulk of their discussions focused on their pending court cases. But Comfort sent the Bureau one piece of important information. She heard Ferenz warn Germans who had not been incarcerated to "be very quiet" and "wait until the time was right," and then they would "strike and strike hard."[22]

On January 20, 1942, Schwinn and Diebel appeared before the Justice Department's Alien Enemy Hearings Board in Los Angeles. Schwinn admitted he had opposed American entry into the European war, but denied any connection between National Socialism and "the ideals and spirit of the German American Bund." He denied being an anti-Semite or ever having called for revolution in the United States. The Bund's main goal, he told them, was to combat anti-German propaganda and promote the greatness of German culture. Thekla Schwinn testified that her husband had no connection to Nazi officials, but the board did not believe either of them, remanding Schwinn and Diebel to prison until federal authorities took further action.[23]

On February 27, Attorney General Biddle ordered the Nazi leaders interned "as alien enemies" for the duration of the war. Schwinn and Diebel were taken in secrecy from the federal prison on Terminal Island and sent to an internment camp. Rumors suggested that the men were imprisoned at Fort Lincoln, North Dakota, but no one, not even Schwinn's wife, knew for sure. In June the FBI reported that ninety-four of the city's German aliens had been taken into custody, with many sent to parts unknown.[24]

Not until July 23, when a federal grand jury in New York indicted Schwinn and Diebel, did their friends and family learn the men had been sent to Camp McCoy in Wisconsin. They were brought to New York along with twenty-five other men (including Fritz Kuhn) and one woman and charged with conspiracy to evade the Selective Service Act, to provoke revolt and disloyalty among the armed forces, and to conceal Bund affiliations in filling out alien registration forms. The indictment marked the culmination of six months of hearings in which federal prosecutors questioned 670 witnesses and gathered 6,800 pages of testimony. U.S. attorney Mathias Correa reminded the grand jury that the Bund "remains an agency and tool of Hitler's Germany," and the only way to stop it was to put its leaders in jail for a very long time.[25]

Less than three weeks later, Schwinn and Diebel were indicted a second time by a grand jury in Washington, D.C., along with Robert Noble, Ellis Jones, and twenty-two other men and women on two additional charges: sedition and conspiracy to undermine morale, loyalty, and discipline within the armed forces of the United States. If convicted, they faced imprisonment for twenty years.[26]

In September Schwinn and Diebel faced their first federal trial in New York. After damning testimony from Lewis's agents Charles Young and Roy Arnold, the two Los Angeles Nazis and their codefendants were convicted of conspiracy to counsel resistance to the Selective Service Act and sentenced to five years in federal prison. In his closing argument, federal prosecutor Howard Corcoran charged the Bund with being the "most militant fifth column group in the United States," one that acted "solely for the benefit of the Third Reich." He warned that the Bund remained "a potential school for sabotage and espionage, and it can still be used, through its connections here and in Germany, to wreak havoc on the United States."[27]

As far as the FBI was concerned, their job was done. On October 3 the Los Angeles bureau filed what it believed was its last report on Hermann Schwinn: "Inasmuch as no further investigation is contemplated by the LA Field Division . . . this case is being closed."[28]

ATTACK THE JEWS

The FBI may have closed its case on Schwinn and the Bund, but Lewis and Roos knew that the fifth-column movement remained alive, and that hatred of Jews had grown stronger since Pearl Harbor. With the FBI focused on rounding up suspected foreign agents, it was up to them to expose any threats to the city's Jewish community. Sylvia Comfort's orders to keep tabs on Ferenz and his friends interned on Terminal Island were only part of her assignment. Taking Hoover's request to heart, Roos asked her and her mother, Grace, to continue monitoring fifth columnists and various hate groups. During the early months of 1942, Sylvia witnessed a dramatic rise in anti-Semitism as greater numbers of citizens blamed Jews for leading the nation into war. At a meeting of the Friends of Progress that February, Robert Noble told the audience, "I am for the Axis powers because they are the liberators of the world." He urged all men of draft age to "refuse to serve in the Army" and risk their lives fighting on behalf of Jews.[29]

Noble's words were to be expected. What startled the two spymasters was Comfort's warning that anti-Semitism had moved from the margins to the mainstream. "Average people around town" were making the kinds of anti-Semitic statements previously voiced only by extremists. Since the outbreak of war, she heard many people say that although they "did not approve of Hitler or the Nazi system of government," they agreed "with Hitler's solution of the so-called 'Jewish problem.'" Comfort listened to ordinary men and women complain about undocumented Jewish immigrants flooding the country and taking away jobs from Christians. Formerly reasonable people were calling Jews "cowards" who needed to "be beaten," and predicted that "we would have a revolution" before war's end.[30]

Americans may have hated Nazis, but many hated Jews even more. Five months before Pearl Harbor, nearly 80 percent of the population had opposed entering the European conflict. Now that the nation had, the city's Jews were in danger. Right-wing isolationists who had pledged to kill Jews if they succeeded in getting the United States into war wanted to follow through on their threats. Five days after Pearl Harbor, Comfort heard a number of America First women insist "We can attack the Jews because now we have gotten the people to a spot where they realize that F. D. Roosevelt is run by the Jews." William Williams told Comfort that he and his allies would continue their work, but "it would now be done in secret."[31]

While Williams spent time thinking about attacking Jews, the National Minute Men and Women of America resumed their campaign of terror. Authorities regarded the group's carving the word "Jew" on storefronts as a minor act of vandalism, but many Los Angeles Jews feared that Germany had come to America. Since Pearl Harbor, 200 of Griffith's loyal followers had been meeting in small groups at people's homes, planning far more deadly assaults. Good Christian citizens, Griffith told Comfort, had finally realized this was "a war for the Jews" and that Jews wanted nothing less than "world control." The Jewish menace needed to be stopped, and his group would take the first steps to do so. He planned on soaking newspapers in gasoline and then fire-bombing Jewish neighborhoods at night when city lights were ordered blacked out. The Minute Men would follow that with a second assault in which cars would drive through Jewish neighborhoods, throwing deadly pipe bombs into homes and businesses. Griffith would make sure drivers covered their license plates so they could not be identified.[32]

Griffith's group committed minor acts of vandalism over the next few months, but it was not until early March, when he met with Ferenz, Comfort, and fifth-column leader David Nutting, that the four decided that "now is the time to act." Griffith and Nutting had been visiting Deutsches Haus on weekends, seeking to recruit fifteen to twenty tough men. Knowing they were being watched, the Germans hesitated to join them. Griffith had better luck at a "peace" meeting in Hollywood, where he met former army colonel Palmer, a rabid anti-Semite and Ku Klux Klan leader who worked at Lockheed Aircraft. Palmer told Griffith that he had been thinking along the same violent lines and that "something would happen" within the next sixty to ninety days. The former officer planned on using his military contacts to airdrop pamphlets alerting citizens that "wealthy Jews have machine guns" and planned to "mow down the populace."[33] The Jews needed to be taken out before they could kill God-fearing Christians who opposed war.

Unsure if Palmer would follow through on his plans, Griffith began working with two chemists to treat needles with poison that could be "shot into a Jew either by rubber band or by a blow gun." The three men also planned to kill Jews by blowing up gas stations in heavily Jewish areas.[34]

Griffith's plots may have sounded insane, but Lewis and Roos were unwilling to take a chance. After receiving Sylvia Comfort's reports, Lewis contacted the FBI and local police and alerted them to the Minute Men leader's death threats. Within a matter of days, a frantic Griffith called Comfort, asking to meet. The police and FBI were after him, and he needed help. Agents had tried to break into his apartment and had questioned his neighbors. Meeting at the Comforts' home that evening, he told Sylvia and Grace that Colonel Palmer had advised him to get a job, "act as if he had quit agitation," and live normally until he was "needed for big stuff." Palmer claimed he had 1,500 "underground workers" waiting for the right moment to come out of hiding and take action.[35]

Fearing arrest, Griffith stopped his activities. Comfort heard of no further talks of murdering Jews. But she did warn Lewis that his life was in danger. In mid-March, she visited popular anti-Semitic radio host G. Allison Phelps, who told her of his plans to broadcast a show in which he would expose the "activities of LLL's group" and give the audience Lewis's office address.[36] Over the next several weeks, the two Jewish spymasters took care as they entered and left their office.

Lewis and Roos were not the only ones in danger. Since their initial meeting in June 1940, the spymasters had asked Sylvia and Grace Comfort to join as many isolationist groups as possible with the aim of sowing dissension among fifth columnists. What they did not expect was that Sylvia Comfort would come under suspicion and face a potentially violent revenge. After Pearl Harbor, she continued working closely with William Williams, Franz Ferenz, Robert Noble, and Ellis Jones. On January 9, 1942, at a peace meeting, one of her America First friends warned Sylvia that Noble had told everyone "not to trust the Comforts," that they were "not what [they] appeared." Noble had thought things over while in jail and had "reached certain conclusions." He was convinced the Comforts were spies.[37]

When an unfazed Sylvia showed up at a Friends of Progress meeting five days later, Noble blocked the door and, in front of dozens of people, told her, "You are not welcome here." The confrontation unnerved the twenty-eight-year-old stenographer. The frightened operative called Lewis for instructions, a thing she did only a few times in the course of her undercover work. Considering Noble a "dangerous psychopath," Lewis told Comfort to leave the meeting immediately. She did, but before she left, Larry Griffith and several attendees who overheard the exchange defended her and spoke of their growing dislike for Noble. Griffith even accused the Nazi sympathizer of working for the FBI.[38]

Over the next several months, ignoring her personal safety, Comfort succeeded in using Noble's accusations to create bitter divisions among former allies. As prominent anti-Semites lined up with Comfort against Noble and Ellis Jones, each side accused the other of spying for the FBI and Jews. When Ferenz failed to defend Comfort in front of Noble, she went to his store and, feigning anger, demanded to know "why he stood for that kind of thing." Ferenz replied that "he felt sure that we [Grace and Sylvia] were 99% alright, or rather that he was 99% sure of us." No one could possibly say "anyone was absolutely alright, because no one could possibly know about anyone else." Ferenz added that other people had accused her of spying, but he had defended her. After they had talked until 3:00 a.m., Ferenz ended their conversation by cautioning, "We live in dangerous times." Sylvia needed to "learn to be more careful" if she did not want to get in serious trouble.[39]

Lines had been drawn. Noble kept telling his followers that the Comforts were "traitors to the cause," but many abandoned him to side with the well-liked mother and daughter. When Ferenz told Sylvia that people wondered where she and her mother got their income from, she replied that people asked her the same question about him, and wondered "if he might not receive something from Germany." Rumors were circulating that he was spying for Hitler. "Ferenz turned a little pale when I told him this," Sylvia reported; for once, he seemed at a loss for words.[40]

Knowing Sylvia Comfort's life was in danger, Lewis and Roos acted to remove the three men who posed the greatest threat to her: Ferenz, Noble, and Jones. They began by providing California state assemblyman Jack Tenney with reams of material to use against the three at his un-American hearings set for late February, hearings that might lead to arrests. Once again spy and spymasters were disappointed. Attending the local proceedings, Comfort reported that Tenney had failed to generate any new knowledge about the "subversives" or curb their activities. In fact, his committee had the opposite effect: Noble, Ferenz, and Jones considered "the publicity that such hearings give them as an asset, and are disappointed if the strong statements they make are not published in the papers." As for Tenney, he had ignored Lewis's reports. Comfort believed the hearings were designed to further his political career, one that would benefit more by focusing on Communists than Nazis and fifth columnists.[41]

Unwilling to retreat, Lewis and Roos turned to California attorney general Earl Warren that spring for help. Unlike Tenney, who would later reveal his strong anti-Semitic streak, Warren hoped to pave the way for his anticipated run for governor by attracting the support of the state's Jewish voters. Mutual friends asked Joe Roos "to come up with some idea which would fulfill that objective, but at the same time would lie in our interest." Roos suggested "that a number of local Nazis be prosecuted for failure to register as Nazi agents with the Secretary of State of California," particularly Noble, Ferenz, and Jones.[42] Warren agreed and instructed deputy attorney general Louis Drucker to work with Roos in developing a case against the men.

Drucker arranged for a truck to go to Ferenz's Continental Book Store and load the vehicle with potentially incriminating evidence. They found so much material that the truck returned for a second load. Even more important, Roos provided Drucker with a complete run of Sylvia Comfort's reports on what had been said, and who had said it, at Friends of Progress meetings from September 1941 until the recent arrests of Noble, Jones, and Ferenz. Drucker and Roos spent weeks preparing for the upcoming trial. As Roos later explained, "I wanted the world to know that Nazis were 'sons of bitches.'"[43]

As state attorneys readied their case, a federal grand jury in Los Angeles charged Noble and Jones with conspiracy to violate the sedition laws of the United States and ordered them to stand trial in Los Angeles district federal court.[44] State and federal authorities were determined to lock up as many subversives as possible.

On April 2, while Noble and Jones remained in county jail awaiting their federal trial, Franz Ferenz appeared at the California attorney general's office in downtown Los Angeles, where Drucker and his team grilled him for three and a half hours. As at past hearings, Ferenz denied ever instructing anyone in "the precepts of the Nazi Party." He denied publishing or distributing anti-Jewish or Nazi propaganda. He denied consulting with Noble and Jones or assisting them with the Friends of Progress. And he denied having any opinion about Hitler's policies in Europe. If asked whether the sun set in the west, Ferenz would have denied that as well.[45]

Government prosecutors were fighting a two-front campaign, state and federal, aimed at destroying the remnants of the Nazi and fifth-column movements. Before taking further action against Ferenz, Noble, and Jones, Drucker and FBI special agent in charge Richard Hood spoke with U.S. attorney general Francis Biddle about coordinating state and federal court actions. Instructing them "to get tough with the subversive gang," Biddle approved their request to arrest the three men and charge them with sedition under California law. Wanting Drucker to be as prepared as possible, Lewis and Roos sent him 113 of their operatives' reports covering the activities of the three men. The spymasters also agreed to maintain their undercover operations and keep "our informants close to these people now under arrest. We could tip off the agencies of contemplated moves by these individuals."[46]

On May 5, 1942, Ferenz, Noble, Jones, and four accomplices were indicted by a grand jury in Sacramento and charged with violating the California Subversive Organization Registration Act of 1941 and the Federal Espionage Act of 1917. The state trial was delayed until July 28 to give federal prosecutors sufficient time to try the jailed Noble and Jones in Los Angeles. By helping put Ferenz and Noble behind bars, Lewis and Roos had thwarted the fascist movement in Los Angeles and saved Sylvia and Grace Comfort from harm. After the arrest of the three Friends of Progress leaders, Lewis observed, "things have become rather quiet on the subversive front." Even those who "have always preferred secret to public meetings" and like to work on "'big' plans and plots have adopted a policy of watchful waiting."[47]

While Ferenz sat in jail throughout May and June, awaiting his Sacramento court date, Noble and Jones went on trial in Los Angeles federal court. On July 20, after a lengthy set of testimonies, the jury found the two men guilty of sedition and conspiracy. Presiding judge Ralph Jenney sentenced Noble and Jones to prison terms of five and four years, respectively. Jenney denied their appeal for probation, explaining that their crime "involves a conspiracy to set in motion an insidious force for disloyalty, disruption, and disunity."[48] If released, the judge feared, they would continue undermining the war effort.

Three days later, Attorney General Biddle indicted Ellis and Jones—along with Schwinn, Diebel, and twenty-three men and one woman—on yet another set of federal charges, accusing them of participating in a nationwide conspiracy to interfere with the war effort. The arrested seditionists included men Lewis and Roos had battled for years, among them Silver Shirt leader William Dudley Pelley and James True, who had plotted with Henry Allen and George Deatherage to overthrow the government. The sole woman indicted, Chicago's Elizabeth Dilling, was a Nazi propagandist who had been among the leaders of the Hermann Schwinn Legal Defense Fund.[49]

Before beginning their second federal court case, Noble, Jones, and Ferenz were taken to Sacramento to stand trial in state court for failure to register as members of a subversive organization. The trial began on August 3, with deputy attorney general Warren Olney telling the jury that Noble and Jones acted as mere fronts for Ferenz, whom he called "an active Nazi agent and the real brains" behind the Friends of Progress. Olney charged the Friends of Progress with being part of "Hitler's strategic plan for dealing with the United States." Two and a half months later, the jury convicted the defendants of violating California's state's antisubversion laws; the judge sentenced them to a six-month-to-five-year term in prison. Ferenz was sent to San Quentin, while Noble and Jones were transported to Washington, D.C., to stand trial in federal court.[50]

On January 4, 1943, in another blow to the fifth-column cause, a federal grand jury in Washington, D.C., issued a third set of charges against Schwinn, Diebel, Noble, Jones, and the twenty-four previously indicted Nazi and fascist figures. The grand jury also indicted Ferenz, Leslie Fry, and George Deatherage. It was an all-star lineup of Lewis and Roos's greatest foes. The Hitler admirers were charged with conspiring to impair the armed forces' morale and promote insubordination and mutiny among them.[51] In August the fifty-two-year-old Ferenz was transferred from Sacramento to Washington, D.C., where he remained imprisoned—like Noble, Jones, and the other defendants—throughout the course of his long trial.

Following the arrests and trials, Lewis and Roos allowed themselves to indulge in a moment of retrospective joy. Thanks to their longtime spy operation and cooperation with state and federal authorities, Schwinn, Diebel, Ferenz, and the city's main Nazi and fifth-column leaders were behind bars. Equally important, Los Angeles, unlike the East Coast, had not experienced a single instance of sabotage. Its numerous aircraft factories, shipbuilding plants, armories, and defense installations remained intact. Nevertheless, the two Jewish leaders remained vigilant about keeping the city and its Jewish population safe until the end of the war.

Epilogue

By early 1942, longtime foes Hermann Schwinn, Hans Diebel, and Franz Ferenz were behind bars and no longer posed a threat. Yet in the months and years after Pearl Harbor, Leon Lewis and Joe Roos faced a far more disturbing enemy: respectable Americans who accused Jews of getting the United States into war. The outbreak of war sparked the formation of new "nationalist" (the term used by former isolationists) organizations—Informed Voters of America, Americanism Defense League, and Americans for Peace—many of whose members called for death to Jews.

With the FBI, naval intelligence, and other authorities on the alert for espionage and subversive activities, Lewis and Roos no longer needed to run the extensive spy network they had employed from 1933 until 1941. But the two men didn't trust local authorities to protect the city's Jews from harm, so they relied on Sylvia Comfort to monitor religious and secular hate groups that openly called for violence against Jews, blacks, and Catholics. Comfort alerted Lewis to the rising tide of anti-Semitism even among well-established organizations such as the California Women's Republican Club. Sylvia was shocked to hear wealthy Republican women complain about "too many Jews" in the city and insist that something had to be done to stem the Hebraic invasion. "One lady," she told Lewis, wanted all Jews to be "hung from lampposts within five years," while another woman complained "that was too slow." Yet another club member "advocated forced sterilization." The anti-Semitism espoused by the GOP group was not unique. Comfort heard similar comments while shopping at the farmers' market on

Fairfax and Third, and told Lewis she had never encountered such rampant anti-Semitism.[1]

Growing resentment of Jews was only one of the problems Lewis and Roos faced over the next several years. On January 10, 1943, the two men awoke to the most disturbing headline they had read since Pearl Harbor: "L.A. Anti-Nazi Agent Killed in Mystery: Neil Ness Dies after Arrest." After drinking at a local bar, Ness fell to the ground and hit his head. A nearby service station attendant called the police, who took him to the Hollywood police station and booked him on charges of intoxication. When his wife arrived to bail him out, she asked the police to call a physician to examine the unconscious engineer. Eight hours later, a doctor finally arrived and concluded that Ness needed hospitalization, but the police waited nearly three more hours before bringing him to the Hollywood hospital, where he died without recovering consciousness.[2]

The county autopsy surgeon ruled that Ness died of a basal skull fracture caused either by a fall or a fatal blow to the head. Police detectives insisted it was the former; Lewis and Roos undoubtedly suspected the latter. The *Los Angeles Daily News* questioned whether Ness was a "victim of enemies he had made while an undercover operative." They wanted to know why it took ten hours after his arrest to transfer him to a hospital.[3]

Ness's death may have been an accident, but given the police department's record of brutality and long-standing relationship with the Bund, it is also possible that officers sympathetic to Nazis and Silver Shirts either beat him inside his cell or allowed him to die by waiting to bring him to a hospital until it was too late. Local Nazis had vowed to kill the American turncoat after Ness testified against them in 1939. The police denied any wrongdoing, but the city council ordered a formal investigation of the department.[4]

Sylvia Comfort's effectiveness ended in late 1943, when a number of local fascists began to suspect her of being a spy. Worst among them was radio broadcaster G. Allison Phelps. The anti-Semitic media host spewed his gospel of hate each week over local radio station KMTR, until Lewis succeeded in getting him kicked off the air. Phelps knew that Lewis and Mendel Silberberg were responsible.[5]

Phelps also accused Comfort of working for the Jews. Someone had seen her going in and out of Lewis's office on several occasions and told Phelps that the Jewish attorney was helping to support her and her mother. Over the next three months, several other right-wing activists

Kathryn Ness and District Attorney B. J. Haworth, January 1943
USC Libraries Special Collections

confronted Comfort about troubling rumors that she had "taken a job for a Jewish organization spying on non-Jews" and was being paid $40 a week to attend meetings and record what was said.[6] She and Lewis both feared for their lives.

Neil Ness was not the only spy to die under mysterious circumstances. A year after Ness's death, John Schmidt, Lewis's first spy, received a presidential subpoena to testify in Washington, D.C., on April 30, 1944, at the federal sedition trial of thirty defendants, including Schwinn, Hans Diebel, Franz Ferenz, Robert Noble, and Ellis Jones. Three weeks before he was set to leave for the capital, the fifty-nine-year-old veteran died after suffering severe stomach pain at home for two days. A preliminary police investigation attributed Schmidt's death to natural causes, but his wife, Alice, insisted that his enemies had poisoned him to prevent him from testifying. She recounted how after dining out on March 31, John fell ill and remained in bed until his death two days later. Alice made sufficient noise to force an autopsy by the coroner and an investigation by two FBI agents, who were ordered to look into the matter "because of frequent threats" to Schmidt's life.[7]

The results of Schmidt's toxicology report never appeared in the press. His only eulogy was a brief quote from Lewis in the *Los Angeles Times*, praising Captain Schmidt as "one of the first men to expose the Nazis here by investigating the work of the groups which were forerunners of the German American Bund."[8]

With her effectiveness as an undercover operative compromised and not wishing to suffer the same fate as Ness or Schmidt, Sylvia Comfort moved to Washington, D.C., to embark upon a career in government. With Lewis's help, she obtained a position as secretary to recently elected Los Angeles Republican congressman Gordon McDonough. Over the next several years, Comfort remained in close touch with Joe Roos, asking for professional advice and sending him government reports about a range of postwar issues. Although there was no further correspondence in the Community Relations Committee files after 1946, she remained in Washington, working for a number of Republican politicians, at least through the late 1960s. Sylvia Comfort died in Washington, D.C., on December 3, 2003, at the age of ninety.[9]

The end of the war also brought a halt to Chuck Slocombe's time as an undercover operative. He continued running his water taxi company in Long Beach for the next twenty-six years, until he went to work for the Pacific Tow and Boat Salvage Company. Long Beach congressman Glenn Anderson entered a tribute for Slocombe in the September 10, 1986, *Congressional Record*, praising him for his longtime work in the harbor and his wartime assistance to naval intelligence. Never once did Anderson mention Slocombe's work for Lewis and Roos. Charles "Chuck" Slocombe died in bed at his Long Beach home on November 15, 1992, his work on behalf of democracy known to only his family and a few close friends.[10]

Lewis and Roos's spy network had helped put many dangerous enemies behind bars. Hermann Schwinn and Hans Diebel spent the remainder of the war in prison, facing three sedition trials. Following their indictment by a federal grand jury in July 1942, both men were brought to New York to stand trial—along with twenty-six Nazis and fascists—for counseling resistance to the Selective Service Act.[11]

Determined to ensure that none of the indicted Southern Californians would escape sentencing, Lewis and Roos spent the next two years traveling back and forth to Washington, D.C., working closely with the U.S. attorney general's office, and hosting government officials who came to Los Angeles to examine their files. On October 19, 1942, following the testimony of undercover operatives William Bockhacker, Charles Young,

Sherry and Chuck Slocombe, 1942
Courtesy Sherry Slocombe

and Roy Arnold, the jury convicted Schwinn, Diebel, and twenty-two other defendants and sentenced them to five years in prison. Four months later, after listening to evidence supplied by Lewis and Roos, a Washington, D.C., jury convicted Schwinn, Diebel, Ferenz, Jones, Ellis, and thirty-one other Nazis and fascists of violating the wartime sedition act. Schwinn was sent to federal prison in Sandstone, Minnesota, while the others remained incarcerated in different parts of the country.[12]

Years of painstaking efforts by Lewis and Roos paid off once again in early 1944, when Schwinn, Diebel, Ferenz, Noble, Jones, and seventeen others were indicted in what became the longest sedition trial in American history. The Great Sedition Trial, as it was called, began in May 1944, with chief prosecutor and assistant attorney general O. John Rogge relying on Lewis and Roos to supply much of his evidence against the defendants. In some of the trial's most dramatic testimony, Rogge had Young, Bockhacker, and Arnold describe Nazi plans to seize control of the government, impose a National Socialist regime on the American people, and kill anyone who stood in their way. Never once did the undercover operatives mention that they were working for Lewis and Roos.[13]

The sedition case was halted in late November 1944, when presiding chief justice Edward C. Eicher died of a sudden heart attack. A month later, judge Bolitha Laws declared a mistrial and dismissed the jury. Schwinn, Ferenz, Noble, Jones, and thirteen Bund leaders remained in jail in Washington, D.C., while they waited for Rogge to begin a new sedition trial. In late November 1946, Judge Laws upheld the defendants' appeal and dismissed the 1944 mass sedition case.[14]

Despite Laws's ruling, the men remained in jail while the Justice Department considered filing an appeal. In November 1947, three months after Justice Department officials finally decided not to appeal the ruling, Schwinn and Diebel were transferred to Ellis Island, where they were held in jail as enemy aliens awaiting deportation. In July 1948, as Thekla Schwinn and her young child waited in New York for the release of her husband, Hermann Schwinn boarded the SS *Uruguay* to join the great mass of Nazis who had escaped to Buenos Aires. Two years later, mother and child left New York and were reunited with Hermann in Argentina. Unhappy in her new surroundings, Thekla moved back to the United States in September 1959.[15]

Deciding he preferred to spend the rest of his life among Americans rather than fellow Nazis, fifty-seven-year-old Hermann Schwinn applied for a visa in December 1962 to live with his wife and child in San Antonio, Florida. In one of life's great ironies, Schwinn spent the remainder of his life in heavily Jewish Dade County, Florida, surrounded by thousands of Holocaust survivors. The former Bund leader died on February 1, 1973.[16]

As for Hans Diebel, it is unclear when he left the United States, but by 1952 he was living in Frankfurt, Germany, where he remained until his death in March 1984.[17]

On April 24, 1945, the Third District Court of Appeals reversed the earlier California convictions of Ferenz, Noble, and Jones on the grounds that prosecutors never proved that the group advocated the overthrow of the government by force and violence.[18] After Ferenz was released from San Quentin prison, he returned to Los Angeles, where he remained until his death in February 1956. Ellis Jones and Robert Noble eventually made their way back to California, where they died in 1967 and 1970, respectively.

When George Gyssling returned to Germany in the summer of 1941, the Gestapo brought him to their headquarters in Berlin, where he was detained and interrogated. Years later, Gyssling told Nuremberg trial investigators he was reproached for inadequate reports on the American military economy and accused of lacking a sufficiently militant National Socialist outlook. "He was detained several times," his daughter Angelica recounted. "He was not put in prison. He was clever enough to get out of interrogation . . . but he told me to keep my mouth shut."[19] Fearing for her safety, Gyssling sent Angelica to live with his longtime mistress Christina Boone, who had settled in the Austrian town of Unterach am Attersee.

Cleared of any wrongdoing, Gyssling continued his diplomatic duties until he was sent to Merano in northern Italy in the fall of 1944, ostensibly to serve as its German general consul. Gyssling would tell American investigators he fled to Merano "as a political refugee" hiding from the Gestapo. The diplomat did not tell the whole truth. When his close friend Friedrich Schwend learned that Nazi officials suspected Gyssling of being too sympathetic to the Allies, he had him transferred to Merano to serve as his chief adviser in Operation Bernard. In an effort to destabilize the British economy, Hitler's government planned to flood the world market with counterfeit pound notes; Schwend and Gyssling were placed in charge of distributing the money.[20]

Gyssling was never fully invested in the operation. The Gestapo had been right: he hated Hitler and wanted the war ended as quickly as possible. In the spring of 1945, while living in Merano, Gyssling became part of Operation Sunrise, working with German officials and Allen Dulles, head of the Office of Strategic Services in Berne, to negotiate the peaceful capitulation of German forces in northern Italy. On May 2, 1945, six days before the end of the European war, an agreement was reached, and German forces in northern Italy and western Austria surrendered to the Allies.[21]

Gyssling was arrested and taken into custody by American authorities in Italy. He remained in prison until brought to Nuremberg, Germany, for interrogation by investigators in May 1947. Seven months later, the American Denazification Board cleared Gyssling on the strength of "resistance rendered."[22]

Evidence of Gyssling's "resistance rendered" came in the form of a character reference sent by Julius Klein. Writing in his capacity as the recently elected national commander of the Jewish War Veterans of the United States of America, Brigadier General Klein explained, "This is the only testimonial I have ever given or would give to any German national who is accused of being a Hitler follower." He told of knowing Gyssling during his tenure as German consul in Los Angeles and found him to be "the only one I met who was willing, at all times, to cooperate for the rebirth of a German Democracy." Gyssling "despised his own superiors" and tried "to do everything to help us in those crucial days," including passing on valuable information about the Hitler regime that proved "of great importance to our government."[23]

Following his release, Gyssling moved to the Austrian town of Unterach am Attersee to be with Angelica and Christina. Shortly thereafter, the couple split up, and Gyssling moved to Bavaria, where he worked as a lawyer and lived with his new mistress, Maria Kleine. The former German consul eventually settled in the small town of Benidorm in southern Spain, where he lived until his death on January 8, 1965.[24]

While Georg Gyssling navigated his way through the difficulties of life in wartime Germany, Leon Lewis was busily preparing for war's end, shifting the focus of the Community Relations Committee to fighting prejudice and protecting the civil rights of a wide range of groups: Jews, blacks, Mexicans, and Japanese. Much to his regret, he discovered that victory against Nazism and fascism did not bring the level of tolerance he had anticipated. "Since V-J Day," Lewis observed in December 1945, "it is all too clear that racial and religious discrimination and inter-group hatreds are becoming more and more pronounced." Despite besting local Nazis and fascists, he could not stem the spread of anti-Semitism in postwar Los Angeles. Two years later, he again warned CRC members about the "intensification of anti-Semitism, especially the reappearance and strengthening of prewar anti-Semitic groups and the anti-Semitic tone of some newspapers."[25]

The memo would be his last. Fourteen years after founding the Community Relations Committee, Leon Lewis stepped down as its executive director. He left behind no explanation. Returning to his law practice, he remained active in Jewish affairs, working with his longtime friend Rabbi Edgar Magnin to promote greater interfaith cooperation and activism. The rest of his life remains a mystery; he spent his postwar years, as he had his prewar years, drawing little attention to himself. What we do know is that after leaving the Community Relations Committee, Lewis moved his family from their midtown home on Keniston Avenue to the more bucolic surroundings of Pacific Palisades, overlooking the ocean.[26]

On May 21, 1954, Leon L. Lewis suffered a fatal heart attack while driving along the Pacific Coast Highway near his home. The constant stress of living so many years under the threat of Nazi retaliation against him or his family may well have hastened Lewis's heart condition and led to his death. The sixty-five-year-old attorney left behind a wife, two daughters, and a considerable legacy.[27]

Joe Roos, the man some committee members found either too quiet or too prickly to occupy Lewis's position as executive secretary, was passed over in 1947 in favor of Fred Herzberg, a dentist and former army colonel whose greatest quality was looking good in an officer's uniform. Herzberg proved "a complete bust." In 1950, Roos was appointed executive director of the Community Relations Committee. Over the next twenty years, he continued Lewis's efforts on behalf of greater racial tolerance and combating right-wing hate groups. In 1961, Roos was given the Judge Henry Hollzer Award, the highest honor bestowed by the Jewish community for outstanding work in the field of human relations. Eight years later, the Jewish War Veterans honored him at their national convention, praising him "for his steadfast and untiring efforts on behalf of our community and state particularly his work in the Community Relations Committee."[28]

Roos retired from the Community Relations Committee in January 1970 and founded his own public relations firm. Over the next three decades, he worked to promote greater tolerance in the city and across the nation. During that time, he helped lay the groundwork for creating the World Affairs Council of Greater Los Angeles, the Los Angeles County Human Relations Commission, and the California Fair Employment Practices Commission.[29]

Not everyone loved the modest Viennese-born Jew. His enemies had long memories. As friend and coauthor Leonard Pitt recounted, following war's end, Joe Roos and his son Leonard were walking down the street when one of his old foes spat in his face. "He told his son that was something to be proud of."[30]

Roos passed away in Los Angeles on December 11, 1999, at the age of ninety-four. When asked what his father would say if he wrote his own obituary, Leonard responded, "Above everything else, he fought his whole life against discrimination. Whether it was against Jews or blacks or others. He fought against those who would discriminate against others, like the Tea Party today and John Birchers in the past."[31]

THERE ARE MANY WAYS to fight an enemy, not all of which require guns. The actions taken by Leon Lewis and Joseph Roos require us to change the way we think about American Jewish resistance in the 1930s. From August 1933 until the end of World War II, with few resources at their disposal, the two men and their courageous undercover operatives continually defeated a variety of enemies—Nazis, fascists, and fifth columnists—bent on violence and murder. Without ever firing a weapon, they managed to keep Los Angeles and its citizens safe.

Democracy requires constant vigilance against all enemies, internal as well as external. Lewis, Roos, and their network of spies refused to sit back and allow their city and nation to be threatened by hate groups. They showed us through their actions that when a government fails to stem the rise of extremists bent on violence, it is up to every citizen to protect the lives of every American, no matter their race or religion.

There can be no better way to honor Leon Lewis than to remember his postwar words. Only in a "unified America," he said, could the nation and its citizens achieve the true "realization of the American democratic ideal."[32]

GUIDE TO SPIES, NAZIS, AND FASCISTS

Spymasters

Leon Lewis (Agent L1)	Chief spymaster; attorney; Anti-Defamation League representative; former army captain; chair of the Americanism Committee for local Disabled American Veterans and the American Legion
Joseph Roos	Associate spymaster; journalist and Hollywood story editor; editor, News Research Service's *News Letter*

Spies

C. Bert Allen (Agent 7)	Former army major; California state adjutant, Disabled American Veterans
William Bockhacker (Agent W2)	Former Burns Agency detective; deep undercover spy at German American Bund; used as an agent by FBI
Walter Clairville (Agent 33)	Former chief investigator for Los Angeles city attorney's office; army veteran; Lewis's assistant investigator for Los Angeles House Un-American Activities Committee hearings
Grace Comfort (Agent G2)	Widow of deceased navy commander
Sylvia Comfort (Agent S3)	Stenographer and daughter of deceased navy commander; worked undercover investigating Nazis, fascists, and isolationist groups

William Conley (Agent WC)	Former army captain; national commander, Disabled American Veterans; Lewis's sole Jewish spy
Neil Ness (Agent N2)	Engineer turned journalist turned spy; former army corporal; main agent inside Nazi groups
Alice Schmidt (Agent 17)	President of the Friends of New Germany's Ladies Auxiliary; wife of John Schmidt
John Schmidt (Agent 11)	Former German military cadet and U.S. army captain; deputy chief of staff for California, Disabled American Veterans; Leon Lewis's first spy
Julius Sicius (Agent S4)	German-born first secretary of Friends of New Germany; unemployed accountant and waiter
Charles Slocombe (Agent C19)	Long Beach water taxi owner; undercover operative working inside Ku Klux Klan, Silver Shirts, and German American Bund
Carl Sunderland (Agent 8)	Former army captain; post commander, Disabled American Veterans, L.A. Chapter No. 5
Charles Young (Agent Y9)	German-born naturalized citizen; former financial investigator; inside agent at Deutsches Haus

The Leading Nazis

Dr. Konrad Burchardi (code name 606)	Physician to consul Georg Gyssling; one of the most militant Nazis in Los Angeles
Hans Diebel	Number-two man in German American Bund; suspected Gestapo agent; replaced Paul Themlitz as owner of Aryan Bookstore
Franz Ferenz	Main distributor of German films and newsreels on Pacific Coast; author of Hitler biography; worked closely with anti-Semitic isolationist groups
Georg Gyssling	German general consul to Los Angeles

Capt. Robert Pape (code name 22)	Former captain in German army; first head of the Los Angeles branch, Friends of New Germany
Hermann Schwinn (code name 27)	German-born bank clerk who became head of Los Angeles branch of Friends of New Germany and western region leader of German American Bund
Paul Themlitz (code name 44)	German-born owner of Aryan Bookstore; Schwinn's number two in Friends of New Germany
Hans Winterhalder (code name 13)	German-born propagandist and recruiting head for Friends of New Germany and local Silver Shirts

The Leading Fascists

Kenneth Alexander	British-born photographer who worked in multiple Hollywood studios; head of Los Angeles Silver Shirts
Henry Allen	American-born fascist involved in virtually every right-wing movement in Los Angeles
Leslie Fry	Publisher of anti-Semitic *Christian Free Press*; worked closely with and funded fascist and Nazi groups
Ingram Hughes	American-born fascist; organized American Nationalist Party
Ellis Jones	American-born cofounder of fascist and anti-Semitic isolationist group Friends of Progress
Leopold McLaglan	Former captain in British Army; jiu-jitsu expert; con artist; fascist
Robert Noble	American-born cofounder of fascist and anti-Semitic isolationist group Friends of Progress

ACKNOWLEDGMENTS

Writing a book is an isolating experience made easier by the support of friends and colleagues. I want to thank the many librarians and archivists who helped me uncover the complex story of Leon Lewis and his spy ring. I owe an enormous debt of gratitude to David Sigler, who guided me through the massive Community Relations Committee collection housed in Special Collections at the Oviatt Library, California State University, Northridge. Closer to home, I received the help and support of a number of archivists at the University of Southern California. My thanks go to Claude Zachary and the Special Collections staff; to Dace Taube of the Regional History archives; and to Ned Comstock of the Cinema-Television Library collection. I also want to thank the many archivists who helped me at the National Archives in Washington, D.C., and in College Park, Maryland; at the Library of Congress; at the New York Public Library; at the Chicago History Museum; at the Columbia University Oral History Collection; at the UCLA Special Collections; and at Margaret Herrick Library in Beverly Hills.

I was fortunate to have a number of excellent research assistants. My greatest debt goes to Andreas Petasis, who worked on two books for me while an undergraduate at USC; one could not ask for a smarter, more dedicated researcher. I received help from two other undergraduates: Ian Carr and Julia Doherty. Thanks also go to two of my graduate students for their research assistance, Simon Judkins and Adam Bloch. I offer a special thanks to Florian Danecke, who conducted research for me in Berlin.

Authors need time to write. I want to acknowledge the funding support I received from the National Endowment for the Humanities, from the provost's office at USC, from the dean's office at USC's Dornsife College, and from the USC Casden Institute for the Study of the Jewish Role in American Life. I also want to thank Peter Hirsch and Jessica Lehman for once again allowing me to escape Los Angeles to write in the quietude of their wonderful mountain cabin.

Many friends and colleagues read and commented on substantial parts of the manuscript, making it a far better book than I could write on my own. I owe a debt of gratitude to Leo Braudy, Tom Doherty, Allison Engel, Buddy Epstein, Wolf Gruner, James Lafferty, Charles Maland, and Jon Wilkman. Likewise, my agent, Sandy Dijkstra, has been a constant source of encouragement and a perceptive reader, helping me refine my arguments. Some friends read the entire manuscript, often more than once. My gratitude goes to two longtime friends from graduate school. Bill Hirsch offered a keen eye toward editing and sharpening key themes. Dick Miller has spent many hours with me on hikes and on the phone, suggesting the best ways to present arguments to a general audience. Phil Ethington has been a constant source of sound advice and inspiration for nearly twenty years; he has also helped me regain my balance by spending many evenings watching movies and talking politics. Bob Slayton has been a great friend, dropping his own work to read through draft after draft of chapters with a keen eye toward getting to the heart of an argument. Jon Boorstin has been an equally valuable friend and critic, always urging me to think less like an academic and more like a writer telling an important story.

I have been fortunate to work with a talented team at Bloomsbury USA. My thanks go to Lea Beresford and especially to Jacqueline Johnson, one of the best editors with whom an author could hope to work.

My greatest debt goes to my wonderful, loving family. My daughter, Lydia Ross, and son, Gabriel Ross, read and edited the entire manuscript with an eye toward refining the writing and making it more appealing to general readers. Gabriel also helped me with research at the Oviatt Library. And finally, my best friend and wife, Linda Kent, has spent countless hours patiently listening to me work through ideas and always offering smart advice. My life, let alone this book, would be far less rich without her.

Finally, I dedicate this book to the memory of my in-laws, Kurt and Olga Kent, who left Germany before it was too late, to my mother, Esther Ross, and to the memory of my father, Benjamin Ross, both of whom survived Hitler's concentration camps and went on to live full and happy lives.

NOTES

Endnote Abbreviations

CRC   Jewish Federation Council of Greater Los Angeles,
                       Community Relations Committee Collection, Part 1
                       (1921–1937), Part 2 (1920–1950), Part 3 (1933–1951), Special
                       Collections and Archives, Oviatt Library, California State
                       University, Northridge

Higham Collection   Charles Higham Collection, Cinematic Arts Library, University
                       of Southern California

PA-AA   Politisches Archiv des Auswärtigen Amts (Political Archives of
                       the German Foreign Office), Berlin

Roos Papers   Joseph Roos Papers, Collection no. 0313, Special Collections,
                       University of Southern California

Summary Report   *Summary Report on Activities of Nazi Groups and Their Allies in
                       Southern California*, Box 10, Joseph Roos Papers, Special
                       Collections, USC Libraries, University of Southern California

Prologue

1 The exhibit can be accessed at http://digital-library.csun.edu/Backyard/.

2 Several years ago, historian Ben Urwand published a highly controversial book, *The Collaboration: Hollywood's Pact with Hitler* (Cambridge, MA: Harvard University Press, 2013). He argued that the Hollywood moguls, overwhelmingly Jewish, did more than just reluctantly cooperate in doing business with the Hitler; they were active collaborators. Yet Urwand's is a highly moralistic history that, in lambasting the moguls for not doing more to prevent the Holocaust, ignores historical contingency. Urwand accuses the moguls of cowardice, complicity, and collaboration. He could not have been more wrong.

3 Adolf Hitler, *Mein Kampf,* trans. Ralph Manheim (New York: Houghton Mifflin, 1943), 470. Goebbels's plans to undermine Hollywood are discussed in Joseph Roos, "Attack on the Motion Picture Industry by Nazis and Anti-Semites in the United States," ca. 1940, pt. 2 (1920–1950), box 110, folder 18, Jewish Federation Council of Greater Los Angeles, Community Relations Committee Collection, Special Collections and Archives, Oviatt Library, California State University, Northridge.

1. "The Most Dangerous Jew in Los Angeles"

1 Leon Lewis to Richard Gutstadt, Sept. 9, 1933, CRC, pt. 1 (1921–1937), box 22, folder 15.

2 *Los Angeles Examiner*, July 27, 1933; *L.A. Record*, July 26, 1933.

3 Leonard Pitt, interview by author, August 5, 2014, Los Angeles.

4 Biographical material is drawn from Julius Schwartz, Solomon Aaron Kaye, and John Simons, *Who's Who in American Jewry, 1926* (New York: Jewish Biographical Bureau, 1927), 382–83; *American Jewish Year Book* 56 (1955): 570.

5 For a sampling of Lewis's early work on behalf of the ADL and the Jewish community, see *American Hebrew and Jewish Messenger*, Nov. 14, 1913; *Chicago Tribune*, Feb. 28, 1914; *American Israelite*, Jan. 21, 1915, and July 13, 1916; *Jewish Exponent*, Dec. 10, 1915.

6 "U.S. World War I Jewish Servicemen Questionnaires, 1918–1921, for Leon Lawrence Lewis," ancestry.com.

7 For his work on behalf of national and international Jewry, see *American Israelite*, Aug. 19, 1920, Nov. 23, 1922, July 26, 1923, and July 10, 1924; *B'nai B'rith News*, Sept. 1920; *The American Hebrew and Jewish Messenger*, Sept. 24, 1920; and Jewish Telegraphic Agency, Dec. 24, 1923, and Jan. 1, 1924.

8 Joseph Roos, who would become Lewis's assistant spymaster, mistakenly wrote that Lewis moved to Los Angeles in 1929; according to newspaper articles, he moved to the city in March 1931. *Los Angeles Times*, June 17, 1931. For an overview of Jewish Los Angeles, see Max Vorspan and Lloyd P. Gartner, *History of the Jews of Los Angeles* (Philadelphia: Jewish Publication Society of America, 1970), 203–05; Ellen Eisenberg, *The First to Cry Down Injustice?: Western Jews and Japanese Removal During World War II* (Lanham, MD: Lexington, 2008), 107; and Samuel C. Kohs, "The Jewish Community of Los Angeles," *Jewish Review* 2 (July–Oct. 1944): 87–126.

9 Vorspan and Gartner, *History of the Jews of Los Angeles*, 203. Boyle Heights statistics are from Ellen Eisenberg and Ava Kahn, *Jews of the Pacific Coast* (Seattle: University of Washington Press, 2010), 261n89.

10 For the Klan's presence in the Los Angeles region, see Joseph Roos, "Draft 3 of Chapter 2: Joining and Shoving [dated July 1990]," 10–11, in "Under the Crooked Cross," unpublished manuscript, box 7, folder "Under the Crooked Cross—Draft and Correspondence 1 of 2," Joseph Roos Papers, Collection no. 0313, Special Collections, USC Libraries, University of Southern California (hereafter cited as Roos Papers); David Chalmers, *Hooded Americanism: The First Century of the Ku Klux Klan, 1865–1965* (New York: Doubleday, 1965), 119–25; Claudine Burnett, *Prohibition Madness: Life and Death in and around Long Beach, California, 1920–1933* (Bloomington, IN: AuthorHouse, 2013), 23. Exclusionary practices against Jews are described in Shana Bernstein, *Bridges of Reform: Interracial Civil Rights Activism in Twentieth-Century Los Angeles* (New York: Oxford University Press, 2011).

11 Edmund Wilson, "An Appeal to Progressives," *New Republic*, Jan. 14, 1931, https://newrepublic.com/article/104618/appeal-progressives.

12 Los Angeles statistics are taken from the [Los Angeles] *B'nai B'rith Messenger*, Nov. 14, 1930. For an overview of the Great Depression, see William Leuchtenburg, *The Perils of Prosperity, 1914–32* (Chicago: University of Chicago Press, 1993); and Colin Shindler, *Hollywood in Crisis: Cinema and American Society, 1929–1939* (London: Routledge, 1996).

13 For overviews of American fascists and demagogues of the era, see Alan Brinkley, *Voices of Protest: Huey Long, Father Coughlin, & the Great Depression* (New York: Alfred A. Knopf, 1982); Charles Higham, *American Swastika* (Garden City, NY: Doubleday, 1985); Scott Beekman, *William Dudley Pelley: A Life in Right-Wing Extremism and the Occult* (Syracuse, NY: Syracuse University Press, 2005); and Arnie Bernstein, *Swastika Nation: Fritz Kuhn and the Rise and Fall of the German-American Bund* (New York: St. Martin's Press, 2013).

14 For a copy of an anti-FDR anti-Semitic flyer issued by the American White Guard, see John Spivak, *Secret Armies: The New Technique of Nazi Warfare* (New York: Modern Age, 1939), 85.

15 *Los Angeles Times,* May 11, 1933; *London Daily Herald,* quoted in *Los Angeles Times,* March 3, 1933.

16 American Jewish Historical Society, "The Anti Nazi Boycott of 1933," www.ajhs .org/ajhsnew/scholarship/chapters/chapter.cfm?documentID=230.

17 Goebbels quoted in ibid. For reports of angry picketing and retribution by Germans before April 1, see *Los Angeles Times,* March 30, 1933.

18 *Los Angeles Times,* April 2, 1933.

19 *New York Times,* July 9, 1933. For an excellent overview of the rise of Nazism in the United States, see Sander A. Diamond, *The Nazi Movement in the United States, 1924–1941* (Ithaca, NY: Cornell University Press, 1974).

20 *California Staats Zeitung,* June 16, 1933; *B'nai B'rith Messenger,* April 14, 1933.

21 *California Staats Zeitung,* June 16, 1933.

22 [Leon Lewis], unsigned memo, June 25, 1933, CRC, pt. 1, box 14, folder 5. For the initial investigative reports received by Lewis, including a report describing the first Nazi meeting, see memos of June 30 and July 1, 6, and 12, 1933, CRC, pt. 1, box 14, folder 5.

23 Quotes are from a speech given in late July or early August 1933, CRC, pt. 1, box 14, folder 6.

24 The city's English residents numbered 100,000, Canadians 100,000, and French 28,000. *Los Angeles Times,* Sept. 19, 1939.

25 For an account of events surrounding the Bonus Army, see Paul Dickson and Thomas B. Allen, *The Bonus Army: An American Epic* (New York: Walker, 2004); for Khaki Shirts, see *New York Times,* July 31, 1932.

26 Dickson and Allen, *Bonus Army.*

27 Lewis to Gutstadt, Sept. 9, 1933, CRC, pt. 1, box 22, folder 15; "Report of the Recommendations of Special Committee on Americanism, Adopted by National Convention of Disabled American Veterans of the World War," Colorado Springs, CO, June 30 to July 7, 1934, box 8, folder "Research—Veterans 1933 & 1934," Roos Papers. Statistics on veterans in Southern California are cited in *Los Angeles Times,* May 18, 1933.

28 Curt Riess, *Total Espionage* (New York: G. P. Putnam's Sons, 1941), 45, 46–47. The number of FBI agents and their lack of training in counterespionage is discussed in "Reminiscences of Henry P. Dolan: Oral History, 1962," 5, 11, Oral History Collection, Columbia University.

29 Rafael Demmler was the man who referred to Lewis as the most dangerous Jew and "the ring-leader of all Jews here." Confidential Report N2 [Neil Ness], Feb. 17, 1936, CRC, pt. 1, box 6, folder 21. According to historian Leonard Pitt, who worked with

Roos on his memoir, Lewis told Roos he had some wartime experience in intelligence work. Pitt, interview by author, Aug. 5, 2014.

30 "Meeting at Judge Pacht's House—August 31, 1933," CRC, pt. 1, box 1, folder 29. The initial advisory committee included Silberberg, Irving Lipsitch, Ludwig Schiff, J. Y. Baruh, Sam Briskin, Tom May, Phil Goldstone, Dr. Maurice Kahn, and I. Eisner. The best source of information about the origins and evolution of Lewis's spy operation is Joseph Roos's unfinished manuscript "Under the Crooked Cross"; see also his drafts of an unfinished manuscript he coauthored with historian Leonard Pitt, "Shadows of the Crooked Cross: An Untold Story About Nazis and Their Sympathizers in America, 1933–1945," box 7, Roos Papers.

31 Lewis included a copy of the Veterans of Foreign Wars resolution in his letter to Richard Gutstadt, Aug. 17, 1933, CRC, pt. 1, box 22, folder 14. For the American Legion resolution, see *B'nai B'rith Messenger*, Aug. 18, 1933.

32 Lewis to Gutstadt, Aug. 17, 1933.

33 "Memorandum [1934]. Data for Committee Meeting File," CRC, pt. 1, box 2, folder 12.

34 Lewis to Gutstadt, March 2, 1934, CRC, pt. 1, box 2, folder 21.

35 For Schmidt's background, see John C. Schmidt, testimony, German-American Alliance Lawsuit, CRC, pt. 1, box 3, folder 36; *Los Angeles Examiner*, Jan. 16, 1934; *Los Angeles Times*, April 4, 1944; "Analysis of Testimony by Capt. John Schmidt in Trial in Los Angeles," March 14, 1934, in Special Committee on Un-American Activities on Nazi Propaganda, HR 73A-F30.1, folder "Emile Normile," RG 233, box 366, entry 5, Investigator Reports, NA (hereafter Investigator Reports, NA). Information about his military records and census reports can also be found on ancestry.com. There are disagreements over Schmidt's date of birth. The *Los Angeles Times* and CRC Records say he was born February 11, 1885; Social Security records show he was born February 11, 1886; the application for a military headstone showed Feb. 11, 1887.

36 *Los Angeles Times*, April 4, 1944; Roos, "Under the Crooked Cross," 26.

37 Lewis to Gutstadt, Oct. 16, 1933, CRC, pt. 1, box 22, folder 15; Lewis speech, ca. 1936, CRC, pt. 1, box 2, folder 13; Roos, "Under the Crooked Cross," 31–32.

38 Joseph Roos, oral history interview by Leonard Pitt and Murray Woods, Dec. 18, 1979, Jan. 7 and 28, and Feb. 14, 1980, p. 15, box 6, folder "Oral Histories-CSUN," Roos Papers.

2. The Spying Begins

1 John Schmidt, report, circa Aug. 20, 1933, CRC, pt. 1, box 7, folder 18.

2 "Unsigned Reports," circa Sept. 1933, CRC, pt. 1, box 14, folder 22.

3 For Pape's background, see Schmidt, reports, Sept. 14 and 27, 1933, CRC, pt. 1, box 7, folder 21; Schmidt, reports, Oct. 11 and 12, 1933, CRC, pt. 1, box 8, folder 1; German-American Alliance Lawsuit transcript, Jan. 1934, CRC, pt. 1, box 4, folder 2. For Pape's direct reporting to Hitler and Goebbels, see Julius Sicius, report, Nov. 30, 1939, CRC, Part 2, box 40, folder 8.

4 Testimony of Hans Winterhalder, Extracts from Executive Hearings, Los Angeles, Thursday, Aug 2, 1934, 501, RG 233, box 361, entry 3, folders Aug. 3–8, 1934, NA. For Winterhalder's background, see Schmidt, report, Oct 10, 1933, CRC, pt. 1, box 8,

folder 1; Winterhalder, testimony, German-American Alliance Lawsuit 1934, CRC, pt. 1, box 4, folders 4 and 5; Diamond, *Nazi Movement*, 135–36.

5 Schmidt's complaints were true. For his ailments and failed efforts to obtain disability payments, see Dr. Louis Felger to Veterans Administration, Aug. 20, 1934, CRC, pt. 1, box 8, folder 13.

6 Schmidt, report, circa Aug. 20, 1933, CRC, pt. 1, box 8, folder 14.

7 Schmidt, report, circa Aug. 19–20, 1933, CRC, pt. 1, box 7, folder 18.

8 Schmidt, report, Aug. 21, 1933, CRC, pt. 1, box 7, folder 18.

9 Schmidt, report, Aug. 22, 1933, CRC, pt. 1, box 7, folder 18.

10 Ibid.

11 Schmidt, report, Aug. 29, 1933, CRC, pt. 1, box 7, folder 18.

12 Records indicate a slight confusion over Sunderland's precise birth date. His original enlistment form listed "about 1883" as his birth date; his social security record has 1884; and one death record suggests 1885. Information on his background and military record is drawn from U.S. Army, Register of Enlistments, 1798–1914; California Death Index, 1940–1997, in ancestry.com; and Report of Eight over Telephone, Sept. 25, 1933, CRC, pt. 1, box 7, folder 20; Reports of 11 and 17, Oct. 6, 1933, CRC, pt. 1, box 9, folder 3.

13 Schmidt, report, Sept. 6, 1934, CRC, pt. 1, box 7, folder 18.

14 A copy of the oath can be found in *The Brown Network: The Activities of Nazis in Foreign Countries*, translated from the German [no author] (New York: Knight Publications, Inc., 1936), 248.

15 Schmidt, report, Aug. 29, 1933, CRC, pt. 1, box 7, folder 18.

16 Schmidt, report, Aug. 30, 1933, CRC, pt. 1, box 7, folder 18.

17 Ibid.

18 Ibid.

19 Schmidt, report, Aug. 31, 1933, CRC, pt. 1, box 7, folder 18. For Allen's background, see *Los Angeles Times,* Aug. 3, 1933; U.S. Veterans Gravesites, ca. 1775–2006, ancestry. com; C. Bert Allen, affidavit, December 1933, CRC, pt. 1, box 14, folder 10.

20 Carl Sunderland, report, Sept. 13, 1933, CRC, pt. 1, box 7, folder 19.

21 Schmidt, report, Aug. 28, 1933, CRC, pt. 1, box 7, folder 18.

22 Schmidt, report, Sept. 1, 1933, CRC, pt. 1, box 8, folder 14.

23 Schmidt, report, Sept. 8, 1933, CRC, pt. 1, box 8, folder 15; Schmidt, report, Sept. 2, 1933, CRC, pt. 1, box 7, folder 21.

24 Sunderland, report, Sept. 8, 1933, CRC, pt. 1, box 7, folder 19. Schwinn told Schmidt that Hynes "was a very good friend" who had designed the shield Nazis wore on their swastika bands. Schmidt, report, Sept. 8, 1933.

25 For Hynes's background and earlier undercover work, see U.S. House of Representatives, Public Hearings before the Special Committee on Un-American Activities, House of Representatives, 73rd Cong., 2nd. sess., *Investigation of Nazi Propaganda Activities and Investigation of Certain Other Propaganda Activities* . . . (Washington, D.C.: Government Printing Office, 1935), 242, 252. Nazi requests for police protection and information passed to police about Red activity can be found in Hermann Schwinn to Captain Hynes, April 3, 1934, Los Angeles Police Department Memo, July 20, 1934, P. L. Phelps to Lt. Luke Lane, Commanding Intelligence Bureau, Nov. 22, 1934, CRC, pt. 1, box 30, folder 7. Winterhalder sent Hynes the names, addresses,

and phone numbers of the group's members on Aug. 7, 1933. Hans L. Winterhalder to Captain Hynes, Aug. 7, 1933, CRC, pt. 1, box 6, folder 13.

26 William Conley, "Brief Report of Interview of Capt. Hynes," Sept. 7, 1933, CRC, pt. 1, box 6, folder 13.

27 Ibid.

28 Ibid.

29 Report of Sunderland to Schmidt, Sept. 9, 1933, CRC, pt. 1, box 7, folder 19. Dollar equivalencies here and throughout this book are taken from www.measuringworth .com.

30 For Davis's background, see Ernest Jerome Hopkins, *Our Lawless Police: A Study of the Unlawful Enforcement of the Law* (New York: Viking, 1931), 152–54.

31 "Memorandum on conference held this morning with Mr. Armin Wittenberg and Chief of Police Davis," Sept. 15, 1933, 11:30 a.m., CRC, pt. 1, box 2, folder 10.

32 Ibid.

33 Ibid.

34 Ibid.

35 N. Nagel to Lewis, April 6, 1934, CRC, pt. 1, box 2, folder 10.

36 Lewis to Gutstadt, Oct. 16, 1933, CRC, pt. 1, box 22, folder 15.

37 Report of Allen, Sept. 25, 1933, CRC, pt. 1, box 7, folder 20; for Lewis on Dunn, see Lewis to Gutstadt, Oct. 16, 1933, CRC, pt. 1, box 22, folder 15.

38 Schmidt, report, Sept. 1, 1933, CRC, pt. 1, box 8, folder 14; *Los Angeles Times*, Jan. 7, 1934.

39 Schmidt, report, Sept. 30, 1933, CRC, pt. 1, box 7, folder 21; William C. Conley, report, Sept. 28, 1933, CRC, pt. 1, box 6, folder 12. Conley served as Commander of the Los Angeles DAV Roosevelt Post #5 in 1930 and as DAV National Commander from 1932 to 1933.

40 Schmidt, report, Sept. 22, 1933, CRC, pt. 1, box 7, folder 20.

41 Ibid.

3. Plots Revealed, Spies Uncovered

1 John Schmidt, report, Sept. 26, 1933, CRC, pt. 1, box 7, folder 21.

2 William Conley to Chief James E. Davis, LAPD, Sept. 28, 1933, CRC, pt. 1, box 14, folder 7; Alice Schmidt, report, Sept. 26, 1933, CRC, pt. 1, box 7, folder 20.

3 Conley to Davis, Sept. 28, 1933.

4 Allen and Sunderland, joint report, Oct. 2, 1933, CRC, pt. 1, box 8, folder 1.

5 Ibid.

6 Ibid.

7 Schmidt, report, Oct. 3, 1933, CRC, pt. 1, box 8, folder 1.

8 Ibid.

9 Conley to Davis, Sept. 28, 1933.

10 Lewis Memo, "Telephone Conversation with Hynes," Oct. 14, 1933, CRC, pt. 1, box 8, folder 2.

11 Lewis to Gutstadt, Oct. 16, 1933, CRC, pt. 1, box 22, folder 15.

12 Allen, report, and Allen and Sunderland, supplemental joint report, Oct. 24, 1933, CRC, pt. 1, box 8, folder 2. See also Lewis to Gutstadt, Oct. 17, 1933, CRC, pt. 1, box 22, folder 15.

13 Allen and Sunderland, report, Oct. 24, 1933, CRC, pt. 1, box 8, folder 3.

14 The naval testimonies were presented at a House Un-American Activities hearing in Los Angeles on August 7, 1934. U.S. House of Representatives, *Investigation of Nazi Propaganda Activities*, 1–25.

15 Allen and Sunderland, report, Oct. 24, 1933.

16 Ibid.

17 Ibid.

18 Allen and Sunderland, report, Oct. 24, 1933; Allen, report, Oct. 25, 1933, CRC, pt. 1, box 8, folder 3.

19 Allen and Sunderland, report, Oct. 28, 1933, CRC, pt. 1, box 8, folder 3.

20 Ibid.

21 Ibid.

22 Ibid.

23 Schmidt, report, Nov. 6, 1933, CRC, pt. 1, box 8, folder 4.

24 Schmidt, report, Nov. 8, 1933, CRC, pt. 1, box 8, folder 4. Georg Gyssling's background and mission to Los Angeles are discussed in chapter 9.

25 Schmidt, report, Nov. 9, 1933, CRC, pt. 1, box 8, folder 4.

26 Ibid.

27 Alice and John Schmidt, report, Nov. 9, 1933, CRC, pt. 1, box 8, folder 4.

28 Schmidt, report, Oct. 5, 1933, CRC, pt. 1, box 8, folder 1.

29 Alice and John Schmidt, report, Nov. 17, 1933, CRC, pt. 1, box 8, folder 4.

30 "Analysis of Testimony by Capt. John Schmidt," NA.

4. Going for Help

1 For a description of the national German-American Alliance, see Diamond, *Nazi Movement*, 56–57. For a look at the Los Angeles organization, see Philip Lenhardt, letter printed in *B'nai B'rith Messenger*, Oct. 25, 1933, CRC, pt. 1, box 15, folder 22.

2 Alice and John Hans Schmidt, joint report, Oct. 11, 1933, CRC, pt. 1, box 8, folder 1.

3 Ibid.

4 Lenhardt, letter in *B'nai B'rith Messenger*, CRC, pt. 1, box 15, folder 22.

5 Schmidt, report, Nov. 2, 1933, CRC, pt. 1, box 8, folder 4.

6 Schmidt, report, Nov. 11, on meeting of the *Stadtverband*, Nov. 10, 1933, CRC, pt. 1, box 8, folder 4.

7 Ibid.

8 Schmidt, report on meeting with John Vieth, Nov. 13, 1933, CRC, pt. 1, box 8, folder 4.

9 Alice and John Schmidt, report, Nov. 17, for the period Nov. 15–17, 1933, CRC, pt. 1, box 8, folder 4. See also Schmidt, report, Nov. 22, 1933, CRC, pt. 1, box 8, folder 5.

10 "Reminiscences of Samuel Dickstein: Oral History, 1950," 28, Oral History Collection, Special Collections, Columbia University. It was later discovered that Dickstein, frustrated by congressional inaction, spied for the KGB. Kurt F. Stone, *The Jews of Capitol Hill: A Compendium of Jewish Congressional Members* (Lanham, MD: Scarecrow, 2010), 120; Allen Weinstein and Alexander Vassiliev, *The Haunted Wood: Soviet Espionage in America—The Stalin Era* (New York: Modern Library, 2000).

11 "Reminiscences of Dickstein," 28, 27.

12 Ibid., 28.

13 The figures for the number of Jews in Kramer's district are taken from *B'nai B'rith Messenger,* July 28, 1933. For Kramer's background and connection to the city's Jewish community, see Joseph Roos, "Under the Crooked Cross," 34.

14 "[Lewis] Memorandum No. 1: Dec. 1933," CRC, pt. 1, box 2, folder 10.

15 Ibid.

16 Ibid.

17 Ibid.

18 Ibid.

19 Ibid.

20 "Reminiscences of Dickstein," 34; Nazis quoted in Diamond, *Nazi Movement,* 141.

21 McFadden quoted in Steven Alan Carr, *Hollywood and Anti-Semitism: A Cultural History Up to World War II* (Cambridge, England: Cambridge University Press, 2001), 108; *Jewish Telegraphic Agency,* January 28, 1934. On May 29, 1933, McFadden gave a speech entitled "In the United States Today, the Gentiles Have Slips of Paper While Jews Have the Gold and Lawful Money." *Jewish Telegraphic Agency,* May 1, 1934. Of the 435 representatives in the 73rd Congress, eight Democrats and two Republicans were Jews. Roos, "Under the Crooked Cross," 35.

22 "[Lewis] Memorandum No. 1."

23 Ibid.

24 Ibid.

25 Schmidt, report, Dec. 8, 1933, CRC, pt. 1, box 8, folder 5.

26 Lewis to Livingston, Nov. 28, 1933, CRC, pt. 1, box 22, folder 16.

27 Charles Kramer to Leon Lewis, Dec. 9, 1933, box 8, folder "Research—Veterans 1933 & 1934," Roos Papers.

5. A Bitter Lesson: The German-American Alliance Trial

1 John Schmidt, affidavit, Jan. 1934, CRC, pt. 1, box 8, folder 22. For Lewis's payment to the plaintiffs' attorneys, see Leon Lewis to Hugo Harris, April 2, 1934, CRC, pt. 1, box 3, folder 32.

2 *Los Angeles Times,* Jan. 10, 1934. A transcript of the trial can be found in CRC, pt. 1, box 3, folder 30, through box 4, folder 5.

3 First two quotes are *Los Angeles Times,* Jan. 16, 1934; *Los Angeles Herald-Express,* Jan. 15, 1934; Sunderland, testimony, CRC, pt. 1, box 3, folder 35.

4 *Los Angeles Examiner,* Jan. 16, 1934.

5 *Los Angeles Evening Herald-Express,* Jan. 16, 1934; Schmidt, testimony.

6 Schmidt, testimony.

7 *Los Angeles Examiner,* Jan. 16, 1934.

8 *Los Angeles Times,* Jan. 17, 1934.

9 Sunderland, testimony.

10 *Los Angeles Times,* Jan. 17, 1934; Schmidt, testimony.

11 Testimonies of these men can be found in German-American Alliance transcript, CRC, pt. 1, box 4, folders 1–4.

12 *Los Angeles Times,* Jan. 17, 1934; also see Hermann Schwinn, testimony, CRC, pt. 1, box 4, folders 4 and 5.

13 *Los Angeles Times*, Jan. 19, 1934.

14 Ibid., Jan. 20, 1934.

15 *Los Angeles Examiner*, Jan. 20, 1934; Leon Lewis, affidavit, January 1934, CRC, pt. 1, box 3, folder 31.

16 Schmidt, affidavit, Jan. 1934, CRC, pt. 1, box 3, folder 31.

17 *Los Angeles Examiner*, Jan. 22, 1934; *Los Angeles Times*, Jan. 23, 1934.

18 *Los Angeles Examiner*, Jan. 24, 1934.

19 Schmidt, affidavit, Feb. 1, 1934, CRC, pt. 1, box 3, folder 32.

20 *Los Angeles Times,* Feb. 10, 1934. For a more complete analysis of the ruling, see David E. Field to Otto Deissler and Philip Lenhardt, March 19, 1934, CRC, pt. 1, box 3, folder 32.

21 Lewis to Gutstadt, Feb. 10, 1934, CRC 22, folder 20.

22 Schmidt, report, Feb. 20, 1934, CRC, pt. 1, box 8, folder 22.

23 First two quotes, CRC, pt. 1, box 8, folder 22; Schmidt, report, April 4, 1934, CRC, pt. 1, box 8, folder 8.

24 Schmidt, report, Feb. 23, 1934, CRC, pt. 1, box 8, folder 22. Schmidt began attending Silver Shirt meetings in December in the same undercover capacity as he had for the FNG. In order to create confusion, Lewis changed Schmidt's code name from 11 to 74. Schmidt, report, Feb. 28, 1934, CRC, pt. 1, box 8, folder 22.

25 For correspondence between the legal team, plaintiffs, and Lewis, see David E. Field to Messrs. Otto Deissler and Philip Lenhardt, March 19, 1934; Leon Lewis to Hugo H. Harris, April 2, 1934; and David E. Field to Otto Deissler and Philip Lenhardt, April 12, 1934, all CRC, pt. 1, box 3, folder 32.

26 Edward Rudy insisted the FNG had 500 members in January 1934. Lewis suggested it was closer to 350. Report of Alice and John Schmidt, Jan. 5, 1934, CRC, pt. 1, box 8, folder 22; "Data for Committee Meeting File," CRC, pt. 1, box 2, folder 12.

27 For Pelley, Winterhalder, and Themlitz's efforts to open a Nazi-dominated Silver Shirt post, see Schmidt, report, March 11, 1934, and affidavit, April 12, 1934, CRC, pt. 1, box 8, folder 23; Lewis to Gutstadt, Feb. 22, 1934, CRC, pt. 1, box 22, folder 20; Mark L. White, report, March 21, 1934, CRC, pt. 1, box 10, folder 11; Jewish Telegraphic Agency, April 22, 1934.

28 For examples of Schmidt reports on Silver Shirt meetings and their starkly anti-Communist, overtly anti-Catholic messages, see John Schmidt, report, July 17, 1933, CRC, pt. 1, box 19, folder 4; Alice Schmidt, report, Sept. 10, 1933, CRC, pt. 1, box 19, folder 4.

29 *Hollywood Citizen-News*, Dec. 14, 1933; Alice and John Schmidt, report, Jan. 5, 1934, CRC, pt. 1, box 8, folder 22.

30 Sunderland, report, Jan. 28, 1934, CRC, pt. 1, box 10, folder 8.

31 Schmidt, report, Feb. 28, 1934, CRC, pt. 1, box 8, folder 22; N. Nagel to Leon Lewis, April 6, 1934, CRC, pt. 1, box 2, folder 10. For police ties to the Silver Shirts and KKK, see memorandum No. 14, "Re: Officer Tate," May 10, 1934, CRC, pt. 1, box 2, folder 11.

32 Memorandum no. 11, phone call from Volney P. Mooney, National Judge Advocate General, DAV, March 9, 1934, CRC, pt. 1, box 2, folder 10. For the report and recommendations the Special DAV Committee made to the national convention in June 1934, see "Report of the Recommendations of Special Committee on Americanism."

33 Summary of operations from June 1933 to March 1934, CRC, pt. 1, box 2, folder 12.
34 "Reminiscences of Samuel Dickstein," 29–30.

6. The Moguls and the Nazis

1 *Silver Ranger*, March 7, Jan. 17, 1934. Capitalized words cited as they appeared in the newspaper. See the *Silver Ranger*'s "Behind the Silver Screen" column for regular attacks on Jewish Hollywood. My discussion of the moguls and their support of Leon Lewis's operation is a stark contrast to Ben Urwand's faulty depiction of them as active collaborators with the Hitler regime. Urwand, *Collaboration*.
2 Memo of [first] meeting held at Hillcrest Country Club, March 13, 1934, CRC, pt. 1, box 1, folder 8.
3 Leon Lewis to Richard Gutstadt, Aug 25, 1933, CRC, pt. 1, box 22, folder 14; Lewis to Gutstadt, Sept. 29, 1933, CRC, pt. 1, box 22, folder 15.
4 Lewis to Gutstadt, Aug. 25, 1933. In September 1930, Silberberg used his influence to orchestrate Louis B. Mayer's appointment as vice chairman of the California GOP. For biographical information about Silberberg, see Roos, "Under the Crooked Cross," 24–37; *Los Angeles Times*, Dec. 14, 1922, June 30, 1965; *Marquis Who Was Who in America 1607–1984*, www.credoreference.com.libproxy.usc.edu/entry/marqwas /silberberg_mendel_b; *Encyclopedia Judaica*, go.galegroup.com.libproxy.usc.edu/ps/i .do?action=interpret&id=GALE%7CCX2587518506&v=2.1&u=usocal_main&it=r &p=GVRL&sw=w&authCount=1.
5 Roos, "Under the Crooked Cross," 25.
6 Harold Friedman, interview by author, at offices of Mitchell, Silberberg, Roth and Knupp, Los Angeles, Nov. 24, 2015.
7 Roos, "Under the Crooked Cross," 27.
8 Lewis to Gutstadt, Sept. 1, 1933, CRC, pt. 1, box 22, folder 15; Lewis to Gutstadt, Nov. 1, 1933, CRC, pt. 1, box 22, folder 16.
9 *Los Angeles Times*, Dec. 10, 1931.
10 Montgomery and *Fortune*'s 1932 article are quoted in Scott Eyeman, *Lion of Holly- wood: The Life and Legend of Louis B. Mayer* (New York: Simon & Schuster, 2005), 204, 152.
11 Roos, "Chapter Headings—For Identification Only," Oct. 6, 1990, box 7, Roos Papers; "Rabbi Edgar F. Magnin: Leader and Personality," ca. 1975, 191, Regional Oral History Office, Bancroft Library, University of California, Berkeley, CA.
12 Lewis to Gutstadt, Sept. 29, 1933, CRC, pt. 1, box 22, folder 15. In the eighteen months between June 1, 1933, and January 1, 1935, Lewis spent $25,508 on his under- cover operation. Lewis to Gutstadt, Jan. 17, 1935, CRC, pt. 1, box 23, folder 3.
13 Lewis to Gutstadt, Nov. 1, 1933, CRC, pt. 1, box 22, folder 16.
14 Lewis to Livingston, Nov. 24, 1933, and Lewis to Gutstadt, Nov. 1, 1933, CRC, pt. 1, box 22, folder 16.
15 Lewis to Thalberg, Nov. 25, 1933, and Feb. 9, 1934, CRC, pt. 1, box 1, folder 11.
16 Memorandum of meeting held on March 9, 1934, CRC, pt. 1, box 1, folder 30.
17 Ibid.
18 Ibid.
19 Lewis to Livingston, May 24, 1933, CRC, pt. 1, box 22, folder 13.

20 Memo of [first] meeting held at Hillcrest Country Club, March 13, 1934, CRC, pt. 1, box 1, folder 8.

21 Ibid. Members of the larger Motion Picture Studio Committee included Thalberg (MGM), Harry Cohn (Columbia), Hennington (Universal), Joseph Schenck (Twentieth Century), Jack Warner (Warner Brothers), Emanuel Cohn (Paramount), Sol Wurtzel (Fox), Pandro Berman (RKO), and Herzbrun (Paramount). Lewis to Gutstadt, March 21, 1934, CRC, pt. 1, box 22, folder 21.

22 Roos, "Under the Crooked Cross," 28.

23 Lewis to Isidore Golden, March 16, 1934, CRC, pt. 1, box 21, folder 18. For industry donations, see correspondence in CRC, pt. 1, box 1, folder 3.

24 The best study of the 1934 campaign is Greg Mitchell, *The Campaign of the Century: Upton Sinclair's Race for Governor of California and the Birth of Media Politics* (New York: Random House, 1992); also see Upton Sinclair, *The Autobiography of Upton Sinclair* (London: W. H. Allen, 1963), 282–91; Leo C. Rosten, *Hollywood: The Movie Colony, The Movie Makers* (New York: Harcourt Brace, 1941), 134–38.

25 The March-Thalberg exchange is quoted in Kyle Crichton, *Total Recoil* (New York: Doubleday, 1960), 245–46. For movie industry salaries, see "Loew's Inc.," *Fortune*, Aug. 1939, in *American Film Industry*, ed. Tino Balio (Madison: University of Wisconsin Press, 1976), 286; Neal Gabler, *An Empire of Their Own: How the Jews Invented Hollywood* (New York: Crown, 1989), 316.

26 See Lewis-Wittenberg correspondence in CRC, pt. 1, box 2, folder 4.

7. Inside the Fascist Front

1 House Resolution 198, 73rd Cong., 2nd sess., 1934.

2 John Schmidt, report, Sept. 15, 1933, CRC, pt. 1, box 19, folder 11.

3 For a biography of Pelley, see Beekman, *William Dudley Pelley*.

4 Pelley first described this extraordinary evening in William Dudley Pelley, "Seven Minutes in Eternity—The Amazing Experience that Made Me Over," *American Magazine*, March 1929, and later in an expanded book-length version: William Dudley Pelley, *Seven Minutes in Eternity with the Aftermath* (New York: Galahad, 1932). Quotes are taken from Harold Lavine, *Fifth Column in America* (New York: Doubleday, Doran, 1940), 171–72; Mitch Horowitz, *Occult America: The Secret History of How Mysticism Shaped Our Nation* (New York: Bantam, 2009), 178; Beekman, *Pelley,* 53–55.

5 *American Magazine* had 2.2 million subscribers. Beekman, *Pelley,* 54–55.

6 William Dudley Pelley, *The Door to Revelation* (Asheville, NC: Pelley, 1939), quoted in Horowitz, *Occult America*, 181; subsequent quotes are in *Liberation*, Feb. 18, 1933.

7 The Silver Shirts' organizational structure and uniforms are discussed in Beekman, *Pelley*, 80–82.

8 *Silver Ranger*, Jan. 17, 31, 1934.

9 William Dudley Pelley, *No More Hunger: The Compact Plan of the Christian Commonwealth* (1933); initial quote appeared in *Silver Ranger*, Jan. 17, 1934; Pelley, *No More Hunger*, quoted in Beekman, *Pelley*, 83; [HUAC Investigator] #89, report, "Pelley," March 7, 1934, Investigator Reports, NA.

10 Report of Alice and John Schmidt for Dec. 10, 1933, CRC, pt. 1, box 8, folder 6.

11 Ibid. From mid-1933 to the end of 1935, national membership in the Silver Shirts rose from 800 to approximately 15,000, with an additional 75,000 nonaffiliated sympathizers. Beekman, *Pelley*, 100–102.

12 Henry Allen to Representative Charles Kramer, U.S. Congressman, Aug. 2, 1934, folder "Allen-Carroll," RG 233, box 367 (HM FY 98), entry 7, Correspondence of Representative Charles Kramer, National Archives (hereafter Corresp. Kramer, NA).

13 For accounts of what was known as the "Business Plot," see Jules Archer, *The Plot to Seize the White House* (Portland, OR: Hawthorn, 1973); Hans Schmidt, *Maverick Marine: General Smedley D. Butler and the Contradictions of American Military History* (Lexington: University Press of Kentucky, 1998); U.S. House of Representatives, *Investigation of Nazi Propaganda Activities*; *New York Times*, Nov. 21, 1934, and Feb. 16, 1935.

14 By February 1934, the Los Angeles county and state Disabled American Veterans had endorsed the creation of a secret investigative committee to continue the work begun by Lewis and the local DAV in August 1933. Leon Lewis to Richard Gutstadt, Feb. 10, 1934, CRC, pt. 1, box 22, folder 20. For Clairville's background, see notes in CRC, pt. 1, box 5, folder 23.

15 Clairville, report, Feb. 19, 1934, CRC, pt. 1, box 5, folder 24.

16 Clairville, report, Feb. 28, 1934, CRC, pt. 1, box 5, folder 24.

17 White's background is taken from information in ancestry.com; Leon Lewis to Mrs. E. M. Lazard, Aug. 6, 1934, CRC, pt. 1, box 10, folder 10.

18 Clairville, report, Feb. 28; Clairville, report, March 8, 1934, CRC, pt. 1, box 5, folder 25.

19 Clairville, report, March 21, 1934, CRC, pt. 1, box 6, folder 1.

20 Leon Lewis, meeting with Mark White, March 21, 1934, CRC, pt. 1, box 10, folder 11; Clairville to Lewis, March 24, 1934, CRC, pt. 1, box 6, folder 1.

21 Mark L. White, report, March 20, 1934; Lewis meeting with White, March 21, 1934, both CRC, pt. 1, box 10, folder 11.

22 Lewis meeting with White.

23 Ibid.

24 White, report, March 22, 1934, CRC, pt. 1, box 10, folder 11.

25 Clairville, report, March 29, 1934, CRC, pt. 1, box 6, folder 1; White, report, April 7, 1934, CRC, pt. 1, box 10, folder 14.

26 Clairville, report, March 23, 1934, CRC, pt. 1, box 6, folder 1.

27 Clairville, verbal report, March 8, 1934, CRC, pt. 1, box 5, folder 25; Clairville, report, March 29, 1934, CRC, pt. 1, box 6, folder 1. For McCord's background as a machine gun battalion commander, see Clairville, report, April 9, 1934, CRC, pt. 1, box 6, folder 2. For Fowler's membership in the KKK and projected army size, see Clairville, reports, March 14 and 15, 1934, CRC, pt. 1, box 5, folder 25.

28 William F. Hynes to E. B. Cornnell, April 25, 1934, CRC, pt. 1, box 30, folder 7.

29 Clairville, report, March 30, 1934, CRC, pt. 1, box 6, folder 1.

30 Clairville, reports, March 26 and April 4, 1934, CRC, pt. 1, box 6, folders 1 and 2.

31 For a fuller report of the special edition, see Jewish Telegraphic Agency, April 22, 1934. For Clairville's *Silver Ranger* work, see Clairville, report, April 4, 1934, CRC, pt. 1, box 6, folder 2; White, report, April 4, 1934, CRC, pt. 1, box 10, folder 11.

32 Jewish Telegraphic Agency, April 22, 1934.

33 White, report, April 12, 1934, CRC, pt. 1, box 10, folder 14; Clairville, report, April 19, 1934, CRC, pt. 1, box 6, folder 3.

34 Clairville, reports, Feb. 19 and March 17, 1934, CRC, pt. 1, box 5, folders 24 and 25.

35 Clairville, reports, April 24, 27, 24, 1934, CRC, pt. 1, box 6, folder 3.

36 Clairville, report, April 25, 1934, CRC, pt. 1, box 6, folder 3.

37 Richard Gid Powers, *Secrecy and Power: The Life of J. Edgar Hoover* (New York: Free Press, 1988); FBI website, "A Byte out of History: 70 Years Ago Rise of Fascism Leads to FBI Casework," www.fbi.gov/news/stories/2004/may/amernazi_050704.

38 "Reminiscences of Henry P. Dolan," 11, 6.

39 See Robert A. Bowen to J. Edgar Hoover, Jan. 7, 1921, RG 65, reel 926 (BS 212657), Investigative Case Files, NA; also see Steven J. Ross, *Working-Class Hollywood: Silent Film and the Shaping of Class in America* (Princeton, NJ: Princeton University Press, 1998), 8, 9, 81, 127, 144; Steven J. Ross, *Hollywood Left and Right: How Movie Stars Shaped American Politics* (New York: Oxford University Press, 2011), 3, 11, 27, 171.

40 F to Capt. Hynes, memo, Sept. 18, 1933, CRC, pt. 1, box 30, folder 7; memorandum No. 14, "Re: Officer Tate," May 10, 1934, CRC, pt. 1, box 2, folder 11.

8. HUAC Comes to Town

1 Richard Gutstadt to Leon Lewis, March 29, 1934 CRC, pt. 1, box 22, folder 22; "Reminiscences of Samuel Dickstein," 29–30.

2 Leon Lewis to Sigmund Livingston, July 13, 1934, CRC, pt. 1, box 22, folder 25. Emphasis Lewis's.

3 Charles Kramer to R. Robert Carroll, May 5, 1934, RG 233, box 367, Corresp. Kramer, NA.

4 Carroll to Kramer, May 20, 14, 1934, Corresp. Kramer, NA.

5 *Los Angeles Times*, May 12, 1934.

6 Robert Carroll to Committee on Un-American Activities, May 15, 1934, and Carroll to Kramer, May 30, 1934, Corresp. Kramer, NA.

7 Kramer to Carroll, June 2, 1934, Corresp. Kramer, NA.

8 Carroll to Kramer, May 22, 1934, Corresp. Kramer, NA.

9 Kramer to Carroll, May 31, 1934; for Lucitt's background, see Carroll to Kramer, May 28, 1934, both Corresp. Kramer, NA.

10 Carroll to Kramer, May 27, 1934; for Spalione's background, see Carroll to Kramer, May 30, 1934, both Corresp. Kramer, NA.

11 Carroll to Kramer, May 29, 1934, folder "Telegrams: Carroll and Kramer," Corresp. Kramer, NA. Kramer changed his mind and told Carroll he could let Sackett read his reports.

12 John McCormack to R. Robert Carroll, to William F. Lucitt, Mrs. Florence Shreve, and to Emile Normile, June 13, 1934, folder "Rich Rollins," RG 233, box 366, Investigator Reports, NA.

13 Emile Normile, report to Committee, June 28, 1934, folder "Emile Normile," Investigator Reports, NA.

14 William Lucitt to John McCormack, July 17, 1934, folder "Florence D. Shreve-Rowan, Reports of William F. Lucitt," Investigator Reports, NA.

15 Florence Shreve, report to the Committee [June 28, 1934], Investigator Reports, NA.

16 Carroll to Committee, Report for the Week Ending June 16, 1934, Corresp. Kramer, NA.

17 Shreve Report to the Committee [July 7, 1934], folder "Shreve-Rowan," Investigator Reports, NA; Carroll to the Committee, July 14, 1934, Corresp. Kramer, NA.

18 Carroll to the Committee, July 1, 1934, Corresp. Kramer, NA; Shreve Report to the Committee [July 12, 1934], folder "Shreve-Rowan," Investigator Reports, NA.

19 Walter Clairville, report, May 30, 1934, CRC, pt. 1, box 6, folder 5.

20 Clairville, reports, May 28 and June 9, 1934, CRC, pt. 1, box 6, folders 5 and 6.

21 Lewis to Gutstadt, May 31, 1934, CRC, pt. 1, box 22, folder 24.

22 Clairville, reports, June 18 and 25, 1934, CRC, pt. 1, box 6, folder 7.

23 Clairville, report, July 24, 1934, CRC, pt. 1, box 6, folder 9; Carroll to the Committee, July 10, 1934, Corresp. Kramer, NA.

24 Carroll to the Committee, June 27, 1934, Corresp. Kramer, NA; Clairville, report, July 24, 1934, CRC, pt. 1, box 6, folder 9. For Demmler's background, see Carroll to the Committee, July 15–21, inclusive [1934], Corresp. Kramer, NA; Clairville, report, June 9, 1934, CRC, pt. 1, box 6, folder 6.

25 F. P. Randolph to Mr. Emile Normile, July 5, 1934, folder "Rich Rollins," Special Committee on Un-American Activities on Nazi Propaganda, RG 233, box 358: NA; the same letter was sent to William Lucitt. Shreve received hers on August 10. Telegram F. P. Randolph to Florence Shreve, Aug. 10, 1934, RG 233, box 359: entry 1, Administrative, entry 2, Draft of Final Report, NA.

26 Carroll to the Committee, July 14, 1934, Corresp. Kramer, NA.

27 Clairville, reports, July 23 and 26, 1934, CRC, pt. 1, box 6, folder 9.

28 Clairville, report, Aug. 1, 1934, CRC, pt. 1, box 6, folder 10.

29 John McCormack to Charles Kramer, circa July 20, 1934, Corresp. Kramer, NA.

30 Herman Schwinn, testimony, RG 233, box 361, Entry 3: folder Aug. 6, 1934, NA; Hans Winterhalder, testimony, NA.

31 For suspicions that Davis and/or Hynes was passing on information, see Carroll to Kramer, July 30, 1934, Corresp. Kramer, NA. For evidence presented to HUAC by the L.A. Police Department, see U.S. House of Representatives, *Investigation of Nazi Propaganda . . .* , 94.

32 Hays HUAC testimony quoted in babel.hathitrust.org/cgi/pt?id=mdp.39015010224 403;view=1up;seq=1062; second quote in *New York Times*, Aug. 8, 1934.

33 *New York Times*, Aug. 5, 1934.

34 For Gray's quote, see babel.hathitrust.org/cgi/pt?id=mdp.39015010224403;view=1u p;seq=1075; for Clairville's testimony, see babel.hathitrust.org/cgi/pt?id=mdp.39015 010224403;view=1up;seq=1078. White's testimony can be found at babel.hathitrust .org/cgi/pt?id=mdp.39015010224403;view=1up;seq=1082. For press coverage of San Diego Silver Shirts and their efforts to overthrow the government, see *New York Times*, Aug. 5 and 8, 1934; *Los Angeles Times*, Aug. 7 and 8, 1934; *Atlanta Constitution*, Aug. 8, 1934; *Washington Post*, Aug. 6, 1934; and *Wall Street Journal*, Aug. 9, 1934.

35 *Los Angeles Times*, Aug. 8, 1934.

36 *New York Times*, Aug. 5, 1934.

37 *New York Times*, Aug. 9 and 10, 1934.

38 Lucitt to John McCormack, July 5, 17, 1934, Lucitt Report to Committee on Un-American Activities, folder "Shreve-Rowan—Reports of William F. Lucitt," Investigator Reports, NA. Only the *New York Times* reported the Gyssling-Riemer check incident. *New York Times*, Aug. 8, 1934.

39 Samuel Dickstein to John McCormack, Aug. 6, 1934, folder "Holden-Kramer," Corresp. Kramer, NA.

40 [Leon Lewis], "Memorandum No. 20," Sept. 28, 1934, CRC, pt. 1, box 2, folder 11.

41 Lewis's suggestions were laid out in a detailed memorandum. "Memorandum No. 18: Recommendations for Legislation," Sept. 13, 1934, CRC, pt. 1, box 2, folder 11; also see Lewis to Judge Harry Hollzer, Sept. 11, 1934, CRC, pt. 1, box 1, folder 13.

42 Committee report quoted in *New York Times*, Feb. 16, 1935. Congress passed the Foreign Registration Act on June 6, 1938.

9. The Most Charming Nazi in Los Angeles

1 Information on Gyssling's life is taken from Mrs. Angelica Gyssling McNally, telephone interview by author, July 15, 2015, and interview in person by author, Aug. 11, 2015, Morro Bay, CA; "Georg Gyssling," translated from German, translate.google .com/translate?hl=en&sl=de&u=https://de.wikipedia.org/wiki/Georg_Gyssling &prev=search; Georg Gyssling, in Bernd Isphording, Gerhard Keiper, and Martin Kröger, eds., *Biographisches Handbuch des deutschen Auswärtigen Dienstes, 1871–1945 [Biographical Manual of the German Foreign Service, 1871–1945]* (Paderborn: F. Schöningh, 2000), 2:141–42; Dr. Georg Gyssling, Freilassing, Upper Bavaria, Schlustr. 5 to the CID Headquarters, Linz, Upper Austria, Sept. 24, 1948, Attachment to "Memorandum Report," Jan. 19, 1949, Criminal Investigation Division, U.S. Forces in Austria, Linz Office, Subject: Jeritza Estate, Records of the Property Control Branch of the U.S. Allied Commission for Austria (USACA), 1945–1950, from "NARA DN 1929. Cases and reports, claims processed by, and general records of the Property Control Commission for Austria (USACA) Section, 1945–1950," in fold3.com. Information on Gyssling is also taken from his personnel files and correspondence in the Politisches Archiv des Auswärtigen Amts (Political Archives of the German Foreign Office; hereafter cited as PA-AA), Berlin.

2 *Los Angeles Times*, Feb. 15, 1932; www.sports-reference.com/olympics/athletes/gy/georg -gyssling-1.html.

3 Luther told his superiors, "I have ordered Gyssling by now to go to Los Angles, because it is necessary that he takes quick actions in 'film business-matters.'" Luther to AA [German Foreign Office], concerning delegation of Gyssling, May 17, 1933, Georg Gyssling personnel file, vol. 5077, 406, PA-AA. For Luther's background, see Diamond, *Nazi Movement*, 105.

4 *Los Angeles Examiner*, June 20, 1933. For Struve and the Einsteins, see *Los Angeles Times*, March 3, 1932, Jan. 1, March 12, 1933.

5 *Los Angeles Examiner*, June 20, 1933.

6 Gyssling letter to *Los Angeles Record* is quoted in Jewish Telegraphic Agency, Aug. 31, 1933.

7 *Los Angeles Times*, March 17, 1939.

8 *Los Angeles Times*, June 11, 1939. I base my argument about Gyssling's social popularity upon my reading of *Los Angeles Times* gossip and society columns from 1933 to 1941. This was the paper of record for the city's social and political elite, and its columnists gushed over Gyssling in a way unlike any other diplomat living in Los Angeles during those years. I found few Jewish names among the lists of guests attending high-profile social events held during Gyssling's time in Los Angeles.

9 *Los Angeles Times*, April 1, 3, July 4, 1934.

10 *Los Angeles Times*, Aug. 26, 1934.

11 Quote is from Gyssling to AA [German Foreign Office], April 27, 1936, Gyssling personnel file, vol. 5078, 75–76, PA-AA. Ingrid was in the sanatorium from Sept. 2, 1935, to Feb. 12, 1936; ibid., 79.

12 *Los Angeles Times,* May 5, 1935, and Dec. 15, 1934.

13 Report on Miss Josephine Alderman, fiancée of Hans Wolfram, Dec. 19, 1940, CRC, pt. 2, box 103, folder 20. For Alderman's salons at Gyssling's home, *Los Angeles Times*, Oct. 5, 1935.

14 [Los Angeles] *B'nai B'rith Messenger*, Oct. 27, 1933, and April 27, 1934.

15 Ralph Heinzen, Paris correspondent of United Press, quoted in "Foreword," 3, in *Summary Report on Activities of Nazi Groups and Their Allies in Southern California*, box 10, Joseph Roos Papers (hereafter cited as *Summary Report*).

16 Ibid., 4.

17 Goebbels quoted in Urwand, *Collaboration*, 114.

18 Goebbels quoted in Thomas Doherty, *Hollywood and Hitler, 1933–1939* (New York: Columbia University Press, 2013), 19. For production statistics and the growth of Hollywood, see Ross, *Working-Class Hollywood*, 115–42.

19 Goebbels quoted in Harry Waldman, *Nazi Films in America, 1933–1942* (Jefferson, NC: McFarland, 2008), 5. Statistics on German nationals and those of German descent are taken from ibid., 8. For an overview of Nazi films and newsreels shown in the United States, see ibid. and Doherty, *Hollywood and Hitler*.

20 Accounts of Goebbels's and the German campaign against Hollywood can be found in Michael E. Birdwell, *Celluloid Soldiers: Warner Bros.'s Campaign Against Nazism* (New York: NYU Press, 1999); David Welky, *The Moguls and the Dictators: Hollywood and the Coming of World War II* (Baltimore: Johns Hopkins, 2008); Doherty, *Hollywood and Hitler*; and Urwand, *Collaboration*.

21 Urwand, *Collaboration*, 48.

22 For further discussion of the film, see *Los Angeles Times*, Nov. 25, 1933; and Urwand, *Collaboration*, 55–58, 74.

23 Quoted in Doherty, *Hollywood and Hitler*, 69. See also Georg Gyssling to Columbia Pictures, Sept. 11, 1933, *Below the Sea* file, Production Code Administration, Motion Picture Producers Association, Margaret Herrick Library, Beverly Hills, CA (hereafter PCA).

24 Frederick Herron to James Wingate, Dec. 7, 1933, *The House of Rothschild* file, PCA.

25 Quoted in Urwand, *Collaboration*, 57.

26 Cooper C. Graham, "'Olympia' in America, 1938: Leni Riefenstahl, Hollywood, and the Kristallnacht," *Historical Journal of Film, Radio, and Television*, 13, no. 4 (1993): 440.

27 For statistics, see Welky, *Moguls and the Dictators*, 15–16.

28 Lewis had been monitoring films in Chicago since before World War I; for his early activities in Los Angeles, see Richard Gutstadt to Leon Lewis, May 9, 1932, CRC, pt. 1, box 22, folder 12.

29 Gutstadt to Lewis, July 31, 1933, CRC, pt. 1, box 22, folder 13.

30 Mayer quoted in Urwand, *Collaboration*, 74.

31 Lewis to Joseph Schenck, Dec. 20, 1933, CRC, pt. 1, box 22, folder 18.

32 Leon Lewis to Rabbi Edgar Magnin, Nov. 25, 1933, CRC, pt. 1, box 1, folder 27; McFadden quoted in *Jewish Telegraphic Agency*, Jan. 28, 1934; for Karloff, see Lewis

Memorandum, Nov. 29, 1933, CRC, pt. 1, box 1, folder 27. Ben Urwand is the historian who has offered a very different, inaccurate, and ahistorical portrait of Gyssling and his relation to the moguls.

33 Eyeman, *Lion of Hollywood*, 343.

34 For a copy of the 1934 PCA Code, see censorshipinfilm.wordpress.com/resources /production-code-1934/.

35 *Los Angeles Times*, Jan. 17, 1934.

36 Gyssling to German consul general, San Francisco, Sept. 20, 1933, Gyssling personnel file, "Politische und Kulturelle Propaganda in den Vereinigten Staaten von Amerika," vol. 22, R 80308, K269260–61, PA-AA.

37 Gyssling to the [Washington, D.C.] embassy, Aug. 8, 1934, in Gyssling personnel file, R 80314, K269944–48, PA-AA. For Gyssling's reports of threats, see *New York Times*, Aug. 9, 1934; *B'nai B'rith Messenger*, Aug. 10, 1934.

38 John Schmidt, report, Sept. 1, 1933, CRC, pt. 1, box 8, folder 14. For rumors of Gyssling having Jewish relatives, see Schmidt, report, Aug. 30, 1933, undated but circa Aug. 20, 1933, CRC, pt. 1, box 7, folder 18.

39 *Summary Report*, 700.

40 Gyssling to German embassy, Oct. 12, 1935, "Politische und Kulturelle Propaganda," vol. 27, R 80319, pp. K270573-82, PA-AA.

41 Conley, "Interview of Capt. Hynes."

42 Testimony of Ernst Wilhelm Bohle at Nuremberg, Germany, Sept. 26, 1945, copy in folder "Ernest Bohle—head of AO," box 80, Charles Higham Collection, Cinematic Arts Library, University of Southern California (hereafter cited as Higham Collection).

43 McNally, interview, Aug. 11, 2015. In his *Collaboration*, Ben Urwand has written the latest and most scathing portrait of Gyssling. For other works dealing with Gyssling, see Doherty, *Hollywood and Hitler*; Welky, *Moguls and the Dictators*; Birdwell, *Celluloid Soldiers*. After finding a character reference written by Brigadier General Julius Klein to Nuremberg investigators in December 1947, I contacted Angelica Gyssling McNally and interviewed her first by phone, then through an e-mail exchange, and finally in person. As the son of two Holocaust survivors, I was prepared to think the worst of her father. Knowing that most daughters would want to paint a positive picture of a parent, I did not tell her what I knew about her father but instead asked vague questions such as "Does the name Julius Klein ring a bell?" "What happened to your mother? Did she leave because she could not practice medicine in the United States?" At every point, her answers fleshed out the skeleton of facts and suppositions I had already accumulated. Every important piece of information she gave me and that I use here can be verified by documents. It is worth noting that from July 1950 to March 1952, Angelica worked as a stenographer for American Military Intelligence in Austria. On March 8, 1952, she married Lt. Colonel Lawrence McNally, who had just finished his assignment working for U.S. Air Force Intelligence. For Angelica's postwar work for Military Intelligence (G2) and marriage to Lt. Col. McNally, see https://www.cia.gov/library/readingroom/docs/DOC_0005359219 .pdf. For Klein's character reference for Georg Gyssling, see Julius Klein, National Commander, Jewish War Veterans of the USA, To Whom It May Concern, Dec. 16, 1947, www.fold3.com/image/311346468.

44 Mrs. McNally was flabbergasted when I told her a *Los Angeles Times* article referred to her mother as an orthopedist. Information about Gyssling's background was taken from my three encounters with his daughter: a preliminary telephone interview on July 15, 2015; e-mail correspondence on July 28, 2015; and a personal daylong visit at her home in Morro Bay, CA, on August 11, 2015. Mrs. McNally passed away on January 25, 2016.

45 McNally, interview, July 15, 2015; McNally, correspondence, July 28, 2015. Ingrid Horn would later remarry and spend most of her time in South America. She apparently died of cancer in 1943.

46 McNally, interview, July 15, 2015; second and third quotes from McNally, interview, August 11, 2015; *Los Angeles Times,* April 2, 1937.

47 McNally, interview, July 15, 2015.

48 Gyssling to German consul, San Francisco, Dec. 18, 1934, "Politische und Kulturelle Propaganda," vol. 23, R 80315, K455349–52, PA-AA.

49 *B'nai B'rith Messenger,* Nov. 17, 1933.

50 Ibid., June 1, 1934.

51 McNally, interview, August 11, 2015.

52 McNally, interview, July 15, 2015.

53 *Summary Report,* 1011; Leon Lewis to Sigmund Livingston, Dec. 7, 1933, CRC, pt. 1, box 22, folder 17; Lewis to Livingston, Dec 7, 1933, CRC, pt. 1, box 22, folder 17.

54 Georg Gyssling to Baron von Reichenberg, Nov. 7, 1933, quoted in *Summary Report,* 1013.

55 Ibid. A copy of the letter can be found in ibid., 1011–15.

56 Note by the German Foreign Office, March 30, 1934, "Politische und Kulturelle Propaganda," vol. 18, R 80310, PA-AA. For fears about the financial impact of banning *The Prize Fighter and the Lady,* see F. L. D. Strengholt to German Foreign Office, March 15, 1934, in "Politische und Kulturelle Propaganda," R 80310, K454505–06, PA-AA.

57 Lewis to Livingston, Dec 7, 1933, CRC, pt. 1, box 22, folder 17.

58 Klein, To Whom It May Concern, Dec. 16, 1947, www.fold3.com/image/311346468/.

59 Ibid. Biographical information on Julius Klein is drawn from *New York Times,* April 9, 1984; Jonathan S. Wiesen, "Germany's PR Man: Julius Klein and the Making of Transatlantic Memory," in *Coping with the Nazi Past: West German Debates on Nazism and Generational Conflict,* ed. Philipp Gassert and Alan E. Steinweis (New York: Berghahn, 2007), 294–308; biography of Julius Klein, en.wikipedia.org/wiki/Julius_Klein; Julius Klein Papers, Library of Congress, Washington, D.C.; and correspondence in CRC files.

60 McNally, interview, July 15, 2015.

61 McNally, correspondence, July 28, 2015; McNally, interview, Aug. 11, 2015.

62 "Interview with Vice Consul Grah," Oct. 4, 1935, CRC, pt. 1, box 15, folder 27.

10. Spy and Divide

1 The proclamation appeared in the *Los Angeles Times* on September 29, 1935. A copy can be found in "Exhibits—Nazi Propaganda in Doheny Memorial Library, 1990," box 6, Roos Papers.

2 For a further discussion of the Nuremberg laws, see Bernstein, *Swastika Nation*, 60.

3 L.A. Police Department, Office of Intelligence Bureau, Metropolitan Division, [unsigned], to Capt. William F. Hynes, "Re: American Nationalist Party, printing and circulating a Proclamation against the Jewish People," Nov. 8, 1935, CRC, pt. 1, box 30, folder 7.

4 Joe Roos left behind an unfinished autobiography as well as numerous oral interviews. However, like many people who write their memoirs or are interviewed later in life, he got a number of dates confused. I have corrected as many of the timing errors as possible. For Roos on his early life, see Roos, "Outline for Beginning of Book in Byographic Style," Oct. 22, 1990, box 7, Roos Papers.

5 Ibid.

6 Ibid.

7 Roos, "Draft 3 of Chapter 2," 4. Roos's various manuscript drafts and oral histories offer slightly different dates as to when he first reported Nazi activities to Roy Keehn.

8 Joseph Roos, Shoah testimony #2996, June 7, 1995, USC Shoah Foundation Visual History Archive Online, http://vhaonline.usc.edu/viewingPage.aspx?testimony ID=3110&returnIndex=0#. For his training with Marshall, also see Leonard Roos, interview by author, Los Angeles, Nov. 2, 2012.

9 Biographical information about Julius Klein is drawn from Roos, "Outline for Beginning of Book." Biography of Klein, en.wikipedia.org/wiki/Julius_Klein; Profile of Julius Klein, National Museum of American Jewish Military History, www .nmajmh.org/exhibitions/juliusKlein.php; Julius Klein Papers, Library of Congress, Washington, D.C.; *New York Times*, April 9, 1984; Jewish Telegraphic Agency, Nov. 13, 1932, April 4, 1933; Jonathan S. Wiesen, "Germany's PR Man: Julius Klein and the Making of Transatlantic Memory," in Gassert and Steinweis, *Coping with the Nazi Past: West German Debates on Nazism and Generational Conflict*, 294–308.

10 Roos, "Outline for Beginning of Book"; "Confidential Report: Subject: Nazi Activities To: The Assistant Chief of Staff, G-2, Sixth Corps Area, 1819 Pershing Rd., Chicago, Illinois, from Joseph C. Hattie, Lt Col, Infantry," Nov. 29, 1933, Special Committee on Un-American Activities on Nazi Propaganda, HR 77A-F30.1, RG 233, box 358, NA.

11 Ibid.

12 Joseph Roos, "Chapter Headings—For Identification Only," box 7, folder "Outline for Book, 'Under the Crooked Cross,'" Roos Papers; Roos, oral history interview.

13 *New York Times*, March 24, 1934.

14 Roos, "Chapter Headings."

15 Michael Melnick, interview by author, April 27, 2016, Playa Vista, CA; Roos, interview by author.

16 Pitt, interview by author.

17 Roos, oral history interview, 10 and 42, box 6, Roos Papers; Harvey Schecter, interview by author, July 29, 2013, Beverly Hills, CA.

18 Ness's biographical background is drawn from information contained in his testimony before the House Un-American Activities Committee on October 5, 1939; archive.org/stream/investigationofu193909unit/investigationofu193909unit_djvu .txt; Neil Ness to Leon Lewis, Jan. 13, 1936, CRC, pt. 1, box 6, folder 16; for his visits to Europe in 1918–20, see ancestry.com.

19 Given the fervently anti-Communist character of HUAC, it is not surprising that Ness omitted his Soviet experiences from his testimony, especially his self-proclaimed links to the OGPU. Neil Ness to Leon Lewis, Jan. 13, 1936, CRC, pt. 1, box 6, folder 16.

20 Neil Ness, "Nazi Agents," book proposal, ch. 1, CRC, pt. 1, box 6, folder 17.

21 Ness to Lewis, Jan. 13, 1936, CRC, pt. 1, box 6, folder 16; Ness, "Nazi Agents." Ship records indicate that Ness sailed from Bremen to New York on May 26, 1932, aboard the *Europa*, ancestry.com.

22 Roos, oral history interview, 35, box 6, Roos Papers; Neil Ness, "The American Entente," published May 1933, CRC, pt. 1, box 6, folder 19. For Goldberg's correspondence with Lewis, see Miles Goldberg to Leon Lewis, Dec. 22, 1933, CRC, pt. 1, box 22, folder 18.

23 Roos, oral history interview, 35 and 36.

24 Ness, report, March 6, 1936, CRC, pt. 1, box 6, folder 16; Roos, Shoah testimony.

25 Leon Lewis to Richard Gutstadt, Dec. 21, 1935; Gutstadt to Lewis, telegram, Dec. 24, 1935, CRC, pt. 1, box 23, folder 8.

26 Ness, confidential report, Dec. 26, 1935, CRC, pt. 1, box 6, folder 20.

27 House of Representatives, "Investigation of Un-American Propaganda Activities in the United States," 5491, archive.org/stream/investigationofu193909unit/investigationofu193909unit_djvu.txt.

28 For estimates of native-born Americans in the Bund, see Hermann Schwinn, interview, Oct. 2, 1935, CRC, pt. 1, box 11, folder 18. For a discussion of Bohle, the Auslands Organization, Kuhn, and changing attitudes toward the FNG, see Diamond, *Nazi Movement*; Arthur L. Smith Jr., *The Deutschtum of Nazi Germany and the United States* (The Hague: Martinus Nijhoff, 1965); Alton Frye, *Nazi Germany and the American Hemisphere, 1933–1941* (New Haven, CT: Yale University Press, 1967); Bernstein, *Swastika Nation*.

29 The edict was quoted in *New York Times*, Dec. 25, 1935.

30 The quote is from Camp Siegfried literature; see Bernstein, *Swastika Nation*, 78. By 1939, Nazis had opened twenty-two camps in the United States. Abraham Chapman, *Nazi Penetration in America* (New York: American League for Peace and Democracy, 1939), 16.

31 Ness, report, May 1936, CRC, pt. 1, box 7, folder 1; Charles Slocombe, report, Dec. 30, 1935, CRC, pt. 1, box 14, folder 13.

32 Ness, confidential report, Jan. 3, 1936, CRC, pt. 1, box 6, folder 20.

33 Ness, confidential report, Jan. 9, 1936, CRC, pt. 1, box 6, folder 20.

34 Ness, report, Feb. 11, 1936, CRC, pt. 1, box 6, folder 21.

35 Ness, confidential report, Jan. 15, 1936, CRC, pt. 1, box 6, folder 20.

36 Ness, confidential report, Jan. 23, 1936, CRC, pt. 1, box 6, folder 20; Ness, report, Feb. 11, 1936, CRC, pt. 1, box 6, folder 21.

37 Ness, report, Feb. 22, 1936, CRC, pt. 1, box 14, folder 16.

38 Ness, report, Feb. 11, 1936, CRC, pt. 1, box 18, folder 29.

39 Ness, reports, Feb. 21 and 20, 1936, CRC, pt. 1, box 14, folder 16, and box 6, folder 21.

40 Ness, confidential report, Jan 30, 1936, CRC, pt. 1, box 6, folder 20. For a fuller portrait of Meyerhoffer, see Spivak, *Secret Armies*, 61–64; *Sunday Daily Worker*, March 14, 1937.

41 Ness, report, Feb. 22, 1936, CRC, pt. 1, box 6, folder 21.

42 Julius Klein to Rupert Hughes, Feb. 20, 1936, CRC, pt. 1, box 6, folder 16.

43 Ness, memorandum, Feb. 22, 1936; Ness, report, Feb. 24, 1936, CRC, pt. 1, box 6, folder 16.

44 Ness, report, Feb. 24, 1936.

45 Ness, report, March 2, 1936, CRC, pt. 1, box 6, folder 22.

46 Ness, report, March 5 and 4, 1936, CRC, pt. 1, box 6, folders 16 and 23.

47 Roos, oral history interview, 36, box 6, Roos Papers; Roos, interview by author; Roos, memo, March 12, 1936, CRC 14, folder 17.

48 Ness, report, March 6, 1936, CRC, pt. 1, box 6, folder 23.

49 Slocombe, report, March 24, 1936, CRC, pt. 1, box 9, folder 10.

11. The Plots to Kill the Jews

1 Charles Slocombe, report, Dec. 31, 1935, CRC, pt. 1, box 14, folder 13. Hughes published his threat in a letter that appeared in the Sept. 22, 1935, issue of the *Weckruf.*

2 For Lewis's initial correspondence with Murphy, see Leon Lewis to Owen Murphy, Oct. 27, 29, 1935, CRC, pt. 1, box 30, folder 12. For the KKK's presence in Long Beach, see Burnett, *Prohibition Madness*, 22.

3 John Barr, report, Oct. 29, 1940, CRC, pt. 2, box 32, folder 10.

4 For Charles Slocombe's background, see census records in ancestry.com; "Advertising Flyer for City Water Taxi Company," ca. May 1936, CRC, pt. 1, box 9, folder 4; and sources mentioned in note 2.

5 Slocombe, report, Oct. 1935, CRC, pt. 1, box 14, folder 13.

6 Slocombe, report, Nov. 21, 1935.

7 For Slocombe's precarious economic situation, see Charles Slocombe to Leon Lewis, Jan. 2, 1937, and Leon Lewis to Dr. Lewis Gunther, Oct. 22, 1937, CRC, pt. 1, box 9, folder 4; for marriage and home addresses, see Slocombe entry in ancestry.com.

8 Slocombe, report, Oct. 1935, CRC, pt. 1, box 14, folder 13.

9 Ibid.

10 Ibid.

11 Slocombe, "Report on Meeting of Friends of New Germany," Nov. 7, 1935, CRC, pt. 1, box 9, folder 5.

12 Ibid.

13 Slocombe, report, Nov. 20, 1935, CRC, pt. 1, box 4, folder 13.

14 A. C. Arnold, Badge 1413, to Capt. Warren L. Justin, Commanding Metropolitan Division, "Summary of Investigation: Re: 'Friends of New Germany and Anti-Semitic Proclamation," Nov. 14, 1935, CRC, pt. 1, box 30, folder 6; Slocombe, report, Nov. 21, 1935.

15 All quotes are from Ingram Hughes, *Anti-Semitism: Organized Anti-Jewish Sentiment; A World-Survey* (Los Angeles: American Nationalist, 1934), 75, 85. A copy of this publication can be found at http://babel.hathitrust.org/cgi/pt?view=image;size=100;id=uc1.b4512544;page=root;seq=7. Biographical information is taken from ancestry.com; *Los Angeles Times,* Jan. 3, 1950; L.A. Police Dept. to Hynes, "Re: American Nationalist Party"; "Ingram Hughes," in *Summary Report*, 292–99.

16 Slocombe, report on contact with Hughes, Nov. 21, 1935 [penciled entry misdated: should be November 22], CRC, pt. 1, box 9, folder 5.

17 Information on Allen's criminal background taken from *Summary Report*, 26; ancestry.com; Slocombe, report, Nov. 21, 1935, CRC, pt. 1, box 9, folder 5.

18 *Summary Report*, 376. For Allen's ties to Mexico and the activities of his wife and son, see Walter Clairville, reports, April 3 and 9, 1934, CRC, pt. 1, box 6, folder 2; Clairville, report, April 23, 1934, CRC, pt. 1, box 6, folder 3.

19 H. Allen to R. W. Caspers, June 24, 1935, CRC, pt. 1, box 11, folder 3.

20 John Barr, report, Oct. 29, 1940, CRC, pt. 2, box 32, folder 10; Slocombe, report, Dec. 13, 1935, CRC, pt. 1, box 11, folder 3.

21 Slocombe, report, Nov. 22, 1935, CRC, pt. 1, box 9, folder 5.

22 Slocombe, report, Nov. 23, 1935 (found on p. 2 of Nov. 22 report), CRC, pt. 1, box 9, folder 5.

23 Ibid.; Slocombe, report, Dec. 6, 1935, CRC, pt. 1, box 11, folder 20.

24 Slocombe, reports, Nov. 25, 26, and 29, 1935, CRC, pt. 1, box 11, folder 20.

25 Ibid.

26 Jewish Telegraphic Agency, May 23, 1934. For Hughes's national fascist allies, see Slocombe, report, Dec. 3, 1935, CRC, pt. 1, box 9, folder 6; for Winrod and the Nazis, see Higham, *American Swastika*, 66.

27 Slocombe, report, Nov. 29, 1935, CRC, pt. 1, box 9, folder 5; Slocombe, supplementary report to that of Dec. 4, 1935, CRC, pt. 1, box 9, folder 6.

28 Slocombe, report, Dec. 30, 1935, CRC, pt. 1, box 9, folder 6.

29 Slocombe, report, Jan. 7, 1936, CRC, pt. 1, box 9, folder 7.

30 Slocombe, report, Dec. 31, 1935, CRC, pt. 1, box 14, folder 13.

31 Slocombe, report, Jan. 7, 1936, CRC, pt. 1, box 9, folder 7.

32 Ibid.; Slocombe, report, Jan. 2, 1936, CRC, pt. 1, box 11, folder 21.

33 "*Fortune* Quarterly Survey," *Fortune*, Jan. 1936, 16; Rufus Learsi (Israel Goldberg), "Jews of America," *Fortune*, Feb. 1936; Gallup poll quoted in Eyeman, *Lion of Hollywood*, 343; for Father Coughlin, see Shana Bernstein, *Bridges of Reform*, 111.

34 Slocombe, reports, Jan. 13, Feb. 9, and Jan. 21, 1936, CRC, pt. 1, box 9, folder 7, box 11, folder 21, and box 9, folder 7.

35 Slocombe, report, Jan. 21, 1936, CRC, pt. 1, box 9, folder 7; Ness, report, April 1, 1936, CRC, pt. 1, box 6, folder 24.

36 Slocombe, reports, Feb. 10 and 19, 1936, CRC, pt. 1, box 11, folder 21, and box 9, folder 9.

37 Slocombe, reports, Jan. 13 and 27, 1936, CRC, pt. 1, box 9, folders 7 and 8.

38 Ness, report, Feb. 17, 1936, CRC, pt. 1, box 11, folder 21. See also Ness, report, Jan. 30, 1936, CRC, pt. 1, box 6, folder 20.

39 Slocombe, reports, April 1 and March 19, 1936, CRC, pt. 1, box 9, folders 11 and 10.

40 Slocombe, report, April 13, 1936, CRC, pt. 1, box 11, folder 21.

41 Slocombe, report, Feb. 10, 1936, CRC, pt. 1, box 11, folder 21.

42 Slocombe, report, April 13, 1936.

43 Slocombe, report, Jan. 4, 1936, CRC, pt. 1, box 11, folder 4.

44 For the case and subsequent appeals, see Slocombe, reports, Jan. 30, March 13, and April 14, 1936, CRC, pt. 1, box 11, folder 4; and David Goldman to Leon Lewis, Feb. 5, 1936, CRC, pt. 1, box 11, folder 4.

45 For Allen's illnesses, see Ness, report, April 30, 1936, CRC, pt. 1, box 11, folder 21: Slocombe, reports, May 21, 1936, CRC 9, folder 13.

46 Ness, report, July 9, 1936, CRC, pt. 1, box 7, folder 3.
47 Slocombe, report, Aug. 10, 1936, CRC, pt. 1, box 11, folder 22.
48 Slocombe, report, Aug. 21, 1936, CRC, pt. 1, box 11, folder 22.
49 Ibid.

12. Nazi versus Nazi

1 Neil Ness, reports, March 4 and 21, 1936, CRC, pt. 1, box 14, folder 17, and box 6, folder 23.
2 Ness, report, March 22, 1936, CRC, pt. 1, box 6, folder 23.
3 Burchardi quoted in Joseph Roos, "Contact with German Government and Nazi Party," in *Summary Report*, 43; Ness, report, Dec. 3, 1937, CRC, pt. 1, box 19, folder 3.
4 Julius Klein to Rupert Hughes, Feb. 20, 1936, CRC, pt. 1, box 6, folder 16.
5 Descriptions of Deutsches Haus are drawn from Roos, "Franz Ferenz," unpublished manuscript, chapter 1, 1–3, folder 1 of 2, "Ferenz Manuscript—Complete," box 7, Roos Papers; Joseph Roos, oral history interview by Leonard Pitt and Murray Wood, Dec. 18, 1979, Jan 7 and 28, and Feb. 14, 1980, 73, box 6, Roos Papers; Spivak, *Secret Armies*, 57; Bernstein, *Bridges of Reform*, 104.
6 Ness, report, March 17, 1936, CRC, pt. 1, box 6, folder 23. For a copy of Deutsches Haus payroll records (which include money paid to Schwinn and Klein), see "Deutschen [*sic*] Haus Restaurant, Payroll and time records, 1935–41," box 3, RG 131: Department of Justice/Office of Alien Property, Entry UD 324: Seized Records of the Los Angles Units of the German-American Bund, 1928–1942, NA.
7 Ness, report, March 22, 1936, CRC, pt. 1, box 6, folder 23.
8 Ness, report, Aug. 3, 1936, CRC, pt. 1, box 7, folder 6.
9 Ness, report, April 2, 1936, CRC, pt. 1, box 6, folder 24.
10 Ibid.
11 Ibid.
12 Ibid.
13 Ness, report, April 28, 1936, CRC, pt. 1, box 6, folder 25.
14 Ness, reports, April 12 and 25, 1936, CRC, pt. 1, box 6, folder 24.
15 House of Representatives, "Investigation of Un-American Propaganda Activities," 5497.
16 Leon Lewis to Mendel Silberberg, March 17, 1936, CRC, pt. 1, box 6, folder 16.
17 Ness, report, March 10, 1936, CRC, pt. 1, box 6, folder 16.
18 Ness, report, April 25, 1936, CRC, pt. 1, box 6, folder 24.
19 For official business quote, see Ness, report, May 27, 1936, CRC, pt. 1, box 13, folder 21. For Kendzia, see *Summary Report*, 19.
20 Ness, report, April 11, 1936, CRC, pt. 1, box 6, folder 24.
21 Ness, report, April 12, 1936, CRC, pt. 1, box 6, folder 24.
22 Ness, report, July 15, 1936, CRC, pt. 1, box 19, folder 2.
23 Ness, report, July 15, 1936, CRC, pt. 1, box 7, folder 4.
24 Ness, report, July 26, 1936, CRC, pt. 1, box 19, folder 2.
25 Ness, report, July 9, 1936, CRC, pt. 1, box 7, folder 3.
26 Ness, report, "Special Meeting," July 9, 1936, CRC, pt. 1, box 7, folder 3.
27 Ibid.

28 Ness, report, July 22 and Aug. 15, 1936, CRC, pt. 1, box 7, folder 4, and box 14, folder 3.

29 John Meiggs Ewen, director, Landon Knox Republican Campaign Committee, to Herman Schwinn, Oct. 19, 1936, "Der Schulungsbrief (Reich Schooling Letter) 1936–38 Thru Scrapbook—Political Cartoons, ca. 1930s," RG 131, NA.

30 Ness quoted in Ferenz v. Superior Court, 53 Cal. App. 2d 639 (1942), aw.justia.com /cases/california/calapp2d/53/639.html. For Sachse, see Ness, report, Aug. 6, 1936, CRC, pt. 1, box 18, folder 29; for Demmler, see Ness, report, Aug. 16, 1936, CRC, pt. 1, box 7, folder 7.

31 Ness, report, July 3, 1936, CRC, pt. 1, box 7, folder 3.

32 The drunkenness and rowdiness did not abate over the next several months. See Slocombe, report, Jan. 20, 1937, CRC, pt. 1, box 9, folder 16.

33 Ness, report, July 27, 1936, CRC, pt. 1, box 19, folder 2.

34 Ibid.

35 Ness, reports, Aug. 1 and 15, 1936, CRC, pt. 1, box 7, folders 6 and 7.

36 Ness, report, Aug. 1, 1936; Slocombe, report, Aug. 19, 1936, CRC, pt. 1, box 11, folder 7.

37 Spivak, *Secret Armies*, 74; Ness, report, Aug. 26, 1936, CRC, pt. 1, box 7, folder 7.

38 *Los Angeles Times*, July 4, 12, 1936.

39 Ness, report, Aug. 20, 1936, CRC, pt. 1, box 7, folder 7.

40 Ibid.

41 Ibid.

42 Slocombe, report, Dec. 1, 1935, CRC, pt. 1, box 11, folder 20.

43 Ness, report, Aug. 20, 1936, CRC, pt. 1, box 7, folder 7.

44 Ibid.

45 For Allen's accusations, see Slocombe, report, Aug. 21, 1936, CRC, pt. 1, box 9, folder 13.

46 Ibid.; Ness, report, April 30, 1936, CRC, pt. 1, box 15, folder 16.

47 Ness, report, Sept. 16, 1936, CRC, pt. 1, box 7, folder 8.

48 Ness, report, Sept. 15, 1936, CRC, pt. 1, box 7, folder 8.

49 Ness, reports, Sept. 16 and 18, 1936, CRC, pt. 1, box 7, folder 8.

50 Ness, report, Sept. 18, 1936.

51 Ness, report, Sept. 28, 1936, CRC, pt. 1, box 19, folder 3.

52 Ness, report, Oct. 3, 1936, CRC, pt. 1, box 7, folder 9.

53 Ness, report, Sept. 6, 1936, CRC, pt. 1, box 7, folder 8.

54 Ibid.

55 Ness, report, Sept. 15, 1936.

56 Ness, report, Oct. 20, 1936, CRC, pt. 1, box 19, folder 3.

57 Ibid.

58 Ness, reports, Oct. 16 and Nov. 13, 1936, CRC, pt. 1, box 12, folder 3.

59 Ness, report, Oct. 6, 1936, CRC, pt. 1, box 7, folder 9.

60 www.measuringworth.com/uscompare/relativevalue.php.

13. Silver Shirts, Nazis, and Movie Stars

1 Descriptions of Pelley's speech are taken from Neil Ness, report, July 21, 1936, CRC, pt. 1, box 7, folder 4; Philo, "Mr. Pelley Comes to Town," CRC, pt. 1, box 2, folder 15.

2 Ness, report, July 21, 1936, CRC, pt. 1, box 7, folder 4; Philo, "Mr. Pelley Comes to Town."

3 Ibid.

4 Slocombe, report, Aug. 3, 1936, CRC, pt. 1, box 11, folder 7.

5 *Los Angeles Times*, May 5, 1935. Biographical information about Alexander was drawn from Charles Slocombe, report, Oct. 13, 1936, CRC, pt. 1, box 9, folder 15; Carr, *Hollywood and Anti-Semitism*, 123–24; and Mark A. Vieira, *George Hurrell's Hollywood: Glamour Portraits, 1925–1992* (Philadelphia: Running Press, 2013); http://en .metapedia.org/wiki/Kenneth_D._Alexander; https://en.wikipedia.org/wiki/Kenneth _Alexander_(photographer); ancestry.com; http://broadway.cas.sc.edu/content /kenneth-alexander.

6 Slocombe, report, Oct. 13, 1936, CRC, pt. 1, box 9, folder 15.

7 Kenneth Alexander, "Who's Who in Hollywood—Find the Gentile," *Liberation*, Aug. 14, 1938, 6, 8.

8 Slocombe, report, Aug. 19, 1936, CRC, pt. 1, box 11, folder 7.

9 Schmidt, report, Oct 19, 1933, CRC, pt. 1, box 8, folder 23.

10 Ness, report, April 10, 1936, CRC, pt. 1, box 6, folder 24; Leon Lewis to Fred Pelton, May 27, 1936, CRC, pt. 1, box 1, folder 9. For Schwinn and Paramount, see Ness, report, Aug. 11, 1936, CRC, pt. 1, box 1, folder 3. For further reports about Nazi and Silver Shirt activity in the studios, see Slocombe, reports, April 20 and May 10 and 14, 1936, CRC, pt. 1, box 11, folder 21; "Memo," Feb. 24, 1936, CRC, pt. 1, box 1, folder 6; Ness, report, April 10, 1936, CRC, pt. 1, box 6, folder 24.

11 Slocombe, report, Aug. 19, 1936, CRC, pt. 1, box 11, folder 7. See also Albert Brown to Neil Ness, May 10, 1936, CRC, pt. 1, box 6, folder 2636. Alexander's most prominent film work included Goldwyn's *Street Scene* (1931) and *Roman Scandals* (1933), and Twentieth Century Pictures' *Bulldog Drummond Strikes Back* (1934) and *The Call of the Wild* (1935). The terms "above the line" and "below the line" are used to distinguish creative and craft labor—that is, workers who negotiate their salaries on a project-by-project basis (actors, writers, directors, and so on) versus craft workers whose salaries are determined by studios and/or unions.

12 Memo, Oct. 6, 1936, CRC, pt. 1, box 11, folder 4. For more on Rodríguez, see John L. Spivak, *A Man in His Time* (New York: Horizon, 1967), 407.

13 For an overview of the Los Angeles Nazi, Silver Shirt, and Mexican Gold Shirt connection, see Riess, *Total Espionage*, 64; Spivak, *A Man in His Time*, 407–18; Spivak, *Secret Armies*, 69–82; Ness, report, Oct. 6, 1936, CRC, pt. 1, box 11, folder 4.

14 Ness, report, Sept. 8, 1936, CRC, pt. 1, box 7, folder 8. Lewis received reports from a trusted source that Police Chief Davis and the Los Angeles city prosecutor were sympathetic to the Silver Shirts. Slocombe, report, Sept. 12, 1936, CRC, pt. 1, box 9, folder 14.

15 Slocombe, report, Nov. 16, 1936, CRC, pt. 1, box 9, folder 15. Roosevelt received 27.8 million votes, compared to Landon's 16.7 million.

16 Slocombe, report, Nov. 17, 1936, CRC, pt. 1, box 9, folder 15.

17 Ibid.

18 Edward G. Robinson to Eleanor Roosevelt, Jan. 20, 1957, folder 3, box 37, Edward G. Robinson Collection, Cinematic Arts Library, University of Southern California. For a discussion of Hollywood politics in the 1920s and 1930s, see Ross, *Hollywood Left and Right*.

19 Statistics are taken from Kevin Starr, *The Dream Endures: California Enters the 1940s* (New York: Oxford University Press, 1997), 367. For Hollywood's émigré

community, see Rosten, *Hollywood*; John Russell Taylor, *Strangers in Paradise: The Hollywood Émigrés, 1933–1950* (New York: Holt, Rinehart & Winston, 1983); Otto Friedrich, *City of Nets: A Portrait of Hollywood in the 1940s* (New York: Harper & Row, 1986); and Saverio Giovacchini, *Hollywood Modernism: Film and Politics in the Age of the New Deal* (Philadelphia: Temple University Press, 2001).

20 George Gallup and Claude Robinson, "American Institute of Public Opinion—Surveys, 1935–38," *Public Opinion Quarterly* 2 (July 1938): 388.

21 HANL Executive Committee Statement, June 8, 1936, quoted in *News of the World*, April 10, 1937. For the Los Angeles origins of the anti-Nazi League, see *Los Angeles Times*, Feb. 21, 1934, Aug. 29, 1935.

22 Leo Rosten, oral history review, 1–2, June 1959, Popular Arts Project, Columbia University Oral History Program 1960. In August 1936, the organization changed its name from the Hollywood League Against Nazism to the Hollywood Anti-Nazi League for the Defense of American Democracy.

23 League activities were regularly reported in the *Los Angeles Times* and *New York Times*. The best overviews of the Hollywood Anti-Nazi League can be found in John Cogley, *Report on Blacklisting, I: Movies* (n.p., 1956), 35–40; Birdwell, *Celluloid Soldiers*; Welky, *Moguls and the Dictators*; Doherty, *Hollywood and Hitler*; Giovacchini, *Hollywood Modernism*; and Carr, *Hollywood and Anti-Semitism*.

24 Leon Lewis to Sydney Wallach, June 4, 1936, CRC, pt. 1, box 29, folder 26; "Memo October 11, 1936," CRC, pt. 1, box 29, folder 27. For Lewis's work with the HANL, see "Memo October 11, 1936"; "Agenda," April 16 and 27, 1937, CRC, pt. 1, box 1, folder 13; and correspondence and memos in CRC, pt. 1, box 29, folder 26, through box 30, folder 2.

25 Slocombe, report, Oct. 12, 1936, CRC, pt. 1, box 9, folder 15.

26 "Hollywood Anti-Nazi Meeting," typescript report, Oct. 20, 1936, CRC, pt. 1, box 29, folder 27. See also *Los Angeles Times*, Oct 21, 1936.

27 *Los Angeles Times*, Oct. 24, 1937.

28 *New York Times*, Nov. 30, 1938. For Mussolini's visit, see *New York Times*, Sept. 26, 1937.

29 Slocombe, reports, Jan. 12 and Feb. 23, 1937, CRC, pt. 1, box 9, folder 16.

30 Slocombe, report, Jan. 20, 1937, CRC, pt. 1, box 9, folder 16.

31 *Sunday Worker*, March 7 and 14, 1937.

32 For a full copy of Spivak's March 1936 interview with Schwinn, see typed report accompanying correspondence, John L. Spivak to Leon Lewis, March 7, 1936, CRC, pt. 1, box 30, folder 31. See also *Sunday Worker*, March 14, 1937.

33 *Sunday Worker*, March 14, 1937; *Daily Worker*, March 25, 1937.

34 Slocombe, report, March 25, 1937, CRC, pt. 1, box 11, folder 5.

35 *Hollywood Now* and Jones quoted in Doherty, *Hollywood and Hitler*, 107.

36 *New York Times*, July 28, 1937; *Los Angeles Examiner*, Nov. 19, 1937.

14. Slaughter the Hollywood Jews

1 Roos, "Contact with German Government," 59.

2 Frederic Sondern Jr., "Captain Fritz: Consul Wiedemann, Hitler's Old Superior Officer, Runs into Trouble Selling Nazism to West," *Life*, June 26, 1939.

3 Quoted in *Los Angeles Times*, Sept. 10, 1937.

4 For a description of the day's events, see Charles Slocombe, report, Sept. 13, 1937, CRC, pt. 1, box 9, folder 20. For a brief biography of von Killinger, see https://en.wikipedia.org/wiki/Manfred_Freiherr_von_Killinger.

5 Slocombe, report, Sept. 13, 1937, CRC, pt. 1, box 9, folder 20.

6 Ibid.

7 Information about Schwinn's German trip can be found in News Research Service, *News Letter* no. 53 (Nov. 9, 1939), box 6, folder "Joseph Roos: Exhibits CSUN, Promotion," Roos Papers; Roos, "Chapter 1: Herman Schwinn-Pacific Coast Leader of the Volksbund," *Summary Report*. For Dieckhoff's view on the German American Bund, see Ambassador Dieckhoff to AA (Under Secretary of State, Count Hans-Georg Mackensen), Nov. 24, 1937, 247–254, R 105009 Deutschtum im Ausland, USA, vol. 1 (June 1936–Feb. 1938) (Germanness [*Deutschtum*] in foreign countries, USA).

8 McLaglan also taught jiu-jitsu and combat techniques to police and military in New Zealand, South Africa, and China. Slocombe, report, Sept. 16, 1937, CRC, pt. 1, box 16, folder 32. For his championship, see *South China Morning Post*, April 3, 1951. McLaglan's books included *Bayonet Fighting for War* (1916), *Infantry Pocket Book: A Concise Guide for Infantry Officers and N.C.Os* (1916), *Jiu-jitsu: A Manual of the Science* (1918), and *Police Jiu-Jitsu* (1922).

9 Pete Ehrmann, "The Informer and the Imposter," www.boxing.com/the_informer _and_the_imposter.html. Biographical information is drawn from the following sources: Slocombe, report, Sept. 16, 1937, CRC, pt. 1, box 16, folder 32; Roos, "Chapter 1: Leopold McLaglen," Part III: Leading Fascist Individuals and Organizations, *Summary Report*, 282–91; ejmas.com/jnc/jncart_McLaglan_1202.htm; www.bull shido.net/forums/showthread.php?t=31181; www.imdb.com/name/nm0572139/bio?ref _=nm_ov_bio_sm; www.nzdoctor.co.nz/in-print/2010/february-2010/24-february -2010/was-it-a-shared-interest-in-undergarments.aspx; frontiersmenhistorian.word press.com/2015/08/11/the-fighting-macks-an-extraordinary-family-of-brothers/; and ancestry.com.

10 Slocombe, report, ca. Sept. 28, 1937, CRC, pt. 1, box 16, folder 33.

11 Slocombe, report, Sept. 16, 1937, CRC, pt. 1, box 9, folder 20.

12 Charles Slocombe Affidavit, Oct. 8, 1937, CRC, pt. 1, box 17, folder 2.

13 Slocombe, report, Sept. 30, 1937, CRC, pt. 1, box 10, folder 1; for Bell and Gompert, see Slocombe, report, Sept. 24, 1937, CRC, pt. 1, box 16, folder 32.

14 Slocombe, report, Sept. 30, 1937, CRC, pt. 1, box 10, folder 1.

15 Ibid.

16 Slocombe, report, Sept. 29, 1937, CRC, pt. 1, box 10, folder 1; *Los Angeles Evening News*, Oct. 27, 1937.

17 Slocombe, report, Sept. 29, 1937.

18 Ibid.

19 Ibid.

20 Slocombe, report, Sept. 30, 1937, CRC, pt. 1, box 10, folder 1.

21 Franchon Simon and Marco Wolff, sister and brother, were prominent movie and theatrical producers. The original list Slocombe sent Lewis on September 30 was incorrect; he had written down the names by memory and had mixed up several people in the process. The correct list was reported in Slocombe, report, Oct. 2,

1937, CRC, pt. 1, box 17, folder 1. For the mistaken list, see Slocombe, report, Sept. 30, 1937, CRC, pt. 1, box 10, folder 1.

22 Slocombe, report, Sept. 30, 1937.

23 Ibid.

24 Attachment to Slocombe, report, Sept. 29, 1937.

25 Slocombe, report, Sept. 30, 1937.

26 Ibid.

27 Slocombe, report, Oct. 1, 1937, CRC, pt. 1, box 17, folder 1.

28 Ibid.

29 "Memorandum," Oct. 1, 1937, CRC, pt. 1, box 17, folder 1.

30 Slocombe, report, Oct. 1, 1937.

31 "Memorandum," Oct. 1, 1937. See also Slocombe, report, Oct. 2, 1937, CRC, pt. 1, box 17, folder 1.

32 "Memorandum," Oct. 1, 1937.

33 Slocombe, report, Oct. 2, 1937.

34 Ibid.

35 [Leon Lewis], "Memorandum," Sept. 30, 1937, CRC, pt. 1, box 10, folder 1; "Memorandum" and Slocombe, report, Oct. 2, 1937, CRC, pt. 1, box 10, folder 2.

36 For Lewis's summary and questions, see "Memorandum," Oct. 6, 1937, CRC, pt. 1, box 11, folder 5. For copies of affidavits, see "Statement of Henry Allen," Oct. 8, 1937, CRC, pt. 1, box 11, folder 5; and Slocombe and Alexander, affidavits, Oct. 8, 1937, CRC, pt. 1, box 17, folder 2.

37 *Los Angeles Evening News*, Oct. 27, 1937.

38 *Los Angeles Daily News*, Oct. 27, 1937.

39 *New York Times*, Oct. 27, 1937; *Los Angeles Examiner*, Oct. 27, 1937.

40 First two quotes from *Los Angeles Herald-Express*, Nov. 15, 1937; *Los Angeles Examiner*, Nov. 16, 1937; *Hollywood Citizen News*, Nov. 16, 1937.

41 *California Jewish Voice*, Nov. 19, 1937.

42 *Los Angeles Times*, March 1, 1938; for McLaglan's testimony, see *Los Angeles Times*, March 9, 1938.

43 *Austin American Statesman*, March 13, 1938.

44 For the sentencing and Victor's role in probation, see *New York Times*, April 6, 1938; *Los Angeles Times*, April 6, 1938.

45 *California Jewish Voice*, April 1, 1938.

46 For Alexander, see Roos, "William Dudley Pelley, Kenneth Alexander, and the Silver Shirts," in *Summary Report*, 302; for Bell and Gompert, see "Report," Jan. 26, 1940, CRC, pt. 2, box 42, folder 3. Crumplar's San Quentin records and photos can be found on ancestry.com.

15. The Most Hated Nazi in Hollywood

1 *Motion Picture Herald*, March 27, 1937; Carl Dreher, "Parade-Ground Art—The German Film Under Hitler," *New Theatre*, June 1936, 12.

2 Motion picture industry statistics are taken from Starr, *The Dream Endures*, 250; and Carr, *Hollywood and Anti-Semitism*, 107.

3 A copy of the letter can be found in Thomas Doherty, *Hollywood and Hitler, 1933–1939* (New York: Columbia University Press, 2013), 70.

4 *Motion Picture Herald*, July 25, 1936.

5 Joseph I. Breen to Alfred T. Mannon, July 22, 1936, *I Was a Captive of Nazi Germany* file, PCA. The New York Board ruling is quoted in Doherty, *Hollywood and Hitler*, 73.

6 McNally, interview by author, July 15, 2015.

7 Joseph Breen to Georg Gyssling, May 16, 1938, *The Three Comrades* file, PCA. See also Gyssling to Breen, Sept. 30, 1936, and Breen to Gyssling, Oct. 2, 1936, in *Three Comrades* file.

8 MGM pressbook for *Three Comrades*, Pressbook Collection, Cinematic Arts Library, University of Southern California.

9 Gyssling to Breen, Sept. 30, Nov. 5, 1936, *The Road Back* file, PCA.

10 Whale quoted in *Hollywood Now*, April 10, 1937.

11 *Hollywood Reporter*, April 6, 1937.

12 *News of the World*, April 10, 1937.

13 *Los Angeles Times*, June 16, 1937. For Dieckhoff's apology, see *Daily Variety*, June 15, 1937. For a perceptive account of State Department reactions to Hitler and their feelings about Jews, see Erik Larson, *In the Garden of Beasts: Love, Terror, and an American Family in Hitler's Berlin* (New York: Crown, 2011).

14 *New York Times*, June 20, 1937.

15 For a further discussion, see Urwand, *Collaboration*, 179–80.

16 Roos, "Contact with German Government," 66.

17 A reproduced copy of Hughes's proclamation can be found in Doherty, *Hollywood and Hitler*, 29. For Allen's stickers and postcards, see *Summary Report*, 121.

18 Ibid., 657. Information on the Continental Theater is taken from *Motion Picture Herald*, April 17, 1938; *Ferenz*, 53 Cal. App. 2d 639.

19 McNally, interview by author, July 15, 2015. Information on Gyssling's cinematic preferences and movie-going habits is taken from McNally, interview by author, August 11, 2015. For Gyssling's "official" attitude toward *The Great Dictator*, see Gyssling to Breen, Oct. 31, 1938, *The Great Dictator* file, PCA.

20 *Motion Picture Daily*, May 12, 1937; *Hollywood Reporter*, April 6, 1937; Welford Beaton, "A Plea to the Jews Who Control Our Films to Use the Mighty Voice of the Screen on Behalf of the Jews Who Are Victims of Nazi Germany," *Hollywood Spectator*, Nov. 26, 1938.

21 *Los Angeles Times*, July 28, 1937; *Los Angeles Examiner*, Nov. 19, 1937.

22 For Gyssling's communications with Berlin regarding espionage, see Gyssling to Under-Secretary of State Ernst Wilhelm Bohle, Jan. 1938, "Chief Auslands Organisation, USA, 1937–1940" (Bureau of the Director of the NSDAP/AO in the Foreign Office), R 27233, PA-AA, 145–47; Bohle to Gyssling, Jan. 1938, ibid., 148; "[Dr.] Hans Helmut Gross," box 80, Higham Collection. All translations from German were done by Florian Danecke.

23 Jill Lawless, "'Nazi propagandist' Hollywood charmer evaded MI5," Aug. 26, 2011, AP report, www.stuff.co.nz/entertainment/5511777/Nazi-propagandist-Hollywood -charmer-evaded-MI5; "Report on Miss Josephine Alderman, Fiancé of Hans Wolfram," Dec. 19, 1940, CRC, pt. 2, box 103, folder 20. In 1941, while in Germany, Plack recruited

British humorist P. G. Wodehouse to make radio broadcasts from Berlin. Lawless, "'Nazi propagandist' Hollywood charmer evaded MI5." For more reports on Plack's activities, see *Los Angeles Times*, Aug. 25, 1946; [London] *Telegraph*, Aug. 26, 2011; Zacharias memorandum, Feb. 9, 1939, CRC, pt. 2, box 42, folder 1.

24 Report by Gyssling on the Bund in Los Angeles, Aug. 1936, R 60114, "Förderung des Deutschtums in den Vereinigten Staaten von Amerika," vol. 11, 102, PA-AA.

25 William Bockhacker, report, "Letter from Burchardi, Staff Meeting, May 16, 1938, dated May 17, 1938," CRC, pt. 2, box 32, folder 13.

26 Bockhacker, report, May 10, 1938, CRC, pt. 2, box 32, folder 13.

27 *Chicago Sunday Times*, Sept. 19, 1937.

28 See note 24.

29 Berlin officials quoted in Urwand, *Collaboration*, 55.

30 Note by the German Foreign Office, Jan. 26, 1938, R 105009, "Deutschtum im Ausland, USA," vol. 1, 286–89, PA-AA.

31 Hitler quoted in Vejas Gabriel Liulevicius, *The German Myth of the East: 1800 to the Present* (New York: Oxford University Press, 2009), 184; Jordan quoted in Thomas Doherty, "Bassler's Letter: How Hollywood's Man in Vienna Escaped the Nazis," March 25, 2014, *Tablet*, http://www.tabletmag.com/jewish-arts-and-culture/167130 /koretz-hollywood-vienna. For local coverage and responses to the Anschluss, see *Los Angeles Times*, March 12, 14, 1938.

32 For Allen's remarks, see Roos, "Chapter 1: Henry D. Allen," in *Summary Report*, 214; for a general description of the evening, see *Los Angeles Times*, April 11, 1938.

33 Naomi Pfefferman, "In Our Own Backyard: A USC Exhibit Explores Nazis in 1930's Los Angeles," *Jewish Journal*, Jan. 19–25, 1990; "Background of Joseph Roos," Box 6, Roos Papers; political animal quote is from Roos, oral history interview, Roos Papers.

34 *Los Angeles Times*, March 29, 1938.

35 Ibid., June 26, 1939. For the June 1937 protest, see ibid., June 13, 1937.

36 *Summary Report*, n.p.; for destruction of documents, see "Chapter 1: Herman Schwinn-Pacific Coast Leader of the Volksbund," in ibid., 12–13.

37 *Los Angeles Times*, Aug. 13, 19, 1938.

16. The Three Most Dangerous Enemies List

1 Leon Lewis to Richard Gutstadt, June 8, 1938, CRC, pt. 2, box 128, folder 15.

2 *Summary Report*, 119–20.

3 A doctor Lewis had provided diagnosed Slocombe with "severe palpitations of the heart" and advised a less stressful life. Leon Lewis to Dr. Lewis Gunther, Oct. 22, 1937, CRC, pt. 1, box 9, folder 4.

4 Roos, oral history interview, Roos Papers; Slocombe, report, April 16, 1938, CRC, pt. 2, box 40, folder 12.

5 For the best account of the day's events, see Slocombe, report, April 23, 1938, CRC, pt. 2, box 40, folder 13.

6 Ibid.

7 Ibid.

8 Leon Lewis had a remarkable memory. In his notes, he wrote down the names of seventy-eight spies he remembered seeing in Allen's diary. "LI [Lewis] Arrest of

Henry Allen, San Diego," April 22, 1938, "Notes from Memory on Names and Data Found in Allen's Brief-Case," [Lewis] Memorandum, April 29, 1938, CRC, pt. 2, box 40, folder 13.

9 Ibid.; also see *Summary Report*, 277. The American Nationalist Confederation comprised the American Nationalist Party, the Militant Christian Patriots, the American League of Christian Women, the Defenders of Christian Civilization, and Christian Constitutionalists.

10 C. F. Ingalls to George Deatherage, Jan. 7, 1938, Supplement 24: "Ingalls Plan for A Military Uprising," in *Summary Report*, 309, 407–8; also see C. F. Ingalls and Laura Ingalls to George Deatherage, Jan. 19, 1938, in ibid., 410.

11 [Lewis] Memorandum, April 29, 1938, CRC, pt. 2, box 40, folder 13; James True to Henry Allen, Feb. 23, 1938, in *Summary Report*, 222–23.

12 Lewis Report, "Arrest of Henry Allen, San Diego, April 22, 1938," April 25, 1938, CRC, pt. 2, box 40, folder 13.

13 For Hull's denials, see Jewish Telegraphic Agency, Feb. 1, 1938.

14 After being tipped off by Roos and Lewis, District Attorney Fitts raided Allen's office in the Bradbury Building and seized his correspondence. For Roos's filing of charges for illegal voter registration and the raid on Allen's office, see [Lewis], "Memorandum," May 13, 1938, CRC, Part 2, box 40, folder 14; Lewis to Gutstadt, June 8, 1938, CRC, pt. 2, box 128, folder 15.

15 *Summary Report*, 279; [L1] Memorandum, April 26, 1938, CRC, pt. 2, box 40, folder 13. Fry published *Waters Flowing Eastward: The War Against the Kingship of Christ* (1931), which blamed Jews for Bolshevism. Her *Christian Free Press* was the official organ of the American League of Christian Women and the American Nationalist Confederation, the organization run by Ingalls and Deatherage. For biographical information on Fry, see Roos and Pitt, "Shadows of the Crooked Cross"; News Research Service, *News Letter* (hereafter cited as *News Letter*), Feb. 22, 1939; Leon Lewis to William B. Cherin, Oct. 26, 1938, CRC, pt. 2, box 24, folder 12; https://en.wikipedia.org/wiki/L._Fry.

16 Slocombe, report, April 26, 1938, CRC, pt. 2, box 40, folder 13.

17 Roos, oral history interview, 31.

18 For Drey's predictions and use of strong-arm tactics, see William Bockhacker [W2] Report, Feb. 16, 1938, CRC, pt. 2, box 32, folder 12.

19 For the best account of the weekend regional conference, see Bockhacker, report, May 31, 1938, CRC, pt. 2, box 32, folder 13.

20 Ibid.

21 Bockhacker, report, Dec. 6, 1937, CRC, pt. 1, box 5, folder 16. For Schwinn's work with fascist groups and Japanese spies, see *Summary Report*, 147–48.

22 Leon Lewis, To Whom It May Concern, June 29, 1942," CRC, pt. 2, box 197, folder 18: Bockhacker William, 1942. The letter was written at Bockhacker's request in case he was ever arrested as a Nazi spy. For Bockhacker's work with the Burns Agency, see Charles Young, report, Aug. 10, 1939, CRC, pt. 2, box 41, folder 16. For Bockhacker being paid by Lewis, see [Reno] *Nevada State Journal*, June 30, 1944.

23 Biographical information on Bockhacker is drawn from sources in previous note as well as his reports to Lewis; *Summary Report*; and data on ancestry.com.

24 Bockhacker, report, Dec. 6, 1937, CRC, pt. 1, box 5, folder 16. Bockhacker had three different code names: WZ, W2, and A. Williams. For more information on the German Radio Hour, see *Summary Report*, 130. For Leon Lewis's efforts to halt the show, see "Confidential Memo: *Herald Examiner*," March 5, 1938, in Leon Lewis File, *Los Angeles Examiner* Clippings, Special Collections, University of Southern California.

25 Bockhacker, report, Dec. 9, 1937, CRC, pt. 1, box 5, folder 16.

26 Bockhacker, report, April 4, 1938, CRC, pt. 2, box 32, folder 12.

27 Bockhacker, report, May 2, 1938, CRC, pt. 2, box 32, folder 13. For Foreign Office and Auslands attitudes toward Kuhn and the Bund, see Diamond, *Nazi Movement*; Susan Canedy, *America's Nazis: A Democratic Dilemma; A History of the German American Bund* (Menlo Park, CA: Markgraf, 1990); and Bernstein, *Swastika Nation*.

28 Bockhacker, report, June 6, 1938, CRC, pt. 2, box 32, folder 14.

29 Bockhacker, report May 10, 1938, CRC, pt. 2, box 32, folder 13; for bringing American military personnel to the Bund, see *Summary Report*, 344–45.

30 *Los Angeles Examiner*, June 9, 1938; Bockhacker, report May 26, 1938, CRC, pt. 2, box 32, folder 13. For Bukowski's visits to Deutsches Haus, see Ben Pleasants, "When Bukowski Was a Nazi, Parts 1 and 2," April 8, 2003, www.hollywoodinvestigator .com/2003/bukowski1.htm.

31 Charles Young, Agent Y, was the most important new recruit that August. Roos's other inside men—whose names were not always written down—included Operative D7, a delegate from Oakland representing the Patriotic Youth of America; D7 Report, Aug. 5 and 6, 1938; Operative E3 [Mr. Elston], an Associated Press correspondent attending the conference, E3 Report, Aug. 6, 1938; operative B6 from Oakland, B6 Report, Aug. 6, 1938; and a Mr. Wiseman, "Telephone Report from Mr. Wiseman," Aug. 6, 1938, CRC, pt. 2, box 211, folder 5. It is unclear who was stationed inside the truck, taking photographs.

32 *Summary Report*, 728.

33 Ibid., 193, 501.

34 Ibid., 490. For a report of the Bund's convention, see *New York Herald Tribune*, Sept. 4, 5, and 6, 1938; and *Los Angeles Times*, Sept. 4, 1938.

35 For a history of the Munich Agreement, see Frank McDonough, *Hitler, Chamberlain and Appeasement* (Cambridge, England: Cambridge University Press, 2002).

36 *Summary Report*, 731–32.

37 Burchardi's letter was dated Sept. 27, 1938. Bockhacker, report, Sept. 29, 1938, CRC, pt. 2, box 32, folder 17; Bockhacker, reports, Sept. 1938, and Oct 3, 1938, CRC, pt. 2, box 32, folder 18.

38 For Bund recruiting activities and the purchase of weapons, see supplement to *Summary Report*, 461–63 and 479.

39 *Summary Report*, 1,056.

40 Slocombe, report, Oct. 8, 1938, CRC, pt. 2, box 40, folder 16. For Fry's knowledge of Allen's Mexican affair, see Slocombe, report, Nov. 3, 1938, CRC, pt. 2, box 40, folder 17.

41 All quotes come from Henry Allen to James True, Sept. 5, 1938, in *Summary Report*, 946.

42 Ibid.; Slocombe, report, Sept. 19, 1938, CRC, pt. 2, box 40, folder 15. For additional information on the kidnapping plot, see Slocombe, report, Oct. 8, 20, 1938, CRC, pt. 2, box 40, folder 16; *Summary Report*, 946–47.

43 Slocombe, report, Sept. 14, 1938, CRC, pt. 2, box 4, folder 15.

44 Ibid.

45 Slocombe, report, Oct. 1, 1938, CRC, pt. 2, box 40, folder 16. For Fry's financial support of the Bund, see Slocombe, report, Nov. 3, 1938, CRC, pt. 2, box 40, folder 17.

46 For a copy of the *Christian Free Press* article, see attachment following Bockhacker, report, Oct. 6, 1938, CRC, pt. 2, box 32, folder 18; for Allen and Katz, see Slocombe, report, Nov. 3, 1938, CRC, pt. 2, box 40, folder 17; for accusations that Fry worked for the Soviets, see *Summary Report*, 949.

47 Ibid., 924.

48 Ibid., 922.

49 Bockhacker, report, May 5, 1938, CRC, pt. 2, box 32, folder 13.

50 *Summary Report*, 33. For the Bund's financial status, suspicion of Schwinn's larcenous activities, and hiding his home address, see Bockhacker, reports, May 5 and 23, 1938, CRC, pt. 2, box 32, folder 13.

51 Bockhacker, report, April 28, 1938.

52 Bockhacker Telephone Report, April 6, 1938, CRC, pt. 2, box 40, folder 12. For Schwinn being shown his reports while in Germany, see Bockhacker, report, May 19, 1938, CRC, pt. 2, box 32, folder 13. On Diebel working for the Gestapo, see *Summary Report*, 14–15.

53 Bockhacker, report, Sept. 28, 1938, CRC, pt. 2, box 32, folder 17.

54 *Los Angeles Examiner*, Dec. 20, 1938; *Los Angeles Times*, Dec. 15, 1938.

55 *Summary Report*, 763.

56 Counting deaths in the camps, 2,000 to 2,500 people died as a result of the pogrom. For histories of Kristallnacht, see Martin Gilbert, *Kristallnacht: Prelude to Destruction* (New York: HarperCollins, 2006); and Walter H. Pehle, ed., *November 1938: From "Reichskristallnacht" to Genocide* (New York: Berg, 1991).

57 Both quotes in *Los Angeles Times,* Nov. 12, 1938. For local coverage of Kristallnacht, see *Los Angeles Times* and *Los Angeles Examiner*, Nov. 11–17, 1938.

58 Gallup and Roper poll results are quoted in Glen Yeadon with John Hawkins, *The Nazi Hydra in America* (Joshua Tree, CA: Progressive, 2008), 187.

59 *Los Angeles Times*, Nov. 17, 1938.

60 For poll results, see *Los Angeles Times*, Nov. 12, 1938; Kusche quoted in *Summary Report*, 484.

17. The Race Is On

1 For descriptions of the ball and subsequent arrests, see *Los Angeles Times*, Jan. 16, 1939; *Los Angeles Examiner*, Jan. 16 and 18, 1939; and *New York Times*, Jan. 16, 1939.

2 *Los Angeles Times*, July 1, 1938. The training of German spies is described in Don Whitehead, *The FBI Story: A Report to the People* (New York: Random House, 1956), 193.

3 For a brief history of the arrests, see Steven J. Ross, "Confessions of a Nazi Spy: Warner Brothers, Anti-Fascism, and the Politicization of Hollywood," in *Warners' War: Politics, Pop Culture and Propaganda in Wartime Hollywood*, eds. Martin Kaplan and Johanna Blakley (Los Angeles: Norman Lear Center Press, 2004), 48–59.

4 By 1945 the number of FBI agents had grown to 4,886. For Roosevelt's orders and for congressional funding, see *Los Angeles Times,* Oct. 8, 1938; Richard Wilmer

Rowan, *Secret Agents Against America* (New York: Doubleday, Doran & Co., 1939), 149; Whitehead, *FBI Story*, 165; and Frances MacDonnell, *Insidious Foes: The Axis Fifth Column and the American Home Front* (New York: Oxford University Press, 1995), 157.

5 For Young's background, see "Memorandum" Nov. 22, 1938, CRC, pt. 2, box 41, folder 12; Bockhacker, report, Oct. 13, 1939, CRC, pt. 2, box 64, folder 20.

6 Roos, Shoah testimony; Roos, oral history interview.

7 Roos, oral history interview, 10, 15.

8 For first quote, see "The News Research Service 1939–1941," cover letter included with Joseph Roos to Helen Ritter, Sept. 9, 1991, box 9, folder "New Research Service, *News Letter*," Roos Papers; Roos, oral history interview, 14. For Gallup poll results, see Robert A. Rosenbaum, *Walking to Danger: Americans and Nazi Germany, 1933–1941* (Santa Barbara: Praeger, 2010), 46.

9 Roos, Shoah testimony; Roos, oral history interview, 14.

10 Bockhacker, report, Nov. 17, 1938, CRC, pt. 2, box 66, folder 25; *Summary Report*, 509.

11 Ibid., 727.

12 Mrs. Friedman, report, April 1, 1939, CRC, pt. 2, box 39, folder 22; Capt. John Schmidt, telephone report, Nov. 28, 1938, CRC, pt. 2, box 40, folder 6.

13 Charles Young, report, May 28, 1939, CRC, pt. 2, box 41, folder 15.

14 Young, report, Feb. 7, 1939, CRC, pt. 2, box 41, folder 14.

15 Slocombe, report, Jan. 17, 1939, CRC, pt. 2, box 40, folder 18.

16 Slocombe, report, Jan 19, 1939, CRC, pt. 2, box 40, folder 18. For Vonsiatsky's contact with Nazi and fascist leaders, see Michael Sayers and Albert E. Kahn, *Sabotage! The Secret War Against America* (New York: Harper & Brothers, 1942).

17 Friedman, report, March 30, 1939, CRC, pt. 2, box 39, folder 22. For Gyssling's remarks, see *Los Angeles Times*, March 17, 1939.

18 Friedman, report, March 30, 1939.

19 Since the money was invested over several years, I based my dollar equivalency on the year 1935. Not wishing to be known, the Stephenses hid their true identity by registering the purchased land under the name of Mrs. Jesse E. Murphy.

20 Hadley Meares, "What Really Happened at Rustic Canyon's Rumored Nazi Ranch?" Sept. 24, 2014, http://la.curbed.com/2014/9/24/10043624/what-really-happened-at-rustic-canyons-rumored-nazi-ranch. The best history of Murphy Ranch, including blueprints for the projected Nazi facilities, is Betty Lou Young, *Rustic Canyon and the Story of the Uplifters* (Santa Monica, CA: Casa Vieja Press, 1975), 117–21; also see Lionel Rolfe, "Body Politics: Retreat of the Master Race," *Los Angeles Times*, Nov. 8, 1992; Chris Roubis, "Heil Hollywood: Hitler's Secret Compound in LA Hills Where He Planned to Rule the World After Winning the War," *Daily Mail,* March 18, 2012.

21 "Memo: Various Unrelated Items of Information," June 27, 1939, CRC, pt. 2, box 64, folder 16; for *Los Angeles Times*, see *Los Angeles Times*, June 30, 1940.

22 Joe Roos to Julius Rice, March 2, 1939, CRC, pt. 2, box 103, folder 1. For Wiedemann's mission and funding, see Whitehead, *FBI Story*, 233; *Los Angeles Times*, March 4, 1939; *New York Times*, March 6, 1941.

23 Martha Dodd, *My Years in Germany* (London: Victor Gollancz, 1939), quoted in http://spartacus-educational.com/Fritz_Wiedemann.htm.

24 Wiedemann quoted in O. John Rogge, *The Official German Report: Nazi Penetration, 1924–1942, Pan Arabism 1939—Today* (New York: Thomas Yoseloff, 1961), 107. For the proposed assassination plot, see *Los Angeles Times*, Nov. 27, 1946; J. Edgar Hoover to Glenn H. Bethel, American embassy, Ottawa Canada, Dec. 31, 1946, and Director to Theron L. Caudle, Asst. Attorney General, memo, Jan. 10, 1947, 65-9483-133, Hermann Schwinn FBI file (obtained by author through Freedom of Information Act); Higham, *American Swastika*, 104–6. The FBI discovered the plot while they were tailing Russell, who had come raise money for the Irish Republican Army from Hollywood directors, stars, and producers.

25 For the training and funding of German and fascist spies, see Michael Sayers and Albert E. Kahn, *The Plot Against Peace: A Warning to the Nation!* (New York: Dial Press, 1945), 172; Rowan, *Secret Agents Against America*, 8.

26 Leon L. Lewis to Commander Ellis M. Zacharias, April 20 and 21, 1939, CRC, pt. 2, box 42, folder 2.

27 Zacharias memorandum, Feb. 9, 1939.

28 For Schiller, see Zacharias memorandum. For Baxter, see Sayers and Kahn, *Plot Against Peace*, 179. For Wiese, see *News Letter*, May 31, 1939, 2.

29 Captain Ellis M. Zacharias, USN, *Secret Missions: The Story of an Intelligence Officer* (New York: G. P. Putnam's Sons, 1946), 200, 204.

30 Sayers and Kahn, *Sabotage!*, 65.

31 "Information on P8 [Park]," July 12, 1938, CRC, pt. 2, box 40, folder 2.

32 Leon L. Lewis to Comdr. E. M. Zacharias, April 20, 1939, CRC, pt. 2, box 42, folder 2.

33 Zacharias memorandum, Feb. 9, 1939. For more reports from Lewis and Roos to Zacharias, see correspondence in CRC, pt. 2, box 42, folder 2. Copies of reports sent by the spymasters to American intelligence agencies can be found in Navy Department Office of Naval Intelligence, Washington, D.C., 10 September 1940, E. B. Nixon to Mr. Clegg, FBI, Colonel Lester, MID, Capt. U.S. Navy, memorandum, file 2801-943, folder 2801-943/1 [Arno Risse], RG165, Military Intelligence Division General Correspondence, 1917–1941, box 166, NA. Lewis and Roos kept sending updated reports that were forwarded to other intelligence agencies.

34 Memo from Lewis to Zacharias, April 20, 1939, CRC, pt. 2, box 42, folder 2.

35 Friedman, report, April 3, 1939, CRC, pt. 2, box 39, folder 22. For Slocombe, see Slocombe, report, April 28, 1939, CRC, pt. 2, box 40, folder 20.

36 *Summary Report*, 445. For a description of the Madison Square Garden rally, see Bernstein, *Swastika Nation*, 177–91.

37 *Summary Report*, 443.

38 Bockhacker, report, May 27, 1939, CRC, pt. 2, box 64, folder 14.

18. Closing In

1 For a history of the making and problems that beset the Warner Brothers' film, see Steven J. Ross, "Confessions of a Nazi Spy: Warner Brothers, Anti-Fascism, and the Politicization of Hollywood," in Kaplan and Blakley, *Warners' War*, 48–59.

2 For Gyssling's various letters, see his correspondence in *Confessions of a Nazi Spy* file, PCA. PCA censor Karl Lischka wanted to reject it on the grounds that it defamed

Hitler and therefore violated the Code. As he wrote, "To represent Hitler *only* as a screaming madman and a bloodthirsty persecutor, and *nothing else*, is manifestly unfair, considering his phenomenal public career, his unchallenged political and social achievements, and his position as head of the most important continental European power." He was overruled by Breen. K. L. [Karl Lischka], "Re: Storm Over America," typed notes, Jan. 22, 1939, *Confessions* file, PCA.

3 Charles Slocombe, reports, Feb. 16 and March 10, 1939, CRC, pt. 2, box 40, folders 18 and 19.

4 *Film Weekly*, May 27, 1939.

5 *Hollywood Spectator*, May 13, 1939. *Confessions* was banned in Japan and eighteen Latin American and European nations.

6 William Bockhacker, report, June 28, 1939, CRC, pt. 2, box 64, folder 16; *Summary Report*, 670. Schwinn and Ferenz issued the handbills under the name of the fictitious Committee on Unemployment, Hollywood Actors and Technicians.

7 Joseph Roos, "Chapter 6: Just Picture It! 'Mein Kampf' Against Hollywood," 119, box 7, folder 1 of 2, "[Franz] Ferenz Manuscript—Complete," Roos Papers.

8 Ibid.

9 Charles Young, report, April 6, 1939, CRC, pt. 2, box 41, folder 15. For FBI interviewing Schwinn, see "Memorandum for the [FBI] Director," Nov. 21, 1940, box 75, Herman Schwinn folder, Higham Collection; for FBI whitewashing of Bund, see Don Whitehead, *The FBI Story: A Report to the People* (New York: Random House, 1956), 163.

10 Slocombe, report, April 28, 1939, CRC, pt. 2, box 40, folder 20.

11 Slocombe, report, June 29, 1939, CRC, pt. 2, box 62, folder 11.

12 Frank Prince to Richard Gutstadt, Sept. 10, 1938, CRC, pt. 2, box 128, folder 17; Lewis to Gutstadt, Aug. 22, 1938, CRC, pt. 2, box 128, folder 16. For LaFollette and Sullivan, see Lewis to Prince, July 15, 1938, CRC, pt. 2, box 24, folder 16.

13 John Schultz to Miles Goldberg, Jan. 16, 1939, CRC, pt. 2, box 128, folder 20; "Telephone Call from Martin Luther Thomas," memo, Feb. 15, 1939, CRC, pt. 2, box 24, folder 13.

14 Leon Lewis to Sidney Wallach, Dec. 13, 1938, CRC, pt. 2, box 24, folder 12; Lewis to Goldberg, Aug. 28, 1939, CRC, pt. 2, box 128, folder 27. Roos's *Summary Report*, which was never attributed to him, was issued in the name of the Americanism Committee of the American Legion.

15 *Summary Report*, 448; Folder: Hermann Schwinn Miscellaneous, RG 131, Dept. of Justice/Office of Alien Property, Entry UD 324, box 8, Seized Records of the Los Angles Units of the German-American Bund, 1928–1942, NA.

16 *Summary Report*, 448.

17 "Statement of William Frank Kendzia and Michael Drey, Los Angeles, June 3, 1939," RG 233, box 13, L.A. Officer Numbered Case Files, NA.

18 Bockhacker, report, June 19, 1939, CRC, pt. 2, box 64, folder 16.

19 Roy Arnold Report, March 15, 1939, CRC, pt. 2, box 64, folder 10.

20 Bockhacker Memo, "Schwinn Loses Citizenship Papers," June 22, 1939, CRC, pt. 2, box 64, folder 16.

21 Ibid.

22 Ibid. For further coverage of the trial and deportation preparations, see *Los Angeles Examiner*, June 23, 1939; Jewish Telegraphic Agency, June 25, 1939; *Summary Report*, 437–38.

23 "Hermann Schwinn and Hans Diebel, Mainstays of the 'German-American Bund,'" 74, Special Report, HUAC Los Angeles (Dies Committee), box 11, RG 233, NA; Young, report, June 26, 1939, CRC, pt. 2, box 41, folder 16.

24 Young, report, Jan. 25, 1939, CRC, pt. 2, box 64, folder 8. For Lewis's continuing contact with Carr, see Lewis to Walter Carr, Nov. 13, 1939, CRC, pt. 2, box 24, folder 14.

25 For a copy of the *Look* article, see CRC, pt. 2, box 129, folder 1; *Summary Report*, 470. The Bund held a brief summer camp in August 1938 as a trial run.

26 *Summary Report*, 465; Julius Sicius, report, Dec. 4, 1939, CRC, pt. 2, box 40, folder 8.

27 Young, report, Aug. 30, 1939, CRC, pt. 2, box 41, folder 16; Slocombe, report, Aug. 23, 1939, CRC, pt. 2, box 40, folder 21.

28 Whitehead, *FBI Story*, 166; *Los Angeles Times*, Sept. 24, 1939.

29 *Los Angeles Times*, Sept. 24, 1939.

30 Bockhacker, report, Sept. 7, 1939, CRC, pt. 2, box 64, folder 19; *Hollywood Now*, Sept. 8, 1939.

31 "Report of C. L.," Sept. 10, 1939, CRC, pt. 2, box 64, folder 19.

32 *Los Angeles Times*, Sept. 10, 1939; for tracking war's progress in Deutsches Haus, see Bockhacker, report, Sept. 7, 1939, CRC, pt. 2, box 64, folder 19.

33 J. H. S. to Robert Stripling, Chief Investigator, HUAC, April 6, 1944, Axis Activities #81, box 12, RG 233, NA.

34 For the San Francisco arms cache, see *Los Angeles Times*, Sept. 13, 1939. For Lewis and Roos sending files and copies of the *News Letter* to government agencies, see Leon Lewis to Commander Ellis Zacharias, May 11, 1939, CRC, pt. 2, box 42, folder 2; FBI Report by Agent D. W. Magee, Aug. 18, 1939, for June 23, 29, and 30 and Aug. 1, 2, and 14, 1939, file 65-214, "Carl Kendzia, Paul Kendzia, Willy Kendzia, character of case: Espionage, German Agents," RG 65, Military Intelligence Division, General Correspondence, 1917–41, box 2857, file #10110-2723-62, NA.

35 *Los Angeles Examiner*, Sept. 26, 1939. See also Bockhacker, report, Sept. 29, 1939, CRC, pt. 2, box 62, folder 12.

36 Slocombe, report, Oct. 27, 1939, CRC, pt. 2, box 40, folder 21.

37 Roos, Shoah testimony.

38 Roos maintained regular correspondence with two trusted men in the State Department: George Messersmith, assistant secretary of state, and R. C. Bannerman, in charge of monitoring foreign propaganda in United States. Both were fans of Roos's *News Letter*. Julius Klein to Roos, Oct. 30, 1939, and Roos to Klein, Nov. 2, 1939, CRC 199, folder 44.

39 "Background of Joseph Roos," box 6, Roos Papers. For a sample of Roos's correspondence with government agencies, see Roos to R. C. Bannerman, Special Agent, Dept. of State, June 14, 1939, CRC, pt. 2, box 226, folder 37; Roos to Bannerman, Aug. 2, 1939, CRC, pt. 2, box 209, folder 31; Paul Maerker Branden to Louis Johnson, Asst. Sec. of War, Aug. 15, 1939, CRC, pt. 2, box 209, folder 32.

40 August Raymond Ogden, *The Dies Committee* (Washington, D.C.: Catholic University Press, 1945), 133n113.

41 Lewis and Ness had lost touch after he left Los Angeles. For their correspondence in preparation for the HUAC hearings, see Lewis to Ness, June 27, July 5, Aug. 14, and Sept. 21 and 27, 1939, and Ness to Lewis, July 16, Aug. 29, and Sept. 30, 1939, CRC, pt. 2, box 39, folder 30.

42 For Ness's testimony, see House of Representatives, "Investigation of un-American Propaganda Activities," 5492.

43 Ibid., 5512.

44 Ibid., 5518.

45 Ibid., 5526 and 5527.

46 Ibid., 5527 and 5514.

47 *Los Angeles Times*, Oct. 7, 1939; *New York Times*, Oct. 7, 1939; *Los Angeles Herald-Express*, Oct. 7, 1939.

48 For a sampling of coverage in lesser-known newspapers across the nation, see daily reports in newspapers.com; for the USS *Arizona*, see *Los Angeles Times*, Oct. 7 and 8, 1939.

49 Roos to Julius Penner, Midwest Institute of Public Relations, Chicago, Oct. 2, 1939, CRC, pt. 2, box 199, folder 44; for Roos's contact with British embassy, see Roos to Klein, Nov. 2, 1939, box 199, folder 44.

50 *Los Angeles Times*, Oct. 8, 1939; Bockhacker, report, Nov. 4, 1939, CRC, pt. 2, box 103, folder 1.

19. Sabotage, Secret Agents, and Fifth Columnists

1 Charles Young, report, Oct. 11, 13, 1939, CRC, pt. 2, box 41, folder 17. For Jaeckel's offer to Schwinn, see Young, report, Dec. 15, 1939, CRC, pt. 2, box 41, folder 18.

2 Young, report, Oct. 14 and 13, 1939, CRC, pt. 2, box 41, folder 17. For their trips to aircraft plants, see Young, reports, Oct. 25 and 28 and Nov. 7, 1939, in CRC, pt. 2, box 41, folder 17.

3 "Memorandum," Oct. 31, 1939, CRC, pt. 2, box 42, folder 2. For Jaeckel's morphine addiction and flight from Los Angeles, see Young, report, Oct. 17, 1939, CRC, pt. 2, box 41, folder 17; Young, reports, Dec. 15 and 17, 1939, CRC, pt. 2, box 41, folder 18.

4 Young, report, Oct. 25, 1939, CRC, pt. 2, box 41, folder 17; Young, reports, Nov. 3 and 9, 1939, CRC, pt. 2, box 41, folder 18.

5 Joseph Roos, "Digest of Report on Meeting of all German Consuls held at the German Embassy—Jan. 11, 12, 13, 1940," 654, in "Behind the Nazi Activities in the United States, First Reports—1933–1934: A Synopsis of the 1933–1934 Investigation and Other Events (1939–1940), compiled by Julius Klein, Lt. Colonel, AMC 33rd Division." A copy of this can be found in ProQuest History Vault Module: U. S. Military Intelligence Reports, 1911–1944, www.conquest-histvault.com.libproxy.usc.edu/pdfs/001717/001717_013_0100/001717_013_0100_From_1_to_700.pdf. After receiving a copy of the memorandum, Roos asked his uncle to answer two dozen questions. The quote is from that document.

6 McNally, interview, July 15, 2015; "rebirth" quote is from a letter Klein sent to Nuremberg prosecutors after the war. Julius Klein, National Commander, Jewish War Veterans of the USA to Whom It May Concern, Dec. 16, 1947, www.fold3.com/image/311346468/.

7 Julius Klein, memo, "Subject: Recent Meeting of All German Consuls Held at the Germany Embassy January 11, 12, 13, 1940—Report of Conversation with important veteran German Consul in Washington, D.C., on Friday, Jan. 12, 1940, and in Chicago on Monday, Jan. 15th," CRC, pt. 2, box 199, folder 44.

8 Ibid.

9 Ibid.

10 Julius Klein to General George C. Marshall, Jan. 6, 1940, in George C. Marshall correspondence with Julius Klein, folder 003255-022-0049, Papers of George C. Marshall can be found online at congressional.proquest.com/histvault?q=003255-022-0049; see also Lt. Col. Kenneth Buchanan (Aide to Chief of Staff), Jan. 10, 1940, ibid. Klein considered Marshall "one of the greatest guys in the world" and had been sending him reports on Nazi activity since 1933—and received appreciative replies in return. For copies of Klein's numerous reports to Marshall, see source in n. 5.

11 General George C. Marshall to Julius Klein, Feb. 29, 1940, and Klein to Roos, March 2, 1940, CRC, pt. 2, box 199, folder 44.

12 Julius Sicius, report, Nov. 16, 1939, CRC, pt. 2, box 40, folder 8.

13 Sicius, report, Nov. 16, 1939, CRC, pt. 2, box 40, folder 8.

14 For a sampling of the information he provided Lewis and Roos, see Sicius, reports, Nov. 27 and 30 and Dec. 26, 1939, CRC, pt. 2, box 40, folder 8; for his relationship with Gyssling, see Sicius, report, Dec. 4, 1939, in CRC, pt. 2, box 40, folder 8.

15 Sicius, report, Feb. 5, 1940, CRC, pt. 2, box 40, folder 9; Julius Sicius's Coroner's Report and Police Report of Death, June 15, 1940, CRC, pt. 2, box 40, folder 10.

16 J. Edgar Hoover to Special Agent in Charge, Los Angeles, March 5, 1940, "Re: Herman Schwinn: Espionage," Schwinn folder, Higham Collection; for local agents asking Roos for help, see Robert Singer to David Coleman, May 24, 1940, CRC, pt. 2, box 39, folder 23. For Hoover and FBI surveillance of anti-interventionists, see Douglas M. Charles, *J. Edgar Hoover and the Anti-Interventionists: FBI Political Surveillance and the Rise of Domestic State Security, 1939–1945* (Columbus: Ohio State University Press, 2007).

17 Charles Young "Memo" attached to Nov. 4, 1940, report, CRC, pt. 2, box 41, folder 12; for Hynes demotion, see "Memos" for June 4 and 17, 1940, CRC, pt. 2, box 70, folder 3.

18 For reports on the Court of Appeals verdict and the move to deport Schwinn, see *Los Angeles Times*, May 14 and June 9, 1940; *Los Angeles Examiner*, June 22, 1940.

19 "'Counter Attack' on Fifth Column Drive Here Advocated in 'Fortune' Survey," Jewish Telegraphic Agency, October 1, 1940.

20 *Los Angeles Times*, May 6, 1940.

21 Young, report, May 26, 1941, CRC, pt. 2, box 41, folder 23.

22 For background information on Grace and Sylvia Comfort and their initial meeting with Lewis, see "Memorandum," June 24, 1940, CRC, pt. 2, box 32, folder 21; further biographical information can be found in ancestry.com and Roos, Shoah testimony.

23 "Memorandum," June 24, 1940, CRC, pt. 2, box 32, folder 21.

24 Sylvia and Grace Comfort, report, July 9, 1940, CRC, pt. 2, box 32, folder 21.

25 Sylvia and Grace Comfort, report, June 26, 1940, CRC, pt. 2, box 32, folder 21.

26 Sylvia and Grace Comfort, report, July 9, 1940. For their contact with Zacharias, see Sylvia and Grace Comfort, report, July 15, 1940, CRC, pt. 2, box 32, folder 21; "Conference with Rupert [Zacharias]," July 18, 1940, CRC, pt. 2, box 32, folder 21.

27 Sylvia and Grace Comfort, report, July 26, 1940, CRC, pt. 2, box 32, folder 21.

28 "S-2 [Sylvia Comfort] Instructed to Establish Contact with Messerschmitt," July 10, 1940, CRC, pt. 2, box 32, folder 21.

29 *New York Times*, Oct. 19, 1940.

30 Ibid., Nov. 17, 1940.

31 "Information Wanted by Berenzweig on Individuals Suspected of Being Pro-Nazi," Sept. 16, 1940, CRC, pt. 2, box 103, folder 2. Lewis and Roos received earlier reports about suspected sabotage at defense plants from Jimmy Frost. Frost, report, July 1, 1940, CRC, pt. 2, box 39, folder 23.

32 A copy of their article can be found in Schwinn folder, Higham Collection. For the Pearson-Allen column and its widespread popularity, see the forward by Richard Norton Smith in Drew Pearson, *Washington Merry-Go-Round: The Drew Pearson Diaries, 1960–1969*, ed. Peter Hannaford (Lincoln, NE: Potomac, 2015). For a sampling of correspondence between Lewis, Roos, and the columnists, see Joseph Roos to Robert Allen, Aug 8, 1940; Lewis to Robert Allen, Sept. 23, 1940; Roos to Robert Allen, April 1 and May 23, 1941; and Joseph Roos to Drew Pearson, Oct. 8 and 13, 1941, all in CRC, pt. 2, box 209, folder 48.

33 Office of the Director to Mr. Tamm, "Re: Washington Merry-Go-Round Column of Nov. 19, 1940," Nov. 19, 1940, Schwinn folder, Higham Collection (a copy of the column can be found in this file); Roos to Capt. Julius Klein, March 7, 1940, CRC, pt. 2, box 199, folder 44; Roos to Lewis, April 3, 1941, CRC, pt. 2, box 9, folder 12. For the hastily written memo the local bureau sent to Hoover, see "Memorandum for the Director," Nov. 21, 1940, Schwinn folder, Higham Collection. The bulk of the local FBI's information on Schwinn came from newspaper clippings; agents cited several earlier interviews with Schwinn that revealed little important information.

34 The cited letter was dated Nov. 22, 1940; for other angry letters to Hoover, see Schwinn folder, Higham Collection. For Hoover's subsequent request to check Schwinn's immigration status, see J. Edgar Hoover to Special Agent in Charge, L.A., Nov. 29, 1940, "Re: Hermann Schwinn; Internal Security," Schwinn folder.

35 Charles Young, report, Nov. 7, 1940, CRC, pt. 2, box 66, folder 23.

36 *Los Angeles Examiner*, Oct. 29, 1940; Charles Young "Memo" attached to Nov. 4, 1940 Report, CRC, pt. 2, box 41, folder 12.

37 Sylvia and Grace Comfort, report, Sept. 12, 1940, CRC, pt. 2, box 32, folder 22. For overviews of America First, see Wayne S. Cole, *Charles A. Lindbergh and the Battle Against American Intervention in World War II* (New York: Houghton Mifflin Harcourt, 1974); Max Wallace, *The American Axis: Henry Ford, Charles Lindbergh, and the Rise of the Third Reich* (New York: St. Martin's Griffin, 2004); Lynn Olson, *Those Angry Days: Roosevelt, Lindbergh, and America's Fight over World War II, 1939–1941* (New York: Random House, 2013). For an overly sympathetic look at Lindbergh that downplays his anti-Semitism, see A. Scott Berg, *Lindbergh* (New York: Putnam, 1998).

38 For Zacharias's offer, see Zacharias to Lewis, Oct. 31, 1939, CRC, pt. 2, box 42, folder 2; for the massive amounts of information Lewis and Roos sent federal agencies, see their files in the Jewish Community Committee Archives, Special Collections, California State University, Northridge.

39 Charles Slocombe, reports, Sept. 4 and Oct. 23, 1940, CRC, pt. 2, box 40, folders 24 and 25.

40 Slocombe, report, Oct. 17, 1940, CRC, pt. 2, box 40, folder 25.

41 John Barr, report, Nov. 7, 1940, CRC, pt. 2, box 32, folder 11.

42 Slocombe, report, Nov. 15, 1940, CRC, pt. 2, box 41, folder 1; for Meader's background, see Sylvia and Grace Comfort, reports, Feb. 4 and 27, 1941, CRC, pt. 2, box 32, folder 25. For former government agents working with Meader, see Slocombe, reports, Nov. 6, 15, 20, and 26, 1940, CRC, pt. 2, box 41, folder 1; Dec. 23 and 27, 1940, folder 2.

43 Slocombe, report, Dec. 5, 1940, CRC, pt. 2, box 41, folder 2.

44 Slocombe, report, Dec. 10, 1940, CRC, pt. 2, box 41, folder 2.

45 Slocombe, report, Jan. 13, 1941, CRC, pt. 2, box 41, folder 3.

46 Slocombe, report, Dec. 20, 1940, CRC, pt. 2, box 41, folder 2.

47 Sylvia and Grace Comfort, report, Oct. 29, Sept. 12, and Oct. 29, 1940, CRC, pt. 2, box 32, folder 22; Jan. 17, 1941, folder 24.

48 Young, report, March 25, 1941, CRC, pt. 2, box 66, folder 24; May 10, 1941, box 41, folder 23.

49 Sylvia and Grace Comfort, report, Dec. 2, 1940, CRC, pt. 2, box 32, folder 23.

50 Sylvia Comfort, report, March 4, 1941, CRC, pt. 2, box 32, folder 26. For Roos's contact with the FBI, see "Memo from Joseph Roos to FBI David McGee, Re: Andrae B. Nordskog," Feb. 17, 1941, CRC, pt. 2, box 32, folder 25; "Various Unrelated Short Items of Information," Feb 4, 1941, CRC, pt. 2, box 18, folder 25.

51 Sylvia and Grace Comfort, report, Sept. 12, 1940, CRC, pt. 2, box 32, folder 22. For their first meeting with Schwinn, see Sylvia and Grace Comfort, report, Dec. 17, 1940, CRC, pt. 2, box 32, folder 23.

52 Sylvia Comfort, report, May 3, 1941, CRC, pt. 2, box 33, folder 1. For a description of the massive crowds who attended screenings, see Sicius, report, March 4, 1940, CRC, pt. 2, box 40, folder 10.

53 Sylvia Comfort, report, May 13, 1941, CRC, pt. 2, box 33, folder 2.

54 For cooperation between Lewis and the local defense industries, see reports contained in CRC, pt. 2, box 18, folders 23–25.

55 *New York Times*, June 1, 1941. See also *New York Times*, June 8, 1941.

56 "Various Items of Information Requested by Federal and Other Agencies: Sept. 16, 1941," CRC, pt. 2, box 18, folder 26. For Lewis and Roos's monitoring of aircraft plants before Pearl Harbor, see correspondence in files from CRC, pt. 2, box 18, folders 23–26.

57 R. B. Hood, [L.A.] Special Agent in Charge, to J. Edgar Hoover, May 8, 1941, Schwinn folder, Higham Collection.

58 Hood to Hoover, May 20, 1941, Schwinn folder, Higham Collection. See also W. C. Hinze, FBI, Washington, D.C., "Memorandum for Mr. Foxworth," May 15, 1941; R. B. Hood to J. Edgar Hoover, May 20, 1941; and Arthur Cornelius Jr. to Hoover, June 4, 1941, all in Schwinn folder.

59 Hood to Hoover, "Strictly Confidential," July 19, 1941, Schwinn folder. Sylvia Comfort's name may well have appeared in the original reports, but FBI records obtained by author Charles Higham through the Freedom of Information Act had all names blacked out.

20. Darkening Skies, New Dangers

1 For a description of the scene, see *Los Angeles Times*, June 29, 1941.

2 *New York Times*, June 17, 1941.

3 Ibid.

4 McNally, interview, July 15, 2015.

5 *Los Angeles Times*, July 9, 1941; Consul General Dr. Gyssling Submitted to Ambassador Dr. Dieckhoff, November 11, 1941, Berlin, letter contained in material submitted to prosecutors at the Nuremburg Trials, "Document 4054-PS [translation]," in *Nazi Conspiracy and Aggression. Supplement A: Closing Address, Closing Arguments, Closing Statements; Documents Introduced in Evidence by British and American Prosecutors, District of Columbia* (Washington, D.C.: U.S. Government Printing Office, 1947), 812–13.

6 McNally, interview, July 15, 2015.

7 Diebel's application for citizenship was denied in March 1941.

8 The 1941 poll is quoted in Nancy Snow, "Confessions of a Hollywood Propagandist: Harry Warner, FDR and Celluloid Persuasion," in Kaplan and Blakley, *Warners' War*, 69.

9 Leon Lewis, "Report on Los Angeles Lewis Community Committee Given at the Annual Meeting of Los Angeles Jewish Community Council on Dec. 22, 1940," CRC, pt. 2, box 8, folder 42.

10 "Paper to be Read by Mr. Leon Lewis at the Detroit Conference on Jan. 27–29, 1940," CRC, pt. 2, box 9, folder 2.

11 Hoover to Special Agent in Charge, L.A., June 17, 1941, "Re: H. Schwinn, Internal Security"; and P. E. Foxworth to E. A. Tamm, memorandum, Sept. 8, 1941, both Schwinn folder, Higham Collection. For orders to investigate Schwinn, see R. B. Hood, SAC, to Director, J. Edgar Hoover, Nov. 28, 1941, "FBI Report: Subject: Herman Schwinn; File No. 65-9483; section 2; Serials 39-67," Schwinn folder. When I requested Hermann Schwinn's FBI file under the Freedom of Information Act, the only files I was sent began in 1942.

12 L[ewis] to Rupert, Oct. 17, 1941, CRC, pt. 2, box 32, folder 9.

13 Roos to Capt. Ralph Riordan, "Re: William P. Williams," Sept. 19, 1941, CRC, pt. 2, box 224, folder 30.

14 "Capt. Riordan Wants Report on Local German Leaders and Organizations—Various Items Turned Over to Him Oct. 7, 1941, Including Dr. Gabriel's Codes," Oct. 8, 1941, CRC, pt. 2, box 224, folder 30. For Young's initial discovery, see Charles Young, report, Sept. 8, 1941, CRC, pt. 2, box 41, folder 24; for Hughes, see James S. Hughes, Captain, MID, Intelligence Officer, Headquarters, Antiaircraft Artillery Training Center, Camp Haan, CA, to Leon Lewis, Sept. 5, 1941, CRC, pt. 2, box 224, folder 30.

15 Correspondence with government agencies can be found in the Jewish Federation Council of Greater Los Angeles, Community Relations Committee Collection, Special Collections, Oviatt Library, California State University, Northridge.

16 For requests from aircraft plants and information sent to their security heads, see correspondence in CRC, pt. 2, box 18, folder 26. For copies of the reports Lewis and Roos sent to army and navy intelligence that were passed on to the FBI, see records in the army and navy intelligence files at the National Archives in College Park, Maryland. For examples, see "Navy Department Office of Naval Intelligence, Washington, D.C., Sept. 10, 1940: Memorandum for Mr. Clegg, FBI, Colonel Lester, MID. From E. B. Nixon, Capt. U. S. Navy. Subject: Suspect Lists," RG 165, Military Intelligence Division Correspondence, 1917–1941, box 1866, file #2801-943, 165-370-72-19-4, NA.

17 Quotations are from ibid. For similar reports, see "German Agents," Military Intelligence file, July 11, 1940, RG 165, Military Intelligence Division Correspondence, 1917–1941, 165-370-72-19-4, box 2857, file #10110-2723-62, NA.

18 For the description of the Royal Order, see *News Letter*, Feb. 5, 1941; Slocombe, report, April 24, 1941, CRC, pt. 2, box 41, folder 4.

19 Sylvia Comfort, report, March 11, 1941, CRC, pt. 2, box 32, folder 26. For Peyton's earlier call for Jewish blood, see John Schmidt, report, Aug. 27, 1940, CRC, pt. 2, box 40, folder 6.

20 Americanism Committee, 17th District American Legion, Department of California, *Report No. 1: Subversive Activities in America First Committee*, Oct. 10, 1941, 18–19.

21 Comfort, report, July 3, 1941, CRC, pt. 2, box 33, folder 7.

22 Comfort, report, July 15, 1941, CRC, pt. 2, box 33, folder 9.

23 Ibid. For Wasson's work with Roos, see Roos to Fred Wasson, Secret Service Dept., L.A., Nov. 17, 1941, CRC, pt. 2, box 209, folder 33.

24 Sylvia and Grace Comfort, report, Oct. 14, 1940, CRC, pt. 2, box 32, folder 22; Comfort, report, July 17, 1941, CRC, pt. 2, box 33, folder 9. For mother and daughter being picked up by Secret Service agents, see Comfort, reports, July 15 and 16, 1941, CRC, pt. 2, box 33, folder 9.

25 Comfort, report, July 12, 1941, CRC, pt. 2, box 33, folder 8. For Ingalls and pro-Nazi women, see Emily Yellin, *Our Mothers' War: American Women at Home and at the Front During World War II* (New York: Simon & Schuster, 2004).

26 Comfort, report, July 12, 1941, CRC, pt. 2, box 33, folder 8.

27 Joseph Roos, "Chapter 1: A Piece of German Earth," unpublished manuscript, 14, box 7, folder 1 of 2, "Ferenz Mss.—Complete," Roos Papers; *Los Angeles Herald-Express*, Dec. 27, 1940.

28 Comfort, report, Sept. 8, 1941, CRC, pt. 2, box 33, folder 15.

29 Comfort, report, Sept. 28, 1941, CRC, pt. 2, box 33, folder 18.

30 For a critical look at America First, see Sayers and Kahn, *Plot Against Peace*.

31 Ibid., 192.

32 Americanism Committee, *Report No. 1: Subversive Activities*, 18, 19.

33 "Memorandum," Oct. 29, 1941, CRC, pt. 2, box 9, folder 1.

34 Nye quoted in Carr, *Hollywood and Anti-Semitism*, 241 and 243.

35 Senate Committee on Interstate and Foreign Commerce, *Propaganda in Motion Pictures: Hearings Before a Subcommittee on Interstate Commerce . . . Sept. 9–26, 1941* (Washington, D.C.: U.S. Government Printing Office, 1942), 71. Nye quoted in Birdwell, *Celluloid Soldiers*, 155; *Variety*, Sept. 10, 1941.

36 *News Letter,* Oct. 1, 1941. See also Wheeler's speech in *News Letter*, Oct. 8, 1941.

37 Comfort, report, Oct. 8, 1941, CRC, pt. 2, box 33, folder 20.

38 Comfort, report, Oct. 5 and 12, 1941, CRC, pt. 2, box 33, folders 19 and 20.

39 Comfort, report, Oct. 17, 1941, CRC, pt. 2, box 33, folder 22. For the Tenney hearings, see Edward L. Barrett Jr., *The Tenney Committee* (Ithaca, NY: Cornell University Press, 1951).

40 Comfort, report, Oct. 18, 1941, CRC, pt. 2, box 33, folder 22. See also *News Letter*, Oct. 22, 1941.

41 Comfort, report, Oct. 29, 1940, CRC, pt. 2, box 32, folder 22.

42 Charles Young, report, March 25, 1941, CRC, pt. 2, box 66, folder 24.

43 Comfort, report, Nov. 5, 1941, CRC, pt. 2, box 34, folder 2.

44 Comfort, reports, Nov. 8 and 15, 1941, CRC, pt. 2, box 34, folders 3 and 4.

45 Poll results quoted in Carr, *Hollywood and Anti-Semitism*, 238.

46 For Roos's description of anti-Communist Christian groups, see *News Letter*, Nov. 5, 1941. Coverage of the America First rally can be found in *News Letter*, June 25, 1941.

47 For a transcript of Lindberg's September 11, 1941, speech, see www.charleslindbergh.com/americanfirst/speech.asp.

48 Comfort, report, Nov. 2, 1941, CRC, pt. 2, box 34, folder 2.

49 Comfort, report, Nov. 23, 1941, CRC, pt. 2, box 34, folder 5.

50 Comfort, report, Dec. 2, 1941, CRC, pt. 2, box 34, folder 6. For photographs of the meeting, see *Life*, Aug. 3, 1942, 32.

51 The A.A.A. on the farmer's sign stood for Roosevelt's Agricultural Adjustment Act. Comfort, report, Dec. 8, 1941, CRC, pt. 2, box 34, folder 7.

21. Pearl Harbor Roundup

1 Charles Slocombe, report, Dec. 10, 1941, CRC, pt. 2, box 41, folder 6. For the occupation of Hindenburg Park, see Young, report, Feb 4, 1942, CRC, pt. 2, box 41, folder 25. Also see *Los Angeles Times*, Dec. 8, 1941.

2 *Los Angeles Times*, Dec. 8, 1941; *Los Angeles Citizen-News*, Dec. 9, 1941.

3 J. F. Buckley to Mr. Ladd, memo, May 26, 1944, 65-94-107, Hermann Schwinn FBI file, obtained through Freedom of Information Act. See also L.A. Office to Director, telemeter, May 13, 1944, 65-9483-110, Schwinn FBI file.

4 Roos and Pitt, "Shadows of the Crooked Cross," 1942 entry.

5 Most of their reports were sent to Lewis's favored contacts at Naval Intelligence, who forwarded them to army intelligence and the FBI. Those lists can be found in army and naval intelligence files at the National Archives. For examples, see "German Known Suspects, Navy Dept. Office of Naval Intelligence, Washington, D.C., 10 September 1940: Memorandum for Mr. Clegg, FBI, Colonel Lester, Military Intelligence Division, from E. B. Nixon, Capt. U.S. Navy, Subject: Suspect Lists," RG 165, War Dept., Military Intelligence Division, Correspondence, 1917–1941, Entry 65: MID General Correspondence, 1917–41, box 1866, file #2801-943; "Supplementary List—Known German Suspects," in "German Known Suspects . . . 10 September 1940: Memorandum for Mr. Clegg," folder 2801-943/1; "German Agents," RG 165, War Dept., Military Intelligence Division, Correspondence, 1917–1941, Entry 65: MID General Correspondence, 1917–41, box 2857, file #10110-2723-62, in NA.

6 J. Edgar Hoover to Attorney General Tom C. Clark, June 22, 1943, 65-9483, Schwinn FBI file; see also L.A. Office to Director, telemeter, May 10, 1944, 65-9483-109, Schwinn FBI file.

7 L.A. Office to Director, telemeter, May 5, 1944, 65-9483-108, Schwinn FBI file; *Los Angeles Examiner*, Dec. 10, 1941. For daily newspaper accounts of the round up of German, Italian, and Japanese nationals and suspected agents, see *Los Angeles Examiner*, *Los Angeles Times*, *Los Angeles Citizen-News*, *Los Angeles Daily News*, Dec. 8–15, 1941.

8 *Los Angeles Citizen-News*, Dec. 9, 1941; Young, report, Dec. 19, 1941, CRC, pt. 2, box 41, folder 24.

9 *Los Angeles Citizen-News*, Dec. 9, 1941. For a list of hourly and daily updates of arrests made by L.A. bureau agents, see "FBI File Memos and Reports on Round-Up of Enemy Aliens," December 7–19, 1941, www.mansell.com/e09066/1941/41-12/IA015.html. The numbers of arrested men and women Hood sent Hoover were slightly different than the ones he gave the press.

10 Descriptions of Ferenz's arrest can be found in Sylvia Comfort, Dec. 19, 1941, CRC, pt. 2, box 34, folder 9; Roos, "A Piece of German Earth."

11 Roos, "A Piece of German Earth," 283, 285.

12 R. B. Hood to J. Edgar Hoover, teletypes, Dec. 9 and 11, 1941, "Reports on Round-Up of Enemy Aliens." Hood told the press the FBI had 422 men and women in custody: 314 Japanese, 71 Germans, and 11 Italians. *Los Angeles Examiner*, Dec. 11, 1941.

13 Noble quoted in Sayers and Kahn, *Plot Against Peace*, 211; *Los Angeles Times*, Dec. 13, 1941. For the arrest of Noble and Jones, see *Los Angeles Times*, Dec. 11, 1941. For dismissal of charges, see *Los Angeles Times*, Dec. 20, 1941. For photographs and an article describing the December 11 meeting and subsequent gatherings, see "Voices of Defeat," *Life*, April 13, 1942, 85, 88, and 90.

14 Hood to Hoover, Dec. 10, 1941, "Reports on Round-Up of Enemy Aliens." For arrests and those under investigation, see Hood to Hoover, Dec. 19, 1941, in "Reports on Round-Up of Enemy Aliens"; *Los Angeles Times*, Dec. 14, 1941; Young, report, Dec. 19, 1941, CRC, pt. 2, box 41, folder 24; Hoover, "Memorandum for the Attorney General: Re: Enemy Alien Problem in the Western Defense Command," Feb. 9, 1942, CRC, pt. 2, box 227, folder 12.

15 Roos, oral history interview, 18; [CRC] Meeting, April 10, 1942, CRC, pt. 2, box 39, folder 26; Roos, oral history interview, 19.

16 Ibid., 19.

17 For examples, see Lewis to Capt. Riordan, Dec. 17, 1941, CRC, pt. 2, box 224, folder 30; "Various Items of Information," Feb. 9, 1942, CRC, pt. 2, box 227, folder 2; Inquiry from Coast Guard Intelligence Section, June 10, 1942, CRC, pt. 2, box 226, folder 29; David Karr, Office of War Information, to Leon Lewis, July 29, 1942, box 1, folder "Corresp.—1940s," Roos Papers.

18 Lewis to Hood, Dec. 11, 1941, CRC, pt. 2, box 227, folder 2. See also Hood to Lewis, Dec. 18, 1941, CRC, pt. 2, box 227, folder 2.

19 J. Edgar Hoover to Joseph Roos, Jan. 24, 1942, CRC, pt. 2, box 227, folder 2.

20 "Covering Reports 7496–7612," [CRC] Meetings, April 10, 1942, and May 15, 1942, CRC, pt. 2, box 39, folder 26. For their work with Steedman and the Dies Committee, see Eisenberg, *The First to Cry Down Injustice?*, 116–17.

21 "Reports 7613-7726," [CRC] Meeting, June 5, 1942, CRC, pt. 2, box 39, folder 26. For Deutsches Haus activities, or the lack of them, see *Los Angeles Examiner*, March 5, 1942; "The German American Bund Has Officially Dissolved," exhibit #6, March 19, 1942, typed report on organizations and people, Special Committee on Un-American Activities on Nazi Propaganda, RG 233, box 11, folder "Nazi Activities #60-I," NA.

22 Sylvia Comfort, report, Dec. 25, 1941, CRC, pt. 2, box 32, folder 8.

23 *Los Angeles Examiner*, Jan. 29, 1942; J. Edgar Hoover to Major General George V. Strong, Assistant Chief of Staff, G-2, War Dept. Washington, D.C., May 5, 1942, Schwinn folder, Higham Collection; and "FBI Report Re: Hermann Schwinn," May 29, 1942, box 79, folder "German American Bund," Higham Collection. There is no

mention of Diebel in either of the aforementioned sources, but since he wound up interned with Schwinn, he was probably sentenced at the same hearing.

24 For Schwinn's internment, see *Los Angeles Examiner*, Jan. 29, 1942; Hoover to Strong, May 5, 1942; "FBI Report Re: Hermann Schwinn," May 29, 1942. For the other Germans taken into custody, see J. Edgar Hoover, "General Intelligence Survey in the United States," confidential report, June 2, 1942, folder "German Intelligence in the U.S.," Higham Collection.

25 *New York Times,* July 8, 1942; also see *Los Angeles Times,* July 8, 1942; J. K. Mumford, Federal Bureau of Investigation, U.S. Dept. of Justice, to Mr. Ladd, "Re: German-American Bund Voorhis Act," memorandum, July 11, 1942, Schwinn folder, Higham Collection. For a history of the sedition trials, see O. John Rogge, *The Official German Report: Nazi Penetration 1924–1942, Pan Arabism 1939–Today* (New York: Thomas Yoseloff, 1961); and Sayers and Kahn, *The Plot Against Peace.* For a book written by one of the defendants, see Maximilian St.-George and Lawrence Dennis, *A Trial on Trial: The Great Sedition Trial of 1944* (Chicago: National Civil Rights Committee, 1946).

26 *Washington Post,* July 23, 1942; *Los Angeles Examiner,* July 23, 1942.

27 *New York Times,* Oct. 22, 1942. For Young's testimony, see ibid., Sept. 30, 1942. For Lewis and Roos's work with the FBI compiling evidence for the federal case, see D. M. Ladd to the Director [Hoover], "Re: German-Am Bund, Voorhis Act, Selective Service Act, Alien Registration Act," memorandum, Oct. 21, 1942, and Agent Hood, FBI L.A., to Director, telegram, Oct. 24, 1942, both Schwinn folder, Higham Collection.

28 FBI L.A. Bureau Report [agent name blacked out], Oct. 3, 1942, Schwinn folder, Higham Collection.

29 "Voices of Defeat," *Life*, April 13, 1942, 86; [Cincinnati] *American Israelite*, April 9, 1942.

30 Comfort, reports, March 10, 9, 1942, CRC, pt. 2, box 34, folder 22: Comfort, reports, March 1942.

31 Comfort, report, December 12, 10, 1941, CRC, pt. 2, box 34, folder 7.

32 Comfort, report on conversation with Larry Griffith, Dec. 18, 1941, CRC, pt. 2, box 34, folder 8, Dec. 1941. The July 1941 poll is quoted in Nancy Snow, "Confessions of a Hollywood Propagandist: Harry Warner, FDR and Celluloid Persuasion," in Kaplan and Blakley, *Warners' War,* 69.

33 Comfort, report, March 6, 1942, CRC, pt. 2, box 34, folder 21.

34 Ibid.; Comfort, report, March 13, 1942, CRC, pt. 2, box 34, folder 22.

35 Comfort, report, March 16, 1942, CRC, pt. 2, box 35, folder 1.

36 Comfort, report, March 12, 1942, CRC, pt. 2, box 34, folder 22.

37 Comfort, report, Jan. 8, 1942, CRC, pt. 2, box 34, folder 13.

38 Lewis to Al Cohn, Jan. 30 1942, CRC, pt. 2, box 196, folder 2; Comfort, report, Jan. 15, 1942, CRC, pt. 2, box 34, folder 12.

39 Comfort, report, Jan. 16, 1942, CRC, pt. 2, box 34, folder 12.

40 Comfort, report, Jan. 24, 1942, CRC, pt. 2, box 34, folder 15.

41 Comfort, report, March 6, 1942, CRC, pt. 2, box 34, folder 21. For Lewis and Roos's work with the Tenney Committee, see files in CRC, pt. 2, box 21, folders 2–8.

42 Roos, oral history interview, 32, box 6, Roos Papers.

43 Ibid., 33; also see files in CRC, pt. 2, box 138, folder 1.

44 For a summary of the often-confusing series of state and federal arrests and trials, see *Ferenz*, 53 Cal. App. 2d 639.

45 "Statement by F. K. Ferenz at Office of Attorney General," April 2, 1942, CRC, pt. 2, box 23, folder 3. For Lewis and Roos's work helping California officials prepare for the hearings, see CRC, pt. 2 files, box 22, folder 7, through box 23, folder 5.

46 [CRC] Meeting, April 10, 1942, CRC, pt. 2, box 39, folder 26.

47 Ibid. The four other arrested "nationalists" were Leone Menier, Daniel Van Meter, Baron Van Meter, and Genevieve Kerrigan.

48 "U.S. Sends Fascist Noble to Prison for Five Years," *Life*, August 3, 1942, 32.

49 *Los Angeles Times*, July 23, 1942; also see J. K. Mumford, Federal Bureau of Investigation, U.S. Dept. of Justice, to Mr. Ladd, "Re German-American Bund Voorhis Act," memorandum, July 11, 1942, Schwinn folder, Higham Collection.

50 *Los Angeles Times*, Aug. 13, 1942. For convictions and sentencing, see *Los Angeles Times*, Aug. 13 and Oct. 27, 1942.

51 *Los Angeles Times*, Jan. 5, 1943.

Epilogue

1 Sylvia Comfort, report, July 17, 1942, CRC, pt. 2, box 35, folder 22. For examples of violent threats made against Jews, see Comfort, reports, May 4 and 18, 1942, CRC, pt. 2, box 35, folders 9 and 11. For anti-Semitism at the farmers' market, see Comfort, report, July 18, 1943, CRC, pt. 2, box 35, folder 22.

2 *Los Angeles Herald-Examiner*, Jan. 10, 1943. For newspaper coverage of Ness's death, see *Los Angeles Herald-Examiner*, Jan. 10, 1943; *Los Angeles Times*, Jan. 10, 11, and 12, 1943; *Los Angeles Examiner*, Jan. 11, 1943; and *Los Angeles Daily News*, Jan. 11, 1943. Ness helped convict Franz Ferenz by testifying against him at his trial for violating the California Subversive Organizations Registration Act; see Neil Ness to Leon Lewis, April 26, 1942, CRC, pt. 2, box 40, folder 1; and *Christian Science Monitor*, Oct. 23, 1942.

3 *Los Angeles Daily News*, Jan. 11, 1943.

4 *Yuma Daily Sun*, Jan. 12, 1943; *Oelwein* [Iowa] *Daily Register*, Jan. 13, 1943.

5 Comfort, report, Feb. 25, 1943, CRC, pt. 2, box 37, folder 6.

6 Comfort, report, July 20, 1943, CRC, pt. 2, box 38, folder 1. See also Comfort, reports, June 3, Oct. 22, and Oct. 26, 1943, CRC, pt. 2, box 37, folder 16, and box 38, folders 10 and 11.

7 *Los Angeles Times*, April 5, 1944. For a newspaper report endorsing Alice's suspicion of poisoning, see *Los Angeles Herald-Express*, April 3, 1944. For local coverage of Schmidt's death, see *Los Angeles Herald-Express*, April 4 and 6, 1944; *Los Angeles Daily News*, April 3 and 6, 1944; *Los Angeles Examiner*, April 4 and 5, 1944. Schmidt was threatened by Nazis and fascists in 1934, 1938, and again in 1940; see [Schmidt], telephone report, Nov. 28, 1938, and report, Aug. 27, 1940, CRC, pt. 2, box 40, folder 6. See also chapter 5 in this volume, "A Bitter Lesson: The German-American Alliance Trial."

8 *Los Angeles Times*, April 4, 1944.

9 For her subsequent work in Washington, D.C., see Leon Lewis to Sylvia Comfort, July 5, 1945, and Comfort to Lewis, Aug. 2, 1945, CRC, pt. 2, box 32, folder 20; *Albuquerque Tribune*, Nov. 22, 1968; *Albuquerque Journal*, Nov. 7, 1968, and Dec. 25, 1969. For

reports she sent Roos, see Sylvia Comfort to Joseph Roos, Jan. 22, April 23, June 10 and 12, and Aug. 21, 1946, CRC, pt. 2, box 197, folder 46.

10 *Los Angeles Times*, May 14, 1944, and Aug. 16, 1984; "Charles P. Slocombe: Congressional Tribute," Sept. 10, 1986, *Congressional Record*, congressional.proquest.com .libproxy1.usc.edu/congressional/result/congressional/pqpdocumentview?accou ntid=14749&groupid=95432&pgId=eedb9b93-e1e5-4f2e-adc9-2a5cd51374fd.

11 For Schwinn and Diebel's internment and subsequent federal indictments, see J. Edgar Hoover to Major General George V. Strong, May 5, 1942; FBI Report [agent's name blacked out], May 29, 1942; and J. J. Mumford to Mr. Ladd, memorandum, July 11, 1942, all Schwinn folder, Higham Collection; *Washington Post*, July 8, 1942; *Los Angeles Examiner*, July 8, 1942; *Wisconsin Rapids Daily Tribune*, July 10, 1942; *Los Angeles Examiner*, July 23, 28, 1942; *New York Times*, July 28, 31, 1942; and *Los Angeles Times*, Aug. 11, 1942.

12 For Young's testimony, see *New York Times*, Sept. 30, 1942. For overviews of the trial and the behind-the-scene-role played by Lewis and Roos, see *New York Times*, Sept. 30 and Oct. 22, 1942; *Washington Post*, Oct. 20, 1942; and J. Edgar Hoover to Assistant Attorney General Wendell Berge, memorandum, Oct. 24, 1942, Schwinn folder, Higham Collection. For general coverage of the trials and Lewis and Roos's involvement, see *Los Angeles Times*, Jan. 5, March 12, and July 8, 1943; Jewish Telegraphic Agency, Jan. 6, 1943; *Los Angeles Examiner*, July 28, 1943; "FBI Report, Jan. 7, 1943: Hermann Schwinn," in Schwinn folder, Higham Collection; Roos to Lewis, March 15, Sept. 24, 1943, CRC, pt. 2, box 9, folder 13; Lewis to Mendel Silberberg, May 6, July 26, 1943, CRC, pt. 2, box 3, folder 28; and James V. Bennett, Director of Prisons, "Memorandum for Mr. J. Edgar Hoover," May 29, 1944, 65-9483-113, Hermann Schwinn FBI File, obtained through Freedom of Information Act, Nov. 6, 2014.

13 Lewis and Roos provided O. John Rogge with much of the information needed for the prosecution. For examples of correspondence with Rogge and other Justice Department officials, see letters contained in "Correspondence—1940s," box 1, Roos Papers. For the testimony of Arnold, Bockhacker, and Young, see *New York Times*, June 27 and 29, 1944; *Chicago Daily Tribune*, June 28 and Sept. 6, 1944; *Washington Post*, July 8, 1944; and [Philadelphia] *Jewish Exponent*, July 14 and 28, 1944. For information about the Great Sedition Trial and the critical involvement of Lewis and Roos, see O. John Rogge to Joe Roos, Jan. 24, 1944, CRC, pt. 2, box 41, folder 13; Special Agent in Charge, Washington, D.C., report, Feb. 26, 1944, and Deputy Director [FBI] to L.A. Office, telemeter, May 5, 1944, both Schwinn folder, Higham Collection; *New York Times*, Jan. 4, May 24, and June 1, 1944; *Chicago Tribune*, April 16, 1944; *Washington Post*, June 5, 1944; Sayers and Kahn, *Plot Against Peace*; and St. George Lawrence Dennis, *A Trial on Trial*.

14 For Laws's decision, see *New York Herald Tribune*, Nov. 23, 1946. For defendants remaining in jail, see Special Agent in Charge, St. Paul, MN, to J. Edgar Hoover, "Re: German-American Bund, Hermann Schwinn, Alien Enemy Control," June 23, 1945, Schwinn folder, Higham Collection; *New York Times*, June 27, 1945; Mr. D. H., Los Angeles Police Department, to E. A. Tamm, Nov. 23, 1945, Schwinn folder; and [Reno] *Nevada State Journal*, Dec. 1, 1945.

15 The departure records for Hermann and Thekla Schwinn can be found on ancestry. com. For government reports on Schwinn's relocation to Argentina, see Special

Agent in Charge, L.A., to J. Edgar Hoover, May 10, 1957, Schwinn folder, Higham Collection; SAC to Director, L.A., memo, May 10, 1957, 100-28689-50, Hermann Schwinn FBI file, obtained by author through Freedom of Information Act, September 26, 2014; and U.S. Embassy, Buenos Aires, to State Department Office of Security, "Security Advisory Opinion," Dec. 20, 1962, 65-9483, Schwinn FBI file.

16 For Schwinn's visa application, see "Security Advisory Opinion," Dec. 20, 1962. Information on their deaths is taken from ancestry.com. Thekla remained in Florida until her death on August 9, 1994.

17 Information on Diebel is taken from ancestry.com.

18 *People v. Robert Noble et al.*, 68 Cal. App. 2d 853 (1945), http://law.justia.com/cases /california/court-of-appeal/2d/68/853.html.

19 McNally, interview, July 15, 2015. For Gyssling's description of events, see Interrogation Summary No. 2260, Georg Gyssling, German Counsel General Los Angeles, Interrogated by: Dr. Kemper, 8 May 1947, Nuremberg, Office of the U.S. Chief of Counsel for War Crimes, APO 696, Evidence Division, Interrogation Branch, Records of the U.S. Nuremberg War Crimes Trials Interrogations, 1946–1949, reel 23, 1019 (I want to thank Jonathan Dentler for translating the interrogation report from German to English); Dr. Georg Gyssling, Freilassing, Upper Bavaria, Schlustr. 5 to the CID Headquarters, Linz, Upper Austria, Sept. 24, 1948, Attachment to "Memorandum Report," Jan. 19, 1949, Criminal Investigation Division, U.S. Forces in Austria, Linz Office, Subject: Jeritza Estate, Records of the Property Control Branch of the U.S. Allied Commission for Austria (USACA), 1945–1950, from NARA DN 1929. Cases and reports, claims processed by, and general records of the Property Control Commission for Austria (USACA) Section, 1945–1950; in fold3.com.

20 Georg Gyssling to the CID Headquarters, Sept. 24, 1948, Records of the Property Control, 1945–1950, from NARA DN 1929. For a record of Gyssling's official postings during his career, see https://de.wikipedia.org/wiki/Georg_Gyssling&prev=search. For a history of Operation Bernard and Gyssling's involvement, see Lt. Charles Michaelis, QMC, memorandum to Commanding Officer, X-2 Germany, re: "RHSA Financial Operations," June 5, 1945; Spitz interrogation, dated 16 May 1945, NARA, RG 226, George Spitz CIA Name File, quoted in Lawrence Malkin, *Krueger's Men: The Secret Counterfeit Plot and the Prisoners of Block 19* (New York: Little, Brown, 2006), 136–37; and Gerald Steinacher, *Nazis on the Run: How Hitler's Henchmen Fled Justice* (New York: Oxford University Press, 2011). The operation was later made into the 2007 Oscar-winning Austrian film *The Counterfeiters* (*Die Fälscher*).

21 McNally, interviews, July 15 and August 11, 2015. For published accounts that confirm Angelica's account of her father's involvement, see Steinacher, *Nazis on the Run*, 169; and Malkin, *Krueger's Men*, 187. For the most complete account of Operation Sunrise, see Bradley F. Smith and Elena Agarossi, *Operation Sunrise: The Secret Surrender* (New York: Basic, 1979).

22 Gyssling to CID Headquarters, Sept. 24, 1948, attachment to "Memorandum Report," Jan. 19, 1949; for Gyssling's Nuremberg testimony, see Interrogation Summary No. 2260, Georg Gyssling, German Counsel General Los Angeles, Interrogated by: Dr. Kemper, May 8, 1947.

23 Julius Klein, National Commander, Jewish War Veterans of the USA to Whom It May Concern, Dec. 16, 1947, attachment to "Memorandum Report," Jan. 19, 1949,

Criminal Investigation Division, U.S. Forces in Austria, Linz Office, Subject: Jeritza Estate, Records of the Property Control Branch of the U.S. Allied Commission for Austria (USACA), 1945–1950, from NARA DN 1929, cases and reports, claims processed by, and general records of the Property Control Commission for Austria (USACA) Section, 1945–1950. A copy of Klein's letter and the 1949 report can be found at www.fold3.com/image/311346468/.

24 For a brief account of Gyssling's postwar history, see "Memorandum Report," Jan. 19, 1949 (see n. 23); "Subject [blacked out names on official document, but appears to be Georg Gyssling and Wilhelm Hoettl], March 18 1952, To: Files," http://www .foia.cia.gov/sites/default/files/document_conversions/89801/DOC_0005359219.pdf. Angelica remained with Boone until April 1947, when she traveled back to the United States. She returned to Austria, where she worked as a stenographer for army intelligence from July 1950 until March 1952, when she married U.S. Air Force Intelligence Lt. Colonel Lawrence McNally, who had just finished his tour of duty. The couple moved to California until their divorce in August 1976. Angelica died in the seaside town of Morro Bay, California, on January 25, 2016, of complications from lung cancer.

25 Los Angeles Jewish Community Committee Annual Report, Dec. 26, 1945, CRC, pt. 2, box 9, folder 2; "CRC Meetings Minutes," Jan. 10, 1947, CRC, pt. 3 (1933–1951), box 3, folder 12. For Lewis's efforts at promoting religious tolerance and greater cooperation among minority groups, see memorandum, March 30, 1944, CRC, pt. 2, box 9, folder 5; Lewis to Mendel Silberberg, memo, March 23, 1945, CRC, pt. 2, box 3, folder 32; and Leon Lewis to Richard Rothschild, March 19, 1945, CRC, pt. 2, box 3, folder 33.

26 *Los Angeles Times*, Feb. 6, 1948.

27 Lewis's obituary can be found in *Los Angeles Times*, May 22, 1954, and *New York Times*, May 22, 1954. Since Nazis and fascists had known Lewis was spying on them since 1933, the question arises as to why no one tried to assassinate him. One can offer only a speculative answer. Given the fact that Lewis had foiled a number of assassination plots, including Leopold McLaglan's plan to murder a number of prominent Hollywood figures, it is likely that had Nazis killed Lewis the Jewish community would have used its considerable influence to pressure government agencies to bring down the Bund and Silver Shirts. Mendel Silberberg, who was as well-known to hate groups as Lewis, would have used his powerful connections to the Republican establishment and local elites (such as the Chandler family) to launch an all-out attack against all Nazi and fascist organizations. This is something these organizations were ultimately unwilling to risk.

28 For Roos's opinion of Herzberg as "a bust," see Roos, oral history interview, Roos Papers, 42; for the Jewish War Veterans, see "[Biographical] Memorandum: Joseph Roos to Dr. Leonard Pitt," June 12, 1990, box 6, folder "Background of Joseph Roos," Roos Papers. There is no documentation on why Roos was passed over, but several people who knew him suggested it was because executive board members thought of him more as a "behind the scenes guy" than a charismatic leader. Melnick, interview by author. Historian Len Pitt, who worked with Roos on his memoirs, suggested he might have irritated some of the board members with his no-nonsense nature, which some interpreted as "prickly." Pitt, Aug. 5, 2014, Los Angeles. Following the

war's end, Roos wrote and produced an award-winning weekly radio show, *For This We Fought*, on the Warner Brother's station KFWB, which focused on national and international efforts at promoting tolerance. *Billboard*, June 28, 1947; *Los Angeles Times*, Oct. 25, 1949.

29 For an overview of Roos's career after he left the Community Relations Committee, see "[Biographical] Memorandum," Roos to Pitt, June 12, 1990, box 6, folder "Background of Joseph Roos," Roos Papers.

30 Schecter, interview by author.

31 Roos, interview by author.

32 Los Angeles Jewish Community Committee Annual Report, Dec. 26, 1945, CRC, pt. 2, box 9, folder 2.

INDEX

Actioneers, 251

Aircraft factories, 178, 257, 300, 321
  potential sabotage, 249, 258, 271, 276,
    279–82, 286, 288, 295–97, 302, 330

Alderman, Jo, 111–13, 222

Alexander, Kenneth, 185, 188–89, 196,
    199–200, 213, 220, 232, 264,
    266, 293
  background, 188–89, 343
  plots with Henry Allen, 188, 193, 197
  plots with Leopold McLaglan, 201–13

All Quiet on the Western Front (1930), 216,
    218

Allen, C. Bert,
  spies for Lewis, 28, 33, 36, 40–42, 58,
    78–79, 341
  suspected of spying by Nazis, 39

Allen, Henry, 83, 158, 178, 180, 187–89,
    200, 220, 225, 228–43, 247, 266,
    282, 300, 330
  background, 157, 343
  plot to overthrow government, 230–31
  plots with Ingram Hughes, 155,
    157–60, 164–65, 175, 184–85
  plots with Kenneth Alexander, 188,
    193, 197,
  plots with Leopold McLaglan, 201–13
  plots with Leslie Fry, 241–43

Allen, Pearl, 158–59

Allen, Robert, 250, 274, 288–89

Allen, Warren, 158

Alt Heidelberg, 7, 14, 21–23, 25–26, 33, 37

Ambassador Hotel, 256

Ambrose, Thomas, 212

America First, 278, 286, 290, 294, 304–9,
    313, 325–26

American Gentile, 301

American Jewish Committee, 13, 73

American Jewish Congress, 13, 73

American Labor Party, 20, 100–3, 105, 121

American Legion, 23–24, 27, 29, 37, 63,
    69, 83, 89
  Americanism committee, 11, 32, 267,
    303–4, 341
  participation in spy operation, 4, 17,
    51, 63

American Magazine, 80

American National Party, 133, 146, 154–57,
    163
  assassination plots, 152, 159–65

American Patriots, 251

American Rangers, 251–52, 303–4, 308

American Warriors, 184

American White Guard, 84, 88, 90, 95,
    158–59

American Vigilantes, 251

Americans for Peace, 331

Americanism Defense League, 331

Anderson, Glenn, 334

Anschluss, 224–26, 228, 236, 237

Anti-Defamation League, 8–10, 14, 17,
    48, 50, 64, 74, 76, 95, 138,
    141–42, 161, 211, 239, 267, 270
  monitoring films for anti–Semitic
    images, 9, 11, 118–20

Anti-Semitism in United States, 9–12, 14,
    20, 33, 49, 52, 61, 67, 72, 79, 118,
    120, 161–62, 192, 205, 212–13,
    236, 250, 252, 308, 312–13
  in Los Angeles, 11, 21, 22, 30, 32, 62,
    98, 106, 125, 133, 145, 156–59, 184,
    189–90, 197, 209, 211, 221, 225,
    245, 247, 251, 255, 286, 293, 303,
    310, 312, 324–26, 331–32, 338
  in U.S. Congress, 49, 62, 119–20, 164
  in motion pictures, 119–20, 220
  in movie studios, 25, 74–75, 188–90,
    249, 264

Anti-Semitism: Organized Anti-Jewish Sentiment; A World Survey, 157
Arnold, Roy,
  background, 249
  spies for Lewis and Roos, 249, 290, 303, 323, 334–35
Aryan Bookstore, 14, 21–22, 24, 28, 40, 98, 100–1, 121, 155, 168, 240, 268, 270, 318, 342
Asheville, N.C., 79–81, 188
Assman, Max, 318
Atlanta Constitution, 104
Auslands-Organisation, 123, 167, 200, 223, 236
Austria, 192, 221, 225–26, 230, 245

B'nai B'rith, 9–10, 13, 17, 30–31, 73, 239, 270
B'nai B'rith Messenger, 15, 30, 45, 113, 125
Baer, Max, 127
Bank of America, 105, 280
Barcelona, 247
Barr, John,
  spies for Lewis and Roos, 290–91, 301, 303
Barrymore, Lionel, 264
Baruch, Bernard, 35, 82, 163
Baxter, William, 256
Beast of Berlin, The (1918), 114
Beaton, Welford, 222, 264
Belgium, 284
Bell, Albert Dunston, 174, 202–4, 208, 213
Bellamy, Ralph, 116
Below the Sea (1933), 116
Benidorm (Spain), 338
Bennett, Joan, 193
Benny, Jack,
  assassination target, 205
Berkeley, Busby,
  assassination target, 160
Berlin, 7, 16, 31, 47, 52, 56, 109–110, 113, 116, 121–22, 126–28, 134–35, 139–41, 149, 160, 167, 171, 174, 177–79, 181, 198, 200, 214–15, 217, 219, 222, 224, 226, 252, 254–55, 277, 280–82, 296, 336
Beverly Hills, 251
Beverly Hills Theater, 263

Biberman, Herbert,
  assassination target, 205
Biddle, Francis, 316, 320, 323, 329
Biltmore Hotel, 226
Biscailuz, Eugene, 103
Black Legion, 176
Blitzkrieg im Westen (1940), 295
Bockhacker, William,
  background, 235, 341,
  spies for Lewis and Roos, 234–36, 240–41, 243–44, 247–48, 250–51, 255–56, 259, 265, 269, 272, 277, 283, 317, 334–35
Boetticher, Friedrich von, 281–82
Bohle, Ernst, 123, 167, 200, 223, 236
Bolger, Ray, 194
Bollert, Helmuth, 256
Bonus Army, 15–16
Boone, Christina, 112, 123–24, 337–38
Borchers, Hans, 307
Bowron, Fletcher, 245
Boyle Heights, 4, 11, 32, 161
Bread and a Home, Protection against Want in Old Age: Program of the American Labor Party, 100
Breen, Joseph, 118, 120, 216–18, 221, 263–64, 308
Bremen, 223, 240
Brett, Ira, 245
Brice, Fanny, 194
Brinnig, Louis, 164
Brown, L. Albert, 189–90
Brownshirts, 8, 10, 12, 24, 31, 36, 39, 47, 81, 101, 134–35, 140, 145, 190, 217, 224, 235, 305
Bruce, Robert, 190
Bruening, Erich, 255–56
Brundage, Avery, 307
Brunsweiger, Walter, 105
Buchenwald concentration camp, 206
Buenos Aires, 336
Bukowski, Charles, 237
Bülow, Ernst Ulrich von, 122–23, 155, 159
  suspected spymaster, 178–80, 196, 276, 291–93, 301
Burchardi, Konrad, 56, 122, 146, 166–67, 178, 182, 200, 222–224, 240, 342
Burns Detective Agency, 235
Bush, Judge Guy F., 52, 54, 57–59, 73
Butler, Major General Smedley, 83–84

Cabot, Bruce, 193
Cagney, James, 106
    assassination target, 205, 212
California Jewish Voice, 211
California National Guard, 4, 29, 36–39,
        103, 105, 127, 136, 176, 182, 189,
        241, 251, 280, 287, 316
California Staats Zeitung, 21
California Weckruf, 147, 150, 167, 180–81
California Women's Republican Club, 331
Camp McCoy, 323
Camp Siegfried, 144
Camp Sutter, 270–71
Canada, 232, 276, 279, 295
Cantor, Eddie, 70, 78, 193, 211, 220
    assassination target, 4, 205, 211
Carnahan, H. L., 54, 56, 58
Captured (1933), 116, 117
Carr, Walter E., 174–75, 183, 213, 244
Carroll, R. Robert, 95–102, 106
Carlson, Albert, 312
Case, Eugene R., 85–91
Catalina Island, 153, 207
Century Club, 256
Chamberlain, Neville, 239
Chancellor, Philip, 202–13
Chandler, Norman, 134
Chaplin, Charles, 92, 221, 308
    assassination target, 4, 197, 205–6, 212
Chicago, 8–11, 13–14, 27–28, 47–48, 50–51,
        127–28, 134–36, 137–38, 141–42,
        159–60, 258, 281, 307, 310
Chicago Daily News, 135, 137
Chicago Herald–Examiner, 135–38
Chicago Times, 198
Chicago Tribune, 59
Christian American Builders, 312
Christian American Guard, 312
Christian Free Press, 164, 232, 243
Christian party, 186
China, 214, 279
City Water Taxi Company, 153, 334
Civilian Army of American Blue Coats,
        184, 194
Clairville, Water,
    background, 84–85, 341
    spies for Lewis, 63, 84–91, 99–102,
        105
Clark, Bennett, 308–9
Cleveland, 240

Cohen, Emmanuel, 76, 78
    assassination target, 205
Cohen, Milton,
    assassination target, 160
Cohn, Harry, 67–68, 76
Columbia Pictures, 76, 116–17, 118, 206
Comfort, Grace,
    background, 286, 341
    spies for Lewis and Roos, 286–87,
        290–91, 293, 303, 305, 324, 326
Comfort, Sylvia,
    background, 286, 341
    comes under suspicion, 326–27,
        332–33
    spies for Lewis and Roos, 286–87,
        290–91, 293–95, 297, 301, 303–7,
        322, 324–27, 331–34
Community Committee (also Community
        Relations Committee), 31, 55,
        62–63, 83, 94, 134, 139, 193, 196,
        225, 228, 248, 334, 338–39
    formation of, 16–17
    funded by Hollywood studios, 67–78
Communist International, 92, 192
Communist Party, 29, 105, 147
Communists, 15, 21, 88, 153, 156, 163,
        188–89, 192, 217, 224, 310, 328
    American attitudes toward, 2, 30, 32,
        43, 62, 92, 95, 97, 101,153,
        195–96, 217, 224, 229–31, 234,
        237, 252, 266, 313
Confessions of a Nazi Spy (1939), 263–65
Conley, William C.,
    spies for Lewis, 19, 30, 34–37, 56, 342
Consolidated Aircraft Corporation, 282
Continental Book Store, 220, 294, 306–7,
        319, 328
Continental Theater, 220–21
Cooper, Gary, 189
Corcoran, Howard, 324
Correa, Mathias, 323
Crawford, Joan, 194
Crosby, Bing, 194
Coughlin, Father Charles, 12, 161
Council of Jewish Women, 73
Crumplar, Edwin, 204, 213
Czechoslovakia, 136, 221, 239, 252, 257

Dachau concentration camp, 1, 206
Davis, Howard, 317–18

Davis, James, 31, 37, 43, 103, 245, 252
    attitude to Hitler and Jews, 32, 62
    attitude to Silver Shirts, 33, 92
Deatherage, George, 230, 242, 330
Deissler, Otto, 52, 53, 54, 59
DeMille, Cecil B., 71
Demmler, Rafael, 100–1, 103, 147–50,
    166–67, 170–71, 176–77, 182–83
Denmark, 284
Der Stürmer, 21, 232
Des Moines, 313
Deutscher Weckruf und Beobachter, 220,
    235, 307
Deutsches Buehne, 150
Deutsches Haus, 149, 151, 155, 162, 165,
    171–72, 176–77, 183, 186, 189–90,
    193, 195, 220, 223, 225–26, 228,
    235–36, 240, 246–47, 252–53,
    255, 257, 268, 272, 277, 279, 283,
    294–95, 310–11, 317–20, 322, 325
    description of, 168–70
Dewey, Thomas, 290
Dickstein, Samuel, 43, 50–53, 59–60, 62,
    72, 78, 183, 196, 222
    calls for investigation of un-
        American activities, 47–49, 63,
        94, 97, 102, 105, 197
Diebel, Hans, 174, 240, 243, 256, 258,
    268, 271, 277, 284, 303, 317–18,
    322–24, 329–31, 333–36, 342
    citizenship troubles, 269–70, 285,
        294, 300
    organizes secret cells, 250–51
Dieckhoff, Hans-Heinrich, 200, 219
Dies, Martin, 226, 266, 275–76, 288
Dilling, Elizabeth, 330
Disabled American Veterans (DAV), 11,
    24, 26–27, 30, 74, 89, 94, 226
    participation in spy operation, 4, 7,
        17–19, 28, 51, 62–63, 84, 235
Dodd, Martha, 254–55
Dodd, William, 254
Dolan, Henry, 92
Doombadze, George, 200, 205, 206, 208
Douglas, Melvyn, 193
Douglas Aircraft Company, 258, 282,
    295, 320
    Nazis and fascists working inside,
        276, 288, 302
Dresden, 255

Drey, Michael, 233–34, 235–37, 239,
    243–44, 257–58, 268
Dreyfus, Alfred, 219
Drucker, Louis, 328–29
Du Bois, W.E.B., 194
Duke, Glenn, 182
Dulles, Allen, 337
Dunn, Joseph, 33

Educational Service Bureau, 286
Egan, Max, 276
Economy Act of 1933, 19
Edmondson, Robert Edward, 157, 159
Egypt, 230
Eicher, Edward C., 336
Einstein, Albert, 110
Elder, Henry, 243
Eldridge, Florence, 193
Embassy Auditorium, 304, 310, 313–14
Ericksen, John, 182
Espionage
    Europe vs U.S., 16, 255
Espionage Act (1917), 271–72

Fairbanks, Jr. Douglas, 116
Fascism, 191, 232,
    and American businessmen, 83–84, 198
    Silver Shirts vs. Nazis, 61
Fascists, 2–3, 12, 29, 138, 187, 190, 201,
    214, 225, 240, 252, 255 (*see also*
        Silver Shirts)
    in Hollywood studios, 74–75, 77–78,
        189–90, 249
    in U.S., 2–4, 12, 20, 29, 31–32, 47–48,
        52, 61–64, 79–83, 95, 97, 100–6,
        133–34, 141, 146, 157–59, 176, 184,
        186, 189, 194, 196–97, 206, 220,
        230–32, 235, 237–40, 249, 251–52,
        254–55, 245, 266–67, 270, 274,
        285, 292, 330, 332, 334–35
Federal Bureau of Investigation (FBI),
    79, 95, 258, 266, 271, 283,
    286–88, 296–97, 307, 310,
    319–20, 322, 324, 327
    lack of counter-intelligence, 16,
        91–92, 248, 256
    receive information from Lewis and
        Roos, 231–32, 257, 267, 273, 277,
        280, 284, 288–90, 293–95, 301,
        306, 315–23

L.A. Bureau investigates Gyssling, 289, 301
L.A. Bureau warns Hoover about Schwinn, 284, 288–89
Ferenz, Franz, 99, 150, 159, 167–68, 225, 265, 293, 303–4, 306–7, 326–28, 342
  exhibits German films, 220–21, 294–95
  works with isolationists, 308, 310–12
  arrested and tried after Pearl Harbor, 319, 322, 328–31, 333, 336
Field, David, 46, 53, 57, 59, 60
fifth column, 281, 285, 309
  in Los Angeles, 223, 276, 278, 281–84, 287–88, 293, 295, 300–3, 315, 324–25, 340
First National Pictures,
  penetrated by Nazis and fascists, 189
Fisher, Preston Harris, Mrs., 251
Fitts, Buron, 185, 208–9, 211, 284–85
  assassination target, 152, 160
Fitzgerald, F. Scott, 217
Flournoy, Robert, 154
Ford, Gerald, 290
Ford, Henry, 22, 143, 307
Ford, John, 193
Foreign Agents Registration Act (1938), 106
Fort Lincoln, 323
Fort MacArthur, 292
Fortune, 285
Fowler, W. C., 85, 88, 90
Fox Studios, 308
Foze, James, 103, 106, 204, 208–9
France, 9, 19, 23, 112, 128, 140, 151, 239, 247, 271, 280
Franco, Francisco, 187, 247
Frankfurter, Felix, 82, 163
Friedman, Anna
  spies for Lewis and Roos, 249, 251, 253, 257–58, 290
Friends of Progress, 304, 308, 310–15, 320, 324, 327–30, 343
Friends of the New Germany (FNG), 8, 18, 21, 23–24, 27–28, 31, 37, 53–61, 67, 121–22, 134, 143, 150, 155, 173, 266, (*see also* German American Bund)
  allied with Silver Shirts and fascists, 61, 79, 83, 87, 89–90, 95, 96–106, 155–57, 159–60, 162–63

anti-Communism, 15, 22, 28–29, 55, 57, 103, 237
anti-Semitism, 24, 55, 61, 122, 146–47, 167, 172
divisions and rivalries within, 33–34, 121–22, 166–67
first meetings, 7–8, 14–15
friction with Georg Gyssling, 121–23, 125, 148–49, 167, 170–74
penetrated by Neil Ness, 142–51
Free Society of Teutonia, 14
Frost, Jimmy,
  spies for Lewis and Roos, 249, 254, 269, 290, 295
Fry, Leslie, 228–40, 245–47, 265, 267, 282, 300, 330
  background, 232, 343
  plots against Lewis, 241–43
Führerprinzip, 172, 244, 259

Gallup Polls, 161–62, 246, 250, 300
Garbo, Greta, 221
Gebhardt, Hans, 318
Gefken, Dietrich, 87, 103
  background, 36
  plot to seize armories and overthrow government, 35–41, 43, 54–55, 58, 189
Generes, Harold, 89
German American Alliance, 31, 44–46, 51–60, 68, 121
German American Bund, 194–95, 225, 236–37, 239–40, 247, 265–66, 271–72, 284, 289, 295–96, 300, 310, 318–19, 322–23, 334 (*see also* Friends of the New Germany)
  allied with Silver Shirt and fascists, 190, 193, 303–4
  anti-Communism, 176, 234–35, 237–39
  creation of, 144
  divisions and rivalries within, 243–44
  friction with Gyssling, 148–49, 167, 170–74, 178, 221–24, 226, 265
  assists spies, secret cells, and fifth columnists, 250–51, 256, 276, 279–80, 290–95
German American League, 172, 176, 239, 318

German Americans, 7, 115, 220–21,
239, 285
arrested after Pearl Harbor, 317–20
divisions within L.A. German
community, 44–45, 51, 143,
167–68, 177, 223
German Day Celebration, 199, 208, 272
German Film Industry, 15, 115–17
German Radio Hour, 235–36
Germany, 3, 7, 9, 31, 34–36, 47, 54, 83, 115,
121, 146, 174, 184, 191, 192, 195,
198, 216–17, 223, 238, 245–46,
265, 270–71, 289, 308, 316
anti-Semitism in, 10, 12–14, 133, 167,
206
espionage in U.S., 180, 196, 222, 230,
247, 254–57, 275, 280, 291–93,
298, 302–03, 306
Foreign Office, 116, 125–26, 148,
219–220, 222–24, 226, 236, 255,
299–300
Reich Ministry of Public
Enlightenment and
Propaganda, 114, 127, 159
sabotage in U.S., 254–55, 273, 275–77,
279, 281, 288–89, 296–97
territorial expansion, 187, 214, 224–25,
239, 247, 251, 252–53, 278
WWII, 271–72, 280, 284, 297, 300,
337
Gestapo,
agents in U.S., 244, 250, 255, 279–82,
301, 306, 342
agents on German ships, 27, 123,
173–74, 275, 336–37
Giesler, Jerry,
assassination target, 160
Gipkins, Julius, 302–3
Gish, Lillian, 188
Gissibl, Fritz, 143–44
Glendale, 251, 302, 304
Glimm, Stanley, 208, 212
Goebbels, Joseph, 14, 16, 21, 23, 56, 149,
220, 245–46, 250, 256, 307, 309
film and film industry, 3, 114–16, 127,
214–15, 263, 265
Goering, Hermann, 282
Gold Shirts, 158, 187, 189–90, 231, 256
Goldberg, Miles, 141
Goldstone, Phil, 76

Goldwyn, Samuel, 188
assassination target, 4, 205
Gompert, Frank, 203, 285
Gray, E.T., 103–5
Great Britain, 9, 112, 232, 271–72, 274,
276, 300, 304, 314, 316
Great Depression, 11–12
Great Dictator (1940), 221, 308
Greenbaum, Louis, 74
Griffith, Larry, 312, 325–27
Gutstadt, Richard, 17, 48, 50, 59, 72–73,
118, 142
Gyssling [McNally], Angelica, 109, 217,
298–300, 337–38
background, 124, 126, 363n43,
364n44
father's secret life, 123–28, 221, 299
Gyssling, Georg, 55, 103, 105, 107–11, 120,
139, 151, 166, 198–99, 213,
225–26, 253, 272, 275, 289–300
and Jewish émigrés in L.A., 125–26
and L.A. social elite, 111–14, 222
attitude to Hitler and Nazi Party,
124–25, 281, 337–38
background, 108–9, 124, 342
dealings with Hollywood studios and
actors, 75, 78, 107, 109, 114–20,
215–220, 221–24, 263–64
friction with L.A. Nazis, 41–42, 75,
110, 121–23, 125, 127–29, 148–49,
167, 170–74, 178, 184, 196,
221–24, 226, 265
post–Pearl Harbor, 336–38
secret life of, 123–29, 221, 280–83,
363n43
secret relationship to Julius Klein,
123, 127–29, 280–83, 299, 337–38
Gyssling, Ingrid, 109, 111–13, 123–24

Haas, John, 182
Hadel, Walter,
spies for Lewis and Roos, 249
Hajaschi, Y., 257
Hamburg, 34, 124, 255, 303
Hamburg American Line, 123
Hammerstein, Oscar, 193
Harold, Hugh, 25
Harris, Hugo, 46, 53, 57, 59
Harrison, Benjamin, 207, 208
Hattie, Joseph, 137–38

Hays, Virgil T., 103–5
Hays, Will, 117–118, 120, 263
Heidenreich, Fred, 291–92
Heinzen, Ralph, 114
Hercules Powder Plant (CA), 276, 287
Hercules Powder Plant (NJ), 287–88, 291
Herron, Frederick, 117
Herzbrun, Henry,
    assassination target, 205
Hess, Rudolf, 143, 149, 195–96, 200
Hillcrest Country Club, 67–78
Hindenburg Park (later renamed La
    Crescenta Park), 144, 198–99,
    201, 259, 270, 272, 285, 316
Histed, Ernest, 188
Hitler: What Every American Should Know
    About the Many Whose Influence
    Is Felt the World Over, 99
Hitler, Adolf, 1, 2, 12, 16, 34, 36, 47, 54,
    56, 58, 61, 71, 73, 75, 80, 83, 99,
    110, 134, 136, 143–44, 149, 151,
    174, 176, 186, 194, 196, 198, 200,
    215, 216, 218, 220, 225–26, 239,
    250, 255, 271, 276, 280, 285,
    292–93, 298, 306–7, 308, 310–11,
    314–15, 324, 330, 338
    divided Jewish strategy over
        opposing, 13, 73
    on power of film, 3, 114–15, 120, 191
    territorial ambitions, 187, 224–25
Hohmann, Arthur, 284
Hollywood,
    politicization of, 191–94
Hollywood Anti–Nazi League, 187, 191,
    192–97, 199–200, 204, 206–8,
    212, 218–19, 237, 239, 243
Hollywood Anti–Nazi News, 193
Hollywood Bowl, 304
Hollywood Now, 196
Hollywood Reporter, 221
Hollywood Spectator, 222
Hollywood studios, 75, 115
    infiltrated by Nazis and fascists, 25,
        74–75, 77–78, 189–90, 249, 264
    refugees in, 191–92
Hollywood studio leaders, 304
    fund Lewis's spy operation, 67–78
Hollzer, Henry, 228, 339
Hood, Richard, 273, 294, 317, 319–22, 329
Hoover, Herbert, 15, 68

Hoover, J. Edgar, 29, 91, 248, 266, 271,
    294, 297, 317, 319–22, 324
    and Schwinn, 284, 288–89, 301, 311
    obsessed with Communists, 92, 289
Hopkins, Jesse, 106
Horn, Henry, 124
Horton, H. A., 303
House of O'Sullivan, 202, 205, 207
House of Rothschild, The (1934), 119–20
House Un-American Activities
    Committee, *see* U.S. Congress,
    House Un-American Activities
    Committee
Howard, Leslie, 116
Hughes, Ingram, 145–47, 151, 154–55, 175,
    179, 187, 196, 232
    assassination plots, 152–53, 159–65,
        184–85, 193
    background, 134, 156–57, 161, 220, 343
Hughes, James, 302
Hughes, Rupert, 149–50
Hughes, T. W., 303, 304
Hull, Cordell, 14, 219, 231
Hungary, 230
Hynes, William "Red," 32, 37–38, 43, 103,
    123, 245, 285
    anti-Communism, 29–30, 60, 105
    friendly relations with Nazis and
        fascists, 25, 29–30, 62–63,
        88–89, 194–95, 237

I Married a Nazi (1940), 308
I Was a Captive of Nazi Germany (1936),
    215–16
Illinois Staats-Zeitung, 134
Immigration Restriction League, 184
Indianapolis, 50
Informed Voters of America, 331
Ingalls, Clayton, 230–31, 242
Ingalls, Laura, 230, 305–6
Isolationists, 192, 278, 285–86, 290,
    300–1, 303–15, 319–20, 322,
    325–26, 331, 342 (see also
    America First and Friends of
    Progress)
Italy, 12, 81, 83, 138, 144, 158, 214, 239, 255,
    316, 337
    Italians arrested after Pearl Harbor,
        317, 319–20
    territorial expansion, 187, 247

Jaeckel, Karl, 279–80, 295
Japan, 27, 193, 198, 204, 214, 235, 238, 252,
      303, 315–16
    espionage in U.S., 178–80, 184, 195,
      202–3, 230, 247, 254–57, 285
    Japanese arrested after Pearl Harbor,
      317, 319–21
Jenney, Ralph, 269, 329
Jewish Community Press, 150–51, 180, 187
*Jewish Telegraphic Ag*ency, 59, 159
Jewett, W. K., Mrs., 232, 243
Jews, Los Angeles, 13
    demographics of, 11, 191
    prejudice against, 11–12
Joint Anti-Fascist Refugee Committee,
      192
Jolson, Al, 78, 220
    assassination target, 4, 205, 212
Jones, Ellis, 303–4, 307–8, 310, 313–15,
      319–20, 326–28, 336, 343
    arrested and tried after Pearl Harbor,
      320, 323, 328–30, 333
Jones, J. J., 196
Jordan, Max, 225

Kahn, Red, 221
Karloff, Boris, 120
Katz, Charles, 243
Keehn, Roy D., 136
Kellogg, Ira, 317–18
Kemp, Willard W., 104, 186
Ken, 243
Kendzia, Paul, 174, 223, 303
Kendzia, Willi, 166, 178, 268, 322
Kennedy, John F., 290
Kerner, Tony, 174
Killinger, Manfred von, 199–200, 206,
      222–23, 231, 254
King of Kings (1927), 71
Klein, John, 247
Klein, Julius, 149
    background, 127–28, 135–39
    secret relationship with Gyssling, 123,
      127–29, 280–83, 299, 337–38,
      363n43
Klein, Peter, 169–70
Kleinberger, Ray, 95
Kleine, Maria, 338
Knox, Frank, 135
Kosher Schächten (1938), 221

Kramer, Charles, 47–49, 83–84, 88, 93, 274
    and 1934 HUAC hearings, 52–53,
      62–63, 79, 94–107
Krims, Milton, 263
Kristallnacht, 245–46, 248
Kron, Carl, 184
Ku Klux Klan, 11, 20, 62, 84–86, 88–89,
      95, 133, 153–56, 159, 162, 194, 252,
      264, 273, 302, 325, 342
Kuhn, Fritz, 143–44, 160, 220, 223, 226,
      236, 239, 252, 295, 323
    speaks in LA, 190–91, 258–59
Kunze, G. Wilhelm, 286, 295, 311
Kusche, Reinhold, 146–47, 166–67, 177,
      181, 195, 199, 246, 318

La Crescenta Park, *see* Hindenburg Park
La Follette, Robert, 267
La Guardia, Fiorello, 258
Laemmle, Carl, 106, 138
Lake Shore Hotel, 281
Landon, Alf, 190
Landthaler, Joseph, 155
Lang, Fritz, 193
Lasky, Jesse, 138
Laws, Bolitha, 336
League to Save America First, 304
Lee, A. Earl, 213
Lehman, Irving, 13
Lehman, Paul, 167, 180–81, 183
Leithold, Ludwig, 56, 58
Lend-Lease Act (1941), 295
Lenhardt, Philip, 45–46, 52–53, 59–60, 172
Lewis, Leon, 2, 4, 9–10, 31–32, 47–52,
      53–60, 62–63, 79, 82–91, 192–93,
      196, 248–52, 255–59, 280, 285,
      288–90, 297, 300–3, 308, 312–13,
      326–27, 334, 338–39, 341
    and HUAC, 47–49, 52, 84, 94–107,
      267–68, 273–77
    assassination target, 152, 160, 205
    background, 8–11
    begins spy ring, 2, 4, 7–8, 16–20
    begins working with Roos, 128–29,
      138–39, 225–26
    foils McLaglan plot, 200, 202, 205–13
    known to and threatened by Nazis and
      fascists, 147–48, 158, 181, 238–39,
      241–43, 270, 293, 312, 326, 332
    foils Gefken's plot, 38–39

monitors Hollywood films for ADL, 14, 64, 71, 118–20
monitors secret cells, 290–95, 301–2, 305
plots against Allen, Fry, and Schwinn, 228–46
raises money from studio heads, 67–78
recruits Bockhacker, 235
recruits Grace and Sylvia Comfort, 286–87
recruits Ness, 141–51, 166–85
recruits Schmidt, 7, 18–19, 27–28
recruits Sicius, 283–84
recruits Slocombe, 153–65, 198–213
works with U.S. government after Pearl Harbor, 316–40
Liberation, 24, 67, 188, 220
Life of Emile Zola, The (1937), 219
Lindbergh, Charles, 47, 290, 306–8, 310, 313–14
Litvak, Anatole, 264
Livingston, Sigmund, 9–10, 48, 50
Lockheed Aircraft Company, 258, 282, 295–96, 300, 302, 325
Lode Star Legion, 20, 101 (*see also* American Labor Party)
Lodahl, Emil, 251
Long Beach, 62, 153–56, 159, 162, 165, 179, 202, 204–9, 229, 242, 257, 291–93, 316, 334, 342
Long Beach Motor Police Association, 205
Look, 270
Loos, Anita, 113
Lorelei Inn, 35
Los Angeles, 3, 11, 15, 191–92
    aircraft factories, 178, 257–58, 276, 281, 282, 288, 295–97, 300, 321
    map of Nazi and Fascist Los Angeles in the 1930s and 1940s, viii–ix
    right-wing extremism in, 3, 11, 12, 251,
    strategic importance, 3, 198, 200, 257, 275, 292, 300,
Los Angeles, Police Department, 102, 247, 284, 318–19, 321, 326, 332–33
    anti-Communism within, 11, 29–30, 32, 43, 60, 88–89, 103, 105–6
    anti-Semitism within, 11, 30, 32, 62, 106
    Nazi and fascist sympathizers within, 29, 33, 62, 89, 92–93, 103, 106, 158, 194, 237, 241

Los Angeles County Sheriff's Department, 11, 102, 204, 208, 211
    anti-Semitism within, 11, 103, 106
    Nazi sand fascist sympathizers within, 62, 103, 241
Los Angeles Daily News, 332
Los Angeles Examiner, 8
Los Angeles Herald-Express, 211, 277
Los Angeles Record, 8
Los Angeles Staats Zeitung, 222
Los Angeles Times, 54, 57, 95, 104, 112, 123, 133–34, 156, 179, 188, 219, 254, 276, 334
Lubitsch, Ernst, 67
Lucitt, William F., 96–98, 101–2, 105
Luther, Hans, 41, 109, 116, 126–27, 171, 219
Luxembourg, 284

MacArthur, General Douglas, 15
MacMurray, Fred, 194
McCord, Walter A., 85, 88, 90
McCormack, John, 63, 97, 101–2, 105–6
McDonough, Gordon, 334
McFadden, Louis T., 49, 62, 119–20, 164
McLaglan, Leopold, 200, 205, 214–15, 225, 228, 232, 252, 285
    background, 201–2, 343
    blackmail and death plots, 202–13
McLaglen, Victor, 201, 212
McPherson, Aimee Semple, 124
McWilliams, Carey, 76
Mad Dog of Europe, The, 118–19
Madison Square Garden, 13, 258
Magnin, Edgar F., 64, 68, 70–73, 75, 106, 138, 338
Malvina Pictures, 215–16
Mankiewicz, Herman, 118, 217
Mannik, Marius, 236
Mannon, Alfred, 216
March, Fredric, 77, 193
    assassination target, 205
Marshall, George C., 271, 280
    receives reports from Julius Klein, 127, 137, 280–82
    trains Roos in spy craft, 136–37, 139, 249
Mayer, Louis B., 64, 67–71, 75, 77–78, 106, 118–19, 188–89, 191, 215, 217, 264, 308
    assassination target, 4, 162, 197, 205, 211, 252

Mayflower Hotel, 280
Meader, Martin, 292, 303, 305
Mein Kampf, 3, 306
Merano (Italy), 337
Merriam, Frank, 77
Messerschmitt, Eugene, 287, 293
Metcalfe, James J., 198
Metcalfe, John C., 223
Metro-Goldwyn-Mayer (MGM), 64,
    69–71, 76–77, 118, 127, 188–89,
    191, 215, 217, 264, 308
  penetrated by Nazis and fascists, 189
Mexico, 18, 23, 207, 230, 241, 254, 291–92,
    296, 301
  Gold Shirts, 158, 187, 189–90, 231, 256
Meyerhoffer, Hans, 149, 177–78, 181, 195
Militant Christian Patriots, 232
Montgomery, Robert, 71, 77
Mooney, Volney P., 62, 94, 102–3
Morgenthau, Henry, 49
Mortal Storm (1940), 308
Motion Picture Artists Committee to
    Aid Republican Spain, 192
Motion Pictures, 308
  imported from Germany, 168,
    220–21, 294–95
Motion Picture Industry, 114–20, 215
    (*see also* Hollywood studios)
Motion Picture Producers and
    Distributors Association
    (MPPDA), 117–18, 120
Müller, Gustav, 117
Muni, Paul, 78
  assassination target, 205
Munich Agreement, 239–40, 246–47
Murphy, Owen, 153, 293
  McLaglan plot, 204–5, 207, 209–10
  works with Slocombe, 153, 204, 257
Mussolini, Benito, 61, 83–84, 138, 187,
    194, 240, 247
Mussolini, Vittorio, 194

National Copperheads, 304
National Free Press, 135, 137
National Minute Men and Women of
    America, 312, 325–26
National Protective Order of Gentiles,
    184, 313
National Rifle Association, 230, 241,
    270

National Socialist German Workers'
    Party (NSDAP), 14, 23, 47, 55,
    100, 102, 110, 121–22, 124, 144,
    147, 200, 222, 243, 270, 335, 337
Nazis (*see also* Sabotage, Nazi plans for)
  estimated number of American
    supporters, 285
  organize secret cells in L.A., 250–51,
    255, 286, 290–95, 302, 304–5
  summer camps in U.S., 144, 196,
    270–71
Ness, Esther, 143, 145, 172, 174
Ness, Kathryn, 332–33
Ness, Neil H., 129, 162, 186–87, 191, 213,
    287–88, 291
  background, 139–42, 342
  comes under suspicion, 151, 165,
    174–75, 178, 180–85
  dies under suspicious circumstances,
    332
  spies on Nazis, 141–51, 166–85
  testifies at 1939 HUAC hearings,
    274–77, 279
  works with Hughes, 152, 163–64, 175
Netherlands, 284
New Gentile, 164
New Jersey, 109, 267, 287–88
New York, 1, 3, 13, 36, 47–51, 56, 63, 70,
    80, 92, 96, 109, 117, 143–44,
    159–60, 188, 192, 216, 226, 232,
    239–40, 246, 248, 258, 263, 268,
    306, 310, 323, 334, 336
New York Non-Sectarian Anti-Nazi
    League, 192
New York Times, 59, 104, 210, 219, 277,
    295, 298
News of the World, 218
News Research Service *News Letter*, 250,
    272–74, 278, 282, 288–89, 294,
    300, 302, 304, 312–13, 320, 341
Ninotchka (1939), 221
*No More Hunger: The Compact Plan of the
    Christian Commonwealth*, 82,
Noble, Robert, 303–4, 307–8, 310–11,
    313–15, 319–20, 324, 326–28,
    336, 343
  arrested and tried after Pearl Harbor,
    320, 323, 328–30, 333
Non-Interventionists, *see* Isolationists
Nordskog, Andrae, 294

Normile, Emile, 96–98, 101–2
North American Aviation, 282, 295–96
Norway, 284
Nugent, Frank, 219
Nuremberg Laws, 133, 157
Nuremburg trials, 336–37
Nuttig, David, 325
Nye, Gerald, 307–9

Oakland, 84, 153, 274
Odd Fellows Temple, 82
Office of Strategic Services, 337
Old Vienna Café, 98
Olney, Warren, 330
Olympics, Berlin (1936), 110, 177–78, 215
Operation Bernard, 337
Operation Sunrise, 337
Orange County, 291
Ordnungdienst (OD), 147, 233–36, 239,
    241, 246, 268
Oviatt Library, California State
    University Northridge, 2

Pacht, Isaac, 68
Pacific Palisades, 253
Paehler, Albert, 143, 144
Palmer, A. Mitchell, 92
Pape, Robert, 24, 26, 28, 33–34, 39, 40,
    41, 43, 45, 51–52, 56, 121, 283
    background, 22–23, 343
    organizes Nazi presence in L.A.,
        14–15
Paramore, Ted, 217
Paramount Studio, 76, 78, 188
    penetrated by Nazis and fascists, 75, 189
Paris, 9, 16, 114, 221, 232, 245, 284
Park, Harwood,
    spies for Lewis and Roos, 249, 257
Parrott, Ken,
    assassination target, 160
Pasadena, 83, 98, 133, 159, 164, 178, 208–9,
    211, 232, 243, 251, 304
Patriotic Hall, 17, 35, 88
Pearl Harbor, 315–17, 320–22, 324–26,
    331–32
Pearson, Drew, 250, 274, 288–89
Pelley, William Dudley, 12, 61, 89–90,
    94, 157, 163, 180, 186–91, 211, 330
    anti-Semitism, 80, 82
    creates Silver Shirts, 79–84

Pennsylvania, 16, 49, 119, 143, 164, 277,
    287–88
Penprase, William, 208
Petsch, Peter, 122
Peyton, Jack, 252, 303
Phelps, G. Allison, 326, 332
Pickford, Mary, 138
Pitt, Leonard, 139, 339
Plack, Werner, 217, 222
Plots by L.A. Nazis and fascists (see also
    Sabotage)
    armed rebellion in San Diego, 87, 91,
        103–5
    Hughes assassination plots, 152–53,
        159–65, 184–85, 193
    rumors of plots, 87, 98, 186, 194, 198
    to kill Hollywood Jews and allies, 4,
        185, 197, 205–13, 252, 265
    to kill Jews, 4, 29, 161, 165, 303–4,
        325–26
    to overthrow U.S. government, 29,
        35–41, 58, 83–84, 230–31,
        276–77, 335
    to sabotage defense installations on
        Pacific Coast, 4, 275–77,
        279–80, 296–97, 303
Poland, 108, 187, 206, 263, 271–72, 280
Porter, John, 159
Portland, 27, 133, 296
Powell, Dick, 193
Price, Gus W., 89, 154
Prize Fighter and the Lady, The (1933), 127
Production Code Administration (PCA),
    118, 120, 215–17, 263–64, 308
Propaganda,
    Hitler and Goebbels on movies as,
        114–15
Proskauer, Joseph, 13
Protocols of the Elders of Zion, 22, 49, 120

Rapf, Harry, 76, 78
Rational Purpose in Government: Expressed
    in the Doctrine of the American
    Nationalist Party, 157
Reichenberg, Baron von, 126–27
Remarque, Erich Maria, 216–18
Republican Party, 47, 49, 69, 77, 119, 176,
    191, 290, 331, 334
Riedel, Peter, 281
Riedlin, Gustav, 280

Riefenstahl, Leni, 194
Riemer, John L., 100–2, 105, 121
Riess, Curt, 16
Riordan, Ralph, 302, 321
Risse, Arno, 145, 199, 235, 239–40, 243, 253, 266
RKO Studio, 69, 76, 118
Road Back, The (1937), 216–19, 221
Robinson, Edward G., 78, 191, 193, 220, 264
Rodríguez, Nicolás, 190
Rogge, O. John, 335–36
Romania, 187
Rome, 214, 243, 252
Roos, Alvina, 150–51, 225
Roos, Joseph 3, 8, 70, 76, 147, 205, 254, 285, 296, 300–3, 308, 312–13, 326, 328, 334, 339, 341
    and Julius Klein, 128, 135, 137–39, 282
    background, 134–39
    beaten up, 233
    begins working with Lewis, 128–29, 138–39, 225–27
    creates News Research Service News Letter, 250, 272–74
    early spying and training, 135–38
    monitors secret cells, 290–95, 301–2, 305
    plots against Allen, Fry, and Schwinn, 228–46
    recruits Bockhacker, 235
    recruits Grace and Sylvia Comfort, 286–87
    recruits Ness, 141–51, 166–85
    recruits Sicius, 283–84
    reorganizes office, recruits more spies, 248–52, 255–59
    provides information to government agencies, 257, 257–68, 277, 288–90, 295
    works with British intelligence, 274, 277
    works with U.S. government after Pearl Harbor, 316–40
Roos, Leonard, 339
Roosevelt, Franklin D., 12–13, 16, 35, 47, 82, 190–91, 234, 271, 298, 300, 307, 313, 316
    hated by Nazis and fascists, 22, 54, 81, 122, 158, 163, 258, 303–4, 311, 320, 325

orders Nazis put under surveillance, 13, 91–92, 248
plot to overthrow or kill, 83–84, 230–31, 237
Rosen, Al, 118–19
Rosten, Leo, 192
Roth, Lester, 74
Royal Order of American Defenders, 303, 308
Russell, H. A., 280
Russell, Sean, 255
Russia, 12, 22, 69, 92, 232 (see also Union of Soviet Socialist Republics)
Russian National Revolutionary Party, 159

Sabotage, Nazi plans for, 4, 27, 34, 37, 39, 51, 67, 177, 235, 248–49, 254–55, 257–258, 264, 271, 273, 275–77, 279–83, 286–88, 290–91, 293–94, 296–97, 299, 301–3, 316, 324, 330
Sachse, Willi, 147, 166–67, 176
Sachsenhausen concentration camp, 206
Sackett, B. E., 97, 100
Sacramento, 322, 329–30
San Diego, 37, 155, 159, 178, 195, 200, 202, 228–30, 232, 241–42, 256, 286–87, 296
    naval base, 122, 179–80, 275–76, 291–92
    Silver Shirts plot armed rebellion, 37–39, 43, 54, 87–88, 91, 103–5, 152–53
San Francisco, 27, 71, 122, 125, 140, 157, 176–177, 199, 206, 222–23, 231, 234, 254–55, 273, 288, 296, 299
    plot to seize control of National Guard armory, 36–38, 43
San Pedro, 27, 121, 198, 203, 228, 275, 277, 287, 291–92
San Quentin State Prison, 157, 164, 213, 330, 336
Sanctuary, Eugene, 159
Santa Barbara, 202, 206, 286
Santa Monica, 302
Schenck, Joseph, 119
    assassination target, 205
Schwend, Friedrich, 337
Schiller, Hans, 256
Schlueter, Kurt, 303

Schmidt, Alice, 25, 28–29, 35, 42, 58, 60–61, 79, 98, 145, 333
  background, 19, 342
Schmidt, Bruno, 160
Schmidt, John, 25, 35–36, 38, 44, 46, 51, 60, 63, 78, 83–84, 122, 173
  and Silver Shirts, 61–62, 79, 83
  background, 7, 18–20, 342
  dies under suspicious circumstances, 333–34
  infiltration of FNG, 21–31, 54
  returns to spying, 251, 290
  suspected of spying by Nazis, 39–42
  testifies at German American Alliance trial, 54–56
  threatened by Nazis, 57–59, 251
Schneeberger, Willi, 178–80, 195, 275, 291
Schnuck, Joe, 182
Schulberg, B.P.
  assassination target, 205
Schwinn, Hermann, 21, 26, 29–31, 33–34, 39, 51–52, 56–57, 60, 87, 103, 105, 108, 125, 138–39, 143–47, 149–50, 156, 160, 166, 194–97, 199–200, 220, 226, 234–41, 247–48, 251–52, 258–59, 265, 267–68, 271–73, 275–79, 282–84, 291, 294–95, 300, 303–4, 306, 310, 330
  arrested and tried after Pearl Harbor, 317–19, 322–24, 329–31, 333–36
  background 34, 269, 343
  citizenship troubles, 174–75, 183, 213, 244–45, 269–70, 285, 289
  gets money and propaganda at L.A. docks, 27, 54, 121, 255
  investigated by FBI, 289, 301
  set up by Lewis and Roos, 228–46
  suspected of sabotage, 288–89, 296–97
  trouble with rivals, 122, 169–70, 177
  trouble with Gyssling, 128–29, 170–73, 178, 184, 222–24
  works with Ness, 144–51, 167, 173–74, 181–84
  works with Silver Shirts and fascists, 90, 159, 162–63, 187, 189–90, 193, 202, 206, 290
Schwinn, Thekla Therese Nagel, 268–69, 323, 336

Scholastic Magazine, 153, 191
Seattle, 27, 276, 296
Sedition Trials, 320, 323, 328–30, 333–36
Selective Service Act, 323, 334
Sellin, William, 270–71
Selznick, David, 76
Shaw, Frank, 245, 252
Shol, Edith, 305
Shreve, Florence, 97–99, 101–2
Shrine Auditorium, 193–94
Sicius, Julius,
  background, 283, 342
  spies for Lewis and Roos, 271, 283–84, 287
Sidney, Sylvia, 193
Sigafoose, Walter, 61
Silberberg, Mendel, 8, 17, 63, 67–69, 71–74, 76, 134, 195, 228
  assassination target, 152, 160, 205
  background, 68–70
  known to Nazis, fascists, and KKK, 89, 158, 239, 332
Simon, Franchon,
  assassination target, 205, 373n21
Silver Legion, see Silver Shirts
Silver Ranger, 61, 67, 81, 91, 98, 155
Silver Shirts (also known as Silver Legion), 20, 24, 33, 60–62, 82, 134, 159, 162, 185–91, 258, 266, 293
  allied with Nazis, 20, 79, 83, 89–90, 95, 96–106, 176, 225
  and HUAC hearings, 95, 97–106
  anti-Communism, 29, 60–61, 81, 83, 87–88
  anti-Semitism, 12, 61, 67, 79, 81–82, 98, 186, 189, 191
  differences with Nazis, 61, 86–87
  discontent within L.A. posts, 85–89
  German Silver Shirt posts, 61, 87, 89–90, 98–99
  growth of and membership in Los Angeles, 61, 79–91
  hatred of Roosevelt, 81–82, 86
  inside Hollywood studios, 74–75, 77–78, 189–90, 249
  San Diego Silver Shirt plot, 37–39, 43, 103–5
  threat to Jews, 61–62, 82
Sinclair, Upton, 77, 92

Slocombe, Charles, 129, 145, 152,
    178, 199–200, 252, 297,
    303, 334–335
  background, 153–54, 342
  begins spying for Lewis and Roos,
    153–65, 187, 277
  comes under suspicion, 232, 242
  and Ku Klux Klan, 153–55, 194
  and Hughes, 156–65
  and McLaglan, 200–213
  and Bülow, 179–80
  comes under suspicion, 232, 242
  discovers plots to kill Jews, 185, 197,
    205–13
  spies on Allen and Alexander, 188,
    190–91, 196, 199–213, 264, 266
  spies on Allen and Fry, 228–32,
    242–43
  spies on Japanese and Nazi agents,
    256–58, 290–93
Slocombe, Sherry, 335
Snelson, C. Earle, 273, 302
Socha, Max, 42, 44–46, 53–56, 58
Spain, 187, 192, 226, 245, 247, 338
Spalione, Mary, 97
Spanknöbel, Heinz, 23, 56, 114
Specht, Karl, 26, 40, 43, 56
Spivak, John, 195–96
St. Louis, 50
Stalin, Joseph, 3, 123, 271
Steedman, James, 322
Steele, Isobel, 215–16
Stephens, Marion, 252
Stephens, Norman and Winona,
  build "western White House" for
    Hitler, 253–54
Steuben Society, 149–50, 167
Stewart, Donald Ogden, 193
  assassination target, 205
Storm Troopers, 14, 24, 37, 39–40, 105,
    214, 225, 245
  in Los Angeles, 7, 26, 36–37, 43, 54,
    56, 58, 90, 98, 100–1, 103–4,
    144, 147, 155, 166–67, 201,
    233, 243, 257, 268, 270, 272–73,
    276, 322
Struve, Gustav, 110
Stuart, Gloria, 193
  assassination target, 205
Sudetenland, 221, 239, 245–46

Sullivan, Edward, 266–67
Summary Report on Activities of Nazi
    Groups and Their Allies in
    Southern California, 267
Sunday Worker, 195
Sunderland, Blanche, 28, 35, 79
Sunderland, Carl, 29, 31, 34–36, 38–42,
    53, 63, 78
  and Silver Shirts, 61–63, 79, 83
  background, 26, 342
  joins spy operation, 26, 28
  testifies at German American Alliance
    trial, 54, 56
Swing Club, 217
Sydney, Sylvia,
  assassination target, 205

Taft, Robert, 290
Tank, Max, 142
Tenney, Jack,
  Fact-Finding Committee, 310–11, 322,
    327–28
Terminal Island, 257, 292, 317–19,
    322–24
Thalberg, Irving, 64, 67–68, 70–71, 73,
    75–77
Themlitz, Paul, 24–25, 29, 39–40, 44, 51,
    56, 58, 60–61, 87, 90, 95, 98–102,
    108, 155, 343
Thomas, Martin Luther, 161, 267
Thompson, Henry Thomas, 178–79
Thomsen, Hans, 280
Three Comrades (1938), 216–17
Tippre, John, 177, 182, 184
To Hell with the Kaiser! (1918), 114
Today, 90–91
Tokyo, 198, 214, 252
Toller, Ernst, 194
  assassination target, 205
Tomid, Nayer, 113–14, 125
Tourrou, Leon, 248, 263
Townsend, Ralph, 257
Treaty of Versailles, 166
True, James, 159, 231, 242, 330
Tucker, Sophie, 194
Turnverein, 45, 168
Turnverein Hall, 15, 28, 42, 45, 51,
    143, 168
Twentieth Century Pictures, 76, 119, 188
  penetrated by Nazis and fascists, 189

United Artists, 76, 188, 225

Union of Socialist Soviet Republics (USSR), 29, 83, 92, 102, 112, 123, 140, 143, 146, 202, 234, 238, 243, 271

United Front, 159–60, 206, 292

United Party Movement, 294

United States Army Intelligence (G-2), 16, 136–37, 248, 256–57, 296
  receive information from Klein, 127, 136, 280, 282
  receive information from Lewis and Roos, 277, 282, 301–2, 317, 321

United States Congress, House Un-American Activities Committee (HUAC),
  1934 HUAC hearings, 47–49, 63, 78–79, 82, 84, 93–107, 121, 123
  1938–39 HUAC hearings, 226–27, 247–48, 266–68, 273–77, 322

United States Department of Justice, 38, 62, 86, 227, 266, 292, 322, 336
  receive information from Lewis and Roos, 33, 91, 97, 100, 104, 175, 184, 302, 304–5, 317, 321

United States Department of Naturalization and Immigration, 302, 321
  works to revoke Schwinn citizenship, 174–75, 184, 213, 244–45, 269–70, 285, 300, 302

United States Department of State, 106, 215, 231, 271–72, 274, 320
  anti-Semitism within, 33, 219
  receive information from Lewis and Roos, 273, 290, 302

United States Department of War, 127, 137, 179, 295
  receive information from Lewis and Roos, 273, 290, 302

United States Marine Corps, 38, 84, 103–5, 179

United States Naval Intelligence, 39, 202–4, 209, 211, 248, 276, 290, 331, 334
  receive information from Lewis and Roos, 38, 93, 104, 152–53, 203, 208, 231–32, 256–57, 267, 277, 280, 284, 288, 293, 302, 317, 321

United States Senate, Investigation of Propaganda in Motion Pictures, 308–9

Universal Pictures, 70, 76, 218–19
  penetrated by Nazis and fascists, 189

Universum Film AG (UFA), 115

Unterach am Attersee, 338

Untermyer, Samuel, 55, 127, 192

Urwand, Ben, 347n2, 356n1, 363n32

Veterans of Foreign Wars, 226

Vienna, 124, 134, 139, 224–25, 306

Vieth, John, 45–46, 59–60

Vindicators, 251

Vonsiatsky, Anastase, 252

Vultee Aircraft Corporation, 282, 295

Wall Street Journal, 59, 104

Warner, Jack, 67, 78, 219, 263, 308

Warner, Harry, 263

Warner Brothers Studios, 70, 76, 116–17, 219, 263–65, 286

Warren, Earl, 328

Washington Conference, 280–83

Washington, D.C., 15, 33, 43–44, 46–49, 60, 70, 96, 110, 222, 227, 230, 232, 256–57, 259, 266, 271, 274, 280–81, 286, 299, 302, 322–23, 330, 333–336

"Washington Merry-Go-Round," 288

Washington Post, 59, 105

Wasson, Fred, 304–6

Welles, Sumner, 298

Wenger, Harry, 142

Whale, James, 218

Wheeler, Burton, 307, 309

Whitaker, Alma, 111–12

White, Joseph, 89

White, Mark L., 104, 105, 158
  background, 85
  spies for Lewis, 85–87, 89, 99–100, 100–2

White Russians, 191, 200–1, 205–6, 208, 225, 228, 230, 252

Wiedemann, Fritz, 198, 214, 254–56, 288, 299, 306

Wiese, Ernst, 256

Willkie, Wendell, 290

Williams, Eugene, 211–12

Williams, Paul, 253

Williams, William Pierce, 286–87, 293–94, 301–6, 312, 325–26
Willis, Henry, assassination target, 160
Wilshire Boulevard Temple, 71, 202
Wilson, Edmund, 11–12
Winchell, Walter, 250, 274, 321 assassination target, 205
Winrod, Gerald, 12, 159, 164
Wise, Rabbi Stephen, 13
Winterhalder, Hans, 7–8, 15, 22–24, 25, 28–30, 33–34, 39, 42, 44, 51–52, 55–56, 58, 60, 99, 102–3, 150
  background, 23, 343
  works with Silver Shirts, 61, 83, 87, 89–90, 98
Wittenberg, Armin, 31–32
Witthoeft-Emden, Robert, 282
Wolff, Marco, assassination target, 205, 373n21
Wolff, Marie, 303
Wolfram, Hans, 113, 222
Wooplemann, Hans, 322
Wood, Robert, 307

Woolvine, Thomas Lee, 11
World War I
  casualties, 9
  discontent among veterans, 15–16, 19, 85–86
World War II, 271–72, 280, 284, 297, 300, 316, 339
Wright, C. J., 157
Wyler, William, assassination target, 205

Young, Charles, background, 248–49, 342
  spies for Lewis and Roos, 248–49, 252, 265–66, 270–71, 279–80, 283–86, 289–90, 293, 302–3, 312, 317, 319, 323, 334–35

Zacharias, Ellis, 231
  welcomes reports from Lewis and Roos, 256–57, 280, 287, 290–91, 293, 301
Zachary, Roy, 237
Zucker, Adolph, 308
Zur Lippe, Prince Kurt, 173–74, 256

Steven J. Ross is professor of history at the University of Southern California and director of the Casden Institute for the Study of the Jewish Role in American Life. He is the author of *Hollywood Left and Right*, recipient of the Academy of Motion Picture Arts and Sciences' Film Scholars Award and nominated for a Pulitzer; *Working-Class Hollywood*, nominated for a Pulitzer and the National Book Award; *Movies and American Society*; and *Workers on the Edge*. He lives in Southern California.